RIDE TO THE SOUND OF THE GUNS

RIDE TO THE SOUND OF THE GUNS

The Life of a Cold War Warrior,
Brig. Gen. (Ret.) Theodore C. Mataxis

LT. COL. (RET.) THEODORE C. MATAXIS JR.

CASEMATE
Pennsylvania & Yorkshire

Published in the United States of America and Great Britain in 2025 by
CASEMATE PUBLISHERS
1950 Lawrence Road, Havertown, PA 19083
and
47 Church Street, Barnsley, S70 2AS, UK

Copyright 2025 © Lt. Col. (Ret.) Theodore C. Mataxis Jr.

Hardcover Edition: ISBN 978-1-63624-580-5
Digital Edition: ISBN 978-1-63624-581-2

A CIP record for this book is available from the British Library

All rights reserved. No part of this book may be reproduced or transmitted in any form or by any means, electronic or mechanical including photocopying, recording or by any information storage and retrieval system, without permission from the publisher in writing.

Printed and bound in the United Kingdom by CPI Group (UK) Ltd, Croydon, CR0 4YY

Typeset in India by Lapiz Digital Services, Chennai.

For a complete list of Casemate titles, please contact:

CASEMATE PUBLISHERS (US)
Telephone (610) 853-9131
Fax (610) 853-9146
Email: casemate@casematepublishers.com
www.casematepublishers.com

CASEMATE PUBLISHERS (UK)
Telephone (0)1226 734350
Email: casemate@casemateuk.com
www.casemateuk.com

All images are from the author's personal collection unless otherwise credited.

The Publisher's authorised representative in the EU for product safety is Authorised Rep Compliance Ltd., Ground Floor, 71 Lower Baggot Street, Dublin D02 P593, Ireland.
http://www.arccompliance.com

Contents

Dedication		vii
Foreword by Lt. Gen. (Ret.) H. R. McMaster		ix
Author's Note		xiii
Preface by Brig. Gen. (Ret.) Theodore C. Mataxis Sr.		xv

1	The Early Years, 1917–36	1
2	The ROTC Years, 1936–40	13
3	Active-Duty Mobilization, 1940–44	21
4	France and Germany, 1944–45	39
5	Postwar Occupation of Germany with Family, 1945–47	65
6	Indian Staff College and UN Observer, Kashmir, 1950–52	77
7	17th Infantry Regiment, Korea, 1952–53	99
8	Fort Benning and the Army War College, 1953–58	115
9	505th Airborne Battle Group, Mainz and Bad Kreuznach, Germany, 1958–61	123
10	Washington, D.C., 1962–64	133
11	Vietnam, 1964–66	139
12	82nd Airborne Division, 1967–68	169
13	Iran, 1968–70	177
14	Vietnam and Cambodia, 1970–72	187
15	Singapore, 1972–75	199
16	Valley Forge Military Academy, 1975–83	207
17	The Committee for a Free Afghanistan, 1983–89	213
18	The Later Years	237

Appendix: Recommendations for Awards, World War II and Early Vietnam	251
References by Chapter	259
Index	267

Dedication

To my wife, Kirby, and my mother, Helma, who both stayed home and raised children when we were off at war. This book would not have been possible without their endless help, support and love. To all of today's family support personnel who stay at home and raise their families, while their loved ones are serving our country.

Also, to the brave men and women of our Armed Forces who risk their lives and limbs defending our nation against all enemies foreign or domestic. Thank you for your service, without it we would not have the freedoms we have today.

These are the words of President Theodore Roosevelt in a speech delivered on April 23, 1910, at the University of Paris, "The Man in the Arena."

> It is not the critic who counts; not the man who points out how the strong man stumbles, or where the doer of deeds could have done them better. The credit belongs to the man who is actually in the arena, whose face is marred by dust and sweat and blood; who strives valiantly; who errs, who comes short again and again, because there is no effort without error and shortcoming; but who does actually strive to do the deeds; who knows great enthusiasms, the great devotions; who spends himself in a worthy cause; who at the best knows in the end the triumph of high achievement, and who at the worst, if he fails, at least fails while daring greatly, so that his place shall never be with those cold and timid souls who neither know victory nor defeat.

Foreword

In *Ride to the Sound of the Guns*, Brigadier General Theodore Mataxis's son, Lieutenant Colonel (Ret.) Theodore Mataxis Jr., has written a memoir of his father that not only illuminates an extraordinary career, but also reveals the character of a man who exhibited tremendous courage, intellect, and compassion.

Brigadier General Mataxis was a prepossessing figure. He seemed intimidating through the eyes of a 14-year-old boy as I arrived at Valley Forge Military Academy and College as a high school freshman in August 1976. When I first saw him, he was in his dress greens army uniform with the stars on his shoulder boards gleaming in the hot summer sun. I thought that this barrel-chested, fit man with a shaved head was a dead ringer for the actor and World War II veteran and son of Greek immigrants, Telly Savalis. I was an avid consumer of military history and movies and was a fan of many of the World War II movies in which Savalis often played the role of a tough, irascible sergeant, like Sergeant Guffy in the 1965 film *The Battle of the Bulge*. I would soon learn that Mataxis's true exploits across three wars far exceeded any Hollywood heroics.

Mataxis's record surpasses fictional stories in literature as well as film. His career and character resonate with Anton Myrer's portrayal of Sam Damon, the strong, principled, and dedicated soldier in the novel *Once an Eagle*. Mataxis commanded a battalion in combat in World War II at the age of 26 and a regiment in the Korean War at the age of 36. He served for four years in Vietnam and Cambodia.

I had the privilege of getting to know General Mataxis well during my high school years at Valley Forge and we stayed in contact after I departed for the United States Military Academy at West Point. We corresponded across most of my subsequent career in our army. His intimidating countenance belied a deep concern for the young cadets of Valley Forge, and I remember fondly our many conversations over those years, even those which followed adolescent indiscretions on my part. Mataxis emphasized the tenets of leadership in our army. He told us that army leaders must always put mission accomplishment and the survival and well-being of those they lead before their own well-being. He described how he fostered trust, confidence, and cohesion among soldiers as the key ingredients for courage in battle. Trust, confidence, and cohesion, he told us, form psychological and emotional bulwarks against fear and inspire soldiers to act in ways contrary to the natural preoccupation with self-preservation. I remember him saying that good army teams take on the quality of a family in which the teammates' sense of honor make them more afraid of letting one another down than they are of the enemy's bullets. All of this rang true to me as I prepared soldiers for and led them in battle years later.

Mataxis had witnessed many changes in the army across three wars, but he was a source of one of the greatest continuities in the profession of arms: the priority of developing the next generations of leaders. I grew to admire greatly that tough, empathetic general. He showed me that the United States Army is a living historical community in which younger generations look to earlier generations for inspiration and to understand better their calling as soldiers.

Mataxis had a profound influence on me and other future leaders through his example and his mentorship. I soon realized that behind our commandant's rugged countenance was a person who always treated everyone with respect. I later understood that Mataxis was also an intellectual, an author, an avid reader, and collector of books. Across my career he sent me the books from his library that he thought were most relevant to my new responsibilities. When I decided to write a doctoral dissertation on how and why Vietnam became an American war, I asked to see General Mataxis for advice. In a letter to him in February 1997, just prior to the publication of that work as a book, I wrote to him: "I often think of you as the book nears publication. It all really began for me with an interview I did with you in the Carolina Inn."

I was fortunate to be with him and his wife, Helma, in the last years of his life when he attended the ceremony in which I assumed command as 71st colonel of the 3rd Armored Cavalry Regiment. He whispered words of encouragement and expressed confidence in me as our regiment was preparing for a second combat mission in Iraq. I told him that I would do my best to live up to his example.

I hope that many young people read this memoir of a great soldier, father, and citizen so that General Mataxis can continue to inspire future generations through his example. Readers will, no doubt, note the contrast between Mataxis's embrace of danger—he received a Silver Star, three Bronze stars with "V" devices for valor, and two Purple Hearts—with the "safetyism" that pervades much of American society. On battlefields there are no safe spaces to which one can retreat and the riskiest course of action is the one that, in seeking the safest course, cedes initiative to the enemy. Young Americans may also draw inspiration from the patriotism of a man whose father arrived, penniless, at Ellis Island from Greece in 1907. The Mataxis family story might help young people challenge the orthodoxy of self-loathing to which so many Americans are subjected in universities and secondary schools. All who read these pages will understand better the rewards of service across lives well-lived. Even after his retirement, when the Soviets occupied Afghanistan in the 1980s, Mataxis went to his fourth war as the field director for the Committee for a Free Afghanistan in Peshawar, Pakistan.

Readers will also gain an understanding of the rewards of service across multiple generations. The author served with great distinction in US Army Special Forces and the Rangers. Brig. Gen. Theodore Mataxis pinned captain's bars on his newly promoted son's uniform when they were both serving in Vietnam in 1971. Theodore Mataxis Jr. went on to serve in two more wars: Grenada in 1983 and in El Salvador from 1988 to 1989. His son, Ted III, carried on the family tradition of service, deploying to combat in Afghanistan and Iraq. All three who wore "Mataxis" nametags on their combat uniforms began service as enlisted soldiers and non-commissioned officers in the reserves before their commission as officers. The author, his father, and his son served their nation in eight wars across their three generations. All three men understood that it is a privilege to serve their nation and their fellow citizens in uniform. And General Mataxis's wife, Helma, exhibited other forms of courage and an equal commitment to service. Married to the general for 65 years at the time of his death, she had lived in bombed-out Berlin in 1946 with two small children, lived in India with no running water and dirt floors with three small children for over a year, was the only parent for three small children for two years while the general was in Kashmir and then in the Korean War, and endured having both her husband and son in combat together in Vietnam for 14 months.

All bore trials and tribulations, but they persevered and experienced the joy of being part of teams committed to missions more important than any individual in which the man or woman next to you is willing to sacrifice everything for the soldier next to them. *Ride to the Sound of the Guns* is a compelling story that should be shared and discussed with others. And it is my hope that it will inspire many more to emulate General Mataxis and his family in service of our nation.

H. R. McMaster
Lt. Gen., US Army (Ret.)
Stanford, California

Author's Note

The views expressed in this book are those of my father, remembered and documented through his letters, written accounts or oral history recordings. All photographs are from his personal collection. My views are closely aligned with his since he was my best friend, mentor, and personal hero. These views do not necessarily reflect the official policies of the Department of the Army, Department of Defense, or the United States Government. There is no consideration of today's political correctness, since those most difficult times were so different to the present moment, and required those of the Greatest Generation to do what they did.

The words for the most part were written by Theodore C. Mataxis Sr. with this book in mind in 2006. I have chosen to use his words where I could throughout this book. So, when the pronoun I is used, it denotes his direct words from one of his resources.

Theodore C. Mataxis Jr.

Henry V "We band of brothers — we happy few.'" SEOUL, KOREA
0500 15 Oct. 2000

MEMO FOR RECORD

SUBJECT: INITIAL CONCEPT FOR MY MEMOIRS:
"RIDE to the SOUND of the GUNS"
The memoirs of a COLD WAR WARRIOR - 1947—1990

1. BACKGROUND

a. For the past several decades I have been "bugged" by my family and friends to write my memoirs. I have thought of it and even made a 100? couple of false starts. But have given up when a new current project would emerge which caused me to put my memoirs aside to involve myself in the "fun & games rush" of involvement in an interesting current project.

b. Ambassador Colby, former Director of the CIA, at a meeting of the Vietnam Center at Texas Tech University noted that I had been involved in some virtually unknown projects which deserved being covered. General and subsequent Secretary of State Haig, when we were discussing the Cold War said "Ted, You've been thru this Cold War from the start to the finish — why don't you get to work on your memoirs. And Dr Jeffy Clarke, the Chief Historian of the US Army chided me for not getting started. He said I know whats holding you and other old goats like you back. You feel that when you start you'll give up your current involvement with current affairs — and feel you're now "out of it - carooned on the beach, another old retiree trying to recall your "days of yore.

c. The first time I really realized that I was at the stage of life when it was time to get to work was at a Conference of the Society of Military Historians in Chicago. After I had presented a paper on "NORDWIND: Hitlers Last offensive in Europe" I was approached by the Editor of Reyman Band of Boulder, Co. who asked me to write my memoirs. He noted that I should send him an Abstract which outlined the subjects I would cover.

Ted Sr.'s initial concept for his book in 2000.

Preface

In October 2005, I returned to Fort Benning, Georgia, for the dedication of the 17th Infantry Brigade monument at Sacrifice Field across from the US Army Infantry Museum. I was commander of the Buffalos during the Korean War, May 6–July 5, 1953 and then became their honorary colonel when Colonel "Buffalo Bill" Quinn passed. There were over 300 veteran Buffalos and their family members there to dedicate the life-sized bronze buffalo monument to their fallen comrades and their combat experiences.

I reflected on my first of many visits to Fort Benning as a young 2nd Lieutenant in July 1940 for the first new weapons course of World War II. It is hard to believe that was over 65 years ago prior to the start of the mobilization for World War II. As a career combat soldier, I was provided an opportunity to "Ride to the Sound of the Guns" in service to our country for my lifetime. As an "adrenaline junky" I was the perennial volunteer. I enlisted in the Washington National Guard when the war broke out in Europe in the fall of 1939 and was commissioned through the University of Washington ROTC in June 1940.

A mere three and a half years later in World War II I was a battalion commander in brutal combat with the 2nd Battalion, 276th Infantry Division during the last German offensive during the winter of 1944. In the Vosges Mountains in northeastern France in the spring of 1945, I participated in the breakthrough of the Siegfried Line and in the subsequent pursuit phase into Bavaria. I had volunteered to go to the Pacific and was en route there when the atomic bombs were dropped, and the war ended. I then returned for occupation duty in Berlin and then southern Germany.

En route to the Indian Army staff college in June 1950, North Korea invaded South Korea. I requested to have my orders changed to Korea. The Infantry Branch chief told me to go on and complete the Indian Staff College and then he would send me to Korea when I completed it. In my next conversation with the branch chief, I was informed that my "utilization tour" for the staff college would be a one-year assignment with the United Nations as an observer in Kashmir. In the spring of 1952, I volunteered again for the Korean War and went directly from Kashmir to Korea, where I was assigned as executive officer of the G-2 (Intelligence Section) of Eighth Army Headquarters. As soon as I arrived, I requested to be assigned to the troops. My boss, the G-2, informed me that I was a regular army officer and would do as instructed. Shortly after, a Department of the Army letter came out stating that anyone who had been separated from their family for more than a year could go home. I said I would stay if they let me go to an assignment with troops. I was assigned to the 17th Infantry Regiment (the Buffaloes), where I was the executive officer and then as the Regimental Commander during the bitter campaigns for Triangle, T-Bone, and Pork Chop hills.

In 1964, I was assigned to General Taylor's staff when he was assigned as Ambassador to Vietnam. He asked me, "Where do you want to go?" I explained that I had visited Vietnam to observe the French in 1952. Shortly after that I had orders assigning me to Vietnam as senior advisor to the South Vietnamese general commanding II Corps. During that 16-month time, the attack on Pleiku in February 1965 heralded the escalation of the fighting by the introduction of regiments of the 325th Division of the North Vietnamese regular army into the central mountain highlands. Upon the arrival of American troops in February 1966, I became the deputy commander of the 1st Brigade of the 101st Airborne Division.

In June 1970, while serving in Iran, I volunteered for Vietnam and went directly from Iran to Vietnam. I was assigned to the Americal division, part of XXIV Corps at Chu Lai, Vietnam, as assistant division commander for maneuver. During the next seven months I served as both the assistant division commander for maneuver and, during August and September, as acting division commander.

In February 1971, with one day's notice, I was assigned as chief of the Military Equipment Delivery Team for Cambodia (MEDT-C). MEDT-C was a unique organization divided into two echelons: a rear echelon in Saigon and a forward echelon in Phnom Penh, Cambodia. It operated under the military command of CINCPAC and the supervision of the chief of the US Diplomatic Mission to Cambodia. Our mission was to assist in the supervision of the Congressionally approved military assistance programs for Cambodia. Congress required us to evaluate requests, coordinate deliveries, observe and expedite distribution. We were also tasked to audit the usage of US-provided military equipment and supplies. I returned in March 1972 after serving 23 months in theater. I had to return to the United States for a forced retirement the next month.

When I retired from Valley Forge Military Academy, during the time the Russians were fighting in Afghanistan, I became the field representative/coordinator for the Committee for a Free Afghanistan (CFA). I visited Afghanistan and Pakistan for periods of two to three months until the Russians withdrew. At age 72, I made my last trip and was behind the lines with the mujahideen. The Russians did not withdraw the last Soviet soldier until February 15, 1989, after the cost of 13,310 killed in action (KIA), 35,478 wounded (WIA) and 311 missing (MIA).

Theodore C. Mataxis Sr.
Brig. Gen., US Army (Ret.)
2006

CHAPTER I

The Early Years, 1917–36

Theodore Christopher Mataxis Sr. (Ted) was born on August 17, 1917. Having been born the same year that America entered World War I, some would claim that Ted was destined for an illustrious military career. Brigadier General Mataxis was born into war, and he would remain in a war zone well into his seventies. He would serve for 50-plus years in and spanning three wars, which he would later describe using the same opening at his numerous speaking engagements stating, "I am a US Army retired brigadier general. I served for 32 years [1940 until 1972] commanding infantry troops in World War II, Korea, and Vietnam." What he leaves out of this description is almost as important as what he includes: Brig. Gen. Mataxis would spend over 15 years in active combat zones throughout the world; he would continue his extensive MAAG duties in Iran and Cambodia; and he was one of the very few to earn the Combat Infantryman's Badge with two stars from World War II, Korea, and Vietnam. Even after retirement, Brig. Gen. Mataxis would go on to serve as a consultant to the Minister of Defense in Singapore, and he would become the commandant of cadets at Valley Forge Military Academy. His career began as a young private and would end with this old war horse gallivanting around the rugged mountains of Afghanistan advising the Afghan freedom fighters in their efforts to defeat the Russians. He would make at least seven trips throughout his 60s and 70s to Afghanistan during their war with Russia. Once Mataxis stopped actively chasing down wars to fight in his mid-70s, he settled into a professorship with American Military University to help others "younger than he" defending the United States against enemies, both foreign and domestic.

Theodore Christopher Mataxis was a second-generation immigrant. His father Christos Peter Metaxas was born on March 25, 1890 in Greece. Chris, as he would be called in the United States, immigrated to the United States when his family's small farm could no longer support any more Metaxas (the correct spelling of the Mataxis name). His family pitched in for a boat ticket to America and $3 for him to get established in this new land. Chris landed at Ellis Island in 1907. He received his US citizenship in Seattle at the age of 26. He was very proud of his new citizenship. According to Christos, in a poem he wrote upon returning to Greece over 50 years later, he was:

> Orphaned by mother, and by father poor.
> Leaving his home country and family
> That's why I deserted everything in Thouria:
> Father, brothers, home, misery, unhappiness,
> And made the decision and left from my country.
> Filled of plans, of dreams and with a secret hope,
> Perhaps my luck will help me,
> And reward my efforts and my hard work.

Arriving at Ellis Island was so intimidating that Chris did not dare correct the burly, red-headed Scotsman that rechristened him "Mataxis" during his immigration processing. For his new life in the United States, Christos Metaxas would be known as Chris Mataxis. Of course, when later asked about the event that changed his name forever, Chris would give a similar but much more entertaining and less deprecating explanation.

Ted's father, Chris, hunting on an unknown date.

According to the General, "When Dad was asked the question [about how Metaxas was changed to Mataxis] he would say, 'Wait, let me tell you a story. Then if you have any questions, you can ask me when it is over.' The story is as follows. In a mining camp up in the hills of Montana a Chinese laundry had the sign Ole Olson's Hand Laundry in the shop window. When the shop owner was asked why a man of Chinese descent had a laundry with a Swedish name, the gentleman would explain his experience when coming through immigration. Apparently, the man standing in front of him when he immigrated from China was a big Swede who, when asked, told the immigration officer that his name was Ole Oleson. The immigration officer sent the Swede on his way and turned next to ask the Chinese gentleman what his name was. When the gentleman replied, 'Mee Tu' the not too bright immigration officer wrote down Ole Oleson on Mee Tu's immigration papers and waved him through. The Chinese gentleman was so happy to be waved through immigration that he didn't try to correct the mistake. The same thing happened to Dad. I must say Dad really enjoyed telling that story, particularly in the 1930s when people were reading of the ruler in Greece, a General Ioannis Metaxas." Yes, the Metaxas/Mataxis family line does indeed include a dictator, as well as ancient nobility, but we will discuss that a little later. For now, it is enough to recognize that apparently a whole generation of Americans were given new surnames as they crossed over the threshold of immigration offices into their newly verified lives as American immigrants.

Ted's father, Chris, and mother, Edla, taken in 1917.

Chris worked his first three years in New York for a man who offered him room and board and taught him English instead of paying him an actual salary. Incomprehensibly to his family, Chris was grateful to the man until his dying day. Chris believed that because this man taught him how to speak English and gave him a foundational understanding of what a trade in produce and food entailed, the man was worthy of his respect. It was hard as the family aged to deny that there was an element of exploitation in the man's actions. Still, despite these suspect motives, it was just as hard to deny that it was indeed this man's actions and the sharing of his knowledge that later allowed Chris to pursue his own American dream.

Chris began his career as a grocer by selling apples from a small pushcart in the streets of New York City. He quickly learned that if one took the time to polish the best of the apples, people would pay a much higher price for the product. Eventually it was time to leave New York. Chris worked his way across America like many immigrants of the time did: by working on one of the many iron roads of the 1900s. By this time the transcontinental railroad that connected the East Coast to the West Coast was a web of lines in all directions. After his transcontinental adventures Chris would meet Edla, Chris's future bride and Ted's mother. Edla was born on August 2, 1891, on the island of Gotland, Sweden. By the time she turned 19 years old, she was ready to venture across the ocean in pursuit of her own American dream. She braved this journey alone, just like Christos did three years before her. Family lore had them both arriving romantically through Ellis Island at about the same time, fated to fall in love several years later in Seattle, Washington. It makes for a charming story, but further research shows that in reality they did not even land on the same coast. Edla Maria Katrin Osterdahl landed on the shores of Montreal, Quebec, on July 28, 1911, and would immediately head to Washington State to join a branch of her mother's family that had originally immigrated before the Civil War. She arrived in Seattle on August 2, 1911. Edla's mother had five brothers and sisters who all immigrated from the island of Gotland in Sweden and eventually settled in the Seattle/Tacoma region. They were all farmers, loggers, and Alaskan fishermen. The American branch of Elda's family originally settled in Wisconsin, where they farmed and logged the land to eke out a living. By the time she arrived, Edla's family had settled on the western slopes of Mount Rainier as loggers and fishermen. The family's children and womenfolk worked on the farm, while Uncle Sieg (a major figure and mentor in Ted's childhood) and his four brothers would pursue soldiering, logging, hunting, and fishing.

Not much is known about how Chris and Edla met or married. One thing is certain: as a first-generation Swedish immigrant and a first-generation Greek immigrant, Chris and Edla made quite the unusual pair. According to their daughter, "They were quite the talk of the town. It just wasn't done back then. It was all considered rather shocking really." Alas, what was shocking then now simply underscores an evolving America. History books would go on to label this new America the melting pot, a somewhat outdated term that modern historians prefer to label the American tapestry/mosaic/salad bowl. Whether one argues for a homogeneous assimilation or a heterogeneous integration, the fact remains that American society was being called on to integrate numerous cultures on her lands while discovering new ways to move forward together as one nation. Edla became a citizen when she married Chris on October 1, 1916. Chris and Edla's multicultural marriage simply reflected how much America was changing during this time: Calvin Coolidge became the first president to deliver a radio broadcast from the White House; Prohibition had taken hold of the country; and J. Edgar Hoover was serving as the head of the FBI. The roaring twenties were swiftly changing America's ideas about what it meant to be an American. The country flourished after its successful campaign in World War I. Both Ted and his country would grow quickly during this postwar boom.

During this time, Ted's family was thriving. His parents owned a successful grocery store, The Kid's Grocery & Bakery, located in the center of Seattle on Sixth and Union. Owning the store meant ten-to-twelve-hour workdays, day after day, every day for six days a week, as was the norm for most of the country's workers. Ted's family had been very successful with their store. As a result of their success, they lived in a large home with plenty of acreage, a tar paper shack, and a garage. Ted's earliest recollections revolved around this home and a woodshed on a large lot located at the corner of 103rd Street and Greenwood Avenue. The family laughingly called the large green lot "Dad's farm" since Chris had planted quite a lot on the property: a couple of cherry trees, several plum trees, and many apple trees. Along the fence line at the end of the lot he proudly planted red raspberries, loganberries,

Ted's father, Chris, in front of The Kid's Grocery & Bakery store in downtown Seattle, Washington, which his family owned and operated for over 40 years and where they worked six days a week.

bushberries, and even some grape vines. The family also had a garden for potatoes and assorted vegetables. They were 18 blocks outside of the city limits and there was even a city trolley to take them downtown, where the local bank, movie house, some restaurants, and other small businesses were thriving.

Ted would always look back fondly at this ideal time of his childhood. One of Ted's most prized possessions was a little wooden boat his mother had carved for him so he could explore the world—the world being the drainage systems throughout his Seattle suburb. It was this sense of adventure and exploration that filled little Teddy's childhood days. He would spend hours simply floating his boat through the streets of Seattle without a care in the world, nestled safely in the comfort of his parents' success. It is unusual to remember much from early childhood, especially once a man is well into his eighties. The little wooden boat, carved with a mother's love, would become a cherished reminder of simpler times before the world fell apart: a talisman to the explorer that Ted (and his mother) believed he was born to become.

Although Ted credits his mother with his desire to explore and see the world, he credits his father with his academic success. Chris loved to read, and his favorites included the classic Greek philosophers Herodotus and Thucydides. Mataxis family guidance was often based on *Aesop's Fables*. Phrases such as "the road to hell is paved with good intentions" and "pressure brings forth oil" were often employed as parental advice for the Mataxis children and grandchildren. According to Ted, "Over the years both my sister and I listened to my father's recounting of the history of our family story with the same attention we paid to *Aesop's Fables*. We thought he was 'gilding the lily' [as] it all sounded so improbable.... This was oral history at its best, one generation handing down their family story to the youth of the next generation. Dad always claimed that legends passed down from father to son, telling of the campaigns and wars had far more validity than some researcher who has read accounts which he then writes down in the history book. [Dad's] favorite saying was, 'And who wrote the history of Carthage?'" Don't all first-generation immigrant families descend from ancient royalty? Aren't they all "great families descended from the court of the Byzantine Empire … [who] fled with their families on the Venetian fleet when Constantinople fell in 1453 … becoming one of the most influential families of the Venetian Empire … taking part in the fight to free the Greeks from the Turks during the 1700s and early 1800s? We thought it was a case of an old man steeped in ancient philosophy and history 'telling stories.' Most families tend to overinflate the history of their families as a point of pride." Chris was not one of those men. As it turns out, and as Ted would later discover while serving as Commandant of Cadets at Valley Forge Military Academy in 1982, these stories were "chapter and verse of Dad's stories to us" and they were recorded clear as day in Michael Pratt's *Britain's Greek Empire*. Ted randomly picked up the book during one of his sister's visits to Valley Forge and according to Ted, they immediately "reviewed the accounts in this book and checked them against [our] recollections of his stories of the Metaxas family and for the first-time credence was lent to Dad's old stories." Turns out the Mataxis family are indeed descendents of a nobility that dates to the Byzantine Empire on his father's side.

At an early age, Ted showed a keen interest in history and the military. His first exposure to the military was initiated by a neighbor who gave him her son's collection of lead soldiers. Between the garden and the woodshed there was a small area which was his playground. Once he was gifted the soldiers, Ted quickly transformed this space into his very own battleground. Ted would constantly wage wars between these little lead soldiers when shooed out of the house by his family and told to go play. Ted would go on to collect foreign soldiers and officers dressed in ornately beautiful uniforms throughout the rest of his boyhood. He would keep his collection for his own son to pass on to his son. The soldiers have peacefully retired to live out the rest of their lives in a rather posh display cabinet.

Ted's newfound obsession with toy soldiers and the military was encouraged by his father's own keen interest in history. Ted would eventually move his soldiers from their sporadic childlike battles in the back yard to their new well-planned campaigns in the living room. As young Ted became older, he and his father spent their free time on Sunday afternoons "war-gaming" key battles of history. Their playbooks at the time were *Wars of Olden Times: Abraham to Oliver Cromwell* by Alfred Miles and Creasey's *The World's Most Famous Battles*. Each Sunday, Ted and his father would select another battle to reenact on their living room rug. Player piano scrolls and books were stuffed under the carpet to recreate proper battlefield configurations and terrain features, and blue ribbon used for rivers. According to Ted in an account later given for posterity, "I would be assigned certain campaigns to read then discuss with my father complete with a prologue of the setting of the battle and an epilogue of the effects on history. I can still remember reading and rereading Xenophon's *Anabasis* (or the march of the 10,000 Greek hoplite mercenaries through Asia Minor after the defeat of the Persian king who hired them as mercenaries). Later, when I took ancient Greek at college, *Anabasis* was our first reading assignment. I must confess that my prior knowledge of the campaign was rather helpful." One can only assume that by the time Ted started school as a first grader in 1924, he was practically a military scholar already.

His fate as a military leader would be solidified in elementary school. During these school years, Ted was allowed the opportunity to star as the circus's ringmaster in his elementary school's yearly play. Once he was allowed to try on his costume (the boots, the top hat, the whip), a little mini tyrant was born. Ted's long line of Metaxas' military heroes and the blood of his people influence the enticement of power and command. It was in this moment, and for months afterwards as he continued to wear the costume every day even after the play had come to an end, that Ted's lifelong passion to lead others while serving his country took root. Ted Mataxis had found his own American dream. He had felt power, strength, leadership, and he wasn't ever going to relinquish them again.

Ted would have a vast understanding of the history of his Metaxas side, but he would have a living relationship with his mother's Scandinavian side. Since the family lived in Seattle, Ted's parents would send him to spend his summers on the farm owned by Ted's youngest uncle, Siegfried Osterdall (known as Uncle Sieg), right outside of the city on Mount Rainier. His first trip was in 1924 at the age of seven, and the trips continued through his high school years. The farm was typical of the time: oil lamps for light, a central wood-burning stove, a water pump on the back porch with a pail to distribute it (there was no indoor plumbing), and a much-needed two-hole outhouse where they regularly utilized the local newspaper. Saturday night was for

This image depicts an elementary school-aged Ted, dressed as a ringmaster in his school's yearly play. This gave Ted his first taste of being in charge, dressed in his boots and top hat, carrying his whip. This is when he decided he wanted to be a leader.

bathing. Family members would take turns bathing after the hot water was brought from the kitchen fire and poured into the old tin tub. Occasionally, if they were lucky enough, one of the local farmers would slaughter a calf or a pig and distribute the fresh meat to all the neighboring farms. There was no refrigeration. A radio was all the entertainment that they had. It truly did not matter though as they seemed to keep each other amused rather easily. Ted fondly recalled these days, stating, "I would take a coal sack along the railway and throw pieces of coal in it." Basically, he grew to love the fresh air, exercise, and the train itself. The task allowed him a peaceful escape from a boisterous family, as well as giving him a purpose. It was his duty to provide a much-needed source of heat for the farm. He learned at a very early age that it was possible to mix business and pleasure in a very seamless way—by foraging forgotten coal along the path of the same railway that carried his father to the West Coast a decade before. Later, Ted would be given another job: "cutting the feeders of the strawberries." It was a task about which he had a lot less to share. Along with his summer visits to the farm there was also an annual family reunion/picnic every summer. The family, along with several cousins (there were always scads of kids), would descend upon the farm for the good old time.

Along with these farm summers, family reunions, and school plays, Ted also looked forward to Seattle's two biggest events of the year: the 4th of July celebration and the World War I Armistice Day parade. During Ted's childhood, patriotism and service to the country was accepted as every citizen's duty. Service was something to be celebrated. Ted's decision to later join the military resulted directly from an Armistice Day parade held during the fall of 1929. It was in that parade that Teddy and his Boy Scout troop followed the Seattle mounted police unit over the streetcar tracks and brought up the end of the parade. Leading the parade were a couple of open touring cars which carried both Union and Confederate veterans of the Civil War. Ted was immediately struck by these enemies who were cordially sitting side by side. These veterans were riding together and communicating to one another as if they were old friends. The Civil War veterans were followed by the middle-aged Spanish-American War veterans, who were then immediately followed by the World War I veterans. The army, navy, and marine troops paraded behind these heroes. Ted was entranced by all the servicemen, as he marched proudly behind them with his fellow scouts.

Ted's scoutmaster at the time was a World War I veteran, so he took the boys to talk with the Civil War veterans after the parade. He would later bring the younger Spanish American and World War I veterans to the scout meetings to talk about their war experiences. During camp that year, the scoutmaster taught the boys how to live in the field, how to read maps, and how to use their compasses to find their way. Ted vividly remembered this experience as life changing; it instilled in him a lifelong love for the Boy Scout program and reinforced his militaristic desires to serve as he became proficient in these skills.

Unfortunately, by middle school, the Great Depression brought all this American prosperity to a jarring halt. What had been a prosperous childhood made possible by his father's successful grocery in downtown Seattle ended thanks to the strain the depression put on every American's spending habits and ability to pay for goods and services. "Dad's farm" eventually became too much for the Mataxis family to sustain, and as a result they were forced to sell their only home in order to avoid being completely destitute or having to liquidate the store. They lost their big house and moved into the small tar paper shack in the back that they affectionately renamed "the bungalow." It was during this same time that Ted had to quit scouting because money was so tight his family could not afford the nickel a week it cost to be a Boy Scout. He became a Boy Scout on his 12th birthday in 1929, the only bright spot in the year as the stock market crashed and the country slid downhill into the depression. He had only become a First Class with one merit badge when money became so short that he had to drop out of scouting. Ted maintained his enthusiasm for the program and continued on his own to consume the *Handbook for Boys (The Scouting Manual)*. He studied it just like his father before him had studied a favorite old English dictionary. He studied field craft, leadership skills, healthier craft, and citizenship while learning the code of the organization through independent study. Throughout his lifetime, Ted Mataxis epitomized the Scout Oath and Law. Looking back over his life, one of his proudest accomplishments was passing on his love for this organization to his son (an Eagle Scout by the age of 12 who was also awarded all three palms—bronze, gold, and silver—and the Explorer Scout equivalent of Eagle Scout—the Silver Award). All five of his grandsons achieved the rank of Eagle Scout. As an aside, later during the draft for World War II when his cadre had to train draftees, the military brass filled the company with those who had Boy Scout experience as acting squad leaders.

What Ted did not study, much to his father's dismay, was his own Greek heritage. According to a later account given by Ted, "As a young boy I was required to take the New Testament in Greek at the Greek language school run by the Greek Orthodox Church in Seattle. I am sorry to say that as I grew older what we call today a 'generation gap' grew and I finally refused to attend Greek school and [I] rejected the 'old country ideas' that Dad used to love to talk to me about.... Fortunately, when I first became an officer [and returned] from World War II as a decorated Infantry Battalion Commander, [my dad and I] could again enjoy discussing ancient history and even philosophy."

During the depression, other aspects of Ted's life changed as well. Now hunting was not simply recreation, but rather a chance to help the family's food budget by killing deer for much-needed food. During the large family's annual reunions at his uncle's farm during the summer, all the boys and men would have shooting contests. At the age of 12, if they had proven they were proficient with the .22 rifles, the

This picture is of Ted in his Boy Scout uniform. Ted had a lifelong belief in the Boy Scouts and what it did for young people. One of his most proud moments was when all five of his grandsons became Eagle Scouts.

young men of the family were permitted to fire both family rifles used in the Spanish-American war, a 45/70 military Springfield, and a Craig 30/40. Uncle Sieg had been in the Swedish army and was in the US Army in World War I. He had been a predatory game hunter on Mount Rainier, then a constable for King County, Washington, after the war. He was also a gunsmith who repaired old guns to be sold later. As one of Ted's earliest mentors/role models, Sieg shared his gunsmithing skills, lifelong love of guns, and his hunting skills with a maturing Ted during these family reunions. This is where Ted developed his love of hunting, which he continued to enjoy all around the world during his many international assignments.

Mataxis was a solid student throughout his academic career, much to the chagrin of his younger sister, Helen, who constantly had to follow in the wake of her "wonderful older brother." Ted grew from an inquisitive child into a proper young man who was well liked by his teachers and fellow students. He was good at group work and able to motivate others (both traits he would lean into as a future officer). He is reported to have been honest and consistent. He connected learning directly to his life and he was a continuous goal setter.

His sterling school career would remain intact even after the uncharacteristic but rather successful "stink bomb" attacks that were launched in the bathrooms and hallways of his high school during his senior year. He received a chemistry set for Christmas in 1929 and tried to make chlorine gas. He had a couple of friends who had to go to the doctor, which ended his chemistry experiments until high school. In his senior year Ted and his group of close friends were initiating coordinated "stink bomb" attacks throughout the halls, as the world was facing its own share of threats.

During the 1930s, the dictatorships of Hitler in Germany and Mussolini in Italy were emerging, threatening the peace established by the defeat of Germany and the Austro-Hungarian Empire during World War I. In the Far East, Japan launched her plan to dismember China and take over the eastern Pacific area through Southeast Asia and Australia. Japan took Manchuria from China. Italy seized Libya and then Ethiopia. It was during this chaos that Mataxis graduated from Lincoln High School in 1936.

Upon graduating from high school, Ted had planned to enlist in the Marines. Family lore claims that it was one of his random moments of fashionable vanity and that he preferred the cut and color of the Marine uniforms to the other branches. Perhaps enlisting in the Marines was merely Ted's attempt to recapture those golden moments of his peaceful childhood exploring the drainage systems of his Seattle neighborhood with his most prized possession, the little wooden boat his mother had carved for him long ago. Despite his reasoning, Mataxis would never join the Marines. His mother would persuade him to go to university for at least one semester before enlisting. Much to his mother's and father's satisfaction, Ted would continue his college education and be the first of his American family to obtain a college degree. In 1940, Ted was commissioned at the age of 23 while still in ROTC at the University of Washington. And the rest, as they say, is history.

Ted at a local lake in a Seattle park in 1943.

As an aside: Ted was introduced to his future wife Helma by his younger sister. Helma was a senior at Lincoln High School and Ted was a Junior at the University of Washington. They were married in 1940. Their official and well-documented military life would begin with their military wedding and end with Ted's military funeral, over 67 years later. Wilhelmina Mary "Helma" Jensen was born in Seattle, Washington on August 1, 1921. Her father was Mr. Emil M. Jensen. He had been born on February 1, 1893, in Denmark. During World War I, he was a sergeant in G Company of the 14th Infantry, stationed at Camp Grant, Rockford, Illinois. At the close of the war, he was discharged with a disability, which was a hidden form of tuberculosis from which he died on February 20, 1926, at the age of 33.

After he got out of the US military, he was a Seattle police officer, where the officers learned to love and respect him. Helma was five years of age when he passed away. His wife, Julia Drankey Jensen, was so distraught over his death that she pined away and died two years later when Helma was seven. Helma was raised in a house in Seattle that was left to her at her parents' passing. Her aunt, along with her family, moved in to raise Helma. In her early years Helma knew little about her family other than having a picture of her grandfather in a Danish army uniform with a huge saber. Years later, when Helma was asked about her family by her grandchildren she embarked on some genealogical research. This is

Helma's mother, Julia Drankey Jensen, and father, Emil M. Jensen, seen at the end of World War I.

Helma's father in the Danish Army before he came to the United States and joined the army for World War I.

what she recounted: "My father had been born February 1, 1893, in Denmark. He had come over from Denmark where his father, my grandfather, had been very successful. Emil's parents were Wilhelmina 'Nelson' Jensen and Christian Jens Jenson, born October 27, 1830. My grandfather had served as a colonel in the Danish army from 1850 to 1870. He was a veterinarian in a horse cavalry division and had been knighted in 1885. We made a trip to Denmark to see where he had lived; the village had the 12th-century church where my great grandfather was married, and my father baptized." In addition to the house and belongings left to her in Seattle by her parents, she also inherited her mother's family farm, which was located on the banks of the Red River in Minnesota. Ted and Helma visited Minnesota to research her mother's family. She had always thought her grandfather on her mother's side was from Oslo, Norway. When researching the Drankey family she discovered her grandfather was born in Oslo, Minnesota not Oslo, Norway. His father had come to Minnesota with a group of Norwegians in the 1850s to homestead that area. They were able to visit the old Norwegian church where her grandparents were buried. It was a very close-knit community and the first church service given in English was not until the 1930s. Helma and Ted enjoyed investigating Helma's genealogy and lineage to answer the questions of their children and grandchildren. Helma took great pride in the fact that her fraternal grandfather's saber was used for cake cutting at their wedding, and her grandchildren's weddings, as well as several retirements. It is now in the Mataxis family for the sixth generation.

CHAPTER 2

The ROTC Years, 1936–40

Family lore continues to argue about who ultimately persuaded Ted to attend university. The one thing that most of the family can agree on is that Ted must have been swayed by the argument and desire of both of his parents for him to be the first Mataxis to attend college. Both parents, as first-generation immigrants, realized the value of an education and stressed its importance to both their son and daughter. In the fall of 1936, Ted Mataxis, because of enrolling in a land grant college where all physically fit male students were required to take Reserve Officers Training Corps (ROTC) for the first two years, was automatically enrolled as a member of the cadet corps. As a result of this compulsory practice, the University of Washington had approximately 2,000 student cadets: 1,800 were Military Science (MS) 1 and 2 students. Their enrollment was in fact required by law. The remaining 200 students were MS 3 and 4. They were handpicked because of their earlier performances and their desire to serve and to be commissioned as second lieutenants upon graduation. MS 1 and 2 students wore blue uniforms that indicated that they had not yet been selected as potential officer cadets, whereas MS 3 and 4 cadets wore the prized army green uniforms with sand brown belts. These brown belts were a badge of distinction, much like the green berets worn in today's army. Ted's goal upon entering college immediately became possession of a sand brown belt of his own. After Ted completed his first two compulsory years of ROTC training, he volunteered and was selected for advanced ROTC. He realized that upon graduating he could earn an inactive reserve second lieutenant commission. This program was designed to turn out reserve second lieutenants who could man the reserves and National Guard divisions and serve as a pool of officers in the event of mobilization. According to Ted, "I wanted to go into ROTC at the U of W because growing up Dad had instilled a sense of pride in myself and a faith in my abilities to succeed. I was after all in America, where 'an immigrant's son had a chance to fulfill his own dreams, if he would take ownership of it and work hard for it.' I truly believed that I owed it to America because my country was a place where a man could come like my father, from Europe with only a few dollars to his name, and end up with a business of his own and provide for a family he never imagined having." Ted was of the generation where the American dream was still alive and well, and where service to your country was a way to pay back society for all your opportunities. Ted's military focus would remain on his ROTC program from 1936 until the summer of 1940.

In addition to the annual curriculum and physical education requirements for the cadets, students participated in two major civic events every year. One of the major yearly events for ROTC during Ted's time was the fall pre-football parade for the Governor. Seattle is rather frigid in the fall. It's cold enough to freeze almost anything. Many of the ROTC cadets had problems with their sabers during these parades. As a result of the wintery temperatures, the cadets' hands would slowly grow numb, and their movements would become more and more difficult. When passing in review, it was more common than not to see a cadet dropping his sword, with the saber sticking securely into the frozen turf. Because of the weather during the fall program, the spring Memorial Day parade, with the American Legion and other patriotic organizations, was the much-preferred ROTC experience amongst the cadets.

Ted excelled in ROTC, and he rose quickly in the cadet corps and joined the Scabbard and Blade Society. The Scabbard and Blade Society is a college-based military honor society founded at the University of Wisconsin in 1904. Membership is open to ROTC cadets and midshipmen of all military services. The society focuses on academic excellence and exposes these future leaders to a wide variety of resources that are based on the foundational qualities of honor, leadership, professionalism, and unity.

During the time he was in ROTC, Ted's Professor of Military Science (PMS), Lieutenant Colonel Delphin Thebaud, made an indelible impression on young Ted. The PMS had been a rifle company commander in World War I and had received the Distinguished Service Cross and a Purple Heart. He made it very clear to the cadets that war was coming, and they must be prepared for what lay ahead. He saw his mission as preparing the young ROTC students to be second lieutenants in an army that would soon go to war. Having experienced the brutality of World War I up close and personally, Lt. Col. Thebaud knew how important it was to prepare for war. Thebaud explained to his cadets, "There's a war coming in which you will be platoon leaders. You need to prepare yourself during mobilization to assume the responsibility of two grades above your rank." According to Ted's account several decades later, "He cautioned us that while doing our job well, we must also try to visualize what those two ranks senior to you were doing, because one day, you may find yourself in the only senior officer's position in the company." Cadet Mataxis would utilize this advice throughout his whole career. He was commissioned in June 1940 as a second lieutenant. A mere three and a half years later during the winter of 1944, Mataxis would command his own battalion in brutal combat as a major. He would be promoted to lieutenant colonel within the same year.

According to Ted, "Lt. Col. Thebaud continually hammered home the idea that these young men needed to 'get mentally prepared to lead troops in combat.'" Thebaud also stressed the need for younger lieutenants to be trained as well or better than their soldiers on all the weapons which could be found in an infantry battalion. He encouraged practicing disassembling and assembling machine guns and Browning Automatic weapons. Basically, he believed all the company's weapons should be mastered by the cadets. According to Ted, "Lt. Col. Thebaud's mantra was that 'someday you may be the only survivor in a position that will be able to fire them.' Needless to say, this is a lesson I never forgot during my next three wars." Lt. Col. Thebaud also stressed that whenever one was given a mission, one must always prepare for the worst-case scenario so one will not be surprised when it happens. He explained that all plans normally change when the first shot is fired. He also advised the cadets not to be worried about making mistakes, but rather to be worried about not repeating them. This philosophy was based on the premise that mistakes happen as it is all part of learning a job. This really contrasts with the era of zero defects which expects perfection. According to Ted's journals, "Thebaud not only told us of his World War I experience—but also held a show-and-tell when he brought some of his souvenirs, to include a German Maxim machine gun which he had captured." Apparently, the pre-existing gun nut nurtured in Ted during the summers with his uncles on the family farm understood, as the newly minted ROTC cadet, that he was going to want to collect whatever he could during his future wartime adventures.

Lt. Col. Thebaud also arranged for decorated World War I veterans and Spanish-American War NCOs to participate in his history class to provide an authentic account of their experiences. Thebaud hoped to illustrate to the cadets that official histories do not always capture life in the field, thus reinforcing a concept Ted's dad had previously introduced during his childhood. Official histories are replete with phrases such as, "The old guard may die but it does not surrender," a phrase attributed to French General Pierre Cambronne at the Battle of Waterloo; however, what he is really supposed to have said was "*Merde*!" According to Ted, Thebaud had these ex-NCO vets "tell it to us as it was—from their viewpoint!"

Ted would go on to admit that, "All good soldiers can identify with the warrior ethos that is the basic cornerstone of esprit and high morale." Thebaud's key teaching points stressed what made a "good lieutenant." He also spent some time on the indications of an incompetent one, as well. Ted would use these early lessons to reinforce the "critical importance of bonding in combat, and the warriors' ethos." He believed these concepts to transcend "our different nationalities, causes, and theaters of war." Soldiers first fought for their cause and country; however, this creates a bonding of men and unit solidarity. Ted was never one for the "fripperies or superficialities" and he warned throughout his career of the dangers of "the trappings of things militaristic or transient fads of the moment." They simply got in the way of the lessons Ted learned early on in his ROTC program at the hands of a "kindred spirit" with "an unspoken passion for soldiering." Lt. Col. Thebaud taught a young, green soldier that the most important endeavors were "training, learning, fighting, and leading by example."

Ted would forever understand the lesson that Thebaud pounded into him as a young officer: "There are no bad units, only bad officers." What is most important to victory on the battlefield, according to General Mataxis, "is the sacred bond between leader and the led which creates the morale that enables soldiers to prevail in combat." Throughout the remainder of his time in the army, Mataxis would stress the value of what he had learned in ROTC, and he would expect the same from his officers, NCOs, and soldiers.

In the fall of 1939, Germany and Russia attacked Poland and divided it, while Britain and France went to war against Germany. Fortunately for the United States, Franklin Roosevelt was a strong president and was able to declare a national emergency in September 1939. He often quoted George Washington: "In times of peace prepare for war and keep your powder dry." He reinforced this by continuing to implement Teddy Roosevelt's dictum, "Speak softly, but carry a big stick."

In September 1939, President Roosevelt declared a limited national emergency. At this time, the regular army consisted of 187,000 personnel, about 200,000 National Guard, plus the reserves and a skeleton force of regular army. This emergency allowed the expansion of the regular army by increasing the army and the National Guard (NG) and calling reserve officers to active duty. As an early adrenaline junkie, Ted was the perennial volunteer. When the war broke out in Europe in fall 1939, Ted enlisted in the Washington National Guard with a group of fellow ROTC cadets. They all went down to join the 41st Infantry Division. The division was operating as a peacetime skeleton crew which was drastically understrength and had immediately approached ROTC members to recruit cadets to assist with the mobilization process. He ended up in the 116th quartermaster. In doing so, he became part of the increase of "other division elements to 75 percent peace strength." At his first weekend drill he was a cook and they served tube steaks, beans, and sauerkraut. At that time, he was shown how to use a meat cleaver to open cans and dump the contents into a large pot to heat over a coal fire. He found this experience to be less organized than his Boy Scout weekends and campouts at JC Hill in Seattle. Mataxis would next be transferred as a corporal to the 205th Coastal Artillery (AAA). He remained in Washington's National Guard from fall 1939 through 1 June 1940, when he was discharged to join the Reserves as a second lieutenant.

All senior cadets had to complete six weeks of training during the summer of 1939. They stayed in Vancouver Barracks in Washington, right across the river from Portland. Throughout America there was bitter division between those who wanted to stay out of the war in Europe and those who wanted to enter to help our old World War I Allies. The isolationists felt that we should stay home. The interventionists felt that we could not let our Allies down. During the time, American campuses were in turmoil, and the University of Washington was no different. There was no consensus on what should be done. According to Mataxis, "The young communist groups used to come down and throw rocks at us during our ROTC drills. Since our regular army instructors wouldn't let us get involved, some students joined Dudley Pellet's 'Silver Shirts' to drive them off." The tension between the young communist groups and the ROTC simply mirrors the chaos of the world that surrounded Ted during these college years. That summer, there was no question that war was looming on the horizon; it was just a matter of when.

This bitter division across the country was not only reflected on college campuses but it also presented itself in the War Department (before the Department of Defense and the Pentagon, the War and Navy Departments ran our armed forces). In the War Department, the Secretary of the Army was a Midwest isolationist, and the assistant secretary was an interventionist. This completely demoralized the civilian leadership and thrust General Marshall into prominence, and he dealt directly with President Roosevelt. The status of the military at this time is best described by a quote from a special study by the Center of Military History: "By 1940, the military establishment had grown into a loose federation of agencies—the general staff, special staff for services, overseas departments, and the Corps areas. Nowhere in this federation was there a center for energy and directing authority. Things were held together by customs, habit, SOP regulations, and a kind of general conspiracy among the responsible officers. In the stillness of peace, the system worked."

By spring 1940, there was no question in anyone's mind that the United States was going to war. Roosevelt was reelected in 1940 on the platform of "I hate war." In May 1940, the president federalized the National Guard. The state National Guard divisions were called to active duty and brought to wartime strength after the regular army had been backfilled with National Guard personnel. In August 1940, Congress authorized the president to impose a draft to bring personnel on active duty for a one-year period. The first draft registration took place on October 16 and was capped at 900,000 personnel. The call went out and a half million people signed up.

Impressed by the German air power in Poland, the United States decided to form 13 brand new antiaircraft (AA) units in the National Guard. The 205th Coast Artillery Regiment (Harbor Defense) was activated and started recruiting soldiers from the division. Mataxis immediately volunteered to go to the new AA unit. With war on the horizon, they were desperate to fill the units. He joined 'A' Battery. His battery commander was a World War I pilot, and his first sergeant was a World War I non-commissioned officer (NCO). He was offered the position of corporal and filled the slot of company clerk. Having explained to them that he couldn't type, he was told that a new 15-year-old high school student would do the typing. His responsibility would be to draw up lesson plans and teach during Army Reserve drills and meetings. When he explained that he didn't know the clerk's responsibilities, he

Ted's ROTC graduation photo prior to his commissioning as a 2nd Lieutenant.

was told to get a field manual and go to the ROTC clerk to find out what his duties and responsibilities would be, which he did immediately. During their scheduled drills, in additional pro bono classes, he taught his assistant how to fill out the forms that were required. During this time, Lt. Col. Thebaud would be an invaluable mentor to Ted. He would continue to show Ted how to maneuver in this new world.

In spring 1940, when his ROTC class was scheduled to join the 96th Infantry Division upon being commissioned, the sergeant who he had been assisting in maintaining rifles recommended that he join the 7th Infantry Regiment as a reserve officer. As stated by Mataxis, "I was due to receive my commission from ROTC in June 1940 and had already received an assignment in the area's local reserve division. I was scheduled to attend a two-week summer camp with them. In addition to the regular army and the National Guard, there existed several army reserve divisions. They were to be called up after the National Guard units and existed mostly at cadre strength. My assignment was as an infantry lieutenant in the 96th Infantry Division, our local reserve division. In addition to the reserve division assignments, we also had regular army assignments." At that time the regular army units were at peacetime strength and only had one officer and approximately 90 enlisted personnel per company. Their Table of Organization and Equipment (TO&E) calls for six officers and 200 plus enlisted personnel. The other five officers would come from reserve augmentation, and the enlisted personnel would come from the enlisted reservist pool of personnel and the draft. This would enable Ted to attend a summer camp of two weeks in June 1940 and would allow him to go on active duty when mobilization started. Ted graduated on June 8 from the University of Washington's ROTC program and by June 16 was training with his reserve regiment at Vancouver Barracks for his two weeks of active-duty summer camp. As a second lieutenant during these two weeks, he trained as an antitank platoon leader. They were armed with only 50 machine guns as antitank weapons. Ted was left perplexed, "I really wondered at our equipment; they were all World War I relics."

While on his two weeks' Reserve augmentation duty he recalled, "I received a TWX notifying me that the army had accepted my request for active duty, and I was detailed to the 20th Infantry at Fort Warren, Wyoming on 1 July 1940, with an initial assignment to Fort Benning, Georgia to attend a special infantry heavy weapons course." His tour with the 7th Regiment was not over until June 30, 1940. "Since it took four days by train, I requested to leave early on a special leave. The adjutant would not let me go! However, he graciously wired the Infantry School the date when I would be released, so that they could calculate my train travel time of four days." It appeared to Ted that the regiment adjutant seemed more interested in making sure that he bought a russet leather Sam Browne belt and boots than the cordovan he had purchased as part of his uniform during graduation. The understanding here was that the adjutant was deemed a self-absorbed chicken shit. By the time he was commissioned in June 1940, Mataxis had traded in his corporal stripes for the gold bars of a second lieutenant with the reserves. Upon completion of his time in the Reserves, Mataxis rushed home to beg his mother to wash his clothes (the poor woman) before he took off the next day for Fort Benning. By the time July 1940 arrived, Ted was discharged from the National Guard; he had served with the reserves for a mere six months. He would later claim that both experiences showed him "the type of tasks that he could be expected to do as a lieutenant."

Ted's first ID card photo after his commissioning as a 2nd Lieutenant in July 1940.

Second Lieutenant Ted Mataxis arrived at Fort Benning the evening of July 4, a mere four days late, where he would begin active duty. Fortunately, he was not missed. It appeared that the whole place was in complete turmoil. With newly commissioned second lieutenants pouring in from all over the country, housing was a problem. It was all hands on deck as they attempted to clear out barracks to make more room. They were also reusing "borrowed mattresses" from the regular army troops. This would become most of the lieutenants' first experience with crabs. The used mattresses they were provided with ended up being infested. Ted would later report to the 20th Infantry at Fort Warren, happily lice free.

CHAPTER 3

Active-Duty Mobilization, 1940–44

At this time, the peacetime army was under 200,000 men scattered in small posts across the United States. Between the World Wars, the United States neglected its armed forces. The US Army ranked as 17th in size among the world's armies. By 1940, the army only numbered 174,079 enlisted members and barely more than 12,000 officers. The National Guard, on the other hand, had 199,491 members in active roles and another 20,980 in inactive positions, all of which were concentrated in 18 infantry divisions and four cavalry divisions. For the first time since the early 1920s, the army outnumbered the National Guard in size. When the guard was mobilized in 1942, the regular army's numbers increased to 264,118, and the guard numbered 241,612. In the book *Mobilization*, published on the 50th anniversary of World War II, the author states that during the summer of 1940, the political climate in the United States can best be described as follows: "The general staff felt reluctant to call for conscription. It continued to assume that conscription would only become possible after a declaration of war. It was feared that proposing a draft now would arouse the isolationist and anti-preparedness forces to endanger the request now meeting general acceptance in Congress." However, by the end of the summer, public and Congressional sentiment had grown so in favor of a strong defense that it outran leadership. Congress enacted the Selective Training and Service Act on September 16, 1940.

This act was the first peacetime draft in United States history. It required all men between the ages of 21 and 45 to register. Mobilization started in September 1940, and the regular army's nine divisions went from peacetime to wartime strength. The draft was initially for 12 months. The draftees immediately coined the phrase OHIO, "over the hill in October of 1941," thus indicating the time the draftees would be released from 12 months of active duty and implying that the draftees would go AWOL at the end of their first year. In 1941, the draft was capped at 900,000 personnel and registered nearly 16.5 million. Over 35.8 percent of the registered draftees were deemed unfit by their medical evaluations. Following Japan's surprise attack on Pearl Harbor, Hawaii, in 1941, Congress amended the act to require that all nondisabled, 18- to 45-year-old men register with their local draft board for military service. Service would no longer be for only one year; instead, draftees would serve for the duration of World War II plus an additional six months after the war ended. This passed by one vote. This change meant that all National Guard and Reserve draftees that were called up to serve a year before were now required to stay for the "duration plus six months" of World War II, a long and bloody war that would last for another three to four years. By the war's end in 1945, 50 million men had registered for the draft, and 10 million individuals were inducted into the military.

FDR ran for his third term and almost everyone acknowledged that the draft was needed, but the country was still divided on the issue. To increase his chances for reelection, President Roosevelt declared, "I hate war!" He even elaborated that "Eleanor, my wife, hates war." Sometimes, he even declared "Fala, my dog, hates war." Political expediency reigned, so the much-needed draft was delayed again. This delay created a crisis in the number of adequately prepared soldiers in the US Army as it slowly transitioned from peacetime to a second world war. Apparently, the great war to end all wars was not the last war America would be forced to fight.

It is important to remember that the United States had allies that carried on the war effort between 1939 and 1941. The Allies' participation allowed the United States the time it needed to mobilize and establish industrial production for new weapons and necessary war equipment. This time also allowed personnel to be drafted, to complete individual and unit training, and to meet various requirements for deployment. Preparing our forces for combat in Europe and the Pacific was critical to ensure the best chances for our drafted soldiers to survive in a combat situation. On September 27, 1940, Germany, Italy, and Japan signed the Tripartite Pact, which became the Axis Alliance.

With World War II's outbreak in Europe, the US armed forces' weakness became a national concern. With the passage of the new draft law, those in the service were caught up in the first phase of the Mobilization Plan, which brought the army's regular nine peacetime-strength divisions up to wartime strength. The Mobilization Plan was based on a small, steady force that would rely heavily on the National Service Draft. The first wave of 1,500 draftees quickly arrived at the battalion level. The second phase of the Mobilization Plan called for wartime strength National Guard divisions (numbered 26–45) to help fill the divisions. During this time, divisions were tasked to send groups out to form two new basic training centers in California and Texas. The 63rd Infantry Regiment was at Camp White, Oregon and the 276th Infantry Regiment was at Camp Adair, Oregon. The third phase of the Mobilization Plan brought peacetime Army Reserve divisions (numbered 76–106) up to wartime strength. This buildup reflected World War I and was designed to support a force of approximately 90 divisions. This constant tasking of division personnel during these transitions significantly affected the experience of officers and NCOs and the unit's morale over time.

During the personnel upheaval in 1940, Lt. Mataxis, a new college graduate, reported to D Company of the 7th Infantry Regiment at Vancouver Barracks. He was there for his two-week-long annual training commitment: the US Army Reserve summer camp, scheduled for the middle of June 1940.

With the end of the US Army Reserve summer camp in June 1940, Lt. Mataxis received his orders for extended active duty. On July 1, 1940, with his freshly-washed clothes courtesy of his mother and a one-way train ticket, he headed for his first active-duty assignment at Fort Benning. He would attend the army's first weapons course since World War I at the Infantry School: a numberless pilot class/test bed focusing on basic squad and platoon tactics, leadership, and the army's new weapons. Even though the course effectively covered the fundamentals of being a platoon leader, a vital element of the course was to familiarize the lieutenants with the new weapons scheduled to replace the current World War I weapons already on hand. The course was used to prepare the Infantry School staff for the upcoming "Basic Weapons Course." The expectation was that the course's graduates would return to their units, and upon arrival of these new weapons systems, they could train the trainers. The dissemination of this information to recent draftees and established officers would be essential for a successful World War II mobilization. The class's lieutenants were well qualified to instruct others on these weapons systems, which included the M1 rifle, the improved Browning Automatic Rifle (BAR), a new light machine gun, a new 60 mm mortar, a new 81 mm mortar, and a new 37 mm antitank gun. When the army finally introduced these weapons to the general military, course graduates knew more than the senior-grade regular army (RA) NCOs.

Upon completing this course at Fort Benning in August 1940, Lt. Mataxis reported to the 1st Battalion, 20th Infantry Regiment, 6th Infantry Division (ID) at Fort Warren, Wyoming. He would remain here until June 1942. When Mataxis arrived during summer 1940, he found that this division was at peacetime strength and neglectfully understaffed. The division was reduced by the transfer of most field-grade officers and many senior captains to the Philippines, where they were charged with helping General MacArthur build up the Philippine Army. So, during summer 1940, Fort Warren was short of soldiers.

Ted and Helma, when she joined him at Fort Warren, Wyoming, when he was assigned to the 20th Infantry Regiment of the 6th Infantry Division.

In this tumultuous environment, Ted's life changed forever. It was not only 2nd Lt. Mataxis who reported for duty at Fort Warren. Two weeks after his arrival, Ted's hometown sweetheart and fiancé, Helma Jensen, joined him to begin her new life as a military wife. She would spend the next 32 years as a devoted military wife and loving mother, graciously moving from one assignment to another in all parts of the world. She would spend numerous years raising the children single-handedly while her husband served in World War II, Korea, and Vietnam. It wasn't until her husband retired in 1972 that she would finally build her dream home in Southern Pines, North Carolina. Helma's first experience with the army came when she arrived at Fort Warren, where she quickly learned that "if the army wanted you to have a wife, it would have issued you one." Since they had not issued Mataxis his wife of choice, they decided they would train her properly upon arrival.

When Helma arrived at Fort Warren, the army and 2nd Lt. Mataxis presented her with a copy of *The Officer's Guide*, which outlined the customs and protocols of the time. Life at Fort Warren in the 6th Division and 20th Regiment reflected the post-World War I peacetime army lifestyle: a culture deep in customs, traditions, and military courtesy. *The Officer's Guide* spelled out precisely what the army wanted and expected of both parties. There was no question that "what the military wanted; it got." The book was essentially the military's equivalent of Emily Post.

Everything a young couple needed to know was in *The Officer's Guide*, and it was followed to the letter by all the new officers. The officers' efficiency reports and promotions reflected compliance. During this time, wives were also "rated for adaptability and sociability." Military wives understood that promotions for their husbands meant more money and a higher social status for them. The connection between the book and being a successful officer was loud and clear. Everything was spelled out in *The Officer's Guide* for those who wanted to succeed. The chapter "Customs of the Service" was 21 pages of small print, and the chapter "Military Courtesy" was 15 pages. Additional support for "Fort/Post and Organization Activities" was spelled out in two more pages of small print. These pages explained what was demanded of an officer and included little gems like: "When the commanding officer states, 'I wish' or 'I desire' rather than, 'I order that you do so-and-so,' this wish, or desire has all the force of a direct order."

At Fort Warren, the officers' club was the base's social center, and the wives' club activities took priority on the post. There were meetings, formal teas, dances, and dinners. All were formal affairs highlighted by crystal and china plates that reflected the ladies' newest hats and gloves. The book prescribed a proper dress code: "Women could not wear pants or shorts to the post exchange or any other office on the post."

One did not want to be caught out of "uniform" during a party, and one did not want to be seen breaking etiquette protocol. Officers could not carry packages. They could not carry children or push baby buggies. Dress blues were standard for the officers' club and mandatory for calling hours during designated evenings beginning at 7 p.m.

Another requirement was calling cards. The calling cards were necessary for the officer and his wife and were required to be left when they made formal calls to other officers in the garrison. After a brief 10- to 15-minute visit, officers and their wives were expected to graciously leave while leaving an elegantly embossed calling card on the silver tray at every home's front entrance. If the senior officer was not there, one would leave a card as proof that they had been there when expected. When it was known that a senior officer was gone, a low-ranking officer was assigned the duty of gathering all the other lower-ranking officers' calling cards to deliver them through the mail slot before the senior officer returned, hopefully none the wiser what his officers had done.

The Officer's Guide also explained in detail what would be demanded of the battalion as it hosted its first formal military wedding on August 18, 1940. The wedding was conducted at the Fort Warren Officers' Club. The regimental commander, Col. George Blair, gave the bride away. Ted was dressed in his "pinks and greens" with his Sam Browne belt and sword. The army reinstated the historical army "pinks and greens" uniform set in 2020, minus the Sam Browne belt. Historically called "pinks and greens," the new army pink and green uniform harkens back to a time when America was helping to save the world from tyranny.

After watching his beautiful bride make her way down the aisle, Helma's enormous sacrifice landed square on Ted's shoulders. Images of his old ROTC instructor standing in front of the class, droning about a soldier's responsibility to prepare their wives for the reality of war, now held a newfound relevance. His ROTC lieutenant colonel's words flashed into his head. Before solemnly repeating his vows, Ted's last coherent thought was: "What the hell? Now I must train my wife to be a widow."

As was the army's traditional way of welcoming the bride to the army, Ted and Helma's military wedding ended with crossed swords. The "Arch of Swords" ceremony is an old English and American custom. It gives a symbolic pledge of the army's loyalty to the newly married couple and welcomes them to their new military

A picture from Ted and Helma's military wedding hosted by the 20th Infantry Regiment's commander. They moved into Quarters #68 at Fort Warren.

family. Tradition dictates that the bride and groom pass through the arch of six or eight swords as they leave the wedding ceremony. Tradition also dictates that the bride is on the groom's left-hand side so the officer can salute.

The ceremony was conducted by the procedures outlined in the Drill Manual (FM 22-5). The participants in the ceremony are in formation facing the exit and given commands to Carry Sabers. They draw their sabers and place them on their shoulders. That is followed by the command Forward March as they march into the designated position. The following command is Halt Center Face; they turn and face the center. The bridal party then walks towards the formation and stops before the first set of sabers. The person positioned in formation left introduces the couple and gives the command Present Sabers when soldiers draw their swords and bring them to their chins. The following command is Arch Sabers when they fully extend their right arms to form a cohesive arch. After they lift the sabers and form the arch, the bride and groom walk through it. They will be the only individuals allowed the privilege. The soldier closest to the bride then gives the bride a gentle pat on her behind and says: "Welcome to the army, Mrs. Mataxis." When the bride and groom reach the last two saber-bearers, the soldiers close their two sabers, bringing them down to cross at the waist level of the newly married couple, and request a kiss as payment for the couple's passage. The soldiers then raise the sabers, and the newly wedded couple passes. The command Sheath Sabers is then given, and the tradition ends. The practice of the bride and groom walking through the arch of swords is meant to ensure the couple's safe passage into their new life together. After the wedding, the reception was conducted with a proper military reception line. The couple used Helma's grandfather's saber for the traditional cutting of the wedding cake.

After completing the wedding reception, Ted and Helma were assigned to quarters 68 at Fort Warren. It was the era of "rank hath its privileges!" These quarters were quite large, with seven bedrooms and three baths. Traditionally, these were the quarters for senior officers. The quarters were vacant because many senior officers had been sent to the Philippines to train General MacArthur's new Philippine Army. Due to the officers' deployment, Ted and Helma, a newly-wedded couple, got to live in these vast quarters. When they moved in, their only possessions were those issued to them by the government: a bedroom suite, a living room sofa, a 9' by 12' area rug, and a dinette table with four chairs. The newlyweds would quickly make these assigned quarters their first home. One of Helma's more peculiar memories about her new living situation was a sign on the porch reading, "Do Not Shoot the Buffalo from the porch," which left her wondering how close the buffalo would roam during her stay.

After the move, the army stopped paying them their $40-a-month housing allowance. Despite the lost income, the couple felt like they had won the lottery. Officers like Ted were assigned an orderly and a soldier to maintain the furnace and cut the grass. As a 20-year-old newlywed, Helma instantly became the housemother for all the young girlfriends of the unmarried lieutenants. Ted and Helma would invite everyone to their home for weekend festivities, provided they bring cots and bedding from the troop barracks. It was the original BYOB party house.

Despite marital bliss and the fantastic living accommodations, Ted quickly shared that significant problems were brewing. When Lt. Mataxis joined the 6th Infantry Division, it was at peacetime strength. The army desperately needed the draft to increase the division to wartime numbers. Ted arrived a couple of months before thousands of draftees reported to the army under the new draft law. However, to help the division reach its numbers when there was no draft, the 1st Battalion, 20th Infantry Regiment and the 3rd Battalion, 63rd Regiment provided fillers for the 6th Infantry Division. Since only regular army soldiers could be deployed overseas, the 1st/20th Battalion and the 3rd/63rd regular army personnel deployed overseas and were then replaced with draftees. Before the draft, ordinary soldiers, NCOs, and officers served in replacement depots, and draftees and reservists were sent to regular units being formed to receive their individual and unit training. After the draft, units continually robbed each other to meet required personnel numbers. There was a constant turnover of leadership and personnel. This exchange between units had a chaotic and adverse effect on readiness and morale.

With the passage of a new draft law in 1940, those in service were caught up in the first phase of the Mobilization Plan. Each infantry rifle company would expand overnight from one to six officers and from 90 to 200 soldiers. The new draft law increased the regular army's six divisions, five infantry divisions and one cavalry division, from peacetime strength to wartime strength. Each activated division was designated a training post with its supply of war reserves from World War I to issue its recruits. The first wave of draftees quickly arrived at the division level and was immediately passed down to regiments and their battalions. At the time, Lt. Mataxis was the battalion adjutant and detachment commander. As the adjutant, he had to supervise the assignment of the thousands of new draftees and supervise the equipment arriving at his detachment. Each battalion received 1,500 personnel, who reported to duty in their civilian clothes. The thousands of uniforms, underwear, and boots that Lt. Mataxis had to provide were older than many draftees. All the government equipment for the battalion was supplied from World War I's leftover war reserves. The old rifles came in barrels of cosmoline, which took days to clean. The aged conditions of the supplies issued did not go unnoticed.

Many officers and senior NCOs were tasked to serve as cadres for new divisions being activated. Once issued everything they needed, the draftees began participation in the mobilization training plan (MTP). The MTP would prepare the 20th Infantry Regiment and the 6th Infantry Division for its upcoming deployment overseas into a combat environment. The MTP was the basic strategy for activating, training, and deploying activated divisions and remained unchanged throughout the war. Before a division could go into combat, it had to complete the MTP and be certified. Under the MTP, recruits underwent basic and advanced individual training for 17 weeks. For the next step, lasting 13 weeks, unit training was conducted. During this time, the platoon and company executed dry fire and live fire exercises, which combined arms training exercises. Finally, as the culmination of a division's training, the division was deployed as part of a corps to participate in a new exercise maneuver area. During this phase, a unit conducted tactical drills to develop techniques used in the field and developed their standard operating procedures (SOPs). After this training, the division was typically relocated to a different fort or camp. Upon arriving at the new location, the unit received an additional eight weeks of training to learn how to use air support, tank support, and antitank warfare techniques. Upon conclusion of these 52 weeks, the division was certified to deploy. As a result, these divisions trained and worked together for at least a year, building unit cohesion and developing teamwork and esprit de corps.

The second phase of the Mobilization Plan called National Guard units to active duty during the winter of 1940–41 to create an entire wartime strength military. This fulfillment resulted in the National Guard units' move to Fort Warren. This displacement moved the 6th Division's 20th Regiment to the summer camp area at Fort Leavenworth, Kansas. Soldiers were ordered to spend the brutal Kansas winter of 1940–41 in tents on wooden platforms outfitted with primitive wood-burning stoves. These heating units would bellow big puffs of dark smoke, sending sparks airborne that would often land on the surrounding tents, instantly burning holes in the very thing meant to protect the men from the harsh winter elements. As the saying goes, "Nothing is too good for our troops," and nothing is precisely what they got.

The wives found themselves on their own once again. As resourceful as their husbands, the wives heard about a few one- and two-bedroom cottages initially built for the Union Electric personnel responsible for creating the Bagnell Dam at the Lake of the Ozarks. The ladies pooled their resources to afford the $15 rent. They immediately outfitted the cottages with purchased hot plates, chaise lounges, and card tables. They slept on army cots. The wives made stools and chairs from nail kegs discarded at construction sites. The wives embellished them with hand-sewn homey cushions for the chairs and stools. They also used dyed target cloth for their curtains and were mindful of creating other little homey touches for the somewhat rustic living conditions on the off chance that their husbands could sneak away at least one day of the week. The officers rarely made it home on the weekdays, if ever. On the weekends, they did manage to sneak away while their wives were there waiting with picnic baskets in hand. The exhausted officers had no desire to stroll through the woods. These little compromises between wives and husbands would reflect the more significant issues of this assignment. The living arrangements provided were the cause of many problems for the division at the

Fort Leavenworth bivouac site. Luckily, the hospitality of Fort Leavenworth only lasted a few months as the military quickly built more suitable accommodations at Camp Leonard Wood, Missouri.

To hear Ted's version of the experience, "In June 1940, the 6th Infantry Division was concentrated at Fort Warren, Wyoming, and Fort Leonard Wood, a newly constructed mobilized training area in Missouri. Per the second phase of the mobilization, the National Guard units were called to active duty after filling all the active-duty divisions. Then in January 1941, a National Guard unit moved into our barracks, and we moved to Fort Leavenworth to the summer campsite, which meant we would spend the winter in tents. Once again, it was the unit tasked to send groups out to form two new basic training centers in California and Texas. Finally, in June 1941, we moved to Fort Leonard Wood, into new wooden barracks. There was nothing around them except small farms, red clay, and wild boar. The newly constructed wooden barracks were it. The nearest town was Waynesville, with a population of 98 people. The small village was outnumbered by hundreds of carpenters who were on site to build the new barracks. Upon arrival, leaders quickly informed the unit that its soldiers had to construct their own supply rooms and the miscellaneous buildings required by the battalion for daily operations. The added challenge was that they would have only scrap lumber to use for their buildings. The task proved to be very time-consuming and arduous. Innovation eventually took hold, as it would to accomplish the impossible, and the 'midnight requisition' was created. After dark, soldiers went out and 'borrowed' the regular lumber they needed to get the job done. As units found that they did not possess whatever they needed to accomplish the mission, the 'midnight requisitions' became an army tradition. We left in July for regimental maneuvers, and then participated in the big Louisiana maneuvers, returning in October 1941."

Helma's side was less military-focused and more oriented towards losing her nice newlywed quarters and even her cozy little cottage. According to Helma, "At Fort Leavenworth, no quarters were available for married officers, which caused additional hardship for us. Everyone was forced to find accommodations off post. Ted and I were forced to live in a small two-bedroom, one-bathroom house with two other couples so we could all split the $140-a-month rent and utility bills. Two couples lived upstairs in the bedrooms, and Ted and I lived in the living room. We went from a big house with three bathrooms to sharing one bathroom between three couples and our combined quarters allowance could not cover the cost. It was less than ideal."

Despite the continued tasking of division personnel, the battalion continued to reboot their training cycle, which included basic training and unit training for the individual draftees and new officers arriving to backfill for the departed officers. At the same time, unit training continued to prepare for the MTP and numerous upcoming maneuvers. According to Ted, "In January 1942, the 6th Division was

The house that Helma and Ted shared with two other couples for $140 a month. It had two bedrooms and one bathroom. Helma and Ted converted the dining room into their bedroom.

converted to a mechanized infantry division and issued armored personnel carriers; we had yet to prepare our personnel to work with these machines. The division had a series of 'Motor Moves' and it required the three regiments to alternate: one unit would start marching, one would shuttle in the trucks, and one would ride for a day in the trucks. Then each day, they would rotate." At this time, the army needed several more divisions for the battle campaign, so they activated several for participation in the war. A lot of the training focused on marching with equipment and strength building for the draftees: the standard for a five-mile march was one hour, a nine-mile march took two hours, and 25 miles was to be completed in eight hours. These benchmarks are not significantly different from today's Special Forces' operation criteria. All marches included rifle, helmet, and backpack.

The move to Fort Leonard Wood was short-lived and only lasted six weeks. In July 1941, Ted's unit reported for regimental maneuvers and then participated in the Big Louisiana Maneuvers. In the middle of this chaos, there was an army-wide shortage of equipment, including track vehicles and tanks. This shortage required that soldiers use trucks with signs on them reading "tank" when training. They simulated antitank guns using pipes, created mortars out of logs, and the rifles they used were old World War I Enfield rifles. Everyone knew these training situations were far from desired; however, they had a schedule to meet. When these maneuvers began in July 1941, many of the wives returned home because their husbands would not return before December 1941. At this time, Helma returned to Seattle, Washington, and enrolled in college courses at the University of Washington.

Up to this point, the army had not functioned at the regimental or divisional level since World War I. As a result, the army had to develop operation procedures based on the lessons learned during the maneuvers; it turned out that many lessons and operation procedures were developed and then revised over time. One realization was that the army had a current shortage of qualified junior officers. In November 1941, military leaders agreed that far too many second lieutenants were serving. This concern led to a procedural revision: the military began to promote second lieutenants after 18 months of service rather than the previously required three years. Second Lt. Mataxis was promoted to First Lt. Mataxis on November 1, 1941. These promotions provided some experienced junior leadership positions of increased responsibility army-wide, thus allowing for new second lieutenants to fill their now vacant ranks.

Once they completed regional maneuvers, the training of the units culminated in the large-scale Louisiana Maneuvers during June–December 1941 between the Second and Third Armies. During these maneuvers, the 6th Division maneuvered as part of the Second Army through Arkansas to Louisiana against the Third Army. The maneuver was designed to give the senior staff at corps and the army practice moving and supplying entire armies in the field, a task not necessary since World War I.

General Eisenhower later said, "The maneuvers were a vast laboratory experiment to prove the worth of ideas, men, weapons and equipment." He said that the lessons learned, and the policies and procedures developed as a result, were "incalculable." As the army was being mobilized, the military personnel had no experience commanding and coordinating anything over regiment size. This exercise was an actual force-on-force, which involved over 400,000 troops. The size of the training maneuvers highlighted the problems and provided a living laboratory where soldiers could work out the solutions to what they encountered in the field. One such problem was the need for the logistical units to teach troops how to operate and maneuver in the arena. These maneuvers also provided the army with an opportunity to look at its leadership. They could evaluate deficiencies and recognize the best and the brightest officers and NCOs presently serving. Many officers participating in the exercise were considered superstars who would rise quickly through the senior ranks during World War II: Dwight D. Eisenhower, Omar Bradley, George Patton, Joseph Stilwell, Mark Clark, Leslie J. McNair, Walter Krueger, and Samuel E. Henderson. In short, the Louisiana maneuvers provided a rapidly mobilizing army with a hands-on opportunity to see what skills and training were necessary before entering the war.

When the Japanese unexpectedly attacked Pearl Harbor on December 7, 1941, America's participation in World War II officially began. Everything changed when America declared war. Rules and attitudes instantaneously altered for all of America; life for Ted and Helma changed drastically. Helma left Seattle, went back to Missouri, and settled in a two-bedroom apartment in a private home in Eldon, Missouri, 65 miles away from Fort Leonard Wood. With the war's escalation and US involvement, the army stopped shipping furniture, and most military-sanctioned moves were temporary. Wives followed their husbands around the country, living in whatever was available, and their possessions were reduced to what they could pack in a car and trailer.

By spring 1942, National Guard divisions were activated, and the next mobilization phase started. The divisions were equipped with the Master Training Plan (MTP) program: a 52-week training cycle designed to prepare a combat-ready division to deploy overseas to Europe or the Pacific in less than a year. The MTP was more detailed and reflected the lessons learned from our bitter World War I mobilization experiences and in the mobilization of the regular army division presently. The army's MTP preparations were designed to increase our armed forces' chance of success during increased danger. As the flood of draftees arrived, the guard divisions were tasked to train them as quickly as possible to survive.

In June 1942, First Lt. Mataxis was selected as a cadre from the 6th Division to a newly activated reserve division, the 91st Infantry Division, at Fort Leonard Wood. This division's nickname was the Wild West Division. The division patch was an evergreen tree. In June 1942, Army Reserve division staff, like Ted, were sent for a month to Fort Benning to attend a new division course of cadre training to better understand how a division should be mobilized and to better handle the influx of new draftees and to help the mobilization run smoothly. Helma accompanied Ted on his drive to Fort Benning. This would be one of the last times Ted and Helma had to spend together for quite some time. Upon completion of the course, Ted was assigned to Camp White, Oregon, and Helma left for Seattle to have the couple's first baby, Shirley Jean Mataxis, born on October 14, 1942.

Captain Mataxis was a company commander in the 361st Infantry Battalion, 91st Division, from June 15, 1942, until January 1943. Ted's relatively new division was ordered to active service and immediately told to reorganize at Camp White, Oregon. Ted remembers the commander, General Gerhart, saying, "I propose to make this new 91st Division the best the United States has ever seen." The commander said that the division's training would be tough but that "what [they] learned could save their lives!" Since they were only a "skeleton," the regular divisions had to furnish cadres to prepare the Reserve Divisions to be filled with draftees and be trained for overseas movement. At Camp White, located near Medford, Oregon, officers and NCO cadres were created to receive brand-new lieutenants or 90-day officers. The cadres were to prepare the lieutenants to receive 15,000 draftees requiring equipment, and individual, team, and unit training. During this time Ted served as Headquarters Company commander, battalion XO, and as the battalion's S-3. His next crisis was when the 91st Division was ordered to form a cadre for another "wave" of activated divisions.

Ted was then assigned to the newly formed 70th Infantry Division, which was activated at Camp Adair, Oregon, on January 18, 1943. En route Ted was required to attend the three-month course of the 12th General Staff Course at Fort

Leavenworth, and then the 13th New Division Course in March–April 1943 to prepare for his new assignment. The division was called the "Trailblazers," whose motto was "Oregon's own." The division's shoulder patch was red in the shape of an ax, laid on a white ax head superimposed on the red background; also in white is a replica of Mount Hood beside the mountain stands of fir tree and green. The first assigned soldiers came in February 1943, when the 91st Infantry Division formed the nucleus of a new division.

According to Helma, "I moved to Eugene, Oregon, to join Ted for a while. After this, I returned to Seattle, since the military moved the division to Camp Leonard Wood, Missouri, in spring 1944 for additional training." On January 22, 1943, IV Corps headquarters changed the 70th Division's orders from Fort Lewis, Washington, to Camp Adair, Oregon. This change caused mass chaos because many of the cadres' families had moved to the vicinity of Fort Lewis earlier when they were told that was where they would be assigned. They set up a "home base" while their husbands participated in training. Because of this change, families now had to move again to the vicinity of Camp Adair.

In April 1943, Ted was assigned as the assistant division G-3. The army was under 200,000 based on mobilization. The division received enlisted cavalry personnel from the 1st Infantry Division. Ted says in a later presentation on the period, "The army was short of officers at that time. I was a young captain with two years of service and was selected to go to the Command and General Staff College (CGSC) in February 1943 to prepare me to become the assistant G-3 in the 70th Division, stationed in Seattle, Washington. This assignment was before I had attended the Advanced Infantry Class, which was required to command a battalion. I finished 12th in the Command General Staff College in April 1943, then attended the Thirteenth New Division Course, March–April 1943, at Fort Leavenworth, and was promoted." During spring 1943, Major Mataxis was again assigned to the 70th Infantry Division cadre by special order: Special Order (SO) 61, March 17, 1943.

The army did not have enough divisions for Europe and the Pacific, so the 91st Division had to fill a cadre for the new 70th Infantry Division before it deployed overseas. The division was initially stationed in Seattle, Washington. Helma and Ted were thrilled since they both were born and raised in Seattle. Unfortunately, they would not be stationed in Washington for long. Soon after their arrival, IV Corps assigned all the designated 70th Division personnel to report to Camp Adair, Oregon. Ted explains that, "Upon arrival at the division the G-3 [in Washington], Col. Bell told me, 'If you stay there for one year to put the division through the Mobilization Training Plan, I will send you back down to a battalion after you complete the Advanced Infantry Class at Fort Benning.'" Ted's first project was to form the Corps "Battalion Field Firing Test" (BFFT) for the 70th Division. According to Ted, "The G-3 asked me to set up the 70th Division in-house BFFT so that the division could train each of the battalions. When each of the division's battalions was taking the BFFT test, they had to have their shortages filled from within our other infantry battalions. I stayed to put the division through the division training cycle. Upon returning to the G-3 and completing my year, they sent me to the Regimental Commander, Colonel Al Morgan, the 276th Regiment, where I became an executive officer in March 1944. I was located at Camp Adair, Oregon, with the 2nd Battalion, 276th. So, as the 70th stood up, the next major event that interrupted was the levies for replacements for the combat losses after D-Day, June 6, 1944." The division was stripped of several thousand infantry replacements during summer (3,000 personnel) and fall 1944 (3,370 personnel), which disrupted the division's advanced Master Training Plan.

As a result of this disruption, the division was not trained to the standards of the time, and they were constantly supplied with thousands of new untrained replacements. Then the division was backfilled with antiaircraft soldiers and miscellaneous supply soldiers from across the country. This situation created another problem. Officer Candidate School (OCS) and the individual basic training centers could not meet training demands. At a conference in 1998, General Mataxis said, "The arrival of untrained or semi-trained fillers required the Division to reorganize and conduct basic training for these new replacements while attempting to continue advanced tactical training. This ad hoc approach derailed the MTP and caused chaotic training conditions and uneven collective readiness. In the summer of 1944, the Division was ordered to move to Fort Leonard Wood, completely disrupting training. From this point on, the unit's fate was not determined by the logical, building-block approach of the MTP, but from the turbulence caused by the growing replacement crisis."

During this chaos, Ted attended a three-month advanced class at Fort Benning to make him eligible to be a battalion commander. Ted explains, "Soon after I finished training, I took over the 2nd Battalion, 276th Regiment as the commander in June 1944." Tensions were high as a battalion commander, with the personnel tasking continually coming down, mandatory training and the upcoming deployment overseas. The situation was less than ideal, and meeting demands was difficult, if not impossible. Mataxis later recalled a heated discussion with the Regimental Commander over a summer parade where the commander required Class A uniforms: "I told him I had directed my battalion to send their 'class A uniforms' out for cleaning, and they would not be available for his rehearsal parade. The commander told me, 'They had better be in their required uniforms.' I responded, 'If you don't like how I run the battalion, you can relieve me.' I learned a precious lesson that August, as I became the battalion executive officer again."

Worldwide shortages of replacements continued through summer and fall 1944. The army continued to rob units in the United States to fill combat casualties for the overseas units that the Basic Training Courses could not meet. To replace transfers for shipment overseas units received college students that had been drafted and kept

A view of the patio and swimming pool at the officers' club, Fort Benning, Georgia, 1942. Ted wrote on the back of the photo, "Boy this sure is fancy. The dance floor is where the lanterns are. It is an especially sweet night when the orchestra is playing."

in school, flying cadets, and AA gunners, and fumigation unit personnel. The AA personnel had been released because the German and Japanese air forces were being shot up. The flying cadets and fumigation units were needed immediately as infantry replacements now! These personnel transfers wreaked havoc with the division and their Master Training Plan.

The reality was that the 70th Division was forced to train 3,871 men into a cohesive group with supplemental training in less than three months before departing for Europe. Some replacements continued to join the regiment until a few days before arriving at the port of departure. The personnel had to be trained in individual infantry skills and unit training. The combined arms training was also cut short. The division never participated in the 12-week, large-scale maneuvers phases of their training sequence, thus losing valuable opportunities to train together and develop the SOPs and unit cohesiveness critical in small-unit survival in combat.

While living in Seattle, Helma would find herself mothering a small toddler while pregnant with their second child. Theodore Christopher Mataxis Jr. was born in September 1944. He was a sickly child who had to be watched very closely. The dresser drawer in Helma's bedroom would become his crib so she could keep a closer eye on him. As a result, Major Mataxis was able to come home on a short emergency leave prior to being deployed to help Helma with the babies. When Mataxis left to report back to duty and deploy overseas, Helma once again found herself a single parent with two small children, while her husband found himself in the thick of World War II preparations. The most ferocious fighting Mataxis would face during all of World War II would occur from December 1944 through February 1945 of Teddy's infancy.

Ted and Helma hold their children in November 1944, two months after Teddy Jr. was born. Shirley was two years old, and it was a month before Ted deployed to France to fight in World War II. This was the first of many times Ted would go off and Helma would be left home with the children.

The division was needed quickly and left for Europe in December 1944, needing more preparation per the required MTP. They were to complete their required training in-country before being deployed in combat. During this time, the 70th Division was required to ship its infantry regiments overseas. The remainder of the division remained behind and conducted further training until February 1945, when they eventually joined their comrades in arms. The 70th, the 42nd, and the 63rd divisions were deployed to France without their supporting units or MTP certification.

The 351st Regiment in the 91st Division, Ted's old regiment and division, was the first all-draftee regiment to see combat in World War II. When deployed overseas, they were immediately sent to Italy in the Mediterranean Theater, where the 351st took part in the Italian Campaign from April 1944 to the close of hostilities in May 1945. During September, the 91st Division fought its most brilliant campaign, which smashed Italy's most formidable defensive position, the Gothic Line. The 91st advanced through elaborately constructed fortifications in mountainous terrain with steadfast determination and unwavering courage.

The 70th Infantry Division went by rail on November 19–20, 1944 from Fort Leonard Wood to Camp Myles Standish, Massachusetts. According to Ted, "A fundamental problem on this trip was keeping our soldiers from 'straying' when the train stopped. Camp Myles Standish was the holding area for the Boston port of embarkation. There was an outcry from the troops of our Cannon Company when they were told that their 105s would be turned into the 'pool' and new ones issued when we landed in France. It turned out that quarts of bourbon had been carefully placed in their artillery tubes." During the next two weeks, they received the equipment that would be necessary to deploy to the European theater of operations, and all required shots. During their stay, they were not allowed to mention their unit for operational security purposes. The 70th Division combat regiments, consisting of the 274th, 275th, and 276th, departed for Europe by troop ship under the leadership of the deputy division commander, Brigadier General Thomas Herren.

Monday night.
Fort Devens, Mass.

Darling Helma,

Tonight I thought I'd drop you a few lines to let you know how much I love and also perhaps to help you understand me better, altho, I guess you should by now after 8 yrs of married life.

You know dear how much I think of being an officer and how much I really feel I owe this country — my country — a place where a man can earn his keep (had I not lost Europe with $10.00 and end up with a business of his own and a substantial amount of money. I know you think he doesn't use it right — but just really well the background is — and how much more it could have been. He at last built up in me a pride in myself and a desire to earn more — and also a feel in my ability to succeed — so now I've the war creates — when an inexcusable to one be a chance if it could be —

it — Well I was lucky as there are now in a position to give much more of a debt to our children.

But don't forget — I am a reservist in the army of Ted I've made myself stand and understand it — as infact a good infantry officer. I that is why you attain desire seen to understand me — just don't forget that I do love you and the children with all of my heart and soul — but it's just the way I've trained myself to act — in fact if I didn't and this war — good never know it. I feel many things so deeply — that you never suspect — and never know of because I don't mention them. The next day of some of the time — so the time I thought I'd let you know you are what I really do think about

2-

and how much I do love you and the children. But don't ever do any thing to make me feel this myself — it I want you to set as a good home wife, mother and daughter should do — look to Poppa also as a noble and put some Ted'l in your household as the children are. Look to see a source of energy and strength. I was this most woman and you've left alone at home again.

And be firm in your Conscience and intuition as I hope I am in mine so you will be able to say to me as it Billy be the 2nd infantry woman was 9½ to think his hub-b, and says — "Well it is up to it." —

Meaning of this Walls — being yourself home in nothing on his journey to attain it. Be proud & do an officers wife and potgomma. I hope you understand my letter dear and that I haven't made you think I'm queer — however I do love you deeply and I want that I was with you now as I am lonely.

So dear I hope this letter helps you understand I am left — because I don't think that you — or you would keep asking do I love you — you know it do I know you love me and the children — I'm pretty like darn sure as I know it'd never say it on the morrow — I believe you really be laying at by — how often and how much I did think I know of you and the children —

So good night darling.
Ted

P.S. — I wish some one read this over because it might think it sounds too corny — but I believe and mean every word.

The troop ship was formerly a luxury cruise liner and had been heavily reconfigured to carry six times its standard passenger limit. The newly reconfigured SS *America* luxury liner would be renamed USS *West Point* (AP-23) and sailed directly to Marseilles, France in December 1944. In 1944, USS *West Point* made five successful voyages as troop transport. In total, USS *West Point* carried 350,000 troops to and from the war during service and even earned the American Defense Service Medal, European-African-Middle Eastern Campaign Medal, Asiatic-Pacific Campaign Medal, and the World War II Victory Medal.

Very little of USS *West Point's* original luxury design remained. The top civilian portion of the ship was taken over by the assistant division commander, regimental staff of the 274th, 275th, 276th, and various nurses. Down in the hold, bunks constructed out of pipes and canvas were stacked four-to-six people high. At the last minute, the ship was overloaded, and the troops had to "hot bunk" below. The luxury liner was now officially a troop ship that could carry 7,600 troops.

As the ship sailed by Gibraltar for the first time in 1944, the regiments on board the USS *West Point* were finally told their destination. These inadequately trained troops arrived in Marseille, France in December 1944 without the necessary division supporting elements. The chaos of service stateside where replacements were being transferred overseas and new and untrained personnel were assigned in their place would quickly be replaced by the deadly chaos of a global war. Major Ted Mataxis had officially entered World War II.

Ted's letter to Helma explaining his love of family, country, and the army, was very similar to one he wrote before leaving for World War II. It contained his advice on raising Teddy as a soldier and instilling in him the Spartan belief to fight for his country and come home with his shield or on it.

CHAPTER 4

France and Germany, 1944–45

The Army needed them in Europe immediately. The divisions had not received their combined arms training nor participated in the large-scale unit maneuver evaluations necessary to certify them officially for deployment. These tough and challenging times required the immediate deployment of three untrained divisions (42nd, 63rd, and 70th). The division commander and support elements were not deployed with their three regiments. and they were led by their respective assistant division commanders. Upon arrival in France, the 42nd, 63rd, and 70th were immediately labeled task forces, not divisions. The 70th was named Task Force Herren, the 42nd was named Task Force Linden, and the 63rd was named Task Force Harris. Major Mataxis was assigned to the 2nd Battalion of the 276th Infantry Regiment in Task Force Herren. Each task force had three regiments with three battalions in each. The idea was that they would complete their training once they arrived overseas. General Eisenhower, in *Crusade in Europe*, referenced the fact that these three infantry divisions not only had their training cut short but had been drained of thousands of soldiers to replace combat losses in the Pacific and European theaters while undergoing their Master Training Plans (MTPs). The arrival of replacements required the unit to restart basic and advanced training over for them to prepare for combat deployment in Europe. The unit had arrived uncertified for combat deployment.

Even before arrival in France, it was clear that Mataxis was heading to war on an overstuffed troop ship full of unprepared, green men and the situation was entirely unsatisfactory. Eisenhower begrudgingly admits, "Nevertheless, the front requirements allowed us to do nothing else." Even General Marshall's report to the Secretary of War in 1945 highlighted that, "To defend the front adequately, full use was made in the Seventh Army of the nine infantry regiments which were just arriving in theater in advance of their division headquarters and troops." General Eisenhower, aware of the predicament in which these units were being utilized, intended to use them in the quiet sectors where there was little likelihood of significant engagement by the enemy. His broad front strategy required men to hold the line. He hoped this limited combat action would provide the necessary time to season the men and, at the same time, permit additional training. General Eisenhower realized that the emergency deployment of these divisions to combat was most unusual without their supporting arms, but nothing could be done.

When Task Force Herren arrived in France on December 15, 1944, the regiment did not have their division support troops of artillery, engineer, quartermaster, medical, signal, or combat service support elements. It was up to the three infantry regiment task forces to figure it out as they went, using the limited resources allotted to their mission. So these troops immediately began unloading the ship that afternoon and were transported to Delta Base Camp # 2 by truck. Each battalion pitched their pup tents in company formation and established bivouac sites. The division had its regiments brought up to Table of Organization and Equipment strength at this location. They were issued rolling stock and wheeled vehicles. They were armed with 57 mm antitank guns and M3 infantry howitzers, and then they were briefed on the latest information regarding the Seventh Army tactical situation.

The day after arrival, December 16, 1944, the Germans initiated their major campaign, the Battle of the Bulge, on the Western Front. The casualties inflicted on the American forces in the Battle of the Bulge demanded immediate and copious replacements, necessitating the general's decision that all combat support troops (for these three divisions) would remain in the United States. The division commander and these support troops would not join their deployed brethren in Europe until February 1945. Before they were ever deployed as a task force, the 7th Infantry Division was required to provide several thousand untrained infantry replacements to the divisions fighting in the Bulge. They were never allowed to season, as Eisenhower had tactfully put it. These men landed in the frying pan and were immediately thrown directly into the line of fire. General Eisenhower, commander at the time admitted, "Hard fighting remains. The enemy that we face has just been reinforced, and defending on his own border, of his own country and would be fighting to defend his homeland. Difficult and rugged terrain confronts us. Rain, cold, and snow will increase the difficulty of our operation. However, I face the future with complete confidence that summoning every obstacle and taking

This is a picture of Colonel Mataxis standing outside of the regimental headquarters somewhere in France in 1945.

every objective in your accustomed manner, you will destroy the enemy before you and will be a vital factor in the final defeat of the enemies of our country."

Before moving out to the Rhine River to take over combat positions facing the Germans, the 276th Regiment, Task Force Herren, was reorganized and lost individual replacement fillers for combat losses on December 20, 1944. On December 20, 1944, Task Force Herren, under the command of Col. Morgan, was assigned to the Seventh Army, Sixth Army Group. They received their orders, were initially attached to the 79th Infantry Division, and moved out on December 23, 1944. They were divided into motorized and dismounted elements, then transported by French troop trains (empty box cars called "40×8s").

Each of the regiments had an infantry cannon company attached, providing direct support to their regiments. The infantry cannon company was the principal organic indirect or direct fire artillery element subordinate to the infantry regiment, manning six 105 mm towed howitzers. It was most responsive when assigned at the battalion level. The infantry cannon company manned the lighter (and shorter-range) M3 howitzer as opposed to the M2A2 assigned to artillery battalions. The company worked closely with the regimental antitank company to handle an effective anti-armor defense. "Appropriate targets for the howitzers of the cannon company are automatic weapons, antitank guns, mortars, infantry howitzers, troop concentrations, roadblocks, pillboxes, strongly fortified buildings, and armored vehicles," as stated in FM 7-37. The 70th Division did not have divisional support elements. The infantry regiment level had a regimental HQ and HQ company, cannon company, antitank company, service company, and attached medical unit to support the three infantry battalions.

As a collection of cattle cars slowly made its way down the tracks towards these newly arrived World War II soldiers, the jokes the World War I veterans had previously made about their horrific wartime transportation became these soldiers' new, very uncomfortable wartime reality. Many of the boxcars had holes in them from strafing. They provided no heat, making the drafty trip bitterly cold. The cold was frigid, and these green soldiers were not only underprepared for combat but underdressed as well. Appropriate cold-weather gear was unavailable, and these poor men suffered immensely. Officers and enlisted alike were caught unaware by Mother Nature's cold disapproval. It had been over thirty years since these temperatures had been seen in these parts of France. Rank had little to no privilege here. The bitter cold and snow caused many medical evacuations for frostbite, trench foot, and upper respiratory diseases. The weather was the first formidable enemy the soldiers had to endure.

The officers were at least afforded rough wooden benches for the arduous journey. The first train to the objective area was commanded by Ted Mataxis, the 2nd battalion XO; the second train to arrive was led by Bob Natzel, the 3rd Battalion XO. Both trains unloaded at Brumath, France and from there, they marched to Bischwiller, located in the French region of Alsace. The two battalions were billeted in an abandoned button factory. There were thousands of brass buttons with the German eagle and swastika embossed—a fine souvenir for the troops.

At the same time on December 24, the motorized element of the 1st battalion began their northward movement and over a four-day motor march covered almost 600 miles. They would join the rest of the regiment at Bischwiller on December 27. Task Force Herren was ordered to establish a defensive posture along the west bank of the Rhine River on the east flank of VI Corps on December 28. After New Year's Eve the mission was changed to stop the German Operation *Nordwind* penetration and strike the enemy at Philippsbourg and Wingen, between Bischwiller and Haguenau.

On December 29, Task Force Herren's soldiers were again impacted when they received a 10 percent cut of their junior soldiers, who were sent immediately to the 80th Infantry Division to reinforce the Third Army, which was presently assigned to attack the Ardennes Salient. Once again, just hours before going into combat, the regiment had received another unavoidable, weakening blow.

Task Force Herren moved by motor and foot into the position of the regimental Command Post at Soufflenheim. They tactically deployed the 1st battalion on the right, the southern half of the regimental sector, and the 2nd Battalion on the left while holding the 3rd Battalion in reserve. Their mission was to deny the enemy access to the area and to prevent the Germans from crossing the Rhine River. The Seventh Army commander, General Patch, hoped that placing Task Force Herren and Task Force Linden in these various locations would finally allow the units time to conduct some of the collective training they were denied earlier.

Alas, the subsequent disruption to the rear area training would come only five days later when Hitler launched his last-ditch offensive, Operation *Nordwind*, at midnight on New Year's Eve 1944. Operation *Nordwind* started with the 256th and 261st Volksgrenadier Divisions moving to the southeast in a two-pronged drive. The Germans penetrated quickly, and overwhelmed American troops positioned along the United States' defensive positions. The lines had been devastated, and the enemy was everywhere; thus, there remained only the practical step of forming of small groups hell-bent on escaping as quickly as possible.

The task forces along the Rhine moved rapidly to reinforce this maneuver. Hitler had hoped to rupture the American defenses between Bischwiller (which the troops lovingly renamed Bitch) and Neunhoffen. General Patch, commander of the Seventh Army, had just taken over the Third Army's sector of the front line so that General Patton's army could launch a mass flank attack against the Bulge. This action spread the front lines thin as they spread out to cover the area General Patton's troops had covered earlier.

The aftermath of Operation *Nordwind* on January 1, 1945 was that the German offensive, conducted with the eight divisions, tore a hole through the Seventh Army's defensive line, which had been stretched thinly over 68 miles. The cavalry screening force and Task Force Huddleston, which covered the area between the Seventh Army's

VI and XV Corps, disintegrated in the German attack, which left a massive gap between the Seventh Army and VI Corps. This gap threatened the front-line infantry divisions of the VI and XV Corps (now cut off or destroyed), which was the entire US Army front in the Ardennes Forest and the Vosges mountains. The German mission was to take Saverne while penetrating the Seventh Army's overstretched positions and attempting to pinch off the Allied forces in France. The Germans attacked the eastern wing of the Seventh Army. The German offensive traveled from the west into the low Vosges mountains, along a 24-mile front from Sarreinsming in the west to Dambach in the east. The Seventh Army started throwing task forces in by regiments and battalions to fill the 15-mile gap the Germans had torn through the Seventh Army's line during their last attack.

Since no infantry troops were available in the corps reserves, the 41st, 63rd, and 70th Task Forces had their infantry regiments' rear area training canceled. Instead, they were deployed immediately, each with their three infantry battalions placed into gaps torn in the Seventh Army's defensive line positions. This gap was covered by extending the west boundary of the 45th Infantry Division west to the eastern border of XV Corps. Four additional infantry regiments and one engineer regiment were assigned to strengthen the 45th Division. Task Force Herren's three battalions were a part of this build-up of the 45th Division. The battalions of the 70th were

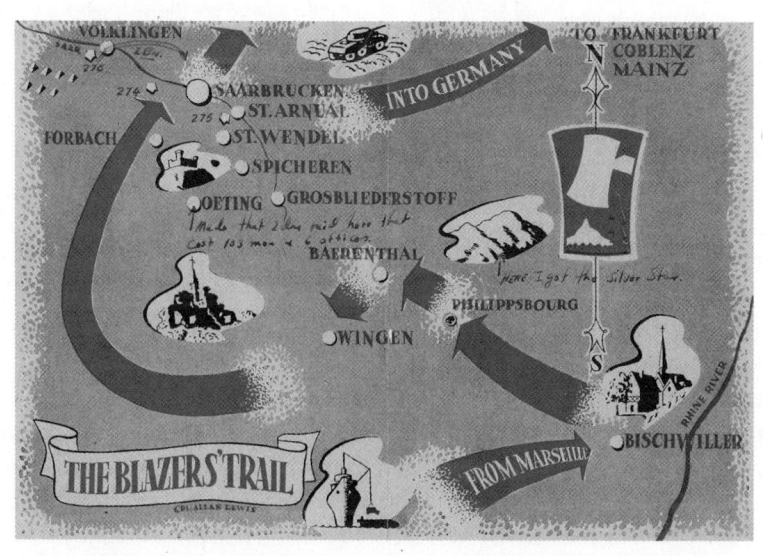

A map published in the 70th Division historical pocket pamphlet with Ted's penned comments. On the right page is written: "Here I got the Silver Star." The comment on the left reads: "This is where our two-day raid on Oeting took place to gather intelligence on the German reactions and composition. This raid on Oeting resulted in 103 men & 6 officers killed in the Battalion I was commanding." (From *Trailblazers: The Story of the 70th Infantry Division, 1944–45*)

Left: Ted with the driver, Sergeant Quintane, that saved his life during their first encounter with the enemy in 1945. Right: Ted with the 276th Brigade commander, Colonel Morgan, in January 1945. Colonel Morgan had relieved Ted of command in the United States over uniforms to be worn in a parade. In 1945, Major General Fredrick told Colonel Morgan he would be relieved if the hill was not taken by morning. When the general left, Colonel Morgan turned to Mataxis and relayed the threat of relief. Mataxis calmly responded, "That's not a new threat, sir! You already relieved me once over uniforms for a parade rehearsal."

quickly assigned to reinforce the divisions along the Sixth Army's lines after Operation *Nordwind*. They struck at the enemy positions at Philippsbourg and Wingen between Bischwiller and Haguenau. The 275th and 274th infantry regiments were assigned to contain the German attacks on the eastern shoulder of the defenses. The 276th regiment was initially designated as the corps reserve position along the Moder River.

On January 2, 1945, the 276th Regiment was attached to the 45th Infantry Division with Gen. Fredricks, the 45th Infantry Division commander. At the age of 37, he was the youngest division commander, and the most decorated. He had been wounded eight times, receiving a Purple Heart with seven clusters, and was awarded two Distinguished Service Crosses. Earlier in the war he had commanded the combined US and Canadian First Special Service Force as a colonel. Upon being promoted to Brigadier General, he was placed in command of the First Airborne Task Force during Operation *Dragoon*, the invasion of southern France. When promoted to major general he took command of the 45th Division, nicknamed the Thunderbirds.

Two days after being attached to the 45th Division, Mataxis records his first contact with German troops: "On January 4, 1945, my unit was fighting a rearguard action. I and several others were returning from one of our companies when we ran into an enemy patrol. I sent a patrol along the east flank to screen for them while

I took a small group to conduct reconnaissance along the road; we were moving along the road when we turned a corner, and there was a German patrol of five soldiers. The meeting was so unexpected that both groups froze in their tracks. I was startled. It was my first 'close eyeball' contact with the Germans. Fortunately, one of my NCOs, Sgt. A. Quintane, serving as the battalion commander's runner, had been with another unit in combat. Before anyone could react, he immediately opened fire with his Thompson. After a couple of the Germans had been killed, the others ran for their lives. Quintane's quick action saved our lives! I collected a pair of binoculars. I kept them with me throughout my military career (Korea, Vietnam, Afghanistan) as a reminder to always stay alert."

Although the first contact Mataxis made with the Germans was brief, it would not be his last encounter. The fighting at this time was harrowing. According to Mataxis's war diaries, "On 9 January 1945 near Rothbach, France, the fighting had been heavy contact." Two company commanders had been killed trying to take Hill 414, and the battalion's progress had stopped. The Headquarters Company commander was also killed after being in command for only two days. The battalion's momentum had been slowed down and could not take the hill. The fighting had been so horrific that one company's lieutenant suffered a nervous breakdown during the battle and had to be evacuated to the rear after being tied down to a litter. Unfortunately, the 2/276th Battalion (Task Force Herren) had stalled, requiring General Frederick to visit their command post. Upon arrival, General Fredrick, with the regimental commander, Col. Morgan, in tow, belligerently relieved the battalion commander. Then he threatened to do the same to Col. Morgan if "Hill 414 was not taken from the Germans by morning."

At this precise moment, fate returned Major Mataxis (from his time with the two rifle companies that had brutally lost their commanding officers) to the command post to deliver a situation update and to reorganize. Later, Mataxis would relate his somewhat unfortunate (some might say fortuitous) timing. According to Mataxis, "At that time, I saw General Frederick yelling at our regimental commander; after relieving our battalion commander since the battalion had been held up in their move forward." During this tirade, the irate General Fredrick unexpectedly turned towards Major Mataxis and told him he was the battalion commander now. Fredricks then explained savagely to Mataxis that if he did not take the hill by morning, then Fredricks would simply find another, more capable commander to take it. Never one to shrink from a challenge or to willingly be relieved of duty, Mataxis accepted the general's belligerent assignment and began strategizing immediately.

When the general left, Col. Morgan turned to Mataxis and said, "If I am relieved, you are relieved." Major Mataxis took this moment to remind Col. Morgan of a past interaction they had shared earlier in the United States. Mataxis calmly responded, "That's not a new threat, Sir! You already relieved me once over uniforms for a parade rehearsal." Col. Morgan could not help but cringe when reminded of the prior argument over parade uniforms when the stakes were now higher for these men and their soldiers.

Major Mataxis took command of the 2/276th Infantry Battalion that day with a very focused mission—take Hill 414. With a quick battlefield assessment of the leadership available, Major Mataxis, having only two company commanders, took the battalion and consolidated the companies into two elements. Mataxis took charge of one and assigned his S-3 as the commander of the other. At dusk, the composite companies began a night attack on the objective. The original plan was that Mataxis would move into position with the two companies (F and G) and try to adjust artillery fire and mortar fire on the German positions on the hill. Unfortunately, the artillery fire was blocked by the trees.

To adapt, Mataxis requested more bazookas that could provide cover along with the mortars. At dusk, Mataxis and his S-3 launched their night attack and stormed the hill. As they moved forward, a German-operated MG-42 machine gun on the rear slope opened fire, forcing Mataxis and company to take cover. In the chaos, Major Mataxis irretrievably lost his carbine in the knee-deep snow, so he immediately retrieved his .45 from his shoulder holster and continued fighting. A barrage of machine-gun bullets whizzed and snapped over their heads, successfully pinning them down. Major Mataxis realized the next step for the gunner would be to depress his gun to fire on those in the prone position. He saw a depression on the left flank with some bushes that could offer him cover a mere 50 yards away.

Mataxis immediately jumped up and ran for this new position. After frantically rolling into the bushes for cover, Mataxis realized that he had unknowingly fallen right into the supporting MG-42; five armed German soldiers presently occupied the position. With only his .45, Mataxis killed three of the Germans and captured the other two. He likens his memory of that event to, "an old 16 mm film jumping its track—vivid flashes ending when I was on my back trying to shoot the remaining two Germans with an empty pistol." Ultimately, his surprise attack allowed the battalion's momentum to continue their brutal uphill attack, eventually seizing the hill that evening.

In June 1945, Mataxis, then a lieutenant colonel, would receive the following letter:

HEADQUARTERS **70TH INFANTRY DIVISION**
APO 461 US ARMY

GENERAL ORDERS
20 June 1945
NUMBER 49

AWARD OF THE SILVER STAR
By direction of the President, under Army Regulations 600-45, 20 June 1945, as amended, the Silver Star is awarded to the following individual:

THEODORE C. MATAXIS, 0-392185, Lieutenant Colonel (then Major), Infantry, Headquarters 2d Battalion, 276 Infantry
For gallantry in action on 10 January 1945, near Rothbach, France. When two companies had lost their commanding officers as a result of enemy action, Lieutenant Colonel Mataxis, then Battalion Executive Officer, went forward to coordinate these units in a night attack. He maneuvered one company into action and aided the other by bringing effective fire upon enemy machine guns which had halted the rifle platoons. Moving forward, he reorganized the front-line troops, in complete darkness and under heavy artillery fire. While thus engaged, he captured two prisoners, and killed three enemy soldiers at an automatic weapons position. His aggressive leadership at a critical juncture was an inspiration to the officers and men of the battalion, and a major factor in the accomplishment of his unit's mission.
Entered military service from Seattle, Washington.

BY COMMAND OF MAJOR GENERAL BARNETT:
JAMES L. RICHARDSON JR.
Colonel, GSC
Actg Chief of Staff

Once the battalion secured their objective, they reinforced their newfound possession with heavy machine guns. Major Mataxis and his men dug in above a small road for the remainder of the evening, expecting a counterattack that never materialized. He called in harassing and interdicting (H&I) artillery on road intersections to his front. He would later learn through POWs that this defensive play decimated the troops the Germans were planning to use later that evening for their counterattack—the one that never came. This was one of the many times that their attached infantry cannon company provided a timely and accurate response. Mataxis could not help but acknowledge that the strategy worked as expected. Like many soldiers after him, he would go on to successfully use the defensive artillery barrage to defend significant roadways and intersections. According to Mataxis, "In the morning a column of German SS soldiers marched route step along the road below. We let them get even with us and opened fire, wiping out the column. The Germans had not realized that we had taken the hill." As a result of that contact, it did not take long for the German SS soldiers to counterattack. When the Germans counterattacked, they managed to cut off the battalion for two days on the top of the hill. SS was the abbreviation of *Schutzstaffel*, German for "Protective Echelon." The unit was identified as the 6th SS Mountain Division, which had been recently brought down from Finland.

At this time, Major Mataxis learned a precious lesson about the critical need for machine guns and proper placement on avenues of approach and in defensive preparation. As a result, Major Mataxis pulled one of his sergeants aside and immediately tasked him. "I told him to get us light machine guns to go with every heavy machine gun we had." The man managed to procure the major's request. As a result, when they advanced on all future operations, the battalion maneuvered with the light machine guns and left the heavy machine guns on the trucks. Whenever they established a night defensive position, the heavy machine guns were tactically employed (one heavy machine gun and one light machine gun were placed in every position). Mataxis also increased the firepower in the rifle companies by adding an extra Browning Automatic Rifle with each light machine gun utilized. According to Mataxis, "At that time, the Germans outgunned us. They had the MG-42 machine gun, and in addition we opposed German units armed with the new MP 44. It was a great weapon. That is why I got the extra machine guns, but we depended heavily on artillery fire from our organic cannon company. When we ran into something, we stopped, called artillery, and shot the hell out of them."

During this time, Mataxis explains, "We ran up against units from the 6th SS Mountain Division, which had come down from Finland. They would ski over the slopes, hit the ground, and start firing on our columns with their MG-42s. One of our sergeants came up with an idea to counter this tactic. He got a 60 mm mortar, filled a helmet with dirt, and fired the mortar without the base plate at the attacking element. The leading element of our formation would be equipped with a 60 mm mortar, and when they saw the German skiers coming down the slopes, they'd open fire with the mortar. When the Germans saw the mortar fire coming in their direction, they wouldn't stop; they continued skiing in search of a softer target. The mortar fire was inaccurate, but it served its purpose as the Germans moved on." By this time in the war the German infantrymen had started to call themselves "front swine."

In one of the contacts Major Mataxis's head was split open by mortar fire. He was medevacked to the aid station with his hand holding his wound; by the time he arrived at the aid station, his hand was frozen to his head. The medic handed him a bottle of whiskey and then told him, "Pour it on the wound to free your frozen hand and disinfect the wound." Major Mataxis was then told to "drink the rest" while the medic stitched up the damage to Mataxis's head. Mataxis's men would later capture the German 60 mm mortar and the forward observer's P38 pistol with its holster and belt to present to their wounded battalion commander. Mataxis would utilize the mortar at his battalion command center as an ashtray for the remainder of the war. Once stitched up, Mataxis returned to the heat of the battle to fight alongside his troops. As a result of the heavy ground fog, the German forward observers could not adjust their artillery; visibility also impacted the ability of the ground forces to use their small arms accurately.

The casualties on the first day of the attack revealed the deadly effectiveness of the enemy antitank and antipersonnel mines, which were unaffected by the fog. When the fog lifted, the effective small arms fire, due to the open terrain and visibility, slowed the regiment down. The coordination between the battalions and within the companies had significantly improved, and they did not lose contact. All units dug in for the night and prepared for the following day. That night the Germans intensified their efforts to defend Rothbach by continuing their mortar and artillery bombardment on all the regiment's positions.

After the regiment's first two weeks in the Saar River region, it was almost like being transferred to an entirely different theater of operations. In the first week of February, the temperature "skyrocketed" into the 30s, and constant rain melted much of the snow. The melted snow turned the ground into mud, impacting the soldiers significantly; everything turned miserable. The mud affected everything, including weapons and equipment. It made sleeping and movement almost impossible. As evacuations continued, the medical impact quickly shifted from frostbite to trench foot and immersion foot, which had the same detrimental effect and continued to take its heavy medical toll on the troops in the regiment as evacuations continued. The terrain and attitude of the local inhabitants changed as the cultural background and orientation of the people did as well; French was spoken, and the churches appeared predominantly Catholic. The ridges in the area were almost as high in altitude as the ones they had left behind; however, it was much less rocky, and the slopes were gentler. The land was much easier to move about on; fields of fire and observation of the enemy were also far more extensive than in the Vosges. In February, Col. Morgan ordered Mataxis's 2/276th Battalion to conduct a raid by four rifle companies against the small town of Oeting.

The rest of the division had arrived in the theater on January 18, 1945, and finally linked up with its commanding general, division staff and three combat regiments. Now the Trailblazers' "redlegs" were once again supporting the "doughfeet" in the way it was intended to be, according to US Army doctrine. In addition to the welcome company of the rest of the Trailblazers, several hundred replacements arrived to fill the depleted ranks of the regiment during this period of relative quiet. Twelve officers and 184 enlisted men arrived on February 3 alone, with another 223 enlisted men eight days later. Some were young men straight from infantry basic training, others were reclassified rear echelon soldiers varying in age. They combined with all the non-infantry support elements and hundreds of replacements arrived at divisions. This improvement was a significant morale booster; now, all wearing and fighting under the same patch, the division's men finally felt united as brothers.

The replacements required training in skills beyond those they already possessed. To that end, the division devised and conducted a brief training program for their newly formed recruits, who were lumped together in a newly formed J company. The uncomfortable game of musical chairs was finally over. The unit no longer bounced from corps to corps, division to division. One evening in February, the division commander, Major General Barnett, directed the division to "cut, slash and drive" its way into Forbach. This was unfortunately easier said than done. The division trained and operationally conducted the liberation of Forbach as a division.

They were no longer an "orphaned unit." It will never be known how many men died or were wounded because of the unfamiliarity with policies and procedures in Task Force Herren stemming from the constant change.

The task force was dissolved on February 4 when the 70th Infantry Division's commanding general and staff arrived in Europe with supporting troops. The 274th Infantry Regiment was returned to the 70th Infantry Division from their previous attachment to the 45th Division on February 9, 1945. The 70th Division found itself a fully functioning division again. The 276th Infantry Regiment transitioned from Task Force Herren to a regiment united with the 70th Trailblazers. The division now had its staff and support elements.

The 70th Division was finally an integral combat entity and had an opportunity to conduct a brief training program for the first time since its arrival in theater. In early February, before the division arrived, a series of raids were designed to keep pressure on the enemy and gather intelligence on their forces for future operations. There were two phases to Oeting's liberation. The raid on Oeting by Mataxis's battalion was the first phase. The purpose of the raid was to discover where the German reserves were located so they could be identified by the air force for bombing attacks when American forces launched their attack on Oeting and Forbach. The air force blanketed the area with recon planes photographing the movement of the German reserves. The raid was very successful and provided the regiment with precise information on the enemy's defensives that lay in front of them and allowed them to take Oeting quickly before the Germans could launch a counterattack. On the evening of February 7/8, the 884th Field Artillery Battalion took over the direct support role for the regiment, along with the Trailblazers' artillery and their attached cannon company. On February 9, the 274th Regiment rejoined the division after many attachments to other divisions to the east during the hectic Operation *Nordwind*.

The regiments were deployed along the defensive line on the west side, with the 275th and the 276th Regiment on the east side. The 274th Regiment was held in reserve. At the same time the division defensive line was shortened by 2,700 meters. This left the division's area responsibility running only about 5,700 meters from Emmersweiler to cover Gaubiving.

In spring 1945, the 70th Division spearheaded the US Seventh Army's drive into Germany, south of Saarbrucken. XV Corps had decided to conduct a limited objective attack line, with the 70th Infantry Division on the eastern left flank and the 63rd Infantry Division on their right flank. With the 45th Infantry Division to their right flank, this would be the most elaborate and extensive attack yet. This limited objective attack would place the 70th Infantry Division in an advantageous position to directly attack the critical industrial and military center at Saarbrucken. The regiments would attack as an integral combined arms team, with the 70th Division staff coordinating and supporting. This arrangement would mark the first time the regiments had participated in an offensive operation together. The division's regiments would not have to accept whatever support that could be scraped together; they had their division supporting them. With the better part of two months of brutal combat experience and significantly more training behind them, the regiments' men would show how far they had come since their first bitter taste of combat in the Vosges last December.

The attack on Forbach began at one minute past midnight on February 1. The 70th Division attacked just below the Saar River and drove to the northwest onto high ground overlooking Saarbrucken and seized Forbach. After securing Forbach, the bondage and suffering of its courageous people finally came to an end.

Forbach was a well-defended French mining center near Saarbrucken, Germany. Anti-Nazi sentiment in Forbach ran rather high for a variety of reasons. Although Lorraine was significantly less German in culture than Alsace, both provinces had been incorporated into the Reich after the capitulation of the French Army in June 1940. For 105 days, death rained down on the starving, yet hopeful inhabitants of the Forbach area. To the inhabitants, this meant that they were not only occupied, they officially became citizens of the Third Reich, subject to all the privileges and obligations pertaining to that. Their sons were eligible for military duty; German became the only permissible language of government, education, and commerce. The anti-German actions were not violations of the terms of occupation, but would now be considered treason. German Nazi party officials were brought in to govern the town and its vicinity. Now the Gestapo was watching. Despite their German occupiers, many citizens of Forbach resisted the Germans. To add to the miseries of the inhabitants of Forbach, most French civilians killed or wounded in and around Forbach died because of their would-be liberators, in acts aimed at the German occupiers.

To reach Forbach, the division had to overcome three imposing terrain barriers: the high ground of the Kleinwald (covered by thick woods), the ancient Schlossberg Castle (towering above a steep hill overlooking Forbach), and a well-protected narrow valley (to the left of the high ground). The 400-year-old tower at Schlossberg served as the enemy observation point to direct artillery and mortar fire against the advancing troops.

All the division's regiments were online under the command of XV Corps. Their operations mainly involved patrolling and continual improvement of the defenses. The division took the opportunity to train, absorb replacements and develop the division's antitank battalion. They finally had time to train, rest, and recuperate while improving their lines. The 2/276th Regiment received orders to relieve the 411th Infantry Regiment and parts of the 106th Cavalry Group. The 276th Regiment's area of operation (AO) extended from Emmersweiler to Bousbach on the right. The 106th Cavalry group was on their left flank, and the 275th Regiment was on their right side. Within their AO, the 2/276th battalion was on the right/eastern flank, and the third battalion was on the left/western flank. The 1/276 battalion was left in reserve. Five miles to the north was the general area of Saarbrucken. The 70th Infantry Division would remain in combat in this AO during the remainder of its time deployed in World War II. This AO was a much quieter section than their earlier deployment near the right flank of the Seventh Army, with the 45th Division, where they were engaged in chaotic combat operations and pressed to their limits.

Mataxis says, "A few weeks later, we took over some defensive positions from the 103rd Division. We were facing bunkers and outposts on the Siegfried Line. The Germans used to have their supplies come up from the rear at night by horse and wagon. At night, troops could hear the squeaking wheels of the horse-drawn wagons the Germans used to resupply their troops. I got four .50 caliber machine guns from our mess truck and gave them to one of my World War I era sergeants. He was one of those guys who would be suitable for 30 days, and then he'd get drunk and get busted. He had been in a machine battalion in World War I and brought his clinometer from that war to this one. They would use indirect machine-gun fire in the trenches. You could put the clinometer on the gun's barrel and use it to adjust the weapon for indirect fire. I had him form four machine gun crews for the 50s. When he got word that the outpost could hear something coming up the road, they would use the 50s for indirect fire into that area. Later, when we picked up some POWs, they told us they had foxholes every 100 yards along the road so they could jump into the hole if they heard artillery coming. But they couldn't hear the machine guns fire and didn't know they were under fire until the bullets started bouncing around them. Those 50 calibers caused a lot of apprehension for them."

In mid-February, the 70th division would begin a month-long campaign in concert with the 63rd Division. The first part of the attack would take 10 days: the two divisions continued fighting in Oeting and Forbach, gained control of Spicheren Heights, and marched toward St. Wendel. From February 15 through February 27, this limited offensive required a two-pronged attack into Forbach and Spicheren to capture the heights along the Saar River south and southwest of the city of Saarbrucken. This had to be retaken to approach the Siegfried Line.

By February 17, 1945, the division attacked just below the Saar River. The 70th drove onto high ground overlooking Saarbrucken, smashed into Forbach, took Stirring-Wendel, and continued across the Saar to take Saarbrucken. While fighting the 6th SS Mountain Division, the Germans were surprised when an American contacted them on a captured radio and suggested, "Let's have a truce and remove our wounded." Both sides gladly removed their wounded personnel. When they pulled out, the Germans left 200 prisoners in a local church (along with their wounded) and their medical doctor to care for all the injured. The medics conducted triage regardless of which uniforms soldiers wore. As the French say, "*C'est la vie.*" When translated, the phrase means, "It's all bread and potatoes." In this case, a wounded soldier was simply an injured person. As promised, the attack resumed on February

18 upon completion of the medical evacuation. They continued reconnaissance missions, and at the same time, improved the defensive positions. The regiment also prepared for an offensive drive.

Colonel Morgan and his battalion commanders decided on the following maneuver schema: 1/276th Battalion advances on the right to capture the high ground overlooking Forbach back in the northeastern corner and seize the high land north of town. The rugged terrain, covered with stretches of undergrowth, was ideal territory for ambushes. Time and time again, enemy patrols were encountered and driven back. The ridge was dotted with a belt of bunkers made of solid eight-feet-thick concrete covered by earth for an additional layer of protection. The battalion pressed forward towards Forbach and passed across the hills north of Oeting as they moved towards their objective in the Kleinwald ("Small Forest") overlooking Forbach. On the most prominent hill, overlooking the small forest, sat the tower of Schlossberg, a late medieval castle. The enemy used this structure, with its thick, artillery-proof walls, as an observation post for artillery and mortar fire adjustment. It was finally put out of commission when a mortar barrage was placed on top of the tower. To the left of the wooded high ground was a narrow valley that could be covered by direct fire almost the entire distance to Forbach, where the German troops were entrenched. Since it dominated the town of Forbach and its approaches, this tower in the "Small Forest" was the key terrain that had to be controlled before Forbach could be liberated. US troops engaged and met solid German resistance. At night, the Germans intensified their efforts to defend the city with heavy mortar and artillery fire on the Americans. The Americans used small arms and hand grenades while trying to force the Germans out of the town.

On February 20, under heavy fire, American soldiers attacked, piercing the enemy's defenses, and broke into the city. They then undertook house-to-house fighting in the town, often involving hand-to-hand combat and bayonets. The multistory buildings presented a different obstacle that needed to be overcome by using small arms, hand grenades, and hand-to-hand combat. Each small house was like a massive bunker with a small basement window that opened on street level, where the Germans were strategically positioned. These basement windows not only allowed devastating fire down the streets but revealed a small target to engage. After a day of house-to-house fighting, the troops returned to their assigned night defensive positions.

On the morning of February 21, they continued the painful house-to-house, block-by-block advance toward downtown. The closer they got to the downtown square, the more intense the fighting became. Enemy resistance was still composed of scattered strong points—German soldiers firing mostly from basement windows. Most of the basement walls were over a foot thick, allowing the enemy to defend from a maze of veritable pillboxes within the city center. Snipers were also a problem. Standing back from upper-story windows, they would wait until a few of the attackers passed, then engage them from behind, shooting them in the back.

Before the Americans could figure out where the shooting had come from, the sniper would displace, going to either a different window or a different building altogether.

In this way, the relatively few German defenders were holding off a much more numerous foe. Although they may have been something less than the elite of the German forces, they still defended with admirable tenacity and had to be dug out one by one or in very small groups. Upon finally reaching the town square, the Americans called in 105 mm artillery support, which enabled the troops to take the railroad station in the center of town on the south side of the main line, which was deserted except for a few disabled freight cars. The rail yards were void of activity; however, when anyone attempted to get near the tracks, all hell broke loose. The soldiers were unexpectedly bombarded by indirect and heavy small-arms fire.

In the middle of this firestorm at the railroad, the Trailblazers were ordered to hold the line. Their mission was to establish a defense until both regiments were

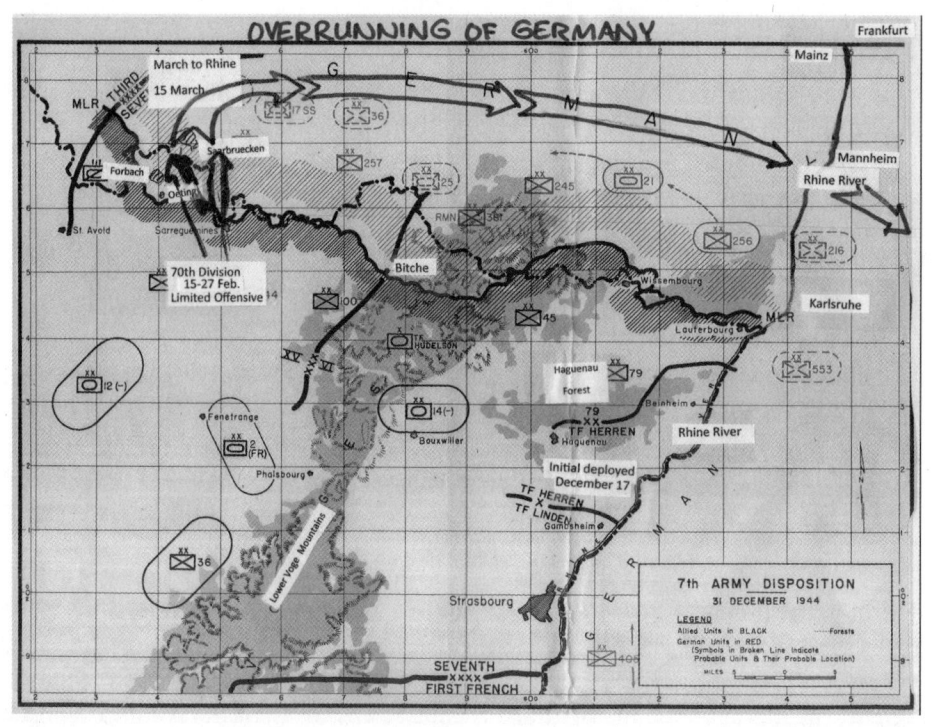

This map from *The Seventh United States Army: Report of Operations, France and Germany 1944–45* covers two pages and shows the Seventh Army disposition on December 31, 1944, the night of Hitler's last desperate Alsace offensive trying to cut off the southeast Saar region of France. The white squares were added by the author to track the movements of Task Force Herren, 70th Infantry Division's combat brigades. The white boxes also identify key terrain features to help orient the reader to the location covered. (US Army)

back online. As a result, the next few days were spent cleaning up their line of German positions bypassed earlier in the attack. Then the battalion consolidated their positions on the line, conducted improvements, and resupplied. The fighting continued door to door, building to building, and block to block through the northern part of the city. They would take over German living facilities, which was quite an improvement over their harrowing existences thus far in dark and cold foxholes, praying for relief. The adage that "there are no atheists in a foxhole" held for Ted's soldiers, and their prayers had finally been answered.

On the night of February 22, Colonel Morgan and his staff issued operating instructions #12. This operation order called for a continuation of the attack to the northwest. The 276th would seize the part of Forbach immediately across the railroad tracks in its present sector. It would then be prepared to resume the advance and take the high ground in its zone northwest of Forbach after conducting a passage of lines through the 3rd Battalion's current position. The 2nd Battalion was to clear Forbach northwest of the tracks; it would be ready on order, to advance further to take the high ground in its zone northwest of Forbach. It would also provide left flank security for the regiment. After the 2nd Battalion had conducted a passage of lines through the 3rd Battalion it would revert to regimental reserve, securing a phase line that followed the railroad tracks to the city and protecting the regiment's right flank.

The plan was to be implemented in consonance with the advance by the 274th infantry, which would attack on the right, providing protection to the regiment's right flank. Beyond the purely tactical significance of this plan, this order indicates the degree of sophistication the regiment had achieved in its operational capabilities. Conducting a passage of lines is an extremely complex task, requiring not only detailed planning, but close cooperation between all elements of the combined arms team. Boundaries must be understood by everyone, to avoid firing on friendly units. Phase lines must be understood and recognized by everyone, to avoid either redundant action or, worse, no action at all in the face of enemy developments. Artillery and mortar fire control measures must be precisely coordinated to provide continuous and responsive fire. Any breakdown of communication can easily cause fratricide or a loss of support at a critical moment.

The benefits of such a coordinated operation are considerable. By passing units through each other in a "leapfrog" fashion, constant pressure may be maintained on the enemy, preventing him from pausing and regrouping. Such tactics also allowed a rotation of friendly units, providing the opportunity for rest and preparation for fresh, well-organized action. If there was ever an indication of how far the regiment's leadership had come since the Vosges, this was it!

The regiment aimed to attack a roughly 3,000-meter-wide corridor to liberate Forbach and clear the hills beyond. Mataxis recalls, "On or about February 27/28, I was ordered to prepare plans to assemble the 2nd Battalion as division reserve and devise a course of action to restore a key hill in the area. I went forward with our S3 and the reconnaissance patrol to conduct an evaluation of the terrain. We came under heavy artillery fire, so we ducked into a stone building. It turned out to be a museum of the 1870 War. I picked up a pamphlet showing the key German attack in 1870. Imagine my surprise when I discovered that our German counterattack had been coming up the same ravine they used in 1870. The old French saying, 'the more it changes, the more it stays the same' really was true!"

On February 28, XXI Corps assumed control from XV Corps of the 101st Cavalry group, the 70th Division, the 63rd Division, the 12th Armored Division, and its supporting troops. They all pivoted to the left and continued to the north-northwest. The second phase of the campaign was the attack on Forbach, beginning on March 7 and taking another 10 days. When the 2/276th was ordered to conduct an attack on Forbach, the 2nd Battalion had to be relieved of its frontline positions by the 1st Battalion. During this time, the division freed 18 towns and captured more than 2,000 German prisoners of war. They breached the Siegfried Line (known as the West Wall), a formidable barrier extending from the Netherlands to the Swiss border in the south on the western border of Germany. It faced the French Maginot Line, which consisted of well-designed and interlocking bunkers, tunnels, and defensive obstacles. The division would begin crossing the Saar River late on March 19 to attack Saarbrucken.

The 70th Infantry Division was on the north flank of the Seventh Army on March 20, 1945; they launched an attack designed to reach the Saar River south of Saarbrucken. After reaching the Saar River, they halted to reorganize and prepare for an offensive that could break through the German defensive positions on the Siegfried Line. Following a heavy artillery barrage, they crossed the river and seized elements of the Siegfried Line in their sector from the withdrawing Germans.

According to Mataxis's journal, "We next took over a town on the northern bank of the Saar River. We immediately deployed the battalion in a defensive posture to prepare for an expected German counterattack. The German burgermeister, the mayor, was waiting in his office with his staff and interpreter to surrender the town. He had decorated his office with a vast Nazi banner along one wall, a life-size oil painting of Hitler, and a marble bust of der Fuhrer. Without speaking to the Germans, I took Hitler's bust and threw it through the oil painting. I was focused then on who would live and who would die, not collecting trophies.

"I immediately ordered that the flag be torn down (it was later cut up as souvenirs for the troops). Once we destroyed the offending Nazi symbols, I turned to the burgermeister to give him our standing operating procedures (SOPs) orders for surrendering his town. All Germans would stay in their homes until further orders. All German military were to report to the town hall to be transferred to a POW compound. In addition, all weapons, including civilian armaments, would be piled in the road in front of the town hall, where they would be destroyed.

"[As a side note,] one treasure caught my eye after completing my procedural responsibilities. The burgermeister had in his office a display of miniature soldiers (ranging from the Hitler Youth through the Waffen SS, two regular German soldiers, plus an array of miniature artillery). I couldn't help but think of my childhood collection of soldiers, so I had my bodyguard wrap them in a curtain and toss them into my jeep."

They would eventually receive orders to turn over the town to the Military Police (MPs) and the Counterintelligence Corps (CIC). At this time, the MPs and the CIC were consolidated under the Provost Marshal General. So, continuing their combat pursuit of the Germans, they participated in the breakthrough of the Siegfried Line and the subsequent pursuit phase into Bavaria.

The weather continued to be cold, about 40 to 45 degrees, and rain continued throughout the following week. Such conditions are favorable to offensive operations. The limited visibility resulting from ground fog and even rain can help obscure the movements of the assaulting troops. Cold tends to make the defenders settle in deeper in their holes and become less attentive. Troops seem to prefer comfort over security. The second battalion of the 276th Infantry Regiment was then assigned to the 313th Infantry Regiment. According to Mataxis, "Our objective was to seize the village of Lichtenberg and defend against a renewed German breakthrough of the corps reserve line along the Moder River on March 20, 1945." The 274th Battalion was then detached and rejoined Mataxis's regiment. Command directed them to move north to seize Hill 402 (the dominant terrain feature in the area). Mataxis's account states, "As we attacked, we drove in the German outpost line, and were halted by the German defensive positions." Pushing through Siegfried Line defenses along the north bank of the Saar, the division took Völklingen and other Saarland cities and towns.

During this harrowing action, the platoon leader in Easy Company won the regiment's only Distinguished Service Cross on February 6, 1945. With his platoon pinned down in a stream of tracer fire from a well-sited German MG-42, Lieutenant Claude Hafner fired a bazooka into an enemy machine-gun bunker, then leaped in and captured the remaining enemy soldiers at bayonet point. He continued to lead the way for his men as he cleared two more enemy defensive positions while taking six prisoners. After daylight, Lt. Hafner led the men back to clear a route for supply parties to come forward, where he killed two more Germans and then captured seven more.

After they crossed the Saar River, the regiment expanded its bridgehead across the Saar and began performing new duties of clearing towns. The Third Army cut across the 70th Division sector from west to east, and then the rest of Seventh Army thrust to the east and northeast on March 21; the 70th Division joined the Seventh Army and was placed in the 7th reserves. As such, the regiment was responsible for clearing the West Wall fortifications north of the Saar and rounding up prisoners, displaced personnel, stragglers, clearing mines, and dismantling enemy defenses and being prepared for encounters with potential Volkssturm members in the greater Saarbrucken/Volklingen area. The Volkssturm was the People's Militia, Hitler's last-ditch attempt to salvage victory from the invaders in the face of defeat.

On April 1, the regiment moved to the west bank of the Rhine River, in the vicinity of Rheinbollen and Bacharach, Germany. At this time, the division was transferred to the control of the Third Army. The regiment continued its occupational activities in the new sector and continued to process displaced people (DPs) for placement into DP camps scattered throughout the area. They also performed duties around the Rhine River bridges and provided heavily armed guards for duty aboard supply trains and security patrols. To complete the missions, the regiment was augmented with various aircraft, Military Police, and engineer units.

Ted stated, "My battalion was the northern most unit, next to a cavalry unit. Along the autobahn there had been a stretch of road 10 to 12 miles covered with trucks, artillery pieces, wagons, dead horses, and casualties which had been caught by US air and engaged as they were attempting to pull out from in front of us as we crossed the Rhine. We then turned up a road toward Steinbach, which we used until we moved into the Mainz area. We crossed at Mainz and followed a bulldozed route through the debris from bombing and moved to Darmstadt." On April 16, 1945, when the battalion was near Darmstadt, the regimental executive officer called Ted on the radio and said he had never seen the commander so pissed off. He was raising hell and wanted to know what his battalion had done now! They had been giving the Germans a tough time, so Ted was worried. He hurried to the command post. Upon arrival there he found the commander in a good mood. It had been a joke. The commander had called him down to let him know he had been promoted to lieutenant colonel. He was officially promoted on that day.

This is a picture of Colonel Mataxis taken as he was giving up command of the 2nd Battalion of 276th Regiment. He had volunteered to serve with the Old Guard to be deployed to the Pacific for the invasion of Japan's homeland. Noteworthy in this picture are his ever-present binoculars that were captured from the German forward observer who wounded him in World War II.

These occupational duties were at the time considered dreadfully dull. An interesting discovery by Mataxis and his troops involved money they had captured months earlier during an ambush of a German paymaster. At the time of capture, they assumed it was useless and acted like big shots, burning the money to light cigars, starting fires, thinking that the war was lost for Germany and the money would be devalued into nothing. It wasn't until the occupation months later that everyone realized their folly; the money they had wasted was in fact the currency of the day.

After VE Day (Victory Day in Europe, May 8, 1945), the division was engaged in occupational duties, with its command posts at Bad Kreuznach and Frankfurt, Germany. The division came under the control of the Ninth Army. During the summer, there was talk about possible deployment to the Pacific Theater of Operations. In June 1945, the 70th Division was filled with high-point soldiers for their upcoming return to the United States and their division's inactivation on October 11, 1945 at Camp Kilmer, New Jersey. In July the division transferred "low point men" to the 3rd Infantry Regiment and the 78th Division.

The 3rd Infantry Regiment, the Old Guard, had been assigned to the 106th Division to replace one of its regiments which had been overrun by the Germans. According to Mataxis, "I volunteered to transfer as battalion commander to the 1st Battalion of the 3rd Regiment, on August 2, 1945. The regiment had been selected to go to Japan for the upcoming invasion. We were in the Suez Canal en route to the Pacific when the atomic bombs were dropped and the war ended. The unit was then reassigned to serve as postwar occupation troops in the fall of 1945 in Limburg, Germany, where my battalion was stationed on occupational duty."

The 70th, 42nd, and 63rd initially fought as task forces when they first arrived and only later, upon arrival of their division's remaining troops, became divisions. They learned lessons as they went on and continually developed as tactical divisions. They would also go on to undertake some of the most challenging and heroic maneuvers in World War II and win significant victories. These soldiers faced some of the war's deadliest and most arduous combat. In the end, many of these soldiers would pay the ultimate price during their service.

Their statistics were:

> 70th Division (Task Force Herren): 86 days in combat liberating 58 towns/villages, 835 KIAs, 2,713 WIAs, 397 Unit members were taken prisoner, and 54 Missing in Action
> 42nd Division (Task Force Linden): 106 days in combat, 655 KIAs, 3,971 WIAs.
> 63rd Division (Task Force Harris): 119 days in combat, 980 KIAs, 4,504 WIAs.

In early October 1943, the Secretary of War authorized the establishment of a new award to be known as the Combat Assault Badge. Later in the same month the name was changed to the Combat Infantryman's Badge. The badge was established to recognize the unique contributions made by infantrymen during ground combat with an armed enemy. General Dwight D. Eisenhower wrote in *Crusade in Europe*:

"Only a small percentage of the manpower in a war theater operates in front of the light artillery lines established by the divisions. Yet this small portion absorbs about 90 percent of the casualties." This coveted award, which ranks with a Bronze Star, has been awarded to infantrymen for their actions during World War II, the Korean War, and the Vietnam War. Colonel Donald A. Seibert researched for three years to locate triple CIB recipients; only 230 such infantrymen were identified. Ted affectingly referred to his, with the two stars, as his "Perfect Attendance Pin."

Years after World War II

On May 8, 1995, the 50th anniversary of the end of World War II, the village of Oetting, France erected a monument to honor the sacrifices of the 2nd Battalion 276th Infantry Regiment at their point of entry to liberate Oeting. When Ted asked the French why they had funded this monument, as in the past the Americans funded their own monuments, the answer was, "Because of the Germans and Waterloo! The Germans had a monument there to their 1870 victory and all we had was a large cross to our dead." Ted said he understood that and asked but why Waterloo? The Frenchman then went on to say, "There are an increasing number of people coming to Waterloo each year as the new generations want to see where their ancestors fought! And that is very good for the local bed and breakfast places in the area."

In May 2005, the 60th anniversary of the end of World War II, the 70th Division monument was placed at Spicheren Heights. It was shaped and designed after the 70th Infantry Division's patch. The engraving says: "Raised in Fire, Always Self-Reliant, and Brotherhood into the Future." This monument proposal had been encouraged by the French and was paid for by the French. The land that the 70th Division had taken in that battle was "Hitler's holy ground." At the start of World War II, when Hitler's army had taken the ground, Hitler made a speech at that location saying, "Alsace Lorraine will be a part of Germany for 1,000 years." The French also wanted a monument on that site to balance the German 1870 monument at the same location stating, "They had captured the land back and won World War II!"

That same year, the Mayor of Oeting recognized Brig. Gen. Mataxis as an honorary village citizen and named a street in the town "Rue du Général Mataxis." Ted had never expected such an honor! The town had named the town square after his battalion, the 2/276th, earlier. Ted's hope was that his children, grandchildren, and great-grandchildren would be able to see Rue du Général Mataxis someday when they visited Europe. Several of Ted's grandchildren have visited the town. The grandchildren were met by the town's mayor and a team of grateful citizens who hosted them for three days. The town historian gave them a day-to-day account of the battle that took place in the liberation of their village. They were provided with an interpreter to translate when they met with many of the survivors of that battle. The grandchildren were able to walk the street named after their grandfather and

Ted's grandsons, Major Ted Mataxis III (center) and his brother Carson (second on the right), visiting Oeting in 2017 to view the street named after their grandfather. The town's welcoming committee joined them at the Rue du Général Mataxis, named in his honor by Oeting during the 60th anniversary of World War II.

came away with a greater understanding of the sacrifice of the villagers, as well as those who liberated them. They also came away with a new perspective on the cost of the freedoms we Americans enjoy each and every day. It is something that each generation must insure is passed on to the next generation to maintain our nation's freedoms.

Laetitia Allard had been the interpreter for the familiy's reception during their earlier visit in 2017. She contacted Carson, Ted's grandson, by Facebook extending an invitation for the family to attend the celebrations for the 80th anniversary of the liberation of Oeting in 2025. She stated, "For the past few months, all over France we have been reminiscing about and celebrating the 80th anniversary of the end of WWII and we are looking forward to the celebrations that will take place in Oeting for the 80th anniversary of the liberation of our town on February 23rd. The freedom that we can enjoy now was only made possible thanks to the bravery and courage of soldiers of different nations and your father [who] was in command of the battles leading to our freedom. We owe him a great debt, that is why we are very deeply honored that you and your family [have] accepted the invitation to join in the festivities in Oeting!"

Despite the Mataxis family's visit to France for the 80th anniversary being rather brief, it was a most enjoyable time because of the warm reception on the part of the town officials, citizens and their families, as well as the participants in the event. Ted Sr.'s role in liberating Oeting with his battalion during World War II was one of the proudest moments of his life, as it was for the men of the 2/276th Battalion. One phrase heard continually from everyone during the visit was "Thank you for giving us our freedom from the German oppressors." The sincerity of the townspeople was almost overwhelming.

During the war, the region was annexed rather than occupied by the Germans. As a result, the citizens were required to speak German, its men were drafted into the German army and then were sent to the Russian front. Any resistance and the Gestapo could execute their entire family, as they were considered traitors. As a result, the citizens felt the pressure of the Germans' hobnailed boots on their throats for four years. Their treatment was more abusive than those regions that were simply occupied. During the battle the citizens moved to basements, where they took refuge not only from the incoming shells of the Germans but also those of the Americans.

Upon the family's arrival in Oeting for the 80th anniversary celebrations they were greeted by Germain Derudder, Mayor of Oeting, and the Town Council. One of Ted Jr.'s overarching takeaways was how much these citizens, as well as the schoolchildren, knew about the war, 80 years later. That afternoon the family presented the town with many artifacts from World War II. This included a portrait of Ted Sr. that was painted in 1947 in Germany, as well as operations orders, maps, other documents and hundreds of photographs from that time. That evening the family were hosted at the school by the townspeople with an outstanding potluck dinner that was unequaled.

The next morning there was a parade that began where the Americans came into Oeting, marked by a monument to the 2/276th Battalion. The parade consisted of local authorities, French armed forces from the infantry regiment from the city of Bitche, old US military vehicles from the Trailblazers, the marching band of Forbach, veterans, residents, several guests including the Mataxis family, along with a US Air Force Color Guard from Ramstein Air Force Base in Germany. The parade's first stop was at Allée Nicolas Greff Street, named after a local resistance fighter who was killed by the Gestapo. The next stop was Rue du Général Mataxis, where flowers were placed on the street sign. The parade continued to the War Memorial next to the Church. Along the way, the Mataxis family paused several times to listen to

The 80th anniversary celebrations of the liberation of Oeting in 2025. Lt. Col. (Ret.) Ted Mataxis Jr. and Lt. Col. Ted Mataxis III attended the anniversary and presented the town of Oeting with many artifacts including operations orders, maps, other documents and hundreds of pictures from World War II and this portrait of Ted Sr.

FRANCE AND GERMANY, 1944–45 • 63

2nd Battalion, 276th Infantry Regiment monument in the town of Oeting. It stands at the point of entry of the 2/276 Battalion when they liberated the town in February 1945. It was erected on the 50th Anniversary 1995, the same year a street was named after General Ted Mataxis, their Battalion Commander during the Liberation.

This monument for the 70th Infantry Division was erected on the 60th anniversary of the end of World War II in 2005, to honor their sacrifices at the significant victory of Spicheren Heights, winning back "Hitler's holy ground." The engraving reads: "Raised in Fire, Always Self-Reliant, and Brotherhood into the Future."

different speeches paying tribute to the men who fought for their freedoms. The parade ended at the reception hall in Rue des Ecoles where there was an exhibition of numerous items from soldiers of World War II along with the artifacts that were donated by the Mataxis family. The anniversary was not only a tribute to the sacrifices of those who fought for freedom, but also an opportunity to ensure that the memory of their bravery is preserved for future generations.

CHAPTER 5

Postwar Occupation of Germany with Family, 1945–47

On August 2, 1945, Lieutenant Colonel Mataxis volunteered to command the 1st Battalion of the 3rd Infantry Regiment (an independent regiment known as "The Old Guard"), which was programmed to go to the Pacific Theater for the invasion of Japan. However, while they were in transit through the Suez Canal, America dropped atomic bombs on Japan and the war ended. Ted remained commander of The Old Guard until November 7, 1946. The military assured Ted that the 3rd Infantry Regiment would be assigned permanently to Berlin, as occupational troops. Its mission was to guard the Allied Council Headquarters, consisting of the four-nation military body governing Germany. (Today The Old Guard remains the oldest active-duty infantry unit in the army, continually serving the United States since 1784. It is the army's official ceremonial unit and escort to the president. It also has the mission of providing security for Washington, D.C., in times of national emergency or civil disturbance.) Being a man of action, Ted also volunteered his family to unite with him in occupied Germany for an additional year of command time. Ted finally came home to his small family in September 1946 to escort them back to Berlin. Berlin at this time was not only wartorn and bombed out, but it was also located deep within Soviet-controlled East Germany. Berlin was a divided city.

His wife, Helma, an exhausted mom of two rather rambunctious toddlers, packed up everything and traveled to Fort Hamilton, New Jersey, to board the army transport ship *Holbrooke* on September 9, 1946. This move is one of the first where Ted was present to help Helma and the kids pack up the household to head to the next assignment. He accompanied his family on the cruise back to Germany. Mataxis had presented the trip to his little family as a 10-day cruise that would take the Mataxis family across the Atlantic to Bremerhaven, Germany.

The ship included the first wave of dependents that would join their husbands already serving occupational duty in Europe. The vessel had 800 wives of soldiers and 27 dependent children. Imagine how the wives felt hauling their little ones across an ocean to a wartorn, foreign land speaking a different language and honoring a

Ted receiving the Purple Heart in Darmstadt, Germany, with the 3rd Infantry Regiment in November 1946 while commanding the Old Guard Battalion after World War II.

A map of the zones of Germany occupied by Britain, France, United States, and the Soviet Union. This was printed in the welcome pamphlet for occupation troops after World War II. (David Rumsey Map Collection, David Rumsey Map Center, Stanford Libraries)

Zones of Occupation in Germany, 1946. (US Army)

different culture. Lieutenant Colonel Mataxis was interviewed for the ship's daily newspaper during the crossing. The interviewer's first question was, "How do you like traveling with 800 women?" Mataxis, always the family man, stated, "I don't." To dig an even deeper trench for himself, Mataxis elaborated, "I would rather be on a troop ship. Then I would sleep on a B deck and eat in the quiet forward mess. These 27 kids sure do make a lot of noise! I've been losing sleep every night. It certainly was much quieter with the troops going over in 1944. I'll need a transfusion when I get there." After an exhausting cruise and a subsequent train ride, the Mataxis family finally reached what they had assumed would be their destination—occupied Berlin. The exchange rate at that time was one dollar for 10 German marks, so US dollars went a long way.

Germany was wrecked and some entire towns had almost been leveled by bombing, while others were heavily damaged by artillery and house-to-house fighting. Back home, many of these buildings would have represented a major catastrophe. Over here they were part of the landscape of the aftermath of World War II. There were thousands of displaced people (DPs), shuffling around like forgotten people, unsure

This passport picture of Helma, Shirley, and Teddy was taken in November of 1945, prior to their deployment to occupied Berlin.

where their next meal would come from, with their wretched belongings on their backs or in their carts. This is a world which requires strength to live in and the force of character to retain balance and judgment. There were many rules and regulations that you were required to live by, both as a dependent and military person.

To say the environment in Berlin was cold understates the relations between the international troops at the time. Upon arriving as occupation forces in Berlin, the soldiers from Soviet combat divisions had established good relationships and interactions with their fellow combat veterans of other nationalities. The troops traded with each other for souvenirs and interacted. Ted learned the Soviet war songs and learned to dance the Cossack sword dance. Unfortunately, these combat soldiers were quickly replaced by young communist troops that immediately created a rather frigid working environment for the British, French, and Americans, who were also occupying Berlin. This frosty environment would later be acknowledged as the precursor to the start of the Cold War.

It was not until Mataxis arrived and settled the family in their new quarters that he learned The Old Guard would be totally deactivated by November 7, 1946. On November 7, 1946, Mataxis was ordered to Frankfurt to activate the 7734th Historical Detachment. With the rapid demobilization, the official military historians had returned home, and the military took over their responsibilities. Mataxis had to leave Helma and the children in Berlin to fulfill his duty assignment until the army could move them. Effectively, this meant that Helma and her two children found themselves stranded in Berlin without Ted until the end of December 1946. The military finalized arrangements to move the Mataxis family to Garmisch in West Germany in early January 1947.

Helma and her two children (Shirley, aged five, and Teddy, aged two) were not left entirely alone; they now had a *Kindermadchen* or nanny, a young German lady named Luba, to look after them. Upon discovering that he was being asked to leave his family alone in a foreign country, Mataxis decided that to keep his little family safe he needed to get them a security guard for when he was not home. He settled on a fine specimen of a German Boxer. So Helma and the kids unexpectedly found themselves in possession of a new family dog, Roscoe. Helma was less than thrilled to have another mouth to feed, so to prove Roscoe's worth, Ted staged a surprise attack to demonstrate the guard dog's abilities to protect his somewhat hesitant wife. Roscoe, true to form, attacked Mataxis the minute he attempted to strike Helma. She immediately felt safer and was more amicable towards Roscoe. Roscoe had effectively "put Ted in his place," and Helma couldn't help but appreciate the dog's spirit. As Roscoe continued to chew up Ted for his transgressions, she acknowledged that the dog was one hell of a protector, and she became a little obsessed with the puppy. Roscoe officially became a member of the Mataxis family.

As if avenging his father, little Teddy was not one to ignore the defeat. One of Roscoe's more endearing family tales involves the poor dog and a demon child with sharp little teeth. Hearing Roscoe whining from the other room, Ted and Helma walked in one day to discover Teddy, sitting on Roscoe's back, teething on Roscoe's ears. The poor dog had resigned himself quietly to allow Teddy to gnaw on his first ear, but by the time those sharp little teeth had moved on to the second ear, even the perfect specimen of a German Boxer could no longer silence his whimpers. The protector that had chewed a hole in Ted Sr.'s ass earlier was not about to harm one of his human puppies.

Roscoe would become one of the few stabilities the Mataxis children would know. During their childhoods, they would trail their father around the globe throughout his military career. Roscoe would accompany the family on all their assignments over the next 14 years because the Mataxis children would refuse to allow him to be left behind. As explained by Ted's son years later, "When we took the around-the-world cruise going to the Indian Staff College, Mom and Dad had planned on leaving Roscoe in Alabama. We children pitched such a fit that they ended up paying for a ticket for him to come along on our India adventure." Roscoe officially became one of the world's best-traveled animals. For the price of half of

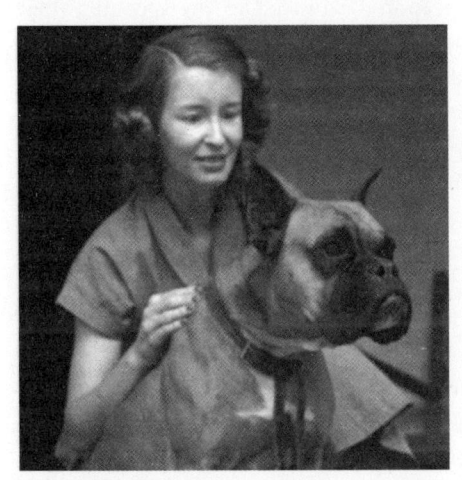

Helma with Roscoe, the children's best friend and protector. Garmisch, Germany, 1947.

Ted has just finished one of his many hunts in southern Germany. Here he poses with Shirley and Teddy in front of their house.

a regular human ticket, the canine protector could accompany the Mataxis family wherever they were stationed.

Once Roscoe was there to secure his family's safety, and the nanny was available as a helper and translator for Helma, Ted reported for an unexpected and somewhat unwelcome duty with the 7734th Historical Detachment. Upon receiving his orders, he reported to Colonel Pence, the commander of the Historical Detachment. Ted quickly informed the colonel that, "he was a battalion commander in combat and was not the type to take a staff job." Once again, Ted was about to learn one of military life's many lessons. General Mataxis laughingly describes the incident in his later accounts: Colonel Pence not so patiently responded, "Young man, shut up and sit down; I was a combat infantry commander in World War I and the commander of the 442nd Combat Team in the recent unpleasantness. Here I am—what do you think you've got to complain about—you are a regular army officer and, as such, will do what you're told." After hitting Mataxis upside of his head with the verbal equivalent of a two-by-four, Pence went on to brief Ted about his new assignment at one of the detachments. Pence's well-worn philosophy that, "it is up to those remaining on active duty to take over and do the best we can" had a significant impact on the young soldier's understanding of duty. Ted had been integrated into the army as a 26-year-old lieutenant colonel.

Mataxis was immediately sent for on-the-job training for a month with a sister historical section working on the Western Front. His mission was to document German operations against the Allies on the Eastern Front. Ted's job was to learn the ropes by attending their briefings and observing their operations. At the end of the month, Mataxis was to head up a new unit of the 7734th Historical Detachment, which would be stationed at Jaeger Kaserne in Garmisch, Germany. Once he finished his report, he immediately requisitioned a jeep and reported to the Occupational Military Government in Garmisch. Ted stated, "I never have been without a 'Worst possible case plan.' When I moved to Berlin, I brought a full basic load of ammo with me that was off the books, which I had gotten from the 70th Division when they were turning it in." Ted's contingency plan had requisitioned field radios, full field gear, individual weapons, and extra Browing Automatic Rifles for the detachment. He organized his detachment personnel into squads and platoons and had maps showing where all US installations were located. By November 1946, Mataxis had moved to the historical detachment at Garmisch, where he was assigned as the commander of the 7734th Historical Detachment Project of the United States Forces European Theater (USFET)—the Eastern Front. The project's mission was to record 300 captured German generals and general staff officers in writing their accounts of the German army's operations against the Soviets on the Eastern Front. The German generals were in a "Prisoner of War Camp."

In Garmisch, the Mataxis family discovered a beautiful little valley that seemed invulnerable to the ravages of the war that had just taken place to the north. The valley rested in the crook of the great arm of the Wetterstein mountain range, sheltering the twin towns of Garmisch-Partenkirchen. The valley was scattered with little colored Alpine houses and winding little streets. Bavarian peasants, ruddy and weathered, wearing the traditional Bavarian lederhosen and green velour hats, strolled through the town looking for their wayward cows. Like most peasant environments, the Bavarians displayed little concern for traffic regulations or the frantic honking of American trucks and jeeps. The town evoked a past version of Germany which had ceased to exist because of the war. With its idyllic charm, Garmisch quickly evolved into one of the army's finest recreation centers in the world.

Mataxis quickly selected billets and a headquarters for his unit so that they could become operational as soon as possible. After a lengthy surveillance period, Ted chose the Schongau Hotel for the staff headquarters' living quarters, and surplus space in the local hospital for the unit's headquarters and office spaces. The staff followed quickly and established operations. Ted then arranged for the Prisoner of War (PW) compound headquarters to support the project's operations. After a month of expediting requisitions for paper, typewriters, necessary maps, and supporting documents, the 7734th Historical Detachment was ready to go, and Ted was prepared to collect his family from Berlin.

So far, Helma had managed to hold down the home front in a foreign country for over a month before Ted unexpectedly reappeared on their proverbial doorstep. Having come on a German train to Berlin, he then hitched a ride with a sympathetic German truck driver who gave him a ride to the Mataxis home. On Christmas Eve, at around 11 p.m., Lt. Col. Mataxis was finally reunited with his little family. Waking up to Mataxis on their doorstep was undoubtedly a considerable Christmas surprise for the family. Having dad home for Christmas must have seemed like a miracle to the children; Santa delivered dad.

Once their Christmas celebrations were completed in Berlin, the Mataxis family was cleared to leave for Garmisch in January 1947. The family started the trip in their assigned car with a trailer tightly packed with all their worldly possessions. The family would spend the first night of their trip at Checkpoint Charlie on the border of the Russian zone. The following day, they would take off for their new home, only to have their car break down. Helma and the children were immediately taken back to Checkpoint Charlie, where they were stranded for a week, living with little food or comforts. A pregnant Helma was stranded again with two young children, a dog, and a problematic German maid with no advanced warning and no help from Ted. Helma, the kids, and the maid lived on powdered eggs and potatoes. The headquarters in Frankfurt had sent a jeep and trailer to get Lt. Col. Mataxis. Unfortunately, they had to send the family car back to Berlin for repair. Once the military could arrange the travel, Helma and the children would eventually travel to Garmisch by train. The family could not stay in military housing in Frankfurt because their German nanny was prohibited. When the time came to depart by train,

Helma and the kids had to smuggle her onto the train through the compartment window because she was not welcomed there either.

Ted did not seem to be faring any better than his family. He found himself single-handedly driving a military-issued jeep with a full trailer attached. Mataxis would wreck said jeep and had to be rescued by the British. Ted's head injury from the accident was severe enough to cause a concussion and require stitches. Ultimately, the severe concussion prevented Mataxis from driving, so he was also required to catch a train to Garmisch. At least he did not travel with two small children and a dog in tow, nor did he have to smuggle anyone through a window.

Finally, despite all the unexpected challenges, the Mataxis family arrived in Garmisch alive and well, if not a little travel-weary. The family was initially housed in the Schongau Hotel in Garmisch with the rest of the detachment. Then, in June, Helma gave birth to their third child, a little girl named Kaye. She was born in the army dispensary in Garmisch since there were no American hospitals in Germany during June 1947. After Kaye was born, the growing family moved into 32 Asnalbechtresse Strasse. Later, this building would be converted into the US Army's Garmisch Officers' Club. Helma and Ted enjoyed their occupational duty in Germany. There were many social events in the storybook setting of Garmisch-Partenkirchen, and the skiing and hunting were incredible. Today, Garmisch remains as one the most ideal of all winter and summer sports resorts, highlighting Germany's highest peak, the Zugspitze, which reaches an elevation of 9,782 feet.

Duty was not all fun and games for the commander; the real work began once he was reunited and settled with his family in Garmisch. The detachment organization was provided administrative headquarters and equipment to gather historical accounts of the German Army's operations on the Eastern Front against the Soviets, including collecting German reports of German efforts against the Soviet and Yugoslavian partisans' operations. At first, the German generals refused to cooperate. Thankfully, the generals swung into action once they were provided, on Lt. Col. Mataxis's orders, with an "approval to participate" letter written by Field Marshal Kesselring. Kesselring assured the generals' participation when he stated, "It is your last duty as German officers to record your operations against great odds so that the German people in the future will appreciate your efforts." The generals could not resist such an honorable and pragmatic call to action. Ted's men were ready to begin fostering relationships and passing out cigarettes at the first sign of cooperation. Ted left several reflections in his many journals about his experiences with these generals. Ted shares some of his favorites below:

"We had a covert mission to obtain accurate maps of Russia for the air force. We collected engineer studies of the terrain for our intelligence. I agreed with General Patton that we would face the Soviets in the future, which provided additional motivation for us all to succeed at our mission here. So, the detachment worked on a covert plan to obtain all the intelligence data we could for future use. We started the project by interviewing the officers who had conducted these missions, including the German generals that served under Field Marshal Georg Carl Wilhelm Fredrick Von Kuchler, the German POW camp commander. Most of the materials we were assessing came from the information these generals gave me while writing their accounts of their operations in Russia.

"The head of the German generals was Field Marshal Kuchler (the writer of the After-Action Report on fighting in Russia for the German Historical Division). In addition to him, we had many other vital German players working with us. Fortunately for the detachment, a German general, the chief historian of the German Army, was also interned in the camp and most cooperative. His typical German thoroughness got things organized. General Franz Hadler, Chief of Staff of the German Army from 1938 through 1942, was interned at the compound and was also most cooperative in providing the information, knowing that we could use it someday against the Russians.

"We developed a time and space matrix for our collection. It covered a whole wall. The dates ranged from the planning phase of 'Fall Barbarossa' through the war's end in the east. The first phase of filling in the blanks of the matrix was to start processing captured records. However, this phase left many gaps in our overall understanding. The Germans then told us that many of them had their diaries and copies of many unit orders and war records in their possessions at home. I immediately approved special travel orders for these officers to return home and recover their documents. Before they left, a committee of senior German generals explained that they would bring shame and discredit to the entire German officer corps if they failed to return. Since I had authorized these leave slips without authority from higher headquarters, I sweated this one out and was incredibly relieved when they all returned.

"We filled in more of the matrix using these records but still had several remaining gaps. So, we set up a system. I had personal monographs written by individual officers. These interviews were researched in advance, had maps with overlays, and were designed to complete the historical document. These historical accounts dealt with army groups, armies, and corps—some covered action at the division level during critical events or large operations. There were several notable projects on Soviet partisan warfare and operations of armored vehicles in the Russian winter.

"The Department of the Army later published many of these accounts in pamphlets highlighting various operations or issues. One interesting report by a division commander who was less than 20 miles outside Stalingrad explained that they could hear the shelling and see the reflections of the flares and artillery. Then, a couple of days before Christmas, they were hit from the flank by two Soviet horse cavalry divisions—they wiped them out, but their formations had been overrun, and their loss was so severe that they had to call off their advance and pull back rather than going to Stalingrad.

"Another fascinating study was triggered by the Nuremberg trials, where the Germans asked themselves, 'When can an officer refuse to obey orders?' It was accepted that an officer could not 'willy nilly' disobey orders if disciplined armed forces were to exist. They concluded that at the army group commander level, the commander could refuse to obey orders from the higher military staff. Their justification was that at the army group level, there were so many human resources and armament that a disregarded order would prevent jeopardizing a severe loss, thus threatening the entire war effort."

Mataxis would later share a fascinating anecdote with anyone who would listen, involving the story of one enigmatic general at the camp. The story initially emerged as the generals were being released from the base. All the generals at the center paid homage to one particular general. Mataxis became curious why this one general was held in such high regard. It piqued his curiosity. So, he asked the question. The unexpected answer he received was that "this particular general officer had participated in World War I, not in World War II." It turns out that when all German generals were told to report to the camp during winter 1946, this World War I German general showed up with all the other World War II generals (apparently, orders never specified from which war generals should report). When Mataxis asked the general why he would stay once he realized his mistake, the German stoically replied, "Why not? I had a roof over my head, a warm place to stay and the food was good. Most of all, it allowed me to be with men of my kind, and I enjoyed discussing operations with many old colleagues. Friendships are so important." The homage paid to an old German general by an old American general was never lost on anyone lucky enough to hear the story directly from General (Ret.) Mataxis.

Another unexpected result of this historical project was that its intelligence-gathering led to the conclusion among intellectual officers that the Soviets were America's next enemy. The intelligence convinced the military brass that Russia would eventually lead a campaign to overtake Europe. The critical focus of the project then became the collection of Russian maps, air photos, town and city plans, and other German intelligence files related to their Russian enemies. One German air force officer released from the PW camp returned from his farm with a portion of the German air force strategic bombing campaign plan that he had previously hidden in his cow barn. Accordingly, much of the data gathered on Soviet guerilla operations and Soviet organization, weapons, and tactics was essential to America's intelligence community for many years after it was initially collected. The term Cold War had not entered the lexicon yet; however, all agreed that something was hovering on the horizon.

Upon the deactivation of this historical project during summer 1947, all records and files were turned over to the Historical Division control at Frankfurt. Mataxis was assigned as deputy commander of the Garmisch military post and recreation center. He would serve in this post until he received orders to return to the United States in December 1947. The former deputy got in trouble and he and his German girlfriend and sport convertible car were transferred out of Garmisch on a day's notice. At the end of the war General Eisenhower issued a non-fraternization policy. It was relaxed in stages and by spring, speaking with German children was allowed. Helma and Ted really enjoyed the occupation duty in Germany with the social events, excellent skiing, and the storybook environment of Garmisch-Partenkirchen.

In Garmisch there was a wonderful club called the Casa Carioca which Mataxis "inspected" at least once a week. It had a sliding roof so you could see the mountains around the valley; it also had a sliding dance floor that could be pulled back and converted into an ice-skating rink where shows were often put on. Ted and Helma had gone there together one night when Helma said she was tired and went home early. Ted stayed and closed the club up in the early hours. Feeling like he was on cloud nine, he invited about 50 people home with him from the club, along with the band. Needless to say, Helma didn't get much rest that evening and when referring to this incident Ted would simply say, "Oh, to be young again!"

Lt. Col. Mataxis's orders were for his young family to return to the United States over Christmas and New Year. He requested a delay for the move until January 1948, which the army turned down. The army felt that a move with three small children over Christmas was not a problem. Lt. Col. Mataxis disagreed and requested that his "books be audited before he left," which allowed the Mataxis family plenty of time to have a wonderful Christmas in Garmisch. In January 1948, the family sailed for New York, where Mataxis was initially assigned to G-2, then G-3 section (Plans and training) of the First Army headquarters at Fort Jay, New York. The family was given quarters at Fort Wadsworth on Staten Island. According to Helma's accounts, "We had one side of a duplex, just as you came in the gate. This time, however, we had to take care of the furnace and the yard ourselves." Mataxis commuted five days a week from Staten Island to Manhattan and to Fort Jay on Governor's Island by ferry. Later, they used a small government boat to bring them directly from Governor's Island to Fort Wadsworth.

During this time, the army was trying to reestablish the old pre-World War II social life, which Ted and Helma had not encountered since their newlywed days. They immediately started socializing with friends at the Fort Wadsworth Club, and they met others in New York City.

The Mataxis children looking like a typical German family. Kaye was born in June 1947 at the local dispensary and the family lived a quiet life in Garmisch until returning home in January 1948. In June of that year Stalin blocked all supplies from Berlin, marking the start of the Cold War and requiring an airlift to supply Berlin's logistical needs.

They found themselves visiting Governor's Island for special events and various parties. It appeared that post-World War II, the army was returning to the idea that "rank doth have its privileges." By this time, Lt. Col. and Mrs. Ted Mataxis had rank.

Ted was always surprised that a staff job he never wanted created his lifelong passion for studying history. The emergence of the Cold War fed Ted's passion for history and its effects on future behaviors for the rest of his military and post-military assignments. The frost that Ted had noticed at the conclusion of World War II and during the occupation slowly progressed into the Cold War, and Mataxis had a front-row seat at the table. The Cold War stemmed from many events: the post-World War II partition of Europe; the Soviet blockade of Berlin that started in June 1948 (including the West's airlift of supplies); the 1949 loss of China to the communists; and the North Korean invasion of the Republic of Korea during the 1950s. During Korea's invasion, President Harry S. Truman committed to "supporting foreign peoples against outside communist aggression." The diplomatic policy (later termed "containment") was a central approach to US foreign policy strategy for years. Even though the United States was fighting a hot war in Korea to contain communism, Germany was widely regarded as the center of the East/West divide and where the next world war would begin.

After World War II ended, as part of the postwar occupation, the victors partitioned the formerly unified Germany into two sovereign nations: the Federal Republic of Germany (FRG) and the German Democratic Republic (GDR). West Germany was under Western sponsorship, and East Germany was under communist support. In the GDR, Berlin was similarly divided into West Berlin and East Berlin in 1949. The troops stationed in West Berlin included American, British, and French forces. Soviet personnel settled in East Berlin. Years later, the Army Chief of Staff would say the Cold War was won without firing a shot. Ted sent him a letter stating that Korea and Vietnam were in fact part of the containment of communism in the Cold War. This letter is the response by the Army Chief of Staff to Ted: "You are right, the battles of the Cold War spanned peace and conflict. Too frequently, in our euphoria over the end of a half-century of confrontation, the service and sacrifice of those that made this great victory possible have been ignored. Thank you for your poignant and proper reminder of the debt we owe to several generations of Americans."

By 1951, the United States' forces in Europe shifted their focus from occupational duty to defense and deterrence against the communist military threat. The Soviets bolstered the Eastern Bloc nations with their military, which contained a million soldiers. The United States formed the North Atlantic Treaty Organization (NATO) and its members had about a third as many soldiers in FRG as the Soviets had in GDR. By late 1951, the European command consisted of three major players in Germany: the US Seventh Army, the US Twelfth Air Force, and US naval forces. Thus, the tense political atmosphere and massive military buildup on both sides made Europe, especially Germany, ripe for potential and devastating future conflicts.

CHAPTER 6

Indian Staff College and UN Observer, Kashmir, 1950–52

In spring 1950, Mataxis attended the Strategic Intelligence School in Washington, D.C. This school prepared officers to serve as defense attachés in embassies worldwide. While attending the school in Washington, the family lived close to Dupont Circle in half of a three-story home on Florida Avenue and R Street. This area is now Embassy Row. During his stint in D.C., Mataxis received a phone call from a World War II friend who now worked at the Department of the Army. He said, "Ted, put in for an assignment to the Indian Staff College." Ted replied, "Friend, I am a Mustang reserve officer, and the West Pointers get priority." Ted's friend was optimistic that if he applied, Ted would get the slot. After Ted agreed to try, his colleague explained the assignment further. Mataxis quickly realized why he would be selected for this assignment over the West Point graduates. The primitive living conditions and unsanitary health issues meant many officers had simply declined the appointment. So, of course, once again, Ted would volunteer himself and his young family to serve in a position that others had rejected immediately.

Ted quickly realized that this next move would take the Mataxis family to the other side of the world. For some historical context, this move occurred well before globalization. The world was not yet as flat as it is now. With this voyage, the Mataxis family would be some of the first Americans to be integrated into India for a substantial amount of time. Being the first American student to attend the Indian school meant this unblazed path created more questions than answers for the Mataxis family about what to expect and what they needed to take with them. He immediately told Helma so that she could begin preparing the family for the move.

Helma discovered information was sparse; however, she was able to learn some specific details about the quarters the family would be assigned. Their new home in India would be rustic: heated by charcoal clay pots, sporting a leaky roof, no running water, and spotty electricity at best. The biggest question in her mind was what they should bring from the United States for their new home in India. What would she need? What would the children need? One had to assume there would be very little available for the family once they arrived. Getting ready for the assignment, Mataxis studied India's history, customs, and traditions, and the organization of its army. Helma became increasingly aware that the travel would be complicated, the language barrier significant, and the unsanitary and primitive living conditions would be challenging with their three young children and the dog. She was not thrilled at the prospect of the move ahead. Ted had to use his only ace to pacify his somewhat reluctant wife and explained to his little family that they would take a world cruise on a United States Line ship to their new home. They would sail out of California and return by way of New York while going to and returning from India. The young family did enjoy their time on cruise ships, so this helped Mataxis excite his little family about another adventure into the unknown.

Travel to India

With Mataxis along for the move this time, the family drove their new 1950 Chevrolet station wagon, with its three-row seating and fancy wood paneling, to their departure point. En route to the port of San Francisco from New York, the family traveled through Fort Benning and Fort Leavenworth. The plan was to swing through Alabama and leave the family dog, Roscoe, with friends who lived on a dairy farm and had room for the dog to roam. Upon arrival in Alabama, as they began to leave Roscoe behind, all three children cried and carried on to the point that Ted made a "command decision" and coordinated the booking of a kennel on the liner *President Monroe* so that Roscoe could accompany the Mataxis children on their world cruise. It was not a cheap endeavor; however, according to Ted Jr., "Dad and Mom realized that their children were being displaced by the move once again, and Roscoe was the only stability we [the children] had in our short lives. So off we went on President Monroe's cruise liner, with Roscoe and our 1950 Chevy station wagon in the cargo hold." When the family departed for India, the children were aged seven (Shirley), five (Teddy Jr.), and two (Kaye); along with Roscoe (aged three and weighing in at 60 lbs).

The family's first stop along the way was Hawaii, followed by: Japan, Hong Kong, Singapore, Penang, Malaysia, and Ceylon, with the last stop at Cochin, Ceylon. Going the western route out of San Francisco and planning to return a year later through the Suez Canal on the eastern path to New York meant that the Mataxis children would circumnavigate the world before the age of 10. This voyage was the children's first taste of Asia, and it was all so fascinating because each port offered a glimpse of a new and different culture. The family was required to dress up for the formal meals. The children loved ordering anything off a menu, like at a fancy restaurant; however, they could also get hamburgers and french fries as a special request.

Roscoe ate well on that trip, too. He enjoyed his cozy sleeping area on the crew's deck rather than his assigned kennel. When the ship arrived at ports of call, Roscoe often accompanied the crew on their shore leave explorations. Ted found the dog's resourcefulness rather endearing. He said, "We discovered [his escapades] when coming back on a launch from Hong Kong. While going ashore, we looked over at another of the ship's launches, and lo-and-behold there was Roscoe on the crew's launch."

After leaving Japan and sailing to India, Mataxis heard the news that North Korea had invaded South Korea. Another war was starting. So, when the ship landed in Hong Kong, Mataxis immediately went to the embassy and cabled the Pentagon to cancel his school assignment with a request to volunteer for combat duty in Korea. According to Mataxis, "I received a cable at the next port in Singapore to continue to school. They assured me they would assign me to Korea when I finished in the spring."

Upon arrival, the Mataxis family was offloaded to begin their new adventure through India. Their car was transported to their new home. Because of the roads and travel conditions, the small family was strongly advised against driving across India and encouraged to take the train. Like in Germany, the family had their assigned compartment outfitted with bunks and an attached bathroom. Their train journey would take three days to their new home. Since it had just gained its independence from Britain three years earlier, there was very little information available on travel. Still, the number one recommendation relayed over and over was to take a valise for train travel (a large canvas bedding roll packed with sheets, blankets, and a pillow for overnight train journeys). Mataxis carried valises for everyone, which made the trip a little better for his young family.

They were immediately surrounded by innumerable hawkers of food, fruit, mineral water, and cigarettes. The sanitation conditions in India during the 1950s were horrible. According to Helma's account of the events, "We had been advised of the golden rule in India: never drink water or use ice from an unknown source. All drinking water should be obtained from a known source and boiled before drinking. No one was allowed to drink water from a tap or put ice in their drinks unless it had been boiled previously." With the small children in tow, Helma also had to ensure that even the milk given to them had been boiled before it was consumed. It was only safe to buy cooked food from personnel wearing an official small metal badge. She explained, "We were warned that if we bought fruit, it should be thick-skinned types such as oranges and bananas. There were many stories of strange diseases in India, so one willingly took the required shots and followed the daily precautions prescribed for day-to-day activities."

Helma was still recovering from her harrowing experience years before on the German trains with nothing but the kids, an illegal nanny, and only limited food options. Helma, as resourceful as her husband in many ways, was rarely one to repeat her mistakes. This time she was prepared with snacks. Helma and the kids, being very apprehensive about eating local food, willingly carried their water, chocolate, biscuits, and snacks to avoid another debacle. Unfortunately, they did not bring enough snacks for a hungry little family. After a day or two, the children became hungry enough that when the train stopped, they disembarked to scout out the area for any remaining British eating establishments where they could all find a hot, cooked meal. When the British pulled out of India, many British establishments remained, and their conditions were much more sanitary than the local establishments.

Helma recalled in her papers, "At every stop along the way, the various stations teemed with people selling food and water. There were also many beggars. We found out that rail journeys are hot, dusty, and dull. We were warned in the heat of the day to keep windows closed. We were also warned to keep our train berths always locked. Roscoe proved to be an additional layer of security. [Despite the dangers] as we traveled across India, we realized what a beautiful country it was in so many ways, and the terrain and vegetation deeply contrasted with the United States."

Captain Patcar, the adjutant for the staff college, met the family at their last train stop. As he drove the family up the road towards the Nilgiri Mountains, they were all mesmerized by how beautiful this part of India was. The Nilgiri Mountains of southern India (at 6,000 ft. of elevation) were home to the oldest regiment in the Indian Army, the Madras Regiment, which was founded in 1644. Before World War I, the British established a staff college in Quetta; however, when the partition of India took place in August 1947, the Muslims were moved to the western part of India, where they founded Pakistan, and to the eastern part of India to form Bangladesh. India became a country of 28 states and eight Union Territories, each with its own cultural heritage and dialect. India established its own staff college at Wellington after the partition. Pakistan continued with the staff college at Quetta. The Defense Staff Service College (DSSC) was in Wellington, India. While Patcar drove the family to Wellington, he told them how much they would love their new home and how much Ted would enjoy the #4 Staff Course.

The college enjoyed its 300-year history and was known as one of the oldest institutions in India. The staff college was a sister to the British staff college in England. Unlike other Commonwealth staff colleges, the college was a tri-service school with a navy wing, an army wing, and an air force wing. Each student participated in the course of their service; however, the three branches combined as a cohort group to study the common core curriculums such as world affairs, military history, integrated operations, theory, and methods of instruction. They spent approximately 70 percent of their working periods on their individual service program and 30 percent on the combined program.

Mataxis was assigned to attend the course offered in 1950, which started on August 1, 1950 and finished on June 1, 1951. This class was the fourth course conducted. There were a hundred students in the fourth course. Most officers represented the

Indian Army, Navy, and Air Force. The Indian student body was comprised of one colonel, 17 lieutenant colonels, 49 majors, and 11 captains, all of whom were drawn from the various regiments of the Indian Army. Class four was the first year the Indians opened the staff college to foreign exchange students. Ted, as the first American, attended with two British officers, two Burmese officers, one Canadian officer, and one Australian. The staff consisted of Indian officers who were lieutenant colonels, and six British officers. This tradition of inviting foreign exchange students has lasted throughout the years. The DSSC ran three separate courses concurrently; each class was 12 months, requiring students to attend the wing of the college devoted to their service. As there were over 22 different languages spoken in India at that time, English was the medium of instruction, and any Indian language proficiency was unnecessary. The Constitution of India declared that Hindi and English were the official languages.

The commandant, Major General Walter Lentaigne, had been awarded several honors: Order of the British Empire (OBE), Commander of the British Empire (CBE), and the Distinguished Service Order (DSO). He was one of only a handful of British general officers to be offered attachment positions to the Indian Army and service after the partition of 1947. This position was reserved for those officers the Indians greatly admired and held in the highest esteem. He was known for his bravery, demonstrated in both World War I and World War II. During World War II, he commanded the 111th Indian Infantry Brigade, which was part of General Wingate's well-known Chindits, and he replaced Wingate after he died in an airplane crash. He was well liked at the interservice staff college by both students and staff alike. He and his wife provided the students with many dinners and parties during the year.

The students were organized into smaller study groups and studied military history throughout the course. The training would culminate with the study groups presenting their research projects to the rest of their fellow students. One group studied the general outline of World War II and constructed a flowchart. Another group, the one to which Mataxis was assigned, surveyed the Russian campaigns in World War II. They all benefited from his interviews with the German generals in Garmisch after the war. Mataxis continually highlighted that the Russians had a very close hold on the location and movements of all their units during the war. The objective of this exercise was for all officers to know something about all the campaigns being studied on the course and for all students to learn a logical, clear, and easily readable method of digesting the campaigns on paper. The overarching objective was for students to learn how to organize their campaign presentations, which was believed to enable them to plan future operations.

The course offered two highlights. The first was a tour of north India. During January 11–24, 1951, students and instructors visited army establishments in northern India on a special air-conditioned train. It took approximately two and a half days to reach Poona College. Many of the students suffered respiratory issues during the train ride. Ted said, "We slept on the train during the tour except for the two nights we spent in tents at Deolali. We had our meals in two dining cars, which we referred to as the Ritz and the Savoy, which were attached to our train. These were staffed by personnel from the officers' mess at the school. Despite all the apparent amenities, the conditions of the tour were not very pleasant. The air conditioning system had to be shut off after 1:00 a.m., and the windows could not be opened, making sleep virtually impossible. Approximately twenty-four students slept in each un-air-conditioned car; no one was surprised that the students and staff began to fall sick with tonsillitis. The mess cars were the most unsanitary. Flies were everywhere, and the plates were not very clean." At least this experience helped these exchange students better understand what their families were dealing with each day in their bungalows.

The tour included visits to the School of Military Engineering at Kirkee, Southern Command Signals at Poona, the School of Artillery at Deolali, and the Armored Corps School at Ahmednagar. Mataxis recounts the visits in his papers: "At the School of Military Engineering, we witnessed various demonstrations such as road construction, bridge building, earthmoving, water supply, and minefield gapping. We were taken to the artillery ranges at the School of Artillery and saw live-fire shooting with 25-pounder, 5.5-inch, and 7.2-inch equipment. At the Armored Corps School, they demonstrated an armored/infantry attack. The tank squadron was equipped with Sheridan tanks from the 5th/3rd Gurkha Rifles."

The second tour was over February 15–27, 1951. The entire class took part in a naval cruise off the coast of India. Each student spent four days on a destroyer or frigate and the remainder on a landing ship. Quite surprisingly, during a firing demonstration of their 20 mm antiaircraft gun, Ted asked if he could fire it at the 55-gallon oil drums used as targets. Lt. Col. Mataxis was temporarily awarded the

Ted wearing a navy captain's hat and his ever-present binoculars. The satisfied look was because on the Indian Staff College cruise he outshot the ship's crew on their 20 mm antiaircraft gun. Ted had been an enlisted soldier with the coastal artillery prior to World War II. Ted had never forgotten the words of his professor of military science at the University of Washington, Lt. Col. Thebaud: "Always know how to maintain and fire all the weapons out there for some day you may be the only one there and need to fire it."

captain's hat for outshooting the navy. They were quite shocked at his proficiency with their weapons. Ted had never forgotten the words of his PMS at the University of Washington: "Always know how to maintain and fire all the weapons out there for some day you may be the only one there and need to fire it." Once again, a lesson from his PMS at ROTC rang true.

For the demonstration, the Indian Navy dedicated two destroyers, three frigates, three minesweepers, one landing ship, and other small vessels for the cruise. The students would participate in a beach assault supported by the Indian Air Force. Toward the end of the course, the college proceeded on a demonstration tour, including exercises at sea with the Indian Navy. As the students traveled to various locations, the tour embraced visits to administrative installations and tactical demonstrations.

Like these excursions, the DSSC was exceptionally well set up and had its own military library, printing press, and extensive buildings for instructional purposes. It also had sufficient married quarters and single quarters for the students, as well as a gym, stables, recreation field, and rifle and pistol ranges.

The center of many activities was the officers' mess, which resembled a luxurious country club and was a beautifully appointed place in the traditional old-world style with antique carpets, an abundance of the finest sterling silver, and magnificent paintings of people and times long passed. In the mess, one was quickly overcome by antiquity and traditions. The building showcased many customs and pageantry of the British colonial period. The East India Company's china plates, which were hundreds of years old, were displayed. Many beautiful things had been presented to the officers' mess during its centuries of operation and memories of the Raj remained in place. At the center of the well-appointed building, there was a majestic fountain.

The exchange students' and officers' housing were within a three-minute walk. There were loads of servants in white turbans wearing regimental colors on the sashes around their waists. The splendor of it all was reminiscent of an old Hollywood movie. The visiting students had been given the best of everything that was available at that time. It was a busy social life spent for the English, Canadian, Australian, and American exchange students, school staff members, Indian students, and wives. Ted recalled, "Occasionally, we would visit the Wellington Gymkhana Club, which was nearby. The club was built in 1885 as a racetrack. It was situated at 6,000 feet above sea level and had an 18-hole golf course and tennis courts, as well as other sporting facilities. The club had its trophies lined along the walls, and they were covered in old pistols, rifles, swords, animal skins, and plaques. It also had an ancient library of dusty old English books, fading away in their locked glass cases, and an old piano bar that remained on the premises. It was a very vivid reminder of how the English lived during the time of their colonial occupation and exploitation of India. We spent many beautiful days and nights with fellow students and old English tea planters in the area. We danced, drank, and made merry on so many occasions. It was wonderful to exist in a place filled with such history."

The Family's Living Conditions

The Mataxis family was assigned a bungalow only a few minutes from the campus. Helma had three children under seven and Roscoe, and she certainly did not expect what she found when they arrived. It was like going back in a time machine. Helma nearly returned home when she saw the conditions they would have to live in for the coming year. However, after much discussion regarding the embarrassment her leaving would cause the American government, she decided to tough it out.

Helma was shocked that the quarters were provided for the officers based on the number of children they had and that the families were expected to run their households and provide cooking utensils, glass, china dishes, and crockery. However, Helma quickly learned that no kitchen equipment was needed because it was unsuitable for Indian cooks or their wood-burning cooking stoves. The lack of a proper American kitchen was only one of the numerous problems Helma would face during her year in India.

The Mataxis home was a typical English bungalow with Poinsettia trees up to the roof. It was a short walk to the officers' mess, the center of all social activities. Despite the furniture provided for the quarters, the primitive conditions were

This picture is of the Mataxis children and their best friend Roscoe, the German Boxer. They are posing with the seven house staff members in Wellington, India. The house had dirt floors, no running water, and a outdoor kitchen.

somewhat intimidating. Carpeting was not encouraged since all the bungalows had dirt floors. The mattresses for the beds were military-issue, and mosquito nets were an absolute necessity. If they owned a mattress, married officers were advised to bring it. All the items needed for the children had to be brought from the United States. Unfortunately, that required planning, and there was no one to explain what was necessary. Since the Mataxis family were the trailblazers, they would be unprepared a few times. It is essential to remember that the turnaround time for packages from the United States was an average of over 60 days. When lucky enough to receive a food parcel from the United States, one had to pay a 40 percent duty on whatever was received. The Mataxis family would have to learn to do without for a while.

Helma later recounted in her reflections that, "The bungalow had four bedrooms and ample living space for entertaining; however, there was no inside plumbing, running water, or regular electricity. Each of the four bedrooms had a separate bathroom, taken care of by a 'wet sweeper' and equipped with a chamber pot. We were provided with five servants. We had a family bearer (butler), a chokra (a young boy about 12 who helped the bearer), a wet sweeper (for the bathrooms), a cook, and a gardener. The bearer wore a large turban adorned in the colors of the college. The stove was in an outbuilding made of metal over a brick foundation. Water was hauled in two large brass pots that were easily balanced on the heads of the servants. A fire was built to heat the stove and oven, and all hot water came from this source, including the water for the tin bathtub. We had a galvanized bathtub in the back of the house. When we wanted a bath, we would notify one of the servants, and they would have to heat the water, transport it, and then pour it into the tub for us. I remember calling out to the head servant during one of my first baths in India, 'Swami, the water is cold.' He answered me immediately, 'Memsahib, I know. The Sabe's bath water is also cold.' I resigned myself to a year of dirt floors and cold baths for the family. We also had what looked like an old icebox and a charcoal fire to keep the food warm. I brought a Norge Midnight Defrost refrigerator, not knowing how problematic electricity was. Everyone thought the American lieutenant colonel was a millionaire with the car and the ice box. It was the talk of the college."

Helma recalled what happened when she asked about a tailor to mend some of their clothes: "The next thing I saw was a tailor followed by a girl with an old pedal Singer Sewing machine on her head, walking up the road to the bungalow. Then the tailor set up shop on the verandah. They could make whatever I wanted. Despite the fact it appeared so primitive, the quality of their work was excellent, and they could copy any design. It was all rather impressive."

The monsoon seasons did not help the unsanitary conditions. Upon arrival, they were greeted by the southwest monsoon (the main monsoon that comes in from the sea and starts making its way up India's west coast in early June). By mid-July, most of the country was covered in rain. The monsoons flooded everywhere, and mud was inescapable. However, when there was no rain for months, all the water was cut off, the dust took over, and you could not keep the dust out of the house. It was a classic case of damned if it rains and damned if it doesn't. There was no easy answer to either of these conditions. There was also no escape. Ted recalled, "Halfway through the tour, we were greeted by the northeast monsoon." The water and dust would be some of the least of their worries. Helma recalled, "It was all extremely unhygienic, and flies were always everywhere. The sanitary arrangements were about as primitive as you can get. There were no septic tanks; everyone from generals to privates used the same sort of lavatory. The whole thing sat on four legs, and it looked like a wooden chair seat with four legs and a cover over it. When you had to use this, you closed the lid and called your sweeper to empty it. Everyone knew what you had been up to."

Helma recalled, "At some time during your stay, your home would have bats, lizards, and rats, known to carry the bubonic plague through their fleas. Additionally, it was almost guaranteed that you would get dysentery if a fly landed on your food." Helma wrote, "The Indians hated killing anything, so critters were allowed to do as they pleased. The catchall phrase was, 'It can't do any harm, Memsahib.' All the children, at one time or another, contracted worms from the flies that were everywhere. I had a rough time with the children. All the dogs and animals were riddled with worms and spread their eggs in their excrement. Not only did the children continually get dysentery, but parasites and worms also plagued them." The dirt floors and the continuous mud did not help dissipate the problem.

Early in the posting, the Mataxis family learned there had been a relatively mild scare of the plague in the town next to Wellington. This was less than half a mile from where the family's cook and house staff lived. The college sent everyone off to get vaccinated against the plague. According to Mataxis, "It had been the first case of the plague for 20 years. So far, there had only been five cases, very mild, that had been reported, but it caused a big stir and a lot of anxiety for the exchange students who remembered the plague in Europe in the Middle Ages! They told people not to worry; they would not permit people to come from that town to Wellington as a precaution. The plague at the next village eventually dried up, thank God. Everyone felt gross discomfort whenever we would see a rat since they carried fleas which carried the plague."

By March, everyone in the Mataxis household had experienced dysentery. Helma explained, "The whole family was often suffering from temperatures well over 103, which was frightening. There was a scare because smallpox was approaching. Everyone in our family had been inoculated against it before coming. The smallpox vaccination was required before our departure to India and was considered essential. Smallpox, typhoid, and cholera shots were required every six months. Other shots could be required when there were outbreaks of yellow fever and the plague. From a health perspective, the only good news was the absence of malaria. Luckily, we had no ill effects from smallpox, so we were as safe as possible."

This picture was taken in Wellington, India, while Ted was attending the Indian Army Staff College. The family was dressed up for the Easter Parade of 1951.

The college ran a British kindergarten for officers' children aged three to eight years. Shirley and Teddy attended. The teacher was an English lady, very stern and stoic, and her assessments of the children were rather harsh. Kaye was too young to attend school and stayed at home with Helma. In September, there was a four-day break in the course, so Ted went on a four-day hunting expedition. Helma sent Teddy and Shirley off to school just like any other day. It wasn't until later that afternoon that problems would arise. Shirley was carried off the school bus, almost hysterical and very ill. She was put to bed early; however, her temperature rose to 105 degrees later that night. The fear of convulsions became a genuine possibility. Shirley did not have any symptoms apart from a headache.

When Helma called the hospital, "A fool of a doctor told me to try eau de cologne on her forehead and to bring her to the hospital in the morning." Eau de cologne, used initially for hygiene and cleansing, was a fragrance that brought freshness and purity. Passed through generations in India, eau de cologne was believed to revitalize and restore energy and vitality. It was meant to make purification a moment of pleasure and well-being, much as our modern infusers are intended to do today.

This insufficient medical attention and her husband's absence during another family crisis caused Helma to panic. She was expecting some medical attention and received none, so she did exactly what any resourceful mother would have done with her child's health in jeopardy; she called the powers that be at the college. They had an ambulance at the house in 10 minutes. Shirley's temperature dropped to 102 by midnight, but she was sick and had violent diarrhea. Shirley had not been treated at the hospital, just observed, which could have been done at home. This sort of thing happened constantly in India and was considered the way of life. Someone always has dysentery. So, lessons were learned that night: if one wants to get better, don't call an Indian doctor, or go to the hospital on any account (especially for tummy problems). Simply stay home and recuperate faster.

When the family moved to India in 1950, Helma decided she wanted to have a typical American Thanksgiving and invite all their friends. She had the cook find a giant turkey, and then the family all spent a couple of weeks trying to fatten it up with grain and food from the tables. Shirley said, "During the meal, somehow, we [the children] realized that we were eating our friend. Tommy had become our pet and we all loved our Tommy. We immediately jumped up and screamed, 'You killed our Tommy; you killed our Tommy!' and ran out of the dining room crying. The parents and their guests quietly finished the meals."

The children weren't the only mischief-makers in India. Shirley remembers her dad pulling a prank of his own. She explained, "While we were in India, another student was visiting Dad, and somehow, they found out that there was a dead cobra snake in the garden. Thinking it was funny; they took it upon themselves to coil it up and put it at the foot of the bed between the sheets of our Indian 'nana's' bed. I never knew a small woman could scream that loud. It's a wonder she didn't have a stroke and a miracle she didn't quit. It was luck that they hadn't tried their shenanigans on Mom, the book would have been a lot shorter."

There was genuine concern that the Korean conflict could turn into World War III at any time and could result in a nuclear exchange. During this time, Lt. Col. Mataxis received a cable stating that since he had volunteered for overseas duty, he was being sent as a military observer to the United Nations in Kashmir with the Indians and Pakistanis. Since he wanted to go to the Korean War, he called to object and was told simply to "obey your orders." He contacted Major General Lentaigne, commandant of the staff college, and Lieutenant General Nimmo, the Australian commander of the UN mission, to explain his situation. According to Ted's account, "They both agreed to fashion a two-week buffer before reporting to the UN mission so I could attend the Indian jump school." That would then be followed by a month's leave to go to Vietnam to observe the French operations against the communists there. The 30-day leave was approved by the Infantry Branch with an additional prohibition. I was not allowed to go to Korea during my leave." Mataxis used the two-week buffer to attend the Indian Army jump school.

Indian Jump School

Ted described his time at jump school in his journals: "During May 1951, I attended the Indian Jump School, styled after the American Jump School. We practiced jumping from a platform on top of the hanger, and a 'Jerry rigged' paddle with the parachute harnesses attached to it. This device enabled us to practice parachute landing falls (PLFs) designed to slow you down when coming in contact with the earth. The jumper disperses his body contact by absorbing the contact with five body parts to conduct a proper PLF. A paratrooper will make an appropriate landing of a parachute fall by hitting all five contact points: (1) Balls of your feet; (2) Calf; (3) Thigh; (4) Buttocks; and (5) Pull-up muscle. The Indians also used the five points of performance: (1) A proper aircraft, exit, check body position, and count; (2) Check canopy and gain canopy control; (3) Keep a sharp lookout during the entire descent; (4) Prepare to land; and (5) Land using proper PLF." Despite this, Mataxis regrettably broke his ankle on the second jump and could not complete the course. He did not get his Indian jump wings. Mataxis explained the experience: "At the India Jump School, they only used one parachute with no reserve. The flight pattern flew over the Taj Mahal and turned a 90-degree bank into the desert for the drop zone. It was quite windy on the second jump, and I tore up my ankle landing."

This picture was taken while Ted was attending the Indian Army's Jump School. Ted broke his ankle on the second jump and did not become airborne qualified at this time due to his injury. It is interesting to note there are no reserve parachutes; the Indian Army did not use them. Of note is the 70th Infantry Division Patch from World War II on his shoulder.

The Path Forward

Mataxis explained what happened next: "I took a month's leave to journey to French Indochina to observe the fighting between the communist-led Vietminh and the French-backed Vietnamese troops." This provided Ted with a visit to a war zone rather than a trip to Denver to visit his family. He had already commanded two battalions: one in World War II (2/276) and one during the occupation (The Old Guard). According to Mataxis, "The army's priority for battalions in Korea was being given to those without combat command experience. The Infantry Branch also noted that I would be assigned to the Marine Corps Amphibious School on return to CONUS after completing the UN mission. This resulted in me taking leave to Vietnam rather than returning to the United States to visit my family. This time I sent a letter to the general who was chief of staff for the Infantry Branch, and he sent me a personal letter that he would have me assigned to Korea when I finished with the UN mission." At the Indian staff college, Mataxis studied the guerrilla aspects of the British Afghan wars in detail and traveled up to the Afghan border detailing the route in case it might be helpful later.

The following was a letter received from the United States Army Chief of Staff dated December 11, 1951: "Lieutenant Colonel Mataxis, I've just received a letter from the general, Commander in Chief of the Indian Army, informing me of your splendid record as a student in the 4th Staff Course in the Indian Defense Service Staff College. The fact is the commandant and staff rated you as the best student in the course. This is a source of real pleasure, and I take great pride in conveying the General's remarks to you. You may be sure that my own congratulations go with General Cariappa's congratulations to you."

The general's endorsement letter stated, "I am very happy to inform you that Lieutenant Colonel Theodore Mataxis of your army, who attended the 4th staff class held at our defense service staff college from 1 Aug 1950 till June 1951, was judged by the commandant and staff of the college as the best student of the course [sic] would you be so good as to convey him our hearty congratulations on his excellent work. My young officers with him on this course were full of praise.... Best wishes, K.M. CARIAPPA."

Upon arriving at the Defense Service Staff College (DSSC), Mataxis was attached to the Defense Attaché's office at the American embassy in New Delhi, India, for administration and military requirements. Despite his numerous attempts to get to Korea, upon completion of the course for his utilization tour, he would be assigned a one-year unaccompanied tour to the United Nations as a member of the United Nations Military Observer Group Kashmir. This assignment meant Helma and the children would return by themselves (once again) to the United States.

The Family Returns Home

In April 1951, Mataxis escorted his family to the ship for their return home. When it came time for the family to return to the United States, they were still determining if the ship would arrive at Cochin, India, or Ceylon. According to Mataxis, "We had received a telegram saying it might continue. If it didn't, Helma and the kids would have to fly to Colombo or Bombay to link up with a ship to travel back to the United States. All household luggage at this time had been sent to Cochin, and if our boat didn't stop there, the bags would be on another ship for the United States, leaving several days later." These types of daily stressors became the norm. Helma could get her things on that ship; however, the family might not be on it. Ted Jr. explains what it must have been like for his mother: "Imagine what it's like for a mom to travel with three kids and a boxer dog for over two months. My dad left her with 52 suitcases and boat tickets to New York City." Little did she know that the one-year separation would turn into two years. Mataxis had once again volunteered to go directly to Korea.

After five weeks of traveling, the family arrived in New York City on June 5, 1951. They returned home via the Suez Canal, Port Said, Alexandria, Naples,

Marseilles, Genoa, and Leghorn, thus completing their first around-the-world cruise. The Mataxis children had now circled the globe, visited 16 countries, crossed five seas, and traversed all ocean meridians including the International Date Line, thus qualifying as circumnavigators. Upon returning to the United States, everyone in the family was made lifetime members of the Magellan Club of World Navigators. These cruises to and from India were terrific lifetime experiences for the family. Life on board the ship was full of various cultural experiences and exciting ports of call, with tours available. There was entertainment, and each evening the passengers in first class would go to a formal dinner requiring a dinner jacket for men, and the ladies and children dressed for dinner. One could select your meal from a menu at dinner as if you were in a large restaurant. Helma recalls, "Occasionally, we visited the ship shop and their duty-free shop. We certainly saw the world, and the accommodations were much better than the cruise to and from Germany for the Occupation in 1947–49. This cruise was an experience the family could never have afforded on a lieutenant colonel's pay."

Before India, Ted and Helma had always lived very carefully, constantly monitoring their spending; they were both Depression-era children. However, once Helma returned from her time in India, her philosophy changed to, "What's the use in saving your money? Everything is going up in price, and you may as well have it and enjoy it all." Helma wanted to live comfortably and enjoy her children and her extended family while Ted was deployed. So, she made it happen.

As told by Ted Jr., "When the family arrived in New York, Mom had to buy a car, a new station wagon, and then drive the family across the country to Denver. Denver was chosen over Arizona because relatives lived there. Then she had to buy a house and move our storage items while getting the household items from India to Denver. She did all this knowing that she would not have a husband for the next year or two while Dad spent a year in Kashmir. That was my dad! I was amazed with what she was able to do and keep her sense of humor." After settling in with the children in Denver, Helma found out Ted would be going directly to Korea, and she would be spending another year alone in Denver with her family. It did not help that the news was full of the heavy daily fighting taking place in Korea.

When settling in Denver, she unpacked the fine china and the sterling silver place settings. Helma immediately ordered a deep freezer and a new 50 cubic foot refrigerator. In Denver, Helma finally had an electric stove, broiler, washing machine, mangle, and many other household items. To her, these were all luxuries. She immediately went about setting up her house with great efficiency. This house was remembered fondly over the years.

With nuclear war looming in her mind constantly, Helma wanted to enjoy her American dream and use her sterling silver set for 12 before it was too late. She wanted to live the American dream and felt Denver would be out of the way in the event of a nuclear war.

After the primitive living conditions in India and the looming threat of war, Helma wanted her family out of harm's way. In her short marriage to Ted, she had already experienced mobilization for World War II, an occupation tour in Germany, two years in New York, and the unsanitary conditions of India. Now her husband had volunteered to go to Korea. She and the children finally had the comfortable home that other Americans had already enjoyed while she and her family were bouncing about the world. When the family left India, little did she know that it would turn into two very long years of separation.

The Kashmir Assignment

Much to his dismay, upon completing the Indian Army staff college, Lt. Col. Mataxis was assigned to the United Nations Military Observer Group rather than Korea. So back in India, after Ted accompanied his family from Ceylon (now Sri Lanka), he reported to the embassy for his instruction on his next assignment to the United Nations Peacekeeping team in Kashmir.

Some historical background needs to be given here. Britain gave up India in 1947 and sent Lord Mountbatten to India in March 1947 to transfer power to India. He consulted with Hindu and Muslim leaders; at this time there were 565 princely states. It was agreed that partition would be done by religion. The individual states were to opt for India or Pakistan depending on whether they were Hindu or Muslim. The partitions took place in August 1947. This resulted in absolute chaos as 5.5 million Hindus fled Pakistan and about 7.5 million Muslims fled India. Hundreds of thousands were murdered, and women and children were injured or carried off into captivity before the two countries got control. When the dust settled all the major states had made their decision, except Hyderabad in central India and Jammu and Kashmir in the north. Jammu and Kashmir had a Hindu maharaja and a Muslim majority population; the Hindu maharaja signed an agreement to join India. Pakistan felt betrayed by this and allowed the Pathan Muslim tribes from the Northwest Frontier to come to the assistance of the Kashmir Muslims. However, they stopped to loot along the road to the capital of Srinagar. This gave time for India to fly troops into the airport and save the capital. Fighting grew as both India and Pakistan sent troops to secure Kashmir. Hyderabad had a Muslim maharaja and a majority Hindu population. India invaded with three divisions and seized control of Hyderabad. Troops from both sides withdrew and established the lines; this line had a faceoff between the troops. Finally, India expanded and brought the troubles to the United Nations. India complained against Pakistan under Article 35 of the UN Charter, and it requested the UN to instruct Pakistan to stop meddling in Kashmir. The UN sent a UN commissioner to India and Pakistan in January 1948; this commission finally succeeded, after much frustration, in obtaining the Ceasefire Line in 1949. By August the UN ceasefire team had been dispatched to the main outpost along the Ceasefire Line. The UN team called a plebiscite; efforts to gain agreement on how to administer the plebiscite resided in a stalemate, however.

Mataxis was assigned to the United Nations as a team observer for the ceasefire commission for India and Pakistan. The teams of the United Nations were located on both sides of the Ceasefire Line and lived with the Indian and Pakistani armies. The UN team's observation posts and living quarters were situated with the host nations and were rotated every couple of months between countries. They would travel by horse or pack mule or hike to the scenes, and it was their job to arbitrate the disputes and decide which side was the aggressor. The United Nations observer team kept the peace by investigating the various incidents as they happened.

Their job was that of an umpire waving white flags and deciding which side had initiated the action. Ted explained: "Both sides were configured in the mountainous area, which consisted of pillboxes looking across the valley to the other side, where you could see the opposing pillboxes. From time to time hostilities would occur. This situation was like Korea's, for both sides stared at each other from static positions. The terrain was also much the same—rolling foothills and rugged mountains—some passes in Kashmir were 12,000 feet. The Indian and Pakistani armies were quite similar in their defensive positions in the mountains. At that time, India had 44 battalions stationed along the border, with about the same number on the Pakistani side."

According to Ted, "While on an investigation covering 90 miles in six days traveling on foot and horseback. All ups and downs in the mountains, up and over an 11,000 ft. mountain pass. Lots of fun, October 1951."

Ted adapted to fit in with the locals during his assignment with the United Nations in Kashmir by growing a mustache and beard.

94 • RIDE TO THE SOUND OF THE GUNS

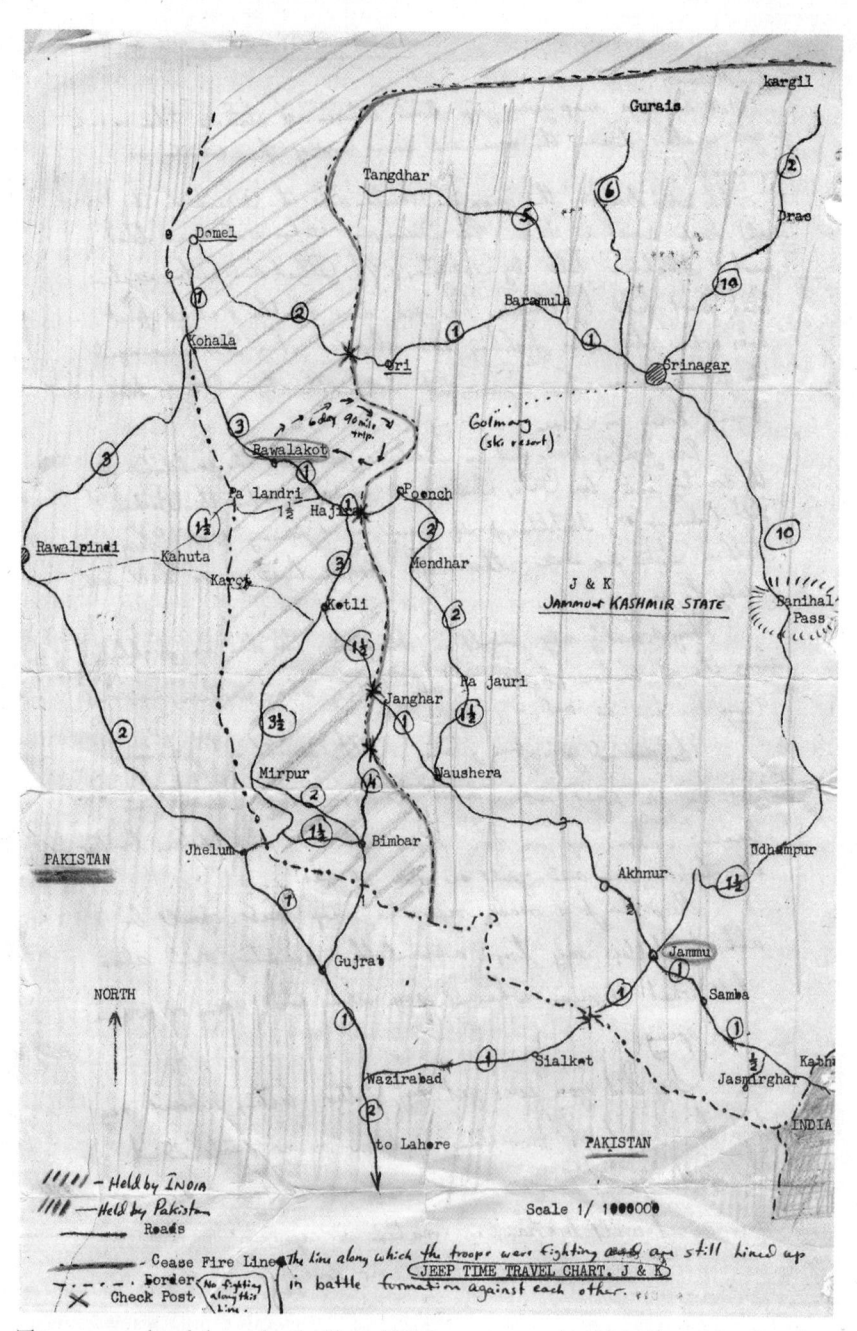

This map was hand-drawn by the United Nations teams and used to stay oriented in their area of operation on both the Pakistani and Indian sides of the dispute. It also shows the travel time from place to place. The terrain was also much the same—rolling foothills and rugged mountains; some passes in Kashmir were 12,000 feet. (United Nations)

General Nimmo, the commander, was responsible for keeping the peace in Kashmir between the Indians and the Pakistanis. The United Nations team was sent to arbitrate the disputes between both nations. This area was considered India from the time of British control until 1947. India was once one of the world's largest and most populated nations and included many different cultures and languages. Kashmir was a natural paradise and a fantastic vacation spot with beautiful scenery and skiing. It was India's equivalent of Vail, Colorado, so it instantly became a global point of conflict. The same conflict that existed then has continued through today.

The UN peacekeeping team in Kashmir was sent to enforce the Ceasefire Line between India and Pakistan. The Ceasefire Line came into effect on January 1, 1949. It was a move that could trace its origins to the United Nations Commission for India and Pakistan's decision in July 1948 asking the Secretary General "to appoint officers and necessary personnel … to supervise the ceasefire if and when it is reached the subcontinent. UN Military observers had arrived and were deployed in the mission area, and an agreement regarding the ceasefire shall continue to be faithfully observed." The group's purpose was to ensure that the agreement regarding the ceasefire would continue to be faithfully observed.

Before the end of the month, the United Nations established military observer groups in India and Pakistan. Initially, this command was only filled with personnel from Britain. Eventually, American and Australian members joined, and other European countries soon followed. In Kashmir, they drew a line on the map, and at the time of the ceasefire, it became the frontline position held by the opposing armies. Running from north to south in Kashmir, the line along which the troops had been fighting and were still lined up in battle formation became the group's primary focus.

Mataxis stated, "The UN teams were stationed for three-month tours at brigade headquarters on both sides of the Ceasefire Line. We lived under primitive conditions in mud huts with sleeping bags and ate in the brigade mess. One three-month tour was with a vegetarian mess from south India. It was horrible. We managed to pick up some rusty #10 tins of peanut butter and using chapatis (like tortillas) we washed them down with glasses of martinis. Thanks to the British tradition of the mess always having gin and vermouth! For medical care you had a kit with bottles of pills, you called a doctor and described the symptoms you had, and he would tell you what pill to take. If you did not feel any better in a week you would get evacuated by litter or pack mule to

United Nations team personnel in Kashmir in 1952. Notice the different uniforms of the British, American, and local personnel.

The Khyber Pass, Pakistan, 1952. Ted and his guides were conducting road reconnaissance for a future date. This was recommended by British Commandant of the India Staff College. It came in very handy when the mujahideen were fighting the Russians in the 1980s and Ted found himself operating in the area again.

a jeep pickup point and be taken to a truck to an airport."

Most positions were up in the hills; only jeep tracks and trails went to them. Ted noted, "In the Northwest Frontier, our area of operation is so far away from the road that it takes five days by mule to get up there and back. Some positions up north near Tibet are at 19,000 feet elevation in the mountains; it takes two weeks to get in and back. Each team has two officers and one enlisted radio operator. Both sides send out patrols, and often a patrol will get lost or wander across the Ceasefire Line. The other side starts shooting at them. In turn, their units start shooting machine guns and mortars back and forth. They are simply trying to stop the incoming fire from the other side to help get their people out. Sometimes these firefights develop into quite a battle. Another type of violation is by the Northwest Frontier tribespeople. They are the ones that never gave in to the Brits' demands. Their favorite sport is coming out of the mountains, raiding a village, driving off the cattle, and stealing the women. Since these tribesmen are from the Pakistan side, the Indians continually complain and have our UN teams gather information on whether it was organized by the regular Pakistani Army or just border raids by the tribesmen." Kashmir's war is not simply religious or based on territory, it's an ideological struggle. For Pakistan, the possession of Kashmir is crucial to the ideology that religion serves as the cornerstone of their state. For India, the integration of Kashmir is important for two reasons: first, it validates India's concept as a secular state and second, the Indians felt letting go of Kashmir would start the break-up of India into smaller Balkan-type mini ethnic states.

The three-person teams shifted sides continuously. The troops on both sides and the UN observers lived in tents, stone huts, mud bunkers, or Quonset huts (half-circle steel buildings). Housing for the team and the field conditions were primitive at best. The sanitation was worse than primitive. The uniform for fieldwork was fatigue uniform or khaki drill brush shirt and trousers or shorts bought locally. Field equipment included binoculars, compasses, sleeping bags, and air mattresses.

The UN observers were not authorized to use firearms on the mission. The diet served in the army mess was indigenous and consisted of curry and rice. However, at the end of April 1951, occasionally there were western dishes served with fresh vegetables and good meat. The UN provided vitamin tablets to supplement most field station observers' deficiencies. A small post store and canteen were available for small purchases.

Mataxis would describe his time in his letters home: "A team would be here for two months, then move on to a new location. We rotate in two to three-month increments from the Pakistani side to the Indian side and then back again. This back-and-forth assignment shows the significant differences between both countries. I like being out in the mountains, except the opposing side randomly shoots across the border. The UN's mission was precise. When there was an engagement along the wall, the UN would send a 'Fact Finding Mission' and check to see whose fault it was. Then it would become a political debate rather than an increasing conflict between the countries. It seemed very interesting for a while; however, it becomes [sic] very tedious once you've been there a few months." Because of this monotony, observers could earn time off with the approval of the Chief Military Observer, and field stations could be granted up to six days of comp time with per diem for each month of continuous service in the field.

General Nimmo, the Australian commander of the United Nations Military Observation Group, had been sympathetically following Ted's troubles and generously gave him two weeks' leave for travel towards the end of the tour. Lt. Col. Mataxis had the local barber give him a Pakistani beard and mustache, and with new military clothes, he went by road to the Khyber Pass and the Afghanistan border. Mataxis was allowed to observe and record information about the bridges and tunnels leading into Pakistan from Kashmir. General Nimmo, also a firm believer in riding to the sound of the guns, encouraged the observers to become familiar with the area because this information might prove significant to their home countries someday.

Upon returning from the Khyber Pass, a frustrated Mataxis attempted again to get an assignment to Korea. He explained, "Before completing my tour with the United Nations and Kashmir, I again asked for combat duty in Korea, which had been promised me. Again, I offered to go directly from India if that's what it took to get Korean orders. Instead, I received orders to attend the Marine Amphibious School in Norfolk, VA." A frustrated Ted left India to fly home to Denver on an around-the-world air force embassy logistical flight for a 30-day leave to be with his family. While home, Mataxis called his friend at the Infantry Branch and was told his name was "mud" among the brass because he already had a "battalion combat command tour in World War II and a bonus of another battalion command after the war during the occupation in Germany." The deputy commander of the Infantry Branch felt Mataxis was hindering their policy and he needed to attend the Marine Amphibious School in Norfolk, Virginia. His friend went on to tell him if the

Infantry Branch knew he was home they would send him immediately to Virginia. So Mataxis did as was suggested and immediately flew "space available" back to India and from there he continued to Japan to report for Korea.

He had a personal letter from the chief of the Infantry Branch that said he would go to Korea after the UN tour was completed. So, he used that letter in place of orders. According to Mataxis, "When I reported to the Headquarters Command in Japan, the next crisis came when the headquarters saw my last duty station had been with the UN. They were desperately looking for officers with experience to draw plans for a 'truce line' between the US and the communists when the Korean War was over. The staff officers were quite enthusiastic about finding someone with my experience." Noting their enthusiasm, Mataxis retrieved his letter from the branch chief and said he had an appointment and would return later. He then went back to the AG's office to look for an NCO working there with a CIB from World War II. He realized that only a combat veteran could relate to his burning desire to return to a combat environment. After hearing Mataxis out, the NCO typed Ted's name on a list going to Korea early the following day. Finally, it appeared that Mataxis was going to war again.

CHAPTER 7

17th Infantry Regiment, Korea, 1952–53

En Route to Korea

As Mataxis reflected in his papers, he found himself heading to Korea during the summer of 1952. After several attempts to volunteer for Korea, he finally made it. Still, his mind could not help but wander back to his time in Japan two years earlier: "En route by ship to the Indian Defense Staff College as an exchange officer, I stopped by Japan and visited friends in the peacetime occupational army in 1950. The combat units at that time were in name only. Tactical training was virtually non-existent, and maneuvers were ignored. In front of the unit's Japanese headquarters was a collection of 37 mm M3 antitank guns and several 80 mm mortars varnished with gaudy regiment insignia and placed out front as decorations. The Secretary of State had said in a previous visit that, 'In Japan, Korea was outside the US defensive perimeter.' The prevalent feeling in Japan at that time was, 'What do we have to worry about?' In Japan, officers who had missed combat in World War II were given a chance to advance their careers by policing and painting their units and maintaining low delinquent report rates rather than by how well they maintained a combat-ready status for their units. I found this personally repugnant." According to Mataxis, "The army is here for one mission, and that is to be prepared for combat at any time, any place. Good training saves lives on the battlefield." He had learned this lesson well from his division's World War II experience and would effectively use it while serving in Korea.

The Korean War

Lt. Col. Mataxis referred to the Korean War as the first hot war of the Cold War. According to Mataxis, "The Korean War should not be perceived as President Truman's 'police action' or, by its common title, 'the unknown war.' It was an attack planned by Stalin and Mao on South Korea and launched using North Korea as their 'cat's paw' to succeed." This close coordination by China and the USSR in

Korea, and the two powers' backing of the communists in Vietnam, culminated in the signing of a 30-year Treaty of Friendship, an alliance and a mutual agreement that formed the Sino-Soviet Bloc in February 1950. This Sino-Soviet Bloc treaty and the North Korean surprise attack on South Korea in June 1950 finally silenced the American liberals (individuals who touted Mao as an agrarian reformer) and alerted the public to the dangers of the ongoing communist expansion of the Cold War worldwide. Finally, the treaty helped establish the Central Treaty Organization (CENTO) to halt the USSR's expansion in the Middle East and the Southeast Asia Treaty Organization (SEATO) to protect southeastern Asia from a communist expansion.

The United Nations (UN) Provides Support During the Korean War

At its peak strength, the UN forces in the field consisted of almost 750,000 men. The breakdown of the UN personnel was about 400,000 South Koreans, 250,000 Americans, and 35,000 personnel from other nations. The following UN countries provided personnel: two British brigades and one Canadian brigade formed their first Commonwealth division; Turkey provided one brigade; Australia supplied two infantry battalions; Thailand, the Philippines, Colombia, Ethiopia, France, Greece, Belgium, and the Netherlands each provided one battalion; New Zealand provided an artillery battalion, and Luxembourg sent one infantry detachment; India, Denmark, Sweden, and Norway provided medical units. Some of these nations also furnished naval and air contingencies. In three years of combat, the United Nations sustained just shy of half a million casualties. The North Korean and Chinese communist losses were estimated at two million men.

Arrival as Deputy G-2, Eighth Army Headquarters

As has now become expected of him, Mataxis was right there in the thick of things. In his papers, he records his experiences in Korea: "Upon arriving in Korea on May 6, 1952, I was assigned to the intelligence section of the Eighth Army headquarters as the deputy of the G-2. I went to see the G-2, an older West Point armor officer, Col. Van Natla, and explained that I wanted to be in combat with the troops rather than on the staff. He locked my heels and told me, 'The trouble with you reserve officers who had lucky promotions in World War II is that you do not know how to follow orders.' He clarified that I was now a regular army officer and would do what I was told. His initial briefings indicated it would be an exciting job, traditionally filled by a full colonel, and I should be all too happy that I got the job. He assured me that it would give me a perspective on how the army is run and an understanding of the importance of intelligence. While filling a full colonel's slot, there would be much responsibility and much to learn."

In a letter home to his wife dated May 9, 1952, Ted wrote, "We've got to learn to live apart quite a bit, I'm afraid, because of the way I'm built. I feel guilty staying out of anything our soldiers are in. I feel guilty sitting up here at army headquarters in relative comfort while those poor buggers in the infantry live in the mud. Don't ever worry, darling, as you know me, whatever comes, you don't have to worry about your old man. I sort of take to the fighting. I feel sorry for those wives separated from their husbands, knowing every minute their husbands are frightened of their jobs, etc. I think I'm giving you 'my creed of life,' darling: All the brothers are valorous—and all the sisters are virtuous. I can forgive anything but a breach of the above. Many people call me old-fashioned, but I'm happy with my creed. And I'm glad to hear you like it also." Many of Ted's letters home included a touch of the husbandly affection expected and the parental guidance most fathers pride themselves in possessing. Still, most of his letters simply discussed the minutia of the wars themselves.

In one letter, Ted explains, "… I've noticed that in Germany, though, we usually operated at a regimental level with all the battalions in there fighting. In Korea, they operate at the battalion level with all the companies in the fight and are left alone to sort it out. I believe this resulted from the rugged mountain terrain." In another letter, the Mataxis family learns that, "In the middle of August, Typhoon Karen whipped into the Eighth Army's zone in Korea." Typhoon Karen's 90 mile per hour wind gusts hit hard at the southwest coast of Korea, grounding all UN aircraft; the typhoon virtually halted all the fighting along the 155-mile front as soldiers on both sides fought the weather rather than each other. Mataxis's first-hand account states, "The frontline soldiers had trenches and fighting positions that quickly filled up with rain, where everything immediately turned to mud, and movement was nearly impossible. The typhoon rains eventually caused the dugouts/trenches to collapse, which raised hell with the frontline infantry companies. In some fighting positions, the rain rose in the trenches so high the machine-gun slots were draining the rain out of the bunkers. Several soldiers drowned while on patrols because the rivers can swell from 14 feet to 36 feet in two hours." Mataxis explains, "You can see how you would get caught if you don't know the country. Just imagine 22 feet of water accumulating in under two hours. Sometimes it will come down like a two- to three-foot wall of water that suddenly catches you … and suddenly you find yourself in the middle of [a rushing river]." Many of Mataxis's letters home to Helma and the children encapsulated detailed descriptions of the battles to be fought, won, and lost. For the Mataxis children, these descriptive letters had to have been preferred over the page-long litanies detailing their father's expectations, the required list of chores he expected them to do, and the constant reminder to help their mother since she was by herself.

In May 1951, the army developed a point system for the big "R" rotation back to the United States. Front line and infantry received four points per month, and support troops received two per month. According to Ted, "When you acquired 36 points, you were eligible to rotate home. This system, like the Combat Infantry Badge in World War II, recognized that the infantry was only 15–20 percent of those deployed overseas in the war. Yet, they received most of the wounded and casualties." The key factor in the battles was that thousands of artillery rounds were used by the enemy, which cut UN communications completely. When the Chinese overran a hill, there was an emergency signal of six white phosphorus rounds exploding in the air over the position. Once that happened, troops had 60 seconds to get undercover before a time on target airburst followed it up. The North Korean artillery was very intense; for example, on May 31, 1952, the North Koreans fired 102,000 rounds on Eighth Army positions. According to Mataxis's journals, "After I had been in the G-2 about a month, the Department of the Army ordered that officers who had been separated from their families for over a year were eligible to go home. Many in the corps headquarters had gone to Korea from Japan, where they had been on a separation tour. This gave them a chance to go home. I checked my time with the United Nations in Kashmir without my wife and family, and this qualified me as eligible to go home. I filled out the form, took it to my boss, and told him I could be out of Korea next week, and then I hedged that if he … 'would release me for an infantry division, I'd stay!' He gave up and called the G-1 to release me for an assignment with an infantry division. I was finally going to return to the trenches and the ongoing battles."

17th Infantry Regiment (Buffalos), as Regimental Executive Officer

Mataxis continues, "I obtained a light plane and visited divisions along the frontline. When I was interviewed by the 7th Infantry Division commander, Major General Wayne C. Smith, he told me his policy was that all infantry field grade officers going to a regiment in his division had to command a rifle company for a month. I told him that I had not only commanded a battalion in combat in World War II, receiving the Silver Star, Bronze Star, and Purple Heart, but I had also led a battalion after the war. [I explained to him that I] was not prepared to become a company commander again. So rather than losing me, I was declared a free agent, and he waived the requirement. I was assigned to the 17th Infantry Regiment in October 1952, where I was the executive officer during the bitter campaigns for Triangle, T-Bone, and Pork Chop Hills. The regiment motto was 'Truth and Courage,' and we were nicknamed 'the Buffaloes.' I was offered the position of executive officer to Colonel Royal Reynolds, Jr. the following month."

Shortly after Mataxis's arrival as executive officer on October 3, 1952, the army released a promotion list for full colonels. In a letter to Helma soon after the list came out, Ted wrote, "The army now has out a promotion list of 900 Lt. Colonels eligible for promotion to Colonel. It is estimated that to go through this list promoting everyone will take a minimum of three to four years. This promotion list is based strictly on age and the date you were promoted to Lt. Colonel. Both promotion criteria leave me way out in the cold. [Ted had been in the army 12 years and four months.] With my current job and during the last war, I would have been promoted to Colonel, but now there's no chance. They promote off that list, so if you are not on it, you better be prepared to live with our Lt. Colonel's pay for at least the next eight to nine years." His disappointment is palpable in his letters home.

In another letter to his wife dated October 22, 1952, Ted writes, "When I arrived at the regiment, heavy fighting was ongoing and took several days for the battle to cool down, and I finally had my first night's sleep in about ten days. Before, we had been going for two to three days without sleep [falling into bed when we could, getting a quick three or four hours of sleep, and then getting up and at it again]. The fighting has been rougher in the 7th Division sector. Most of the fighting was conducted at the rifle company level, with the commanders leading by example in heavy combat battles. You must give a lot of credit to these youngsters fighting for their country under these horrible conditions. Despite the conditions, I realize I am at my best with the troops in extreme conditions like this. I'm glad I'm back in combat with troops, and I love it. I have again fallen into the same old routine–up at 6:30 a.m. and returning to bed at 11:30 p.m. [I am woken] several times at night; such is life. It is however a great experience, damn good for the record; also, and I do love troop duty in combat. I now realize I can run a good regiment; all I needed was the opportunity. I should have been here in 1950; however, the army had India and Kashmir planned for me. At least I finally made it here now! The pressure is on every day to prepare something for the next day that will help the soldiers in the front, that keeps you from worrying about yourself and focused on the soldiers."

Unbeknownst to Helma at the time, she would provide her husband with a large part of the inspiration he used for his success in Korea by sending him (upon Ted's request) one of her father's old military books. Fortunately, Lt. Col. Mataxis remembered a book published in 1917 called *Trench Warfare* by Major James A. Moss in his father-in-law's collection, and he had Helma send it to him. Helma's father was Emil M. Jensen, a sergeant in G Company of the 14th Regiment during World War I. He died of tuberculosis, a disease he acquired in World War I when Helma was just a child. He left several military books to Helma when he passed, and she eventually gave them to Ted. According to Mataxis, "*Trench Warfare* instantaneously became the most useful book in the regimental headquarters. It appeared to be the only field manual that covered static warfare adequately. It became the source material for many regimental poop sheets that outlined tactics and techniques regarding the 7th Division's trench warfare." General Trudeau, the division commander, remarked when he saw the book being carried under the arm of Mataxis that, "There is nothing new under the Sun!"

The Battle for Triangle Hill (October 14–November 25, 1952)

In 1952, the 42 days of fighting during the Battle for Triangle Hill would be marked as one of Korea's most significant and bloodiest contests. Two United Nations divisions of the Eighth Army went up against elements of the Chinese People's Volunteer Army (PVA). Despite massive United Nations artillery and US Air Force support, the two PVA corps (the 12th and 15th) maintained their control of Triangle Hill. The PVA had constructed a massive, tunneled complex and constantly received personnel replacements, ammo, and other supplies through the tunnels. Despite suffering over 11,000 casualties, the North Koreans maintained that this validated North Korea's belief in its ability to sustain such losses while they would ultimately exhaust the US Eighth Army. It shows that the Chinese and North Koreans could fight a battle of attrition with the Americans and that a war of attrition was a helpful strategy against the United Nations fighting forces.

Ted recounts this time: "When I became a regimental commander of the 17th Regiment, they were conducting peace talks, and because of the peace talks, the US was trying to disengage and minimize the loss of personnel. The Chinese launched a series of attacks from Pork Chop Hill on the rest of the surrounding outposts. In late October 1952, the 7th Division was visited by the American Ambassador to Japan, Robert Murphy; Far East commander, General Mark W. Clark; Eighth Army commander, General James A. Van Fleet; Major General Reuben E. Jenkins, IX Corps commander; and other army and air force officials. They were escorted by Major General Wayne C. Smith, 7th Infantry Division commander; Brigadier General Derrell M. Daniel, assistant 7th Infantry Division commander; and Brigadier General Andrew P. O'Meara, 7th Infantry Division artillery commander." The UN forces were concerned about casualties, which led to the cancellation of more significant upcoming offensive operations for the remainder of the war; moving forward, all US operations of more than one battalion had to seek approval at the highest level of US staff.

Months later, in December 1952, two battalions were assigned to POW Camp Koje-Do, a North Korean POW camp (1st and 2nd Battalions), on temporary duty as guards through January 1953. At that time, they raised a grave issue regarding the severely mistreated and even brutalized North Korean POWs through their chain of command. Prior to their raising the issue, the United States MPs were ordering the combat units assigned to them to beat the POWs using their rifles. They were able to get these orders discontinued. The North Korean POWs considered themselves unarmed combatants.

In May 1952, there was a revolt at the camp, and the North Korean POWs took the commander, General Dodd, as a hostage. Dodd was forced to confess that the Americans had abused the POWs during his command. These actions were the observations that Ted's unit had reported during the time they were assigned to the

Lieutenant Colonel Mataxis with his regimental staff and Captain Hal Moore in December 1952. This picture was taken at Koje-Do POW camp.

Lieutenant Colonel Mataxis at the entrance of his sleeping trailer at the 17th Infantry Regiment, 7th Infantry Division in Korea, 1952. He is standing at the entrance of his sleeping trailer. He finally got where he wanted to be after years of volunteering.

camp. General Ridgway was commanding then and gave the order to use everything, including tanks, to overrun the resistance. Ridgway explained that he "would not stand for a dissident group showing that the Americans couldn't control their POW camps." He was a soldier first. He responded to political ramifications afterward. Mataxis went on to explain, "I think that … we don't like to think about [these things] as soldiers, but the politics drive us."

In a letter written on February 23, 1953 to Helma after this duty, Ted recalls, "I was acting as the regiment commander because Col. Hardick went to Seoul for a couple of days for a required conference. I commanded the regiment for a couple of days in his absence. Two of our combat patrols, platoon size, of the 1st and 2nd Battalion were hit by a large enemy on patrol, and the forces were moving south on both sides of the T-Bone Hill while sweeping the area. A critical company outpost was just south of T-Bone Hill, where the 7th Division had conducted a raid. The fight went on all night and finally finished the next afternoon. The 1st Battalion was directed with its set of reinforcements to pull back, so we could prep the area with artillery fire, a Time on Target (TOT), on the objective, which destroyed them before deploying the troops. After the artillery TOT, we deployed a couple of platoons again to seize the battle area by about 5:00 in the morning. The 2nd Battalion had to deploy their replacements and commit to their reserves. Then I committed our regimental infantry reserve at dawn and got some additional division assets deployed into the battle. With these troop deployments, we controlled the battlefield and destroyed the enemy. It all went very well."

Mataxis continues, "That afternoon, the general was really pleased. He requested I go up and brief the division headquarters on the encounter. He was going down to the Eighth Army to provide a briefing on the fight to the Eighth Army commander. It was the biggest battle the regiment had fought since October 1951, when I arrived as XO. The after-action review estimated that we fought a reinforced enemy battalion. As the acting commander, I could finally conduct successful regimental battle in combat. I always thought I could do it, but now I know I can, and I am very proud of our unit. I was called to Seoul to present that special briefing to the army commander, General Maxwell Taylor, General Adams, the Chief of Staff, several other generals, and many army staff personnel. I had the thing laid out well. I introduced the background materials about the area and its terrain analysis. I then covered the fight from a regimental viewpoint. Then I had Lieutenant Colonel Smith, the second battalion commander, present the pictures from one Battalion's point of view, and finally, I had a sergeant there who led the reinforcements out to the area. I was so proud when General Martin introduced me as the acting commander for directing this action. Afterward, he and the army commander shook our hands and congratulated us on having such a courageous group of men in the regiment. It was quite a successful battle, followed by a successful briefing at the highest level. I was so proud to have the opportunity of leading these brave men."

The letter continues, "Later, I heard in the generals' mess that they were discussing the policy of having regimental commanders called to the rear and told to stay overnight for required meetings with the army commander. The general was against it because it took the colonels away from their regiments when the Chinese might attack, like in our case the night I served as the acting regiment commander. Someone pointed out that everything turned out okay while the commander was away, to which the general simply replied, 'Yes, it was okay that time, but every regiment doesn't have a Mataxis.' You can imagine how I felt about what I had just heard!" General Taylor later sent a letter of commendation for the battle and the briefing Mataxis provided. Mataxis explains how his own combat regiment was his life's dream: "I had to pinch myself to see if I was dreaming. It was worth all the effort it took to get to Korea and continually volunteering for the hard jobs and family separation." He would always go after the combat positions where he thrived and felt most alive.

He had now been placed higher up the ladder from the bracket of a battalion commander to that of a regimental commander in combat. Ted stated, "I guess I'm just cut out for combat. I made my best record during World War II as a battalion commander with troops also in combat, and now I just did it with my regiment!" Lt. Col. Mataxis hit the jackpot on his Officer Efficiency Report from Col. Hardick: he received a seven, the highest possible score. Previously, most Lt. Col. Mataxis efficiency reports were sixes. It appeared Mataxis was meant for combat, and he excelled at it. At the same time, Mataxis realized that he had become an adrenaline junky who would continuously "ride to the sound of the guns."

In his own words, Mataxis reinforces that, "The one thing going for me [is that] I have proven to myself that I really can run a regiment and do it well. That was acknowledged at the highest staff level in the country when I was previously the acting commander. That is one thing about getting the regimental commanders who have not had troop combat experience before is that [sic] they leave all the details up to you, just wanting their tickets punched, and there's no better way to learn. However, it burns me up seeing all the commanders who have never had troop duty, let alone combat duty. I am made for combat duty. I enjoyed it. It seems like a giant game of chess you're playing with the enemy, matching you against them for real high stakes!! [sic] When you are in combat with your unit and the men carrying the load with you, [sic] it is an unequaled feeling, a bond that is never equaled in any situation!! [sic]"

In another letter sent to Helma, Mataxis explains how the conflict had progressed, "By early March, the thaw set in, and with the additional rain, the troops were really bogged down in the trenches. Nothing but mud, mud, and more mud! I would much rather have snow and ice on the ground like in World War II. This mud is really bad: since many of the bunkers caved in, trenches fill up with mud, and roads and resupply routes become almost impossible. In other words, everything grinds to a halt along the front and really becomes quite dull." The weather conditions made it even harder for the infantry. The weather, once again, drastically impacted soldiers in every aspect of their personal and tactical lives. According to Mataxis's accounts, it seemed as if each war he participated in had unique and challenging weather conditions that the soldiers had to endure while fighting, and Korea was no different.

That summer, Ted would receive two bronze oak leaf clusters to his Bronze Star as a result of the fighting in February 1952. The first was awarded for his actions on the night of February 6–7:

HEADQUARTERS
7TH INFANTRY DIVISION
APO 7

GENERAL ORDERS
4 June 1953
NUMBER 298

Section I
AWARD OF THE BRONZE STAR MEDAL (FIRST BRONZE OAK-LEAF CLUSTER)
By direction of the President, under the provisions of Executive Order 9419, 4 February 1944 (sec. II, WD Bul. 3, 1944), and pursuant to authority in AR 600-45, the Bronze Star Medal (First Oak-Leaf Cluster), with Letter "V" device for heroic achievement in connection with military operations against an enemy of the United States is awarded to the following-named officer:

Lieutenant Colonel THEODORE C. MATAXIS, 034035, Infantry, United States Army, a member of Headquarters, 17th Infantry, distinguished himself by heroic achievement near Song Ch'on-dong, Korea. On the night of 6–7 February 1953, Colonel Mataxis, in his capacity as Regimental Executive Officer, moved up to the scene of enemy action in order to obtain a more exact and complete report for his superior officers. When Colonel Mataxis reached the lines, he found the friendly troops nervous because they believed the enemy was within their tactical defensive wire. Colonel Mataxis talked to the men to bolster their morale and personally led a group of men to screen the defensive wire.

While moving to the wire, an enemy searchlight illuminated Colonel Mataxis and his men. Taking cover until the searchlight had swung its arc in another direction, Colonel Mataxis, with complete disregard for his personal safety, moved to an exposed position to observe the enemy and call in heavy mortar fire on them. After the hail of friendly fire had demolished the enemy, Colonel Mataxis continued on his original mission to check the defensive wire.

The heroic actions of Colonel Mataxis reflect great credit on himself and the military service. Entered the Federal service from Washington, D.C.

The second was awarded for his actions on the night of February 20–21:

GO 285 Hq 7th Inf Div APO 7, 2 June 1953
Section II

AWARD OF THE BRONZE STAR MEDAL (SECOND BRONZE OAK LEAF CLUSTER)

By direction of the President, under the provisions of Executive Order 9419, 4 February 1944 (sec. II, WD Bul. 3, 1944), and pursuant to authority in AR 600-45, the Bronze Star Medal (Second Oak Leaf Cluster) with Letter "V" device for heroic achievement in connection with military operations against an enemy of the United States is awarded to the following-named officer:

Lieutenant Colonel THEODORE C. MATAXIS, 034035, Infantry, United States Army, a member of Headquarters, 17th Infantry, distinguished himself by heroic achievement near Haugae, Korea. On the night of 20–21 February 1953, when a friendly patrol was engaged by a numerically superior enemy force, Colonel Mataxis, upon hearing of the ensuing action, hurried to the Fire Support Coordination Center where he oriented himself on the situation and advised the battalion commander on courses of action.

Colonel Mataxis also heard that communications to the supporting tanks had failed and that their fires were endangering friendly units sent to relieve the original patrol. Realizing the gravity of this new development, Colonel Mataxis went two hundred yards forward of friendly lines to locate the tank platoon. When he arrived, Colonel Mataxis calmly redirected their fire to give maximum support without endangering the friendly forces. The heroic actions of Colonel Mataxis reflect great credit on himself and the military service.

Entered the Federal service from Washington, D.C.

BY COMMAND OF MAJOR GENERAL TRUDEAU:
OFFICIAL:
THOMAS J. ELDER
Lt. Col., GS
Acting Chief of Staff

The North Koreans changed tactics on March 26, 1953 and decided to raise hell and attack several platoons and company outposts across the division front. Mataxis explains, "It was similar in our sector to the attack we had in February. They attacked simultaneously across the front lines. Three attacks in the 31st Division and two large and one minor attack in our division's area of operation. We were very successful and stopped them in their tracks.... The misery of this war is the story of the bravery of the platoons and company commanders leading their men in brutal combat. At that level [of fighting], the only concern is staying alive and keeping their men alive, even at the expense of their own lives. This is where the warrior ethos and esprit de corps shine through. These poor guys are in muddy trenches with no lights, constant mortar and artillery fire, horrible weather, and C-rations. But I guess I went through that in the last war at the battalion level when we were carrying the load of the combat up close with brutal daily combat. Having been in that situation, I can better visualize what they're doing and going through. This situation requires the leader to set an example in everything he does, which allows me to focus on the unit and do things that will help them."

On April 1, 1953, Mataxis wrote in another letter to Helma that, "Things have [quieted down] again. We're going back into division reserve again. Our movements are classified because the enemy is trying to monitor them to make their plans. At this time, rumors are flying thick and fast here in Korea due to the radio announcement that we might use atomic weapons in the country. President Eisenhower's conference with his advisers followed this closely with the offer to repatriate sick and wounded POWs, followed by an offer to accept the principle of voluntary reparation. There are two schools of thought here. The first is that the Reds are ready for peace here in Korea. The second is that they are afraid that we will go all out this spring, so they will try to blame the renewed war on us, saying that we attacked just as they were ready for peace. I believe we should accept their offer on the condition that there is a 30-day deadline to see if they are serious. If nothing happens by then, we will let go of everything we've got! And get this thing settled once and for all!"

First Battle of Pork Chop Hill, April 16–18, 1953

There was a lot to settle as the 7th Infantry Division defense sector was part of the UN Main Line of Resistance (including several exposed hill outposts defended by a company or platoon with sandbagged bunkers connected with trenches). The United Nations, primarily supported by the United States, won the first battle when the Chinese broke contact and withdrew after two days of fighting. The second battle involved many more troops on both sides and was bitterly contested for five days before UN forces conceded the hill to the Chinese forces by withdrawing behind the main battle line. Ted received a Purple Heart inspecting the position after the UN counterattack. Captain Hal Moore commanded a rifle company at the grass roots level during this time. He then became the regimental S-3, working with Ted. These battles were fought while the UN negotiated with the Chinese and North Koreans on the Korean Armistice Agreement. Stateside, these battles were controversial as many soldiers were killed over terrain that had no strategic or tactical value. Both sides used military operations to gain leverage or make political statements relevant to the armistice negotiations. The 7th Division rebuilt its defenses on Pork Chop Hill during May and June 1953.

17th Regiment Commander

As a direct result of his leadership and combat capability displayed in February, Lt. Col. Ted Mataxis became the commanding officer of the 17th Buffalo Regiment on May 6, 1953. His command was wedged between the outgoing commander, Colonel Hardick, and the incoming commander. The command would only be for three weeks. In World War II, he was a battalion commander in combat at age 26, and now at 35 years of age, he was regimental commander in combat. During Ted's time with them, the regiment had conducted battles on Old Baldy and Pork Chop Hill—some of the war's most intense fighting.

A proud Ted immediately wrote to Helma to share the news: "Well dear, it's happened. I am now the regimental commander of the 17th US Infantry Regiment!!! Hold your breath; it will only be for two or three weeks until the new colonel reports from the States, but still, darling, it is a regiment in combat. My dreams are coming true. Now I can say I was a battalion commander at age 26 and a regimental commander at age 35!!! Sorry if I sound silly, but you know what this means to me, darling! I now have proven what I felt all along—that I can run a regiment! So, darling, you can rest assured that I will be home in June or the start of July, as I've been waiting, hoping that something like this would happen. As I have explained, the regimental commander is a full colonel sent out from the States to take over for six months. Sometimes there are two to three weeks between an old commander going out and a new commander coming in; that's when a guy like me has a chance based on previous performance or displayed potential. Colonel Hardick got orders and had to leave today, so here I am. After I get relieved as commander, there will be no reason to stay longer due to the orders that an officer who has been separated from his family for over a year is eligible to go home. We have been separated for 24 months with Kashmir and my year in Korea. So, when the new colonel comes at the end of May or the first of June, I will leave then. The Department of the Army put out this 12-month rule to ensure the people were not away from families too long at any given time. For us, the separation has been since you and the children departed from India."

The 17th Regiment had United Nations battalions attached. One battalion assigned was from Colombia, South America. Mataxis had the South Korean 101st

Regiment and an Ethiopian battalion attached for a short time. While accepting his position as the Buffalo Regiment's commanding officer, Mataxis was quoted in the *Buffalo Bugle*, May 1953, "I am very pleased to have the opportunity to take command of the Buffalo Regiment. I realize it is a great responsibility to follow in the footsteps of the former regimental commanders. I hope that I will be able to carry on with the success, high standards, and accomplishments set by Col. Quinn, Col. R. Reynolds, and Col. W. Hardick. I trust in the future that the Buffalo Regiment will continue to enjoy the same high morale and outstanding record of performance it has in the past."

Upon assuming command of the regiment in early May, one of his first duties was participation in the Colombian battalion memorial service to pay tribute to their heroic comrades who had given their lives earlier in Korea. They had been attached to the 31st Regiment under the command of Col. William B. Kernan when the heaviest fighting by a Colombian battalion took place. They had just been reassigned to the 17th Buffalo Regiment under the command of Lt. Col. Ted Mataxis. They were part of the Battle for Old Baldy, where 48 Colombians were awarded their country's Medal of Honor. In the savage struggle to hold that outpost, 59 of their soldiers had been wounded.

Mataxis recounts, "Shortly after, we were attacked at one of our outposts; I sent one platoon up to reinforce it. I was called back to brief the Eighth Army commander, General Taylor, and I gave him the briefing (you know, a dog and pony show). After my briefing, General Taylor said, 'I am putting out an order down the chain of command that states that the regimental

Ted (far left) presiding over an attached United Nations Colombian Battalion award ceremony on Old Baldy honoring their war dead in April 1953. In September 2017, the family provided Buffalo artifacts of the regiment to the Columbian Army Museum.

Lieutenant Colonel Ruiz Novoa, the Colombian Battalion commander, is holding a regiment initiation certificate for the Buffalos and a jug labeled "Buffalo Piss." Lieutenant Colonel Mataxis holds a "buffalo goad" which has on it the unique blue and white name tag of the regiment.

commanders will not be able to use more than one platoon without checking with a division commander before a company element is committed. The reason for that is our biggest danger now is the Chinese are trying to bleed us. If we did like we did on Triangle Hill, we would lose a battalion a day worth of casualties. They'd have to be replaced with another battalion. We couldn't afford it. So don't commit.' Then he said, 'This is not a good order for me to give. I think it's terrible; however, I must give it, but the overriding consideration is holding the casualties down.' Preserving troops was more important than fighting to the last man for a hill out there. So, this is where the political impact comes through to the army commander and impacts the last guy standing on the front line. So, you do what you do at times not because it's what you should or want to do. The overriding consideration was to minimize casualties."

There were two opinions regarding General Taylor's decision to keep casualties low in Korea. One view believed that increases in deaths would diminish US and Allies' political will. The other side believed that increases in losses would inflame political will. General Taylor was concerned that the American public would become more enraged as the death toll climbed and that their anger would bog American troops down even more in Korea. The United States had accepted the fact that there was going to be an armistice. Ted explained, "So, you did your best to hold onto what you could while moving forward."

In June 1953, Lt. Col. Mataxis had an unexpected visitor while in command: Sergeant First Class A. Quintana visited him for two days at Buffalo's command post. As a sergeant, Quintana had served as the battalion runner in Mataxis's World War II battalion, where he had saved Major Mataxis's life. In the Buffalo newspaper, Lt. Col. Mataxis stated, "The Germans launched an offensive during the winter of 1944. My unit was engaged in the fighting of a rearguard action. I and several others were returning from a visiting inspection of our companies when we ran into an enemy patrol. The meeting was so unexpected that both groups literally froze in their tracks. Sgt. Quintana quickly recovered and opened fire on the surprised Nazis with his Thompson submachine gun killing two, and the rest fled for their lives. That prompt action saved my neck." Mataxis and Quintana toured Pork Chop Hill and went on several front-line inspections during the visit. Sgt. First Class Quintana found many differences in this ongoing action. Quintana stated that, "He especially noticed that Lt. Col. Mataxis was ducking more quickly these days than when the artillery rounds went overhead in Germany." Mataxis simply laughed. The *Buffalo Bugle* article on May 6, 1953 said that the commanding officer of the 17th Infantry "at age 35 was most likely the youngest regimental commander in Korea at that time." On June 4, 1953, Lt. Col. Mataxis turned over command of the 17th Infantry Regiment to Colonel Benjamin T. Harris, and he rotated home to his wife and family after two years of separation.

During the Korean War, while serving with the 17th Infantry Regiment, Mataxis was awarded the Legion of Merit, two oak leaf clusters for Valor with the Bronze Star, one oak leaf cluster for the Purple Heart, and the second award of the Combat Infantry Badge (which was indicated by one star placed between the reefs). Despite all his accolades, the funniest story regarding Ted's time in Korea is the somewhat irreverent joke that Ted's most impressive achievement in Korea involved the growth of facial hair. When Mataxis first arrived at the regiment in October 1952 as executive officer, he decided to grow a mustache. Since he was only 34 then, Mataxis thought the mustache would make him look older. He ultimately grew a full mustache, and it became a trademark in the regiment. Regimental mustaches were immediately dubbed "Buffalostaches," and everyone began growing them. Even the new commander grew one. On July 4, 1953, the regiment conducted a contest for the best "Buffalostaches." The best was awarded $300. Ironically, this contest was conducted as Lt. Col. Mataxis was becoming reacquainted with his wife and three young children stateside, so Ted's "Buffalostache" never even got a chance to compete.

The month after Mataxis left command, the Second Battle of Pork Chop Hill occurred. The 7th Division was ordered to evacuate its troops from Pork Chop Hill. The final ground combat occurred and resulted in 43 KIAs and 316 WIAs. Ultimately, the 7th Infantry Division suffered 3,905 KIAs and 10,858 WIAs. On July 27, 1953, the Korean War ended. And the Korean armistice was signed.

The peak of US ground troops' strength on July 31, 1953, was 302,483. Deployed American troops totaled 1,587,040 during the Korean War; some 198,380 (or 12.5 percent) participated in combat. The total impact of US casualties in the war was 33,629 KIAs, 103,284 WIAs, and 7,140 MIAs. Two months later, on September 6, 1953, during Operation *Big Switch*, the last of 3,597 US POWs were released, effectively bringing this chapter of American military history to a close.

Several decades passed before Mataxis would return to Korea. As he recounts in his papers, "We returned to Korea for the 50th anniversary of the war. The government of South Korea created a metal called the Korean War Service Medal, for the 50th anniversary of the ending of the Korean War. It was showing their appreciation for veteran United Nations soldiers who helped Korea fight its war against the North Korea and China invasion. All nations but one were authorized to wear their Korean War Veterans' medal. For some reason never explained Americans were prohibited from wearing it. Then in 1999, the Pentagon finally approved the metal as an official award to be worn with military uniforms." It would be nearly a decade before Mataxis would later meet again with his band of brothers. During October 2005, Mataxis returned to Fort Benning for the dedication of the 17th Infantry Brigade monument at Sacrifice Field across from the US Army Infantry Museum. He recalls "I was the 'Honorary Colonel' of the Regiment Association. Over 300 veteran 'Buffalos' and their family members were there to dedicate the life-size bronze buffalo monument to their fallen comrades and their combat experience."

Mike Guardia wrote a book shortly after General Moore's death titled *Hal Moore on Leadership: Winning When Outgunned and Outmanned*. The following is a direct quote, "For Hal Moore, being the Regimental Operations Officer also reinforced the importance of mentoring. 'The Regimental Executive Officer, Lt. Colonel Ted Mataxis, took a liking to me,' said Moore. 'He had served as an Infantry battalion commander in the European Theater during World War II, and as a United Nations Observer when India and Pakistan were formed as independent countries in the late 1940s. He would frequently talk to me late at night instructing me, giving me the benefit of his experiences and guidance.' As Moore recalled, these mentoring sessions were helpful because, 'a leader must realize his subordinate leaders will be killed or wounded. He must prepare and train other leaders to step up and take over.' He, himself, must train his next-in-line to take command in the event he is killed, wounded, or evacuated." These words sound a lot like the voice of Lt. Col. Thebaud, the PMS at the University of Washington before World War II. Mentoring is one of the most important responsibilities any military leader has.

CHAPTER 8

Fort Benning and the Army War College, 1953–58

Upon returning from Korea in summer 1953, Mataxis was assigned for the next four years as an instructor with the Tactics Committee and the Atomic Committee to the Tactical Department at the Infantry School in Fort Benning. The first requirement for an instructor arriving at Fort Benning was to attend the army's two-week course on military instruction to become certified. After this course, students were required to present a class to a committee of current instructors, fondly called the "Murder Board." Presenting to contemporaries is always challenging and these final presentations were no exception. In his recollections of the experience, the relief Mataxis and his contemporaries felt to have the challenge behind them was palpable.

Upon completing the course and for the remainder of his time at the Infantry School, Mataxis served as an instructor and was the committee chairman and departmental head. His first assignment, as explained by Mataxis in his own words, "I was to chair a panel that analyzed our current infantry tactics to see how we would have to change our doctrine to accommodate the atomic firepower of the newly developed 280 mm atomic artillery round. A Military Occupation Skill 5 (MOS) was developed for nuclear specialists to identify those the military provided with appropriate training."

During his time teaching atomic courses, the Army Chief of Staff encouraged all service schools to have their faculty publish unclassified articles to get the word out. Mataxis published several articles on atomic tactics in the *Infantry Magazine* and other military-affiliated magazines. Mataxis served on the committee responsible for rewriting the infantry field manuals (FMs) for the Infantry School. He became one of the army's subject matter experts (SME) on using atomic weapons. The manuals were constantly revised and updated as more desirable techniques and tactics were developed, tested, and adopted.

Mataxis attended several special nuclear weapons tests and courses to provide the necessary background to work on revisions of the fundamental army doctrine. They also rewrote the tactical field manual to include the effects of tactical nuclear weapons on ground combat. While at the Infantry School from 1953 through 1957, he participated in staff studies, maneuvers, planning, and field testing, designed to reorganize, and modernize the army for possible employment on a nuclear battlefield. Mataxis was also responsible for writing the official FM on atomic tactics. While attending an Army Association meeting, a military publishing company approached him about writing an unclassified version of *Nuclear Tactics*. He received the army's permission to write the book, and everything he wrote was drawn from unclassified information. However, when the book was submitted, it was pointed out that when linked, the compilation of the materials made unclassified materials classified. Its classification was officially changed and required several workarounds. Lieutenant Colonel Seymour L. Goldberg co-authored the book, called *Nuclear Tactics*, which is still being used as a reference in military schools. This book was published in seven languages. As instructors with the Tactics Committee, they were responsible for the various platform classes conducted at the Infantry School. Once a year for four years, the draft FM and Training Texts were sent to the Continental Army Command (CONARC) Headquarters for use during the army divisions' summer maneuvers to validate their content by providing application and feedback from the divisions.

For the Mataxis family, this was an extraordinary time. The move to Fort Benning was the first time the Mataxis family had lived together as a typical family in the United States. There were only a handful of times that Mataxis lived for extended periods with his family. Helma and the children briefly had a husband/father during the occupation in Germany, then a short time later in Staten Island, New York, and for a year in India. Their short stay as a family together in India while he attended the Indian Army staff college was anything but ordinary. Before that time, he had been deployed worldwide, serving God and country while chasing the windmills of the time. After India, Mataxis served a year with the UN in Kashmir and volunteered to go directly from Kashmir to the Korean War. The family lived in Denver during that time. At Fort Benning, the Mataxis family had the opportunity to live as an actual family under the same roof. There was no longer a need for the long letters Mataxis wrote directing the children's activities and chores. In 1953, the children (Shirley, 11, Ted, 9, and Kaye, 7) wondered, "Who is this full-time stranger living with us? He sure is bossy—doesn't he know Mom is in charge?" Fort Benning, the home of the Infantry School, has always been a family-friendly post that offered various activities for youth and wives sponsored by the military personnel assigned to the post. This post facilitated maximum family time and interaction since military life often required separation from their infantry fathers.

The time at Fort Benning from summer 1953 through summer 1957 was the first time that the Mataxis family lived the American notion of "everyday family life." Living at 121 Rainbow Avenue at Fort Benning was an excellent environment for the family. They had a lovely house with a corner lot with plenty of room for outdoor activities. Since the children had bounced around from school to school over the years, Helma and Ted sent their children to Trinity School, a private school located in Columbus, Georgia. Their classmates included President Eisenhower's grandchildren, whose father was also stationed at Fort Benning.

Benning was the first military post the Mataxis family had ever lived on, so the children were surrounded by military children their age in various clubs, activities, and social events. Life at Fort Benning for those four years reflected a pre-World War II army social life. Life once again revolved around the officers' club, with formal parties and a great social life with family and friends! The officers' club at Fort Benning was the center of the universe for activities, and almost everyone lived on the post then. It was located directly behind the original Infantry School building, and everything evolved around the school and club. The club had swimming pools, tennis courts, golf courses, a package store, a barbershop, and dozens of small cottages available for rent by anyone coming or going from Fort Benning. Fort Benning even had its resort center, located at Destin, Florida, which provided the families with a seaside location close to Fort Benning.

There were no longer calling cards and required weekly visits to the commander's house every Friday, but there were still expectations to be upheld. Everyone was expected to live on post, very few (if any) wives worked, and everyone participated in the activities, as was expected of them. The Class A uniform at that time was pink and green, and mandatory dress. The officers' club required dress blues or dress whites. The ladies' clubs and coffees still required the ladies to wear hats and white gloves. All officers were expected to be active club members, and wives were expected to support club activities.

The officer's efficiency reports at that time reflected the family's conduct. The officers knew that "if [they] could not control [their] family," there was no way the army would believe that they could control their soldiers. Delinquent reports (DRs) could be issued to dependents who did not abide by the rules and regulations of the installation. This practice was considered a hefty hit for the family whose dependent committed the transgression. When deployed overseas, dependent children could be sent home for egregious activities.

Fort Benning was an excellent location for everyday family life. In the 1950s, military life reflected the old customs and traditions of the military. Many men on base had Deactivated Military War Trophies (DMWTs). These weapons were proudly displayed in their homes. A captured weapon seemed to validate their active participation in World War II and Korea. The Mataxis children grew up around these weapons, thinking everyone had participated in the wars and collected war souvenirs. This tradition ended in Vietnam and became a punishable offense by the army.

The Mataxis family's years at Fort Benning were a wonderful time for the children, Helma, and Ted. The family started getting accustomed to having a father around the house. For the first time, Ted participated actively with his children in all the opportunities available for families. The family was often found at the base's various craft shops completing crafts, such as ceramics, pottery, and woodworking. Benning also hosted a Youth Activity Club, which provided social events and sports for all of the kids: flag football, T-ball, baseball, and basketball. The instructors were senior-grade field officers and senior-grade NCOs, many of whom had played various sports on army teams or in college. At that time, the cadre of Infantry School instructors had participated in both World War II and Korea.

As soon as Ted Jr. turned 11, Ted Sr. was exposed to scouting again, rekindling his love of the program. Ted Sr. worked with Ted Jr. every morning before school on the Scouts' advancement requirements and they connected for the first time as a father and son. With the schooling Ted Jr. could have been a better student; however, he excelled in Scouting, blasting through the ranks. He became a Tenderfoot in September 1955, Second Class in December 1955, First Class in June 1956, Star in August 1956, Life in December 1956, and Eagle Scout in June 1957. He became an Eagle Scout before his 13th birthday. Boy Scout Troop 27, the Benning scout troop, had its own building, which displayed completed projects and accomplishments of its Scouts. The Scouts and their troop leadership carved a 12-foot totem pole at one of their summer camps and placed it in front of the troop's building. This Boy Scout troop has continually been at Fort Benning since 1923 and has produced over 200 Eagle Scouts. There was a wide variety of adult leadership and support from the active-duty personnel assigned to Fort Benning. The volunteers filled Boy Scout leadership positions, and gave support as merit badge counselors and as coaches for sports teams. When Lord Baden Powell, a famous English general and hero to his countrymen, developed Scouting and started the movement, he had no idea it would spread around the world.

In transferring from one military installation to another, you could always rest assured that there would be a Scout troop wherever you were assigned. There has always been a strong connection between Boy Scout activities and military skills.

Lt. Col. Mataxis was not the only parent that had a chance to revisit their old Scouting days. Helma was a Girl Scout leader for the Brownies and then the Girl Scouts, in which Shirley actively participated. Shirley earned the Curved Bar Award, the highest award in Girl Scouts from 1940 to 1963. This award had previously been called the Golden Eagle from 1916 to 1940 and after 1963 it was called the Girl Scout Gold Award. Shirley was also in the Junior American Red Cross and later volunteered at the hospital on post. The post hospital, consisting of several World War II buildings connected by enclosed walkways, was just out the back door and across the parking lot from the family home on Rainbow Avenue. When the hospital was later torn down, the Infantry Museum was constructed on the site.

Almost all families on base participated in the National Rifle Association (NRA), Junior Division, where their activities took place at the Fort Benning Rifle and Pistol Club. Since Fort Benning was the army's home for the Infantry School, it meant that everyone valued their sons' and daughters' shooting and hunting abilities. They all loved guns, hunting, and the outdoors. Saturday mornings were reserved for the Junior NRA program where the dependent children learned how to handle a .22 rifle and pistol safely. The NRA provided a series of patches and pins that the children would earn based on their skill level: Pro-Marksman, Marksman levels 1–7, and Sharpshooter. The children took great pride in their advancements, as did their parents. Mataxis was surprised to discover that his oldest daughter, Shirley, was the best shot in the family. Every Saturday morning, they would work on gun safety and marksmanship with the children. This club was one of the favorites among the instructors at the Infantry School.

Fort Benning, in addition to being the Infantry School, is the home of the army's Jump School. Among Fort Benning's key landmarks are the three jump towers, standing 250 feet high. The World's Fair in New York in 1939 had constructed these towers as amusement rides. It was recognized that the towers could be used to teach paratroopers how to control a parachute while descending to earth. They have been used continuously since their construction in 1941 and 1942. Four towers were built initially, but one was destroyed in 1954 by a tornado. The Jump School has used these towers in the training of paratroopers since the school was founded. The towers were a rite of passage, not only for the soldiers' training; it also became a goal of the dependent children to have that experience. As a real "military brat" at Fort Benning you had to participate with the 34-foot and the 250-foot tower. First, all dependents were introduced to the 34-foot tower. At this station, the children learned all the actions that took place inside an aircraft, and were then taught the commands inside the plane. They were then hooked up to the static line. They exited the mock tower, instantly feeling the static line connect with the parachute pack as they quickly slid down a cable to a berm, where they immediately disconnected and promptly returned to the tower to receive a jump critique. Each of the 250-foot towers had four arms, and each one took a fully inflated parachute to the top, where it was released, giving the students exposure to what it is like under a full canopy, how to maneuver the chute, and how to conduct a Parachute Landing Fall (PLF). The real thrill for the children was the 250-foot jump towers. Unlike for the Jump School students, these were rigged with a bench that slid down cables to the base of the tower, permitting room for an adult. The soldiers would be released at the top and float down controlling their parachutes. The Mataxis children were just as enamored with jumping out of planes as their father before them.

During this assignment at Fort Benning, Col. Mataxis attended the American Jump School, followed by the Jump Master's Course. This time, he did not break an ankle (as he had previously at the Indian Jump School in 1951). Mataxis and Ted Jr. ran together to prepare the 37-year-old "old man" for the physically demanding program. "And let me tell you," Mataxis later confessed, "trying to keep up with the young studs in the Airborne class was difficult. I'd come back home at night, practically crawling. I was proud when I finally got my Airborne wings." He would eventually punch those same Airborne wings into Ted Jr.'s chest in 1963, and his grandson Ted III's chest in 2000.

At the end of his tour at Fort Benning, Ted spent the last six months on temporary duty assignment (TDY) as the deputy chief evaluator and test evaluator, for Exercise King Cole. This training was designed to try the newly proposed Pentomic unit structure and test the developing theories and techniques used with nuclear devices on the battlefield and methods for operating in an atomic combat environment. His detailed background with the Pentomic concept allowed the test-evaluated group to look at and evaluate the idea objectively. While Ted was off TDY, Helma and the children had been instructed to eat the four years of leftovers from their chest freezer. After completing this exercise, he joined his family at the Army War College. Once again, Helma had moved the family while he was TDY.

After four beautiful years full of family, contemporaries, and friends, it was time for Mataxis to move on to the Army War College in Carlisle, Pennsylvania. The 10-month course was number 11, the class of 1957, attended by lieutenant colonels and colonels that were perceived to be the best of the best. They displayed potential and upward mobility and were deemed more capable of significant and increased responsibility. The curriculum of the college provided many intellectual opportunities related to a leader's ability to think, communicate effectively, and execute at the strategic level. University-level graduate school opportunities were also available while attending this course.

The college did not have dorms; however, bachelor quarters were available for unaccompanied and unmarried officers. Tiny houses were provided for families. They were so small that most families had to store some of their household belongings. Kaye and Shirley had to share a bedroom, and their constant bickering made family life difficult at times. Despite this difficulty, the assignment was quite pleasant. Many of the War College students knew one another from previous assignments; they were contemporaries of the same age and rank.

The same opportunities at Fort Benning were available for families at the War College. The family's social life revolved around college activities, the officers' club, and the students' homes. The "mother-at-home lifestyle" was in place, everyone lived on post, and none of the wives worked but stayed very busy with ladies' activities and family activities, as well as providing transportation to the wide variety of children's activities. Ted Jr. had a newspaper route on post, delivering the Sunday newspapers. He delivered four different newspapers: the *New York Times*, *Washington Post*, *Herald-Tribune*, and *Philadelphia Inquirer*. Col. Mataxis was the first to hear about no newspaper or a wrong newspaper being delivered, as his classmates gave him hell whenever there was a mistake. So, the paper route turned into a family event every Sunday morning.

Mataxis and another friend, Bill Kernan, an instructor in the Tactics Department with him at Fort Benning, were chosen to attend the War College. While attending, they went to the Pentagon to ask for command assignments. They were both laughed at and told, "You've both been lucky commanding battalions and regiments in combat. Many of your contemporaries haven't even been in command yet. Both of you are due for Pentagon duty." They had similar combat backgrounds, battalion commands in World War II, and in Korea they commanded regiments next to each other. So, when the personnel assignment team came to Carlisle, they both sat in the back of the room, knowing what their assignments would be. When they were in the auditorium listening to classmates' assignments being announced, Col. Mataxis heard: "Bill Kernan, command duty, the Berlin Brigade in Germany," followed by his name, "Ted Mataxis, command duty in Germany." They were both quite surprised. They went down and talked to the assignments chief and asked for assignment clarification. The chief responded, "Well, it seems the Seventh Army commander is fed up with 'one-year ticket punching tours' for his commanders. This resulted in far too many disciplinary problems, tactical inexperience, and lack of training standards." The Seventh Army commander told his chief of staff, "Get me some combat-experienced commanders!" Colonels Kernan and Mataxis fit the bill perfectly.

By the end of the course, a war had begun in Lebanon. So once again, Ted left immediately. Ted's hasty deployment meant Helma was left alone to clear out their quarters, pack the house, put things in storage for the next three years in preparation for the family's next assignment in Germany, and get the family, dog, and car to the port of embarkation. When asked decades later if their dad had any shortcomings, Mataxis's son admits, "My dad's most significant shortcoming in life was abandoning my mother every time it came to a permanent change of station move or a chance to volunteer for an adrenaline-filled activity. He would volunteer and do a disappearing act. I always believed he used the wars as an easy out." His siblings are quick to agree with his assessment of the family dynamics.

CHAPTER 9

505th Airborne Battle Group, Mainz and Bad Kreuznach, Germany, 1958–61

In July 1958 the Mataxis family left on the SS *America*, sailing out of New York bound for Bremerhaven, Germany. Ted stopped at a bookstore to stock up on reading material for the trip. The family were old hands at traveling on ships and loved the time. Roscoe was heading back to his home country, which he had left in 1948. Upon arriving at Bremerhaven, the family went by train to Bad Kreuznach, home of the 8th Division headquarters.

By 1958, Germany had changed significantly from when the Mataxis family had been there during the Occupation at the end of World War II. The occupied zone of West Germany had merged into a West German state, the Bundesrepublik Deutschland (BRD) or in English, Federal Republic of Germany (FRG). This was done with the help of the US Marshall Plan, named after the Secretary of State and former US Army Chief of Staff General Marshall. It enabled West Germany to rise out of the ashes of war like the historic phoenix, developing a stable democracy. The same was true in the Allied-occupied part of Berlin, which was very well developed in contrast to East Berlin. The signs of World War II were no longer everywhere, and the bombed-out buildings and rubble had been cleaned up. The Occupation officially ended for the war zone in 1949. Ted and family left Germany in January 1948.

The Soviet Union's once-friendly relations turned hostile, and they wanted to absorb Berlin into the Soviet Eastern sector. The Berlin Airlift crisis started on June 24, 1948, when Soviet forces blockaded the rail, road, and water access to Allied-controlled areas held by the United States, French, and British. The Allied nations were forced to supply by air everything needed for the people there to survive. The Berlin Airlift was conducted around the clock from June 24, 1948 until the Soviets lifted the blockade on May 12, 1949. The Western administrations calculated that if the Soviets opposed the airlift with force, it would be an act of aggression against an unarmed humanitarian mission and a violation of an explicit agreement. The crisis in Berlin was caused by competing occupation policies and rising tensions between Western powers and the Soviet Union. In June 1948, without informing the Soviets, US and British policymakers introduced the new deutschmark to West Berlin. The purpose of the currency reform was to wrestle economic control of the city from the Soviets, enable the introduction of Marshall Plan aid, and curb the city's black market. Despite the desire for a peaceful resolution to the standoff, the United States also deployed B-29 bombers to the United Kingdom, which could carry nuclear weapons. The airlift proved difficult and Western diplomats asked the Soviets to seek a diplomatic solution to the impasse. The Soviets offered to drop the blockade if the Western Allies withdrew the new deutschmark from West Berlin.

Once the Soviet Union achieved a nuclear capability, US citizens began to prepare for a possible nuclear attack back in the United States. Stephen E. Ambrose's observation was that "the United States in early 1955 came closer to using atomic weapons than at any other time in the Eisenhower Administration." The American presence changed in Europe in August 1958. After Korea everyone believed that limited wars like Korea were a thing of the past, with tactical nuclear weapons available on both sides. Nuclear weapons dramatically changed the concept of the concentration of large forces at one point to provide overwhelming combat power. Now they simply provided a lucrative target for a nuclear device. The threat of that time became the fear that the Russians would try something like a blitzkrieg through the Fulda Gap, invading Western Europe, with the possible use of nuclear weapons.

The army radically changed the structure in 1958 by converting the infantry division to what became known as the "Pentomic Division." The Pentomic structure was designed to allow infantry units to survive and fight on an atomic battlefield. Structurally, it eliminated the regiment and battalion, replacing both with five self-contained "battlegroups," each of which were larger than an old-style battalion, but smaller than a regiment. A full colonel commanded the battlegroup, and his captains commanded four, later five, subordinate rifle companies. The Pentomic division structurally reflected that of the World War II European theater airborne divisions. Since three World War II European airborne commanders dominated the army's strategic thinking after the Korean War, this was no surprise. These commanders were Army Chief of Staff General Matthew Ridgway, Eighth Army commander General Maxwell Taylor, and VII Corps commander Lieutenant General James Gavin. In World War II, though theoretically triangular in design, the two airborne divisions, the 82nd and 101st, fought as division task forces reinforced with additional parachute regiments and separate battalions. For most of the northern European campaign, both divisions had two additional parachute regiments attached to them, giving them five subordinate regiments, each commanded by colonels. Parachute regiments were smaller than standard infantry regiments by organization, and attrition often made them even smaller, giving the 82nd or 101st commander a perfect prototype of the structure that later became the Pentomic division.

The Pentomic organization, officially known as the Reorganization of the Current Infantry Division (ROCID), went through frequent modifications from its conception in 1954 to when it was finally adopted in 1958. The original tables of organization (TOE) that were implemented included a small brigade headquarters commanded by the assistant division commander, a brigadier general. This headquarters was designed to provide command and control of attached units to the division, as directed by the division commander, and to act as an alternate division command post. The concept was not really used in practice, and when Pentomic TOEs were modified in February 1960, the brigade was eliminated.

In the first weeks of August 1961, nearly 10,000 refugees a day fled to West Berlin seeking freedom and a new life. On the morning of August 13, 1961, the East Germans, with Soviet acquiescence, began sealing off the Soviet sector of the city from West Berlin. This set off a shock across the Western world. The East Germans were now prisoners in their own city, and West Berlin was an island of freedom isolated by the Berlin Wall. Checkpoint Charlie, the transition point between the East and West, went on to become a hot spot of the Cold War. The Berlin Wall remained one of the most powerful and enduring symbols of the Cold War. Thirty years after the wall was erected, on June 12, 1987, President Reagan stood 100 yards away from the wall dividing East from West Berlin. In his speech he challenged, "Mr. Gorbachev, tear down this wall." On November 9, 1989, East Germany announced that citizens of the GDR could cross the border whenever they pleased, and the wall was torn down. This is often said to be the end of the Cold War.

Ted's first assignment in Germany was as chief of staff of the 8th Infantry Division and then the deputy commanding officer, in July 1958, of the Reorganization of the Current Infantry Division (ROCID). These divisions were made up of five infantry battle groups (rather than three regiments/brigades.) Two of the battle groups, the 504th and 505th, were airborne and had just rotated to Germany from Fort Bragg, North Carolina. As the "airborne task force" for Europe, the units had two sets of equipment. One set was for mobile airborne missions and another set was for NATO missions. The battle groups had five infantry companies and a lieutenant colonel as the executive officer and deputy commander. This concept was developed by General Maxwell Taylor so that the battle group could be divided into two task forces, along with a reserve. Tactical nuclear weapons like the 280 mm artillery cannon were part of the unit's equipment. As a result of the dual missions these battle groups spent twice the time in the field in comparison with the other units. This was required to maintain their tactical proficiency. Once, during trouble in Congo, the unit was pulled out of winter maneuvers and ordered to go to the airfield, drop off winter clothing, draw some summer clothing, and be prepared to fly to Africa to parachute into Congo.

When the newly airborne troops arrived from Fort Bragg, the 8th Division commander saw no reason for the airborne troops to dress differently from the rest of his division. He was not a fan of the airborne! So, he sent a memo to the newly arrived airborne units stating that they would not be allowed to wear the airborne overseas cap or jump boots. One of the airborne sergeant majors called the corps commander and explained what the memo stated. The corps commander, who had commanded an airborne division in World War II, wrote to the division commander, and said that he understood he now had airborne troops assigned and that there were certain traditions in the airborne units that needed to be maintained. For example, being allowed to wear their unique headgear and jump boots as part of their duty uniform. The division commander relieved both battle group commanders of the airborne battle groups. Until that time these commanders were very well thought of by everyone in the airborne community and many felt it was not justified.

The division commander called Colonel Mataxis in September 1958 and told him he was giving him command of the 505th Airborne Battle Group. He went on to explain how disappointed he was with the unit's Delinquent Reports (DRs) rate, as it was the highest in the division. He felt that all these troops needed was "firm discipline" and if Ted couldn't provide that, he would also be relieved. The airborne troops were a rather high-spirited lot and had volunteered to become airborne. They were a group of people willing to take risks that many others would not take and produce tactical results above and beyond regular soldiers. The airborne "high spirits" and "morale" resulted in outstanding soldier skills but also resulted in receiving more DRs than less enthusiastic peers.

Both the 504th and the 505th Battle Groups were in Mainz, Germany, at the Robert E. Lee Barracks. The barracks were named after US Army Captain Robert Edward Lee, who received the DSC posthumously for his bravery at the Battle of the Bulge in World War II. Mainz was the home of the airborne troopers and as such was a sought-after assignment for young, gung-ho, and enthusiastic officers, NCOs, and enlisted personnel. These airborne units instilled great esprit de corps and attracted very capable and physically fit personnel who immediately bonded with one another. After all, they were the cream of airborne troopers. These troops took pride that their units were considered the best in the army, and they remained as physically fit as possible. They worked long and hard to maintain the units' high standards. The leadership and mentorship of these enthusiastic young officers and

Colonel Welsh presenting Ted with the symbol of the 505th Battle Group, a black panther, for his desk.

troops were a dream come true for Ted since the troops thrived on hard work and physically demanding and realistic training. The belief was that "sweat in training saves blood on the battlefield."

This was aided by good leadership at all levels of command, a good training schedule, internal battle battlegroup sports programs, and a challenging physical fitness program. Teams were representative of the units to which they belonged. The airborne unit started the program in excellent shape, so the conditioning phase could be skipped, and all efforts were spent on the basics and team building. This enabled them to constantly win whatever event they entered. Nowhere was this more visible than in unit competitions and sport competitions between the USAREUR units. Upon the Mainz troopers winning the championship in 1959, the division commander wrote Col. Mataxis. He stated, "The splendid unit spirit displayed by the personnel who supported the football team far outdistanced any rival. Mainz not only had the outstanding football team in USAREUR, but it also had the outstanding supporting unit spirit."

There is an old army saying: "A commander never wants enthusiastic soldiers to be bored and looking for something to do because there is no telling what they will come up with! Chances are the commander would never think of it!" As commander, the first thing Ted had to do was solve the Delinquent Report (DR) rate of his high-spirited personnel. Ted recalled, "I met with the Mayor of Mainz and explained the problem I had with DRs. The mayor explained to me, 'We have been dealing with foreign troops since the time of the Roman invasion and we can certainly resolve this issue.' The mayor called in his Chief of Police and together they developed a system to prevent any delinquency reports being submitted from that time going forward. This was quickly done by assigning a senior-grade 505th NCO to accompany the Military Police on their rounds. As events occurred, participants were assembled, and an investigation immediately took place on the spot. A solution was found to everyone's satisfaction and closure was reached. If any damages occurred,

The change of command ceremony, the passing of the colors, upon assumption of command of the 505th Battle Group in Mainz, Germany, from Colonel Lemar Welsch to Ted. Colonel Welsch went on to be the jump school commander at Fort Benning for years.

the Germans were told they would be paid for the next payday by whomever was responsible. This way the Germans did not have to wait for the paperwork to go through, justice took its course, and the relationships quickly changed for the better." The division commander pulled Ted aside and reminded him it was just like he said: "All they need is strong discipline."

There were many interesting policies Ted put in place at the unit. First was to prohibit anyone but him using a green pen; this would let those reading the document know it was his directive. An interesting vignette came about when he had a certain innovative idea and wanted to implement it. He called in his operations officer, who proceeded to explain that the division had a policy against that particular idea. Ted quickly said, "I can't believe the division prohibits it. I want to see it!" His operations officer sheepishly returned with the document that Ted had signed in his green ink when he was chief of staff for the division. He quickly responded, "Where you sit on an issue can often determine where you may stand on an issue."

This was Ted's first assignment to an airborne unit, placing him on jump status, so he became eligible to start working towards the Senior Parachute badge. To earn this badge a paratrooper must make at least 30 jumps, which included 15 jumps with combat equipment; two night jumps, for one of which he must be the jumpmaster; and two mass tactical jumps. Once the Senior Parachute badge is earned, as long as the paratrooper remains on jump status, he then works towards the Master Parachute badge, which is the highest level. This has very demanding prerequisites of time on jump status and jumpmaster requirements. It really separates the experienced jumpers from the inexperienced, as does the Eagle Scout award in Boy Scouts. They are both very respected in their respective communities. Many of the young airborne personnel assigned to the 505th as fresh second lieutenants and young enlisted personnel would years later show up in other airborne units at increased rank and experience, having been exposed to professional mentorship and experienced officers and NCOs who were older and wiser. One of the best feelings that a leader has is watching his young personnel develop and grow as professional soldiers over the years. It seems as if they are forever remembered at the rank they held at that first assignment. In 1980 Ted was visiting one of his second lieutenants from Mainz (in 1960), who was now a three-star commander at Fort Benning. He remarked to Ted, "I will always remember you as a colonel; no offence!" Ted's immediate response was, "No problem, I have always remembered you as a second lieutenant!"

As a direct result of being the Airborne Task Force for Europe, these units were always maintained at overstrength in manpower. This way the normal leaves, TDYs, and injured personnel would not make the unit understrength in personnel in case of deployment. The 504th and the 505th were the only battle groups that were airborne and if deployed it could possibly take a long time for reinforcements to arrive. As a result, Colonel Mataxis drew up a new organization, using some equipment from both sets. He fleshed out his reconnaissance and antitank units so that they could be employed with the task force. A Ranger platoon consisting of almost 100 members was formed out of the assets available.

He then decided to go out on his own and recruit a couple of "studs" for the battle group: one for the reconaissance platoon and the other for the Ranger platoon. He sent the word out through the sergeant major network. He couldn't go through normal personnel channels, because he would be perceived as stealing people. The type of personnel he was looking for would have certain "characteristics" that wouldn't be listed in personnel channels, but the sergeant majors would know who these guys were. Almost all the senior ranking officers and NCOs in the 504th and 505th were veterans of combat in World War II and Korea. He needed two junior officers that were combat proven to lead these units. In Germany at that time there were always experienced airborne qualified personnel who had "gyroscoped" from the 82nd Airborne Division and were in "leg units" trying to get to an airborne slot. The wives really liked the extra jump pay they received while their husbands were in an airborne unit; the officer received $110 and an enlisted man $55. The two lieutenants he tried to recruit for the 505th had excellent combat records in Korea and each had received multiple Silver Stars and Purple Hearts. Ted was successful in having Lieutenant Herbert assigned. Lieutenant Hackworth could not be assigned but they kept in contact and would later serve together. Both Lieutenants Hackworth and Herbert would go on to continue their bravery in combat in Vietnam as they had previously in Korea. Col. Mataxis thought they were both "cut out of the same bolt of cloth." Simply put, they were great combat soldiers, fearless and always gravitating towards the sounds of the guns. However, as it turned out both had remained in combat so long that they became burned out to such an extent that they believed regulations were only to be followed if they helped your mission. Both were recognized for the warriors they were but fell out of the good graces of the army. Lt. Col. Herbert wrote the book *Soldier* about his experiences in the army. Colonel Hackworth wrote *About Face* covering his experiences. He went on to become a syndicated columnist, speaker, writer, and multimillionaire.

The battle groups had a difficult time with tactical communications on exercises, with the five companies' commanders communicating directly with the battle group commander. For the NATO Exercise Winter Shield in 1960, the 505 had an attached German tank battalion with a heavy tank company and an armored personnel carrier (APC) unit. This made a difficult communication issue even more difficult, with the span of control increasing with the addition of the attachments. Col. Mataxis quickly organized his task force into three echelons. His deputy commander was assigned echelon one with two 505th rifle companies and a German tank company. His XO was assigned echelon two with two 505th rifle companies and the German heavy tank company. Echelon three was the remainder of the German battalion, assigned to a 505th rifle company. The three echelons proved to work very well for the task force. His organic 505th elements were with each echelon while changing

Ted and Lieutenant Tony Herbert, a commander of his Ranger platoon, on a Winter Shield exercise in 1960. Tony was said to be the most decorated enlisted man in the Korean War.

the span of control to three echelons, not the five companies and the additional attachments. He later stated, "This was like I reorganized my battalion in Europe because of casualties inflicted on my unit. The task force's three echelons were able to penetrate the enemy's artillery positions far to the rear of the opposing force, forcing the end of the exercise by overwhelming the opposing force. I briefed the Seventh Army commander on the difficulties I had with current communications in the organization of the battle group and how this Pentomic organization triggered me to reorganize into three echelons within my task force. I also stuck my neck out and recommended that another look be taken at the Pentomic organization. The command structure currently went from five captain rifle company commanders, directly to the battle group commander, who also had the additional elements consisting of: a combat service company, a tank company, an engineer company, and an artillery battery with the atomic cannon! The army commander asked me to write up my recommendations and send them to him at the Seventh Army headquarters, where they would be studying the restructure of the Pentomic division."

Because of his background in nuclear weapons, Col. Mataxis also participated in a series of lecture tours throughout Europe on the Pentomic Division and its potential utilization of atomic fire support. His last two years there he spent commanding the 505th Airborne Battle Group in Mainz, Germany. At that time the army was a very experienced and professional force, with the majority of the senior-grade officers and senior NCOs veterans of World War II and Korea. Just prior to turning over command Ted took several of his officers and NCOs to the German Parachute School in Schongau, Germany.

Many of the 505th Battle Group personnel had jumped into Sainte-Mère-Église on D-Day, June 6, 1944, making it the first town in France to be liberated. On the 14th anniversary (1960) of D-Day the veterans who participated in the original jump with the 505th were encouraged to go to the celebration at Sainte-Mère-Église along with the unit's color guard. The unit had a mannequin with parachute gear to be presented to the small town museum. In fact, one member of the command happened to be the soldier who was hung up on the church tower in Sainte-Mère-Église, Pvt. John Steele, and he was very popular with everyone. The town named two streets that year to honor the American war efforts: Rue de 505th and Rue de General Gavin. The Mataxis family attended the ceremony.

Ambassador Gavin, an airborne division commander in World War II, attended this celebration and was asked for money to help establish a museum there. He said, "I cannot do that before Americans donate to an established fund." A bond between the 505th and the town was quickly formed, and the unit donated $505 to build a museum. Over the next few years, the unit continued to donate many artifacts and personal effects from that action. The town's mayor, Mayor Maslin, and his wife Jacquelin became lifelong friends with the Mataxis family. Years later the Maslin family came to the United States several times and the Mataxis family visited them in France. Their children continued this relationship over the years, enriching their family's lives.

As the possibility of a nuclear war existed, there needed to be an evacuation plan for the dependent families. This increased the stress levels for those living in Western Europe. The dependent families were provided maps with evacuation routes and were required to have extra gas cans, food and to-go bags at their homes for dependent evacuation in the event the Russians came through the Fulda Gap. The 1950s and 1960s were also very tense times, with some believing that the Soviets could possibly use nuclear weapons. Young dependents could get their driver's licenses early in the event they might be needed to drive. At the same time, in the United States, exercises were being conducted, and public shelters and bomb shelters were under construction. Students in schools throughout America were instructed what to do in the event of a nuclear attack: "Don't look and get under the desk."

The United States' presence in West Germany had significantly changed since the family were there for the occupation following the war. US Forces in Europe had grown to 300,000. The United States Government had established enclaves that resembled living on post. There were army and air force bases strategically situated throughout Germany. The dependent families lived in homes, duplexes, or large apartment buildings in areas that had all the special facilities you would have on post in the United States: post exchanges, commissaries, gas stations, barbershops, etc. In addition, there were recreational areas for bowling alleys, swimming pools, and gyms. They also had officers, NCOs, enlisted and dependent children's clubs designed to make them feel like they were living in the United States. There were Department of Defense schools available for the dependents of all grade levels. When we arrived, Kaye was in elementary school, Ted Jr. was in middle school, and Shirley went to the air force Wiesbaden High School, which was an hour away by the school bus. They even had military hospitals. The children joked to Helma that she would not have to go to a dispensary this time, and she could have two American and two German children. She thought she had her hands full with three children, Roscoe and Ted.

The family lived in a duplex and life for the next two years was wonderful. There were no servants; however, all the amenities that were not available in India were there, such as indoor plumbing, water, electricity, and TV. There was a very busy social life among the members of the airborne community in their personal quarters, the officers' club, and in the local establishments. Our quarters were just across from the officers' club in Finthen housing area in Gonsenheim. Today, large parts of the Mainz-Gonsenheim district are located on the property that was occupied by the United States' facilities of that era.

This period in Germany provided the family with a wide variety of travel opportunities across all of Europe and the Mediterranean. In Germany after World War II the exchange rate was 10 marks to one dollar. In 1958 the exchange rate was four marks and 20 pfennigs to a dollar. Col. Mataxis's favorite vacations were visiting all the historic battlefields of Europe. This was not limited to World War II, but covered all the famous battles of history. These visits always followed the same process he and his father used when he was a child. As we toured the battlefields, we often stayed in the bunkers that were used in World War II. Ted said it was to provide a more relevant experience. The children's take on it was, "He was too cheap for a hotel." It did not take long for Helma to learn the locations of the best buying trips. One of the benefits of living all over the world was that it enabled a family to acquire things at affordable prices compared to what they would cost in the United States. This was Helma's greatest enjoyment as she was a true believer in retail therapy. Another benefit of living abroad was the cultural experiences this provided. These were used to balance out the battlefield trips.

One of the most memorable family events was the trip to Brussels, Belgium, to visit the World's Fair in 1958. It was the first official world fair since the end of World War II. The various nations each had their own pavilion which displayed their nation's culture, art, food, and current technologies. The focal point of the fair was the Atomium monument, which was constructed as the main pavilion. It consisted of the base, which served as the reception center for the fair, and nine orbs, spherical bodies, in the shape of an atom suspended above it. It was intended to be temporary; however, it quickly became one of the city's most popular attractions and one of Europe's most iconic buildings. Even today it serves as the city's most popular attraction, hosting a museum, restaurant, gift shop, educational and art displays, and a wonderful panoramic view of Brussels. Despite all the fair offered, the children's most vivid memory was a small bronze statue of a naked boy urinating into a fountain's basin known as the Manneken Pis. This is also a very popular tourist sight.

In September 1961, the family returned to the United States on an army transport ship from Bremerhaven to New York. After landing in New York, they spent a couple of days in the old stomping ground. One night in New York, the family went to the movies and could not believe that the cost of a movie ticket was several dollars; in Germany, at the military theaters it was only 25 cents. On that occasion they realized how good life in Germany had been. A new adventure was about to start for the family. Ted had been assigned to the US Army Strategic & Tactical Group, located in Bethesda, Maryland. This required the purchase of a home. This time the Mataxises would be there as a complete family, unlike in Denver.

CHAPTER 10

Washington, D.C., 1962–64

In August 1961, Mataxis returned to the United States, where he was assigned as deputy chief of the army's Strategic and Tactical Analysis Group (STAG), a computerized wargaming organization located in Bethesda, Maryland. The mission was to support the Department of the Army in operational planning and evaluation activities by wargaming and aligned techniques. STAG's definition of wargaming was "a technique whereby the various courses of action involved in a problem set were subjected to analysis under prescribed rules of play representing actual conditions and employing planning factors which were as realistic as possible." STAG considers operational research "as the analytical study of military problems, undertaken to provide responsible commanders and staff agencies with a scientific basis for decisions on actions to improve the military operations." STAG was organized to provide military, scientific, and computer integration necessary for solving problems, which lend themselves to gaming or simulation-type techniques. General Hamlet, the deputy chief of staff for operations, was responsible for daily operations and missions. The organization utilized 92 personnel (41 in the military and 51 civilians). STAG consisted of four distinct divisions: the chief's office, the administrative office, the plans division, and the operations division.

In July 1962, Colonel Mataxis was appointed as the military assistant to General Lemnitzer, chairman of the Joint Chiefs of Staff. General Lemnitzer's tenure as chairman ended on September 30, 1962. President Kennedy did not appoint him to a second term. There had been a fundamental difference between the two over how best to deal with the anticipated increase in communist-sponsored "wars of national liberation." President Kennedy was confident in the efficacy of special forces and other counterinsurgency capabilities. Lemnitzer believed that, historically, regular military forces had played a key role in defeating insurgencies and should be dealt with in that manner. On November 1, 1962, President Kennedy appointed Lemnitzer commander in chief of the US European Command (CINCEUR). In January 1963, he was appointed commander of the Supreme Allied Command Europe (SACEUR). The commander of SACEUR is one of NATO's two strategic commander positions and is at the head of Allied Command Operations (ACO). SACEUR is responsible to NATO's highest military authority, the Military Committee (MC), for the conduct of all NATO military operations. He served as SACEUR until his retirement on July 1, 1969.

After retiring from active duty in July 1959, General Maxwell Taylor criticized US strategic planning and joint organization in one of his books, *The Uncertain Trumpet*, published in 1960. In his book, General Taylor presented a practical program for combining new and old weapons to correct the threatened imbalance of our military strength with that of the communist bloc of the Cold War. This book influenced President John F. Kennedy's decision to adopt a "flexible response" strategy. In 1961, President Kennedy requested General Taylor return to public service to become his military representative at the White House. As a direct result of the request to return to active duty, General Taylor's philosophy was that he was not a military officer who had been promoted "up the chain of command" to be chairman of the Joint Chiefs of Staff but an individual selected personally by the President to reflect the President's philosophy. His feeling was that as a presidential appointee he should reflect the President's position, unless it was a position that threatened the country's security. For example, he was in favor of calling up the reserve forces for Vietnam and was turned down on this repeatedly. However, one of his last acts as chairman was to prepare a paper for the President reflecting the position of the Joint Chiefs that to gain the support of the public the reserves should be called to duty. The Joint Chiefs felt that it would be prudent to involve the public and Congress in the decision to move to a full-scale war. Regrettably, this was not done and perhaps is one of the reasons why the public, who initially favored assistance to South Vietnam, turned against the war.

One of the first tasks the President gave Taylor was to lead a group to investigate the Bay of Pigs debacle. This CIA operation had shaken the President's confidence in the Joint Chiefs of Staff and the CIA. The President declared that in the future, the Joint Chiefs were expected to be "more than military men" and wanted "dynamic and imaginative leadership" in all future Cold War operations. In his capacity as Military Representative at the White House, General Taylor became involved in the expanding US military effort in Southeast Asia. After visiting Saigon, General Taylor recommended sending 5,000 to 8,000 US advisors and support troops to help South Vietnam resist the growing Viet Cong (VC) insurgency. The President was very impressed with General Taylor's capabilities and the advice he gave. On October 1, 1962, Kennedy appointed Taylor as chairman of the Joint Chiefs of Staff, thus replacing General Lemnitzer. Col. Mataxis was selected to remain General Taylor's military assistant and remained in that position until General Taylor was appointed ambassador to Vietnam in 1964.

After two weeks as the chairman, Taylor had proof that the Soviet Union secretly established missile sites in Cuba and had developed an offensive nuclear capability just 90 miles from American shores. The Cuban Missile Crisis became the new high-water mark of the Cold War and the two countries appeared to be sliding toward a nuclear conflict over the placement of these missiles. Intelligence later discovered that in addition to their intermediate-range ballistic missiles, the Soviets had nine tactical nuclear missiles in Cuba for use against any possible American invasion force. The Soviet field commanders on the ground, ranking colonels, had been granted release authority to fire these weapons without any further direction from Moscow.

General Taylor was in the group of daily advisors to the president. Speaking for the Joint Chiefs of Staff, Taylor recommended air strikes against Cuba, a naval quarantine of the island, and preparation for an invasion. On October 22, rather than immediately attack Cuba, President Kennedy decided to implement the first blockade. Kennedy's blockade was designed to prevent the Soviet Union from finishing the installation of missiles that could reach the continental United States. A naval quarantine of Cuba was immediately followed by alerting about 250,000 men of a possible invasion force. The United States called upon the Soviet Union to withdraw its missiles. Kennedy reserved air strikes as a last resort. The Soviet Union removed the missiles in mid-November, and the crisis passed.

Two weeks later the Joint Chiefs took the Chinese attack into India very seriously because they believed it could be part of a joint Soviet and Chinese initiative to break out of their current political boundaries. The Joint Chief believed this was an effort coordinated with the Cuban Missile Crisis to tempt the United States to overextend itself. The Cold War situation at that time was that NATO had blocked the USSR threats to Europe; our defenses in Korea had blocked that approach.

It was believed that the United States was on the edge of a nuclear war. General Taylor's staff was issued evacuation passes to go to their alternative underground command post. The most difficult thing Ted ever did in his life was to make a quick visit home to his wife to tell her to move to the basement and not get out on the highway. Mataxis believed it would be safer than any other available option. At this time, Shirley was working in D.C., Kaye was in high school, and Ted Jr. was a senior at Walter Johnson High in Bethesda, Maryland. On October 20, 1962, Ted Jr. enlisted in the US Army Special Forces Reserves. Like father, like son (and eventually like grandsons and a great-grandson).

The Sino-Indian War between China and India, mimicking other border skirmishes throughout the decades, occurred in October 1962. The Chinese invaded the Indian Himalayan border, called the North-East Frontier Agency. The Indians discovered Chinese individuals on Indian land and requested them to leave immediately; instead, the Chinese attacked in force. The Indians were routed and lost 16,600 square miles of their land. The Indians suffered many losses (1,383 KIAs, 1,698 MIAs, and 3,968 POWs). The Indian prime minister, Jawaharlal Nehru, had to ask for help from Washington and London.

1. ON ALERT SIGNAL - evacuate the city per Civil DEFENSE INSTRUCTIONS

```
DEPARTMENT OF DEFENSE EMERGENCY INSTRUCTION CARD
LAST NAME, FIRST NAME, MIDDLE INITIAL          GRADE OR RANK
MATAXIS, Theodore C.        COL, USA
TO:
UPON EVACUATION GO TO THIS EMERGENCY HEADQUARTERS OR ASSEMBLY AREA
The Pentagon Building
SPECIAL INSTRUCTIONS
Report to the PENTAGON - then
as directed (CATEGORY I).
KEEP THIS CARD WITH YOU      SIGNATURE OF HOLDER
AT ALL TIMES
DATE OF ISSUE                SIGNATURE AND TITLE OF ISSUING OFFICIAL

DD FORM 886
```

PRIORITY HELICOPTER EVACUATION WITH CHIEFS

This card was to be used in the event of the evacuation of Washington, D.C. due to nuclear deployment during the Cuban Missile Crisis in October 1962. Ted said the hardest thing he had to do in life was visit his family in Bethesda, Maryland, and tell them it would be safer to stay in their home than try to evacuate in the event of a nuclear threat.

General Taylor received a briefing on the Chinese attack and was told that they could not find an experienced US military person to accompany Ambassador Herriman on the special presidential mission. The consensus of the Joint Chiefs was that in conjunction with the Soviet movement of atomic missiles into Cuba, the Sino-Indian War was simply a minor part of a larger ploy by the Chinese and the Soviets to put pressure on the United States. These acts became a distinct part of the Cold War containment strategy against communist expansion. President Kennedy immediately sent the Harriman Mission to India, and the mission was recognized as part of a presidential diplomatic mission responding to the Chinese attack.

General Adams was the commanding general of Strike Command (STRICOM), and since India was outside his area of responsibility, he needed an Indian specialist on his staff. General Taylor knew Col. Mataxis had years of experience in the area and asked him to consider the task. Ted called home and had Helma pack his Blues, fatigues, passport and $400 in cash. At his office he always maintained a fld duffel bag, which was most helpful. Helma then had to take this to the River Entrance of the Pentagon to drop off for Ted. The State Department insisted that getting immediate passports would be out of the question. After a brief phone call from the president's office the State Department immediately set up a passport team at the Pentagon and made it happen. The team left that night, flying in the "Drainpipe," which was a converted US Air Force tanker. Ted gave the ambassador a briefing enroute and the ambassador thanked him for presenting his thoughts to him. Ambassador Harriman realized there was a political side to the issue and a military side and told each group to work on their respective parts. When they arrived, the Indian staff was in a panic. Ted's job was to meet with his Indian Army staff college classmates and verify the information they were getting from the Indian staff during their briefing. The ambassador's team worked with a joint mission from Britain and Canada.

Upon arrival at the airport, Mr. Harriman told newsmen, "The American people and Government are keen to help India in their situation." All missions focused on assessing India's needs and making suggestions and recommendations for appropriate military assistance. As explained in Mataxis's papers, "Upon our arrival, the US and the British visited the Chinese attack sites in the northern frontier and the Kashmir region. We then met with Prime Minister Nehru and the Indian military, advising them on a phased build-up for their military, including what aid to request from the US, Britain, and Canada. The US even released a mothballed ammo factory from their war reserve stock."

While General Taylor was chairman, the deteriorating situation in South Vietnam increasingly occupied the attention of the Joint Chiefs of Staff. In early November 1963, a coup in Saigon resulted in the assassination of South Vietnam's President Ngo Dinh Diem, unleashing further political instability in South Vietnam. The Viet Cong and their North Vietnamese patrons exploited the turmoil by intensifying attacks in the countryside and against US military advisers in South Vietnam. In March 1964, Lyndon B. Johnson directed the Joint Chiefs of Staff to draw up plans for retaliatory air strikes against North Vietnam. Following trips to Saigon in spring 1964, General Taylor and Secretary of Defense Robert S. McNamara urged continued support of the South Vietnamese counterinsurgency effort, stopping just short of suggesting US ground combat involvement. They recommended planning air strikes and possible commando raids against North Vietnam, but the United States did not follow that course of action until later.

In 1963 Mayor Maslin from Ste-Mère-Église, France, and his family came to visit the Mataxis family, who were still living in Bethesda, Maryland. While Dr. Maslin visited the Pentagon to see General Taylor, he asked for assistance in obtaining material for the new museum Sainte-Mère-Église was building. General Taylor authorized Ted to research the captured German files in Washington to see what material would be useful for their museum. They also visited Vice President Johnson's office while in D.C. General Taylor then coordinated for both families to visit Eisenhower's farm at Gettysburg for a weekend. The Eisenhowers graciously showed them their farm and some of his

General Taylor presenting Ted with the Joint Service Commendation Award for his service to the Joint Chiefs of Staff.

paintings. The Maslin family concluded their visit with a trip to Fort Bragg, where they witnessed an airborne drop on Sainte-Mère-Église Drop Zone. The Maslins also presented the town's flag and a French flag to the 82nd Airborne Division's war memorial museum. This museum is in the center of the 82nd Division area and open to the public. It was dedicated to the 1,142 paratroopers killed in the 82nd during the campaign in World War II. Years later, Ted's grandson was a captain serving in Germany and visited the museum in Ste-Mère-Église. He was quite surprised to see his grandfather's picture on the wall with an explanation of his involvement with the museum.

In June 1964, on the 20th anniversary of D-Day, General Taylor and Colonel Mataxis went to Sainte-Mère-Église for the official opening of the museum. At the 1960 celebration, Colonel Mataxis, as the commander of the 505th Battle Group, had donated money to get the museum started. The 20th anniversary was a real gala event. General Taylor was supportive and contacted the army to release weapons, materials, and photos for the museum. The army also released copies of captured German maps and documents. Helma had gone to France a week earlier to visit the Maslins and was staying with them in Sainte-Mère-Église. While visiting the museum, she found out that the Seventh Army had not delivered the uniforms needed for the mannequins. So, she called the Seventh Army chief of staff and told him about the crisis. She explained that Generals Taylor, Gavin, and Ridgway were going to be in the official party for the opening of the new museum and celebrations. The next day, Sainte-Mère-Église had helicopters arriving with uniforms for the mannequins. Helma had saved the day.

On July 1, 1964, President Johnson named General Taylor the United States Ambassador to South Vietnam, and General Taylor retired from military service for a second time. In Saigon, Ambassador Taylor witnessed the introduction of American ground combat troops into South Vietnam. Upon arrival, Ambassador Taylor and General Westmoreland welcomed a brigade from the 101st Airborne Division. Both men had previously commanded the division and General Taylor's son was a captain in that unit when it arrived.

CHAPTER 11

Vietnam, 1964–66

After General Taylor retired, he was appointed as the Ambassador to South Vietnam by President Johnson and served in that position from July 14, 1964, through July 30, 1965. Ambassador Henry Cabot Lodge replaced him in August 1965. Before General Taylor retired, he asked Ted what he would like for his next assignment. Col. Mataxis said that he had visited Vietnam for 30 days when the French were fighting there and he had commanded an infantry battalion in World War II in Europe and the 17th Infantry Regiment in Korea; therefore, he would prefer field duty as a senior advisor to a corps in Vietnam. At that time, Vietnam was divided into four tactical corps, each with a US Army colonel as the senior advisor to the Army of the Republic of Vietnam (ARVIN) corps commander. In preparation for his upcoming deployment, his first assignment was to the Defense Language Institute at the Presidio of Monterey in July and August 1964 for language training. In September and October 1964, he attended the Military Advisor Training Academy (MATA) at the Special Warfare School, in Fort Bragg. The school prepared conventional US Army officers and NCOs for assignments as advisors and trainers to Vietnamese army units, familiarizing them with the tactics and techniques needed and a brief overview of their culture and language.

Mataxis was scheduled to arrive in Vietnam in January 1965; however, the senior American advisor in IV Corps was sent home due to a coup. The colonel designated to become the II Corps advisor was shifted to IV Corps. As a result, in October 1964 Mataxis received orders to proceed to Vietnam to become the senior adviser to II Corps in Pleiku, as part of Advisory Team 21. Mataxis said, "When I first came to Vietnam, I'd come from the Joint Chiefs with a background of the currently available intelligence. We knew the North Vietnamese were beginning to move their troops toward South Vietnam, stockpiling new weapons, and so forth in the area. So, when I came to Pleiku in October 1964, I looked at what we had in II ARVIN Corps, and we were running a peacetime Military Advisory Group (MAAG). We were housed in an excellent compound with flowers and so forth, and it was lovely."

General Westmoreland had a colonel as the United States' senior advisor at each of the four corps areas of operation to coordinate and execute the war as well as the internal development in each corps. In a presentation at TTU Mataxis stated, "During this advisory period, 1964/1965, the four corps senior advisors were General Westmoreland's field commanders, not only controlling advisory teams at corps, division, regiment, and battalion level, but also supervising the logistical and special unit advisory teams throughout the corps area."

Upon arrival in Vietnam, Mataxis reported in at Pleiku during the Montagnard Revolt, which became the focus of attention during his initial briefings at the ARVIN corps headquarters. While visiting Pleiku, he first met his counterpart, General Hue Co, the II Corps commander. The revolt took place in the fall of 1964. A Montagnard tribe uprising had taken place against a US Special Forces camp, and the Vietnamese advisors that were stationed at that camp, on the Cambodian border. The Montagnard tribes were the mountain people of Vietnam and were looked down upon by the Vietnamese. Early in the war, the CIA had initially organized, paid, trained, and equipped Montagnard camps, which were scattered throughout the border area to act as buffers to the Ho Chi Minh Trail. In 1964, the US Army was assigned these missions in an advisory capacity.

According to Mataxis, "These camps were assigned to the 5th Special Forces Group, who placed an A-Team at each location. The Montagnards revolted in several

Ted as senior advisor to the Commanding General of II Corps, which consisted of almost 50 percent of the land mass of Vietnam. So a lot of time was spent in helicopters checking the area of operations.

camps, killing some Vietnamese military advisors, and holding others captive. The Vietnamese moved in an infantry battalion against the camps, and the Montagnards surrendered. The Vietnamese identified 35 or 36 of the Montagnards' senior organizers who had been NCOs under the French in the 1950s and were going to execute them. I talked to the corps commander, General Hue Co, and suggested that this would be a disaster and raise human rights issues at home. I said, 'Now, I can resolve this for you. If you give them to me, I will form an "Eagle Flight Strike Force," and I will furnish half of an A-Team to put in charge of the men. Then anytime we get into action somewhere, and it looks like the advisors are threatened, we'll immediately launch the Eagle Flight reaction force, and you will provide an A1-E to provide tactical air support when we insert the Eagle Flight into the area.' General Co thought that was a good idea, and the Eagle Flights worked well." The A1-E Skyraider was propeller-driven, had excellent maneuverability at low speeds and it could carry a large amount of ordnance (bombs, cannons, and bullets). It had a long loiter time for its size and could continually stay on station, providing accurate fire with its ordnance. Mataxis observed, "These Montagnard leaders of the revolt were supposed to be executed for their part and were instead turned into an Eagle Flight Strike Force to support our advisors. Up until now, all we had were clerks and cooks in the advisory group, with nothing to hit back in the event of an attack except for these men and their personal weapons. Now we had a group of experienced guys, with air force dedicated aircraft support, led by our Special Forces. Now that was a win for all." Special Forces A-Teams are configured to have the capability of being divided equally so they are able to conduct two simultaneous operations. Mataxis recalls, "The Montagnards were very good, the Special Forces leading them were also outstanding, and they quickly developed a combat bond, a deep friendship, and respect. We had some other cases where a camp was surrounded, and the guys fought like hell, so it all depended on the psychological feeling of the people in the camp at that time. 'Maybe I can save my ass if I fight like hell.' They would go for it. But the Special Forces camps up there held the highlands. If we hadn't had those Special Forces camps, the other side would have taken it over completely, but we kept the highlands, so that was a very strategic move for us to have Montagnard tribes under us, led by our Special Forces."

"On my initial inspection in fall 1964, I found that our advisory compound was secured only by ARVIN troops. Having served in summer 1951 as a military observer with the French in Indochina, I vividly remember the advice of the French military, 'Never depend only on the Vietnamese troops for security—always secure your billets with your own troops.' When I asked where the US troops were to secure the compound, I was told that none were assigned, and the security was the responsibility of the ARVIN. Well, I knew we would soon have security problems, so I tried to put some security efforts in place such as barbed wire around the compound and having guards posted. Well, my deputy told me, 'The Vietnamese are guarding us; we don't need our security,' and I said, 'Hey, I've been there, done that, twice, and I won't accept American troops exposed to being surprised.' I didn't want to be blindsided, so I got a guard roster published. I next had complaints from the sergeant major that these people were working too hard to put them on guard in the middle of the night. I said, 'Well, I'm sorry, I hear you, but now do it!' They did it; however, they did it very reluctantly. So, I got up one night at 3 o'clock and went around to check my guard posts. Here I am, a colonel in the army checking a sergeant out on a guard post. I found the guy sound asleep at the entrance to the compound. I picked up his rifle and gave it to the duty officer, who was also sleeping instead of being awake. I gave him the gun and said, 'Hey, I want orders written for a General Court, which I will send to Saigon.' I knew it would not go through then; however, I wanted a wake-up call to our guys that we were in a dangerous position here and under the threat of an imminent attack. The senior JAG flew up from Saigon and said, 'Hey Ted, have you lost your mind?' And I said, 'No. Now you tell me what you recommend.' He said, 'Well, why don't you have a summary court.' I said, 'Fine. We'll put one in.'"

Additionally, Col. Mataxis placed a curfew on parties in rooms at the MACV compound. Mataxis noted, "One Forward Air Controller [FAC] didn't like the idea of having the bar shut down at 2300 hours. He was determined to let his feelings be known. The FAC calculated the pitch of the roof of my quarters. He decided it was such that they would drop their aircraft over the peak of my roof and run landing gear over the tile roof, making a loud noise in my room below. Their 'victory rolls' quickly stopped after I set the radio antennas up next to my room."

"However, I made my point; it was a dangerous environment that we were in. And I was proven right later because when they did launch their attack on the compound during Tet 1965, the guard at the gate, Specialist 5 Jesse A. Pyle, opened fire on the sappers coming in. The enemy lost the element of surprise and retreated under fire with their satchel charges only partially placed. Specialist Pyle was killed at the entrance, but that alerted the people in the compound. In preparation for an attack, I also had cement blocks to buffer the bottom rooms. Before they could shoot down the aisle and hit all the doors when they were opened, with the cement blocks, the guys could dodge in between and fire back. So, prudence paid off. 'Prior planning prevents piss poor performance.'" As a result of the attack, Specialist 5 Pyle was the only person killed while warning the compound; he was awarded the Distinguished Service Cross. There were 24 WIAs during the attack.

"II Corps was also known as Military Region 2 (MR2), covering almost half of Vietnam. It was referred to as the Central Highlands of Vietnam and situated to the north of the capitol of Saigon. The corps boundaries extended from the mountains on the western boundaries of Cambodia and Laos through the lowlands to the areas of sand flats on the coast. The Annamite Mountain chains were jungle-clad and merged into Laos and Cambodia; a high plateau lay between. The heavily populated areas in the plains were near the ocean and were populated by Vietnamese peasant rice farmers. The II Corps area consisted of 12 provinces from north to south: Kontum, Binh Dinh, Pleiku, Phu Bon, Phu Yen, Dariac, Khanh Hoa, Quang Duc, Tuyen Duc, Ninh Thuan, Lam Dong, and Binh Thuan. The corps area of operation was so large, I spent a lot of time in helicopters going from unit to unit. I used to fly around daily and had my sergeant major carry a Browning Automatic Rifle (BAR) with many clips. If we ran into action somewhere down the road, we could provide some covering air support from our chopper. We also had a box of water glasses with hand grenades; we'd fly high and shoot with the Browning Automatic Rifle at the area where the enemy was. Then we'd fly over the place, pull the pins, and drop the glasses so they'd break on the ground and the grenades would go off. That was the total of advisory fire support circa 1964."

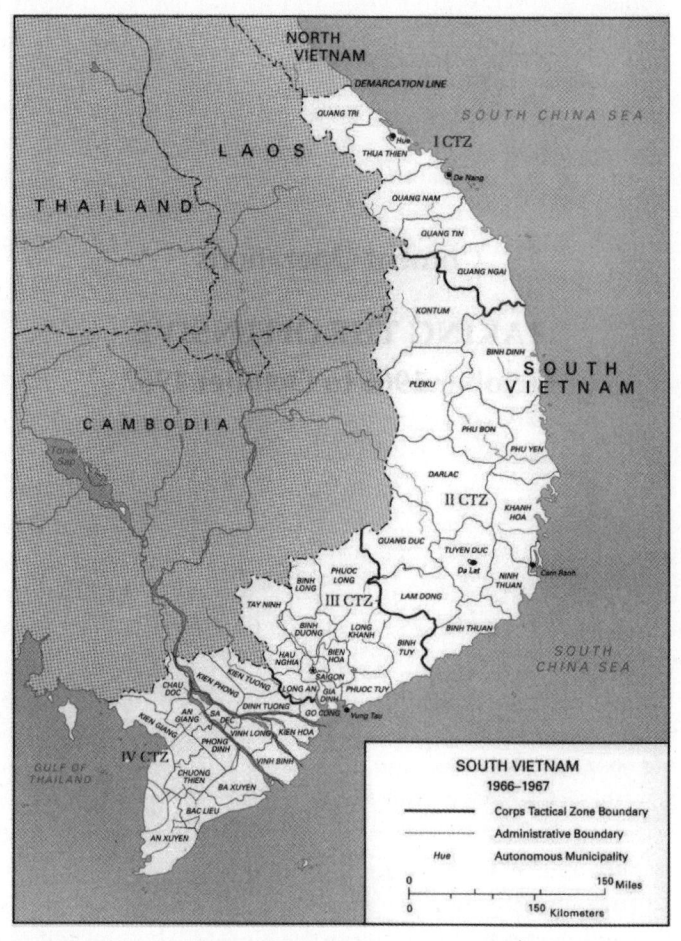

A military map of the II Corps area of operation in 1966–67. (US Army)

"General Taylor made a trip to Washington, and he was told by the president and the secretaries of Defense and State that there were too many coups in Vietnam. He was told to get those ARVIN generals together and ask them to get out of the coups and become unified. Ambassador Taylor had a great big dinner for them and gave a talk to them. A couple of days later, they had a mini coup. Taylor called in the senior generals and chewed them out. The ARVIN generals were extremely unhappy being talked down to like that, and they cut all conversation with the US military. They wouldn't accept telephone calls or anything else. Right after that happened, General Co, the II Corps commander, called me to his headquarters, and he said, 'Look, both sides are firm; each one's waiting for the other to come around.' He went on to say, 'Now you have worked for Ambassador Taylor, and he knows you. We want you to go down there and talk to him. This situation is impossible. You see what you can develop and let us know what we can do.' So, I flew down to Saigon, reported in first to General Westmoreland, and said, 'Sir, I'm down from II Corps.' He says, 'Don't tell me anything else, I don't want to hear anything about it.' Now, this was plausible deniability. He'd known through the agency what was happening, so he simply said, 'You just go see the ambassador, and then you can go back and talk to General Co. I don't want to hear about it.' I went in to see the ambassador, who said, 'Oh Ted, I'm glad to see you. How are things going and the wife?' because I worked very closely with him, being his speech writer in Washington. I finally said, 'Sir, I'm down here to bring a message from the corps commander. A group of three of the four ARVIN corps commanders are willing to get together with the Americans and resolve this affair.' He said, 'Ted, stop there. I am a representative of the president. I deal with the Vietnamese government. I cannot talk to dissident corps commanders; do you understand that?' 'Yes, sir, you're the ambassador. You can't talk to these dissidents.' And then he said, 'I understand you have my son up in the area with the 101st Brigade,' and then when I got ready to leave, he said, 'Colonel,' and I stood at attention and said, 'Yes sir!' He says, 'I'm giving you an order. What did I tell you?' 'You said, sir, that you cannot deal with dissident corps commanders,' He said, 'Do you understand me?' I said, 'Loud and clear, Mr. Ambassador, loud and clear. I will carry that message to the corps commander.' And then he said, 'Goodbye,' and I took off to II Corps. On return to Pleiku, I saw the corps commander, and he wanted to know what went on. So first, I was very prudent. I said, 'Ambassador Taylor heard what you had to say and so forth and so on, and he thinks it's very loyal and patriotic of you to try and take these actions on your own, which could be misconstrued by your contemporaries.' So forth and so on. 'But he recommended for you people to go and see his deputy, Hugh Alexis Johnson. In that way, it removes a confrontation between our two countries. Here you guys can negotiate out the back door.' And that's what they did. General Co was pleased with that. They got together, and the problem was resolved." General Nguyen Ky's book, *How We Lost the Vietnam War*, covers this issue. He gives their approach, how the Vietnamese generals felt, how unhappy they were with Ambassador Taylor, and presents the ARVIN perspective of their side of the incident.

Mataxis said, "When I initially reported to the highlands, the roads from Pleiku to Saigon were open. The VC guerrillas intermittently interdicted them. We could drive a sedan down from Pleiku on Highway #14 to Ban Me Thuot, then on to Saigon. Highway #1 was open along the coast and the railroads ran from Saigon to Hue. The railroad was interdicted and was also blown up from time to time. They would go along with work trains and repair the bridges and so forth so they could run the trains. Now all this started to change in November 1964. At this time, the VC and the North Vietnamese stepped up the war considerably. They started interdicting the roads more seriously and going after the gasoline trucks. The gas trucks could use the roads by paying taxes, thus allowing the big gas tankers to run up and down the roads and supply the highland cities. Gas and food trucks were critical in supplying the province of Bien Dien. One of the initial attacks there, by the VC, was the attack laid on in December 1964 against the city of An Loc and the An Loc valley. The VC came out of the hills in estimated regiment strength in this area, knocked off An Loc city, and destroyed an ARVIN unit with a strength of about 300–400. We deployed a counterattack with a couple of battalions in the area. Our first battalion going into the valley got hit badly, taking out some of their armored personnel carriers. When we realized the VC would stay here in strength and fight, we moved several other battalions by helicopters right into An Loc city. However, we had so much pressure throughout the region that the VC moved back to the hills after staying around and operating with several battalions. We eventually had to pull out and turn the An Loc valley over entirely to the North Vietnamese. That was the first time this had happened. The second time the NVA [North Vietnamese Army] came out with regimental units, attacked and fought us to a standstill, we had to give up a section of the II Corps."

On February 16, 1965, a North Vietnamese 100-ton naval trawler was attempting to unload supplies and munitions in South Vietnam. A medevac helicopter spotted the unloading. The South Vietnam Air Force then launched an A-1 Skyraider aircraft, which sunk and capsized the ship. The ship was located in Vong Ro Bay. Recovered from the trawler were an estimated 100 tons of Soviet and Chinese-made war materials, including 35,000 rifles, submachine guns, a million rounds of small arms ammunition, 1,500 grenades and 2,000 mortar rounds and 500 pounds of explosives. This was the first proof positive that North Vietnam was using ships to infiltrate supplies into South Vietnam. The NVA had five sea routes in addition to the Ho Chi Min Trail.

Mataxis remembers, "Then in January, things went along very smoothly. Very little happened, and we started getting rumors of many VCs in the area from all friendly civilians and military and the Vietnamese peasants. The morning of February

Ted inspected captured weapons and equipment after a North Vietnamese ship was grounded in Vong Ro Bay. The sinking of the North Vietnamese ship was the first proof that the North was supplying arms in South Vietnam by sea. The NVA had five sea routes in addition to the Ho Chi Min Trail.

7 at 2:00 a.m., their attack came on Pleiku. The attack on Pleiku was not a single attack. They attacked the compound where the advisory group lived and attacked the airfield. The airport was attacked, with forces blowing up the airplanes with charges on the planes and heavy mortar fire on the living quarters of the 52nd Combat Aviation Battalion. When this happened, Bill Mauldin, of World War II fame, was in my hooch at Pleiku, and his son was the airfield officer on call that night. The following day Ambassador Taylor came up with Mr. Bundy from the president's staff and toured the barracks. This was a real shock for our good civilian friend Bundy; he came into some living areas just a few hours after the attack, and there were still sections of the bunks blown down with pieces of flesh and body parts lying around. He was pretty shaken up. Soon he and Ambassador Taylor returned to Saigon. When they returned, they immediately called for an air attack on North Vietnam. At the same time, the VC launched their counterattack on the Thuy Hoa Airfield and city and set fire to the gas lines at Thuy Hoa. We lost the whole northern section of the Bien Dien province. There were several district capitals lost at this time. South of Bong Son, the road was completely cut off to the Phu Cat area."

"In fall 1964, ARVIN troops had gone into pacification operations, and we were 'going to win the hearts and minds of the people.' General Westmoreland wanted to break up the ARVIN regiments and put their battalions down in various district levels to help the people pacify the countryside. General Co resisted this; the ARVIN II Corps commander finally agreed when General Westmoreland insisted this be done. General Co said okay. They would implement the instructions and see what happened."

Mataxis observed, "In the northern district, we had one battalion of the 40th Regiment placed up against the II Corps boundary in the north of the district. Then around the Bong Son area, he had placed another battalion, then south of Bong Son, there was a third battalion. When the enemy attack was launched against a smaller force, most of the ARVIN 40th Regiment was wiped out. We had about one battalion and a couple of companies left. General Co was very unhappy about this, and he had said this was the danger of breaking down units when large-scale enemy troops were in the area. Unfortunately, this situation is one case where the advice I'd given was wrong. General Co had warned me of the dangers ahead. MACV had pressed me so much to be a good soldier that I did what I was told. General Co feared that would happen, and it did happen; and the advisors were wrong. You can't break down your front-line troops to support pacification when large-scale enemy troops are concentrated against you. The attack on Pleiku was a coordinated, significant-scale attack that nearly wiped out a regiment and took the whole northern area of II Corps. Taking the whole northern Bien Dien area from the Vietnamese, they cut the road north and south of Thuy Hoa on Highway #1 and blew the railroad throughout the entire section. The railroad was unable to open for some time. Then a week later, VC came in and blew up the four-story hotel, which collapsed completely. The next day they then attacked Quan Yen. It was a very dangerous time."

"You can imagine the chaos. The hotel was blown up, the city was completely cut off, and the fishing boats were coming across. We had rules of engagement and so forth at this time. The province chief came into the office. He asked for help from the gunships, so we quickly got some gunships in the air, flew over the harbor area, and they shot the hell out of the fishing fleet that was invading across the canal. This point was tricky since some State Department people thought we were shooting at poor fishermen that the VC forced to do their bidding. All the ARVIN and their advisors agreed that if we let these two or three companies get into the middle of town, we would have lost that city completely. That would have thrown Bien Dien into VC's hands."

In October 1965, Ted wrote an *Army Times* magazine article called "The War in the Highlands—Attack and Counterattack Along Highway 19." The article covered the close air support operations during the advisory campaign on Highway 19. Mataxis stated, "The ARVIN had a unit trapped along the HW. There were no ARVIN lift helicopters to pull them out. This battle was the first use of US fighter-bombers in Vietnam. We had sent a request down to MACV. I called General Westmoreland and told him that, 'The Vietnam troops are failing, they had been completely whipped in the battles in February; they are isolated along HW 19. We sent a regular battalion down HW 19 to free one of the isolated units, it was defeated very bitterly and driven back. The Vietnamese wouldn't move anymore, saying it was just like in 1954, the same area where the French Group Mobile had been wiped out in 1954. One of the trapped units was within the site of the monuments of the French failure on Highway 19 in 1954.' Some arranged for fishing boats on the coast to flee to the Philippines." Mataxis stated, "General Westmoreland gave the OK to use US fighters and bombers in the area. We had F-100s go in on the north side of the road, B-52s on the south of the road, with helicopter gunships firing at both sides of the road.

The lift helicopters came in and landed at the three isolated surrounding units. We were able to extract all units by the suppressive air fire from gunships. Only the last chopper to lift off received a few rounds of mortar fire and had a couple people wounded but it was a very successful operation. Westmoreland had approved moving the US 173rd to Pleiku to free up ARVIN forces for the operation."

Following the attack along Highway 19 and the cutting of the highlands, things quieted down for a couple of months; then the summer monsoons started. The VC came out of the hills and used even more NVA regiments. Mataxis wrote a draft manuscript called "The Monsoon Offensive of the Highlands," covering the plans that MACV headquarters made. He said, "The decision was made to use the troops that we had available, the Vietnamese Marine battalions and an airborne battalion, flying them with C-123s and shifting them from one place to another. We were taking the risk of scraping all available ARVIN troops from the areas that were not under attack and moving them to reinforce the areas under attack. This was a massive gamble at a critical time. Therefore, Tet 1965 was significantly more dangerous than 1968. At this time, the VC launched a series of attacks in the highlands, cutting off every district town from every province town and every province town from one another. All the Special Forces camps were cut off as well. We ran into a big problem running out of food in some locations. All resupplies had to be done by helicopter."

"Now operations between the Vietnamese and Americans started to take place with the arrival of the first American troops. This timing seemed to coincide with introducing the NVA regiments and American soldiers into the highland area and along the coast. The concept of operational coordination between the ARVIN and US troops was first announced by Secretary McNamara in spring 1965. McNamara had a press conference and announced the introduction of NVA units in South Vietnam had resulted in such an increase in enemy forces that the ratio of combat power had become unfavorable against the South Vietnamese. There had been no prior 'Concept of Operation' between the allied and ARVIN forces. McNamara stated, 'Therefore, we are seeking to correct the unfavorable land power balance by additional combat forces from other nations: Australia, United States, and Korea.' His announcement to deploy US troops and free world forces in South Vietnam initiated a series of questions by the reporters regarding the mission that would be assigned to US troops and Allies when they reached Vietnam. As the Secretary of Defense explained, their initial mission was to protect the base where the US heavily concentrated fighter-bomber aircraft, etc. McNamara also said, 'If the Vietnamese military commanders requested the assistance of US troops, they have the authority to send our troops and Allies troops in combat to support the Vietnamese.' This triggered a lot of questions by the Vietnamese reporters, and they asked what the future of the combat relationship between the US and Vietnam was to be? At this time, the secretary answered that the basis of future operations in Vietnam, the joining of US and ARVIN troops in a typical battle, was to be as follows: the battlefield would be split into segments, and the South Vietnamese forces would operate under their commanders as one component, and US troops and their commanders in support of Vietnamese forces as another. Now this announcement by McNamara was staffed by the Pentagon and MACV headquarters and formed the basis of operations for US and Vietnamese troops the whole time I was in Vietnam on this tour. Initially, II Corps would get together with General Jenna Lawson, who became the US 2 Field Force commander; he and I would get together to decide what we thought should be done. Then we would meet with the Vietnamese II Corps commander, II Corps forces, and the II Field Force Vietnamese and lay out a plan on what the 1st Cavalry Division could carry out on the one hand and the ARVIN 22nd Division and 23rd Division would carry out on the other. They were joined together to coordinate their areas of operation, each expected to stay in their sector of the battle."

"We had the concept of operational coordination at this time, and this was one thing that sounded good; however, it was challenging to live on the ground. In February 1965, the operations of the VC and NVA against the Vietnamese II Corps started with combined VC and NVA. Initially, our operations during the advisory startup period were relatively small-scale. We occasionally planned a few battalion operations; we would sometimes mount a full-scale regimental operation. Usually, this was mounted against the VC. By the time we got our troops together and moved out on operation, the VC had gotten information of it and had moved out of our way. At this time, most operations were done by a combination of US and ARVIN staff. When I was an advisor in II Corps, we had very few restrictions from higher authority, but there were some restrictions. Traditionally these rules of engagement, such as not firing until fired on and so forth, fell by the wayside once the firing started. We were not observed when we got on the ground and a man used his common sense."

"The advisor-counterpart relationship before US troops came in was straightforward; much of it depended on your relationship with your counterpart. Being an advisor is an interesting and subtle experience. You do it by raising questions. You listen to the general's analysis of a problem or proposal for the deployment of troops and request for US support. You offer comments stressing a bit of information not previously mentioned. You ask, 'Has the general thought of this?' or 'Has the general thought of that?' and that is how you get your point across. Certainly, we bring our views, but we do not necessarily prevail when there are differences, and there are relatively few differences."

Mataxis recalls: "I had two counterparts as the senior advisor to II Corps. The first one was General Hue Co, from September 1964 until June 1965. He went on to become the deputy prime minister of Vietnam. General Co was a very confident military commander, and most of our planning was done with my S-3 and his S-3. We'd sit around the table with a map and decide what would be done jointly. I would often travel by chopper with him or his chief of staff to ongoing battles to aid in any way we could, often helping with fire support, maneuvering, and medical evacuations. Then I would make the helicopters available for him and get together with the US Special Forces, and we would go forth and carry out our plans. The Special Forces occupied many camps scattered along avenues of approach into Vietnam throughout the area. At that time, as the senior American advisor, I was responsible for ensuring the coordination and safety of all US operations in the corps." When General Co departed, he gave a farewell party to the corps staff's US advisors. The highlight of the party was a presentation to Col. Mataxis, his senior adviser, of a stuffed tiger. After the party, Colonel Mataxis proudly carried the gift to his room in the MACV compound and plopped it on the floor. Colonel Mataxis owned a living cat of uncertain parentage. Mataxis described his cat's reaction as follows. "As the tiger took up its place in the center of the room, my cat took one horrified look, his hair on end, arched his back, ripped his claws vaguely in the direction of the jungle version of his genus feline, and retreated stiff legged under my bed. He has remained there ever since. He takes his meals under the bed, one wary eye on the monstrosity that has come to live with him. I haven't yet figured out a solution, but the tiger is such a conversational piece that the domestic cat must adjust to the intruder." A young II Corps advisor, S. Vaughn Binzer, recalled, "On a hot night, I was in his quarters for comments and approval of an operations order. Mataxis read through the mammographic master, made a few suggestions, and approved the order. All the time he was reading, I was seeing something that looked like a huge tiger, in the darkness of his room. It was a real stuffed tiger." Mataxis always enjoyed the various responses of those who entered his quarters.

Mataxis goes on, "The next counterpart was General Vin Loc, and our relationship was a little more difficult initially. When working together we would have to develop a plan through the advisory side and decide what we thought should be done. Then I would personally go to General Vinh Loc and sell this to him. This was rather difficult at times because initially when he was assigned, he was unsure of himself and wanted to ensure that I got with him so that he could have a plan that looked pretty good. Then we would call a meeting of his staff and mine

Ted's tiger was presented to him by his counterpart, General Hue Co, the II Corps commander. Given as a sign of respect, it was killed with a spear by a Montagnard of II Corps near Pleiku.

Lieutenant General NGUYỄN-HỮU-CÓ
　　Deputy Prime Minister
　　　Minister of War
　Secretary of State for Defense

REPUBLIC OF VIETNAM

Colonel Theodore C. Mataxis
Dep. Dir. of Operations
ODCSOPS, DA
Washington, D.C. 20310

Dear Colonel Mataxis:

　　　I have just received your and Colonel Nguyen Vinh Xuan's letters. The missives reached me at a time when I was preparing to leave for the Second Corps Area where I shall spend Christmas with some of the units stationed there, especially in the Highland. It is my intention to commemorate this year the birth of Christ with a front line unit in Kontum province.

　　　But I have to tell you I shall cherish forever the happy memories of Christmas 1964 in Pleiku and, more particularly, the sight of you drinking glass after glass in an effort to share with us our joys and sorrows. Neither shall I ever forget the many visits I made to Lam dong and Quang duc on New Year Day.

　　　These were also the happiest days of the Second Corps Area for, two short months after, new developments took place in the mountains that mark a new phase in the history of South Vietnam. History will say that during the darkest days of the Second Corps Area, I had the unlimited assistance of U.S. officers then serving at my headquarters. It was thanks to our common determination as well as the spirit of service that animated all of us that the people of Kontum and Pleiku resisted the ever-increasing pressure of the enemy so successfully that my last six months there resulted in the victories at Kannack, Hoai an, Bong son, Tam quan, etc...

　　　Early last November, I revisited the 22nd Division now under the command of Colonel Hieu and I had the opportunity to re-live some of the experiences I had with that unit. On the coming Christmas, I shall also have similar occasions and shall pray for the rapid restoration of peace in this our land.

　　　My wife joins me in extending our very best wishes to you and your family for a most enjoyable Yuletide season and a successful New Year for you and your country.

　　　　　　　　　　　　　　　　Sincerely,

　　　　　　　　　　　　　　　　Nguyen Huu Co

This letter was sent to Ted by General Hue Co, Ted's first counterpart, with Christmas wishes for Ted and Helma six months after his return to the United States.

```
              HEADQUARTERS
       II CORPS AND TACTICAL ZONE II
       Office of the Commanding General   Số ϕ/44  /VPT
            APO 4579, VIETNAM
                                    27 January, 1966
```

Colonel THEODORE C. MATAXIS
   C.O. II Corps Advisory Group
               PLEIKU

Dear Col. MATAXIS,

    I have read with great pleasure your article "The VC Summer Monsoon Offensive in the Highlands" and found it, not only highly informative but also most interesting.

    I think that nobody else could have described, with more accuracy and details than you have done, the deplorable situation which reigned over the Highlands during the 1st semester of last year. With our common efforts, ARVN initiative has been regained and VC inflicted the heaviest losses they have ever suffered. The storm is over and now it is the finest weather ever enjoyed by the Highlands. From now on, ARVN and US FFV build-up would never allow the VC to gain back their initiative in II CTZ.

    I thank you very much for having endeavoured to present the true situation in the Highlands and the efforts and progress made by II Corps units.

    I only regret that not much has been said about the worst hardships and tremendous job endured and achieved by the US Advisors and too much has been said about me, which I myself sincerely feel not so praiseworthy.

    I believe that your article will be of unvaluable benefit for all advisors having cooperated with us and also for those to come in the future and kept as a souvenir of the time they have spent in the Highlands.

    Once again, I highly appreciate your friendly kindness reserved for me in the review of your fine article and look forward to its publication.

                                    Major General VĨNH LỘC
                                          Commanding,

This letter was sent to Ted by his second counterpart, General Vinh Loc, in January 1966. These show the significant relationships that were formed when he served as a senior advisor.

VIETNAM, 1964–66 • 153

jointly. He would come out, look at the map, walk over, and put on quite a play of estimating the situation. Running down the various courses of action of what we could do, finally selecting the one we had decided was best for him in the previous meeting. So, this was a case of an advisor having to try and figure out what his counterpart wanted, how he worked, and how to get done what Saigon wanted done."

"It is fascinating that if the commander wanted to avoid doing what was suggested, they would hesitate, beat around the bush for a while and just sit there and not move out of their office. We discussed everything under the sun until we got it across that this would make General Westmoreland very happy, and he wanted it done. I would assure them, 'Yes, General Westmoreland wanted this done, and I have talked to him.' Well, things would fall in place about that time, and they'd start moving on it. When we finally worked it out this way from the G3 level to chief of staff to the commanding general, we usually got things done. I'd say about 50 percent of them would get done at the staff level, another 40 percent done at the Chief of Staff level and the last 10 percent or maybe a little less would be done by the general himself."

General Vinh Loc and Ted at a ceremony in front of II Corps in Pleiku, Vietnam.

A second significant escalation came in June 1966, when the North Vietnamese regular army units (NVA) covertly infiltrated the II Corps ARVIN Highlands. This coincided with the arrival of the first American units in Vietnam. They then attacked the Duc Co Special Forces camp on the Cambodian border and isolated the district headquarters in Kontum and Pleiku provinces. The 1st/173rd Infantry Regiment was first followed by the 1st Cavalry Division and the Marines. As US troops were being deployed into Vietnam, they were authorized by the Pentagon to assist the Vietnamese by offering security to II Corps headquarters. The 1st/173rd was assigned to assist the Vietnamese II Corps, protecting Plieku. Plei Me was under siege by the North Vietnamese at that time. After the Vietnamese were relieved at Plei Me, the II Corps ARVIN commander, General Vin Loc, and his senior advisor, Col. Mataxis, could form a Vietnamese task force to relieve the besieged Duc Co Special Forces camp. They felt that the relief column to Duc Co would be ambushed, as was the case in Phu Bon the month before. They prepared the troops for this order to roll up in a defensive position when attacked and had the air force on strip alert.

They looked at this as an excellent chance to clobber the NVA troops which were concentrating for the attack.

Mataxis describes the events: "I was flying over the column when the NVA attacked the column. The initial attack came from the woods to the right of the column by about a battalion-sized element. They attacked in classic platoon rushes and cut the column, which rolled up into defensive 'bastions.' The close air support butchered these enemy troops in the open. All through the night, we continued the air strikes on the area surrounding the ARVIN. By morning, the enemy had withdrawn, and Duc Co was relieved. General Westmoreland and the senior Vietnamese general arrived to celebrate this victory to highlight the win over the North Vietnamese regular army. So, when Plei Me was threatened, the 1st Cavalry not only sent a brigade to garrison at Pleiku, as with the Duc Co Operation, but also offered artillery support when we were ready for a rerun on Duc Co. I took the assistant division commander (ADC) of the 1st Cavalry on a recon of the road to Plei Me and explained this was the third example of the 'Lure and Ambush' tried by the enemy this summer, even guessed correctly where the ambush would be when our relief column was en route to Plei Me. The ambush was a return to the Duc Co; a killing field."

The personnel on site at Plei Me were US Special Forces ODA-217, commanded by a captain with his team sergeant, MSG Everette M. Hamby, and 10 Special Forces soldiers, 14 South Vietnamese Special Forces troops, and a CIDG unit of 400 Montagnard tribesman with their families. At the time of the attack, two Americans and 85 Montagnards were on a mission 9 miles northwest of the camp, 40 Montagnards were conducting security patrols in the area around the camp, and 20 were at each of the listening and observations posts to the north and southwest of the camp.

The attack began around 5 p.m. on October 19 by initiating contact with a patrol and overrunning the post to the southwest. At the same time the camp received incoming from mortars and recoilless rifle fire. This was followed up with NVA attacks from the north and northwest and an hour later attacks from the south and east. This continued to be the pattern to keep the pressure on the camp. The camp received priority air support and fighter-bombers arrived at the station about 4 a.m. and more than 100 strikes followed over the next 26 hours. Reinforcements were requested as anticipated. That night Vinh Loc authorized a relief force consisting of an armored cavalry squadron, a Ranger battalion, and a few other units. It was known they would be ambushed along the way; after all there was only one route available. It was expected to take several days to get to Plei Me. Knowing this, it was critical to reinforce and resupply the base. The relief effort fell on the commander of the 5th SFG, Col. William A McKean, and he proposed that Maj. Charley Beckwith with 175 ARVIN Rangers conduct a parachute drop into the enemy's surrounding camp. Col. Mataxis disagreed and rejected the idea. Mataxis said, "It not only would be safer but also quicker to conduct an air assault to a location close to the camp and go overland for the link up." Beckwith's team was inserted early on the 21st about three miles from the camp and moved overland nearer to the camp but delayed, since the camp defenders might take them for the enemy. The next morning Beckwith told his men to "run like hell to the gates."

When Beckwith arrived inside the camp, he took over command. Col. McKean ordered them to "get outside the camp, rummage around, clear the enemy out of there." Beckwith complied and sent out two ARVIN companies and their advisors. They had 14 friendly KIAs, one of which was an American advisor. Beckwith recalled that later, saying, "We were all beginning to realize that we would be damn fortunate to get out of this camp alive." The 33rd Regiment continued to keep up the ground fire but did not launch the expected ground assault. The camp continued to pound the enemy regiment with American artillery and air power from the navy and air force. The following is quoted from an enemy soldier from the 25th Battalion: "The 33rd had taken more punishment than it could stand. Two of the regiment's battalion commanders were dead; the 2nd battalion had lost nearly 250 men, about half of its strength; the 1st and 3rd had suffered heavily."

Meanwhile, dispatch of the main relief force had been delayed by a disagreement between General Vinh Loc and Col. Mataxis. Mataxis wanted a larger relief force to counter the ambush everyone expected. Vinh Loc, however, considered the attack at Plei Me a possible ruse to lure South Vietnamese forces away from Pleiku, thus leaving the city unprotected. On October 22, General Larsen broke the stalemate by promising Vinh Loc that the 173rd Infantry Brigade troops would ensure the safety of Pleiku if he would commit his reserves to Plei Me's defense. Had the size of the relief force not been increased, the estimates would have been right on the mark. The relief force was increased to 1,400 and moved out tactically prepared for the ambush. The reserve battalion and a Ranger unit were airlifted into a position behind the suspected ambush site of the relief column with orders to sweep towards the highway on order. The ambush was initiated by the 32nd NVA Regiment of about 1,800. We had anticipated their move and planned for it with F-100 jet fighter aircraft and Huey gunships. Artillery support had been planned and was immediately provided. Some parts of the column did not fare as well, but the tactical air support paid off and by morning it was obvious the ambush by the 32nd Regiment had failed. It started to withdraw north of Ia Drang, near the Cambodian border. Despite the enemy being driven back, the convoy commander would not move until resupplied a couple of days later and was provided American artillery support. For the remainder of the way, the relief column only received harassing fire.

The 1st Cavalry Division conducted the first major battle between the United States Army and the People's Army of Vietnam in the Battle of Ia Drang. General Westmoreland had ordered this because of the strong attack on Plei Me and at Dak To. It was part of the Pleiku campaign, conducted early in the Vietnam War, which started with the siege of Plei Me at the eastern foot of the Chu Pong Massif in the

156 • RIDE TO THE SOUND OF THE GUNS

This iconic photo was taken in August 1965 after the Duc Co Operation in the II Corps region, with then-Major Schwartzkopf, General Westmoreland and Ted immediately after the battle. This was Major Schwartzkopf's first tour. Years later, he and Ted would serve together again. General Schwartzkopf went on to plan and lead Operation *Desert Storm*.

Central Highlands of Vietnam, in 1965. The 1st Cavalry Division, which had recently arrived in South Vietnam, took the fight to the NVA.

The Ia Drang Valley, South Vietnam, November 1965: the 1st Battalion, 7th Cavalry, under the command of Lt. Col. Hal Moore, was dropped by helicopter into a small clearing in the jungle on top of 2,000 North Vietnamese soldiers, who immediately surrounded them. A sister battalion, only 2.5 miles away, was chopped to pieces three days later. The actions at these sites constitute one of the most savage and significant battles of the Vietnam War. The Ia Drang battle took place November 16–20 at 1st Cavalry landing zones X-Ray and Albany. These airmobile insertions were on top of the NVA staging areas. During that period of four days the Americans had 234 men killed, and more than 250 wounded. The Ia Drang campaign lasted 43 days, resulting in 545 US KIAs with an estimated 3,561 NVA killed. This battle marked the term "Body Count" as the scoreboard of the Vietnam War.

Years later, Retired Lt. Gen. Hal Moore and reporter Joseph L. Galloway, both lifelong friends of Ted, wrote *We Were Soldiers Once… And Young: Ia Drang—The Battle That Changed Vietnam*. This became a movie of the same title, starring Mel Gibson and Barry Pepper, playing Lt. Col. Moore and Joe Galloway, respectively. This movie, from 2002, was said to be Hollywood's about-face, finally showing the Vietnam GIs in a less than dismal light. Up until this time the veterans of Vietnam were almost always portrayed in a bad light. This movie corrected that stereotype. Vietnam veterans finally received some credit for serving their nation. Retired Col. David Hackworth was the most decorated soldier in Vietnam, earning two Distinguished Crosses, nine Silver Stars, and nine Purple Hearts and according to him, "Moore's book is the best account of infantry combat I have ever read, and the most significant book to come out of the Vietnam War." After the book, YouTube did a tribute to Retired Lt. Gen. Hal Moore. Then, later, Mr. Joe Galloway narrated a tribute to all helicopter pilots of the Vietnam War called "God's Own Lunatics," which appeared in the 2004 documentary *In the Shadow of the Blade*. In May 1988, the US Army awarded Galloway the only Bronze Star Medal for Valor given to a civilian during Vietnam for helping rescue the wounded GIs in the Ia Drang Valley during the battle. Years later, the movie *Shock and*

Awe portrayed a group of journalists doing coverage of President George W. Bush's 2003 planned invasion of Iraq. Joe Galloway was played by Tommy Lee Jones.

In 2023, with the changes of names of military bases to politically correct ones, Fort Benning was renamed in honor of Retired Lt. Gen. Hal Moore, who served as both an infantry and a cavalry officer during his career. Fort Moore is the location of the schools for infantry and armor officers to receive their basic and advanced training. It also remains the home of the army's airborne and Ranger training centers.

This picture was taken with Ted's counterpart, General Vinh Loc, and Colonel Hal Moore at the ARVN II Corps headquarters. It dates from shortly after the famed battle of Ia Drang Valley. Hal Moore was promoted to colonel and took over the brigade. Hal Moore and Ted remained lifelong friends. Colonel Moore was Ted's operations officer during the Korean War. Fort Benning, Georgia, was renamed Fort Moore when the names of many military installations were changed in 2023.

As told by Mataxis, "In fall 1965, after Dak To and after the 173rd came up to Pleiku, things settled down for a while. Then the enemy relaunched a series of attacks. They attacked Plei Me, doing the same thing they did at Dak To. After the ARVIN relieved Plei Me, General Westmoreland gave the order to the 1st Cavalry to pursue the NVA into the Ia Drang. I had known Lieutenant Colonel Hal Moore from the 17th in Korea, when he was a young captain and when he was promoted to major; he became my operations officer for my regiment. I had also known Joe Galloway from his coverage of the summer offensive. General Vin Loc's troops were to be engaged along with American artillery support. I went to the 1st Division and got their artillery and air to support the ARVIN attack. We had anticipated where the attack would be on the column, and we blanketed the area with heavy artillery fire with devastating effectiveness. As a direct result the NVA attacked the column but didn't have enough troops to overpower the ARVIN troops."

According to Mataxis, "During this period, the ARVIN and American troops captured quite a few prisoners and were able to interrogate them and build a better picture of what was happening. Interestingly, numerous prisoners provided intelligence for the first time, allowing us to return to each province, particularly Pleiku and Kontum. We screened the reports on VC activities that we had gotten from the Montagnard villagers, with other information received by other villages. We matched up these reports to see which were true and which were not. This proved to be an intelligence windfall. About 15 percent of the information we were getting about the VC activities was factual. The VC knew the villagers would pick up on their movements, so they passed several cover stories and rumors. We got such a flood of information we were not able to ascertain what was true and what was not."

At this time, the US I Field Force Vietnam (IFFV) had moved in, and Lieutenant General Larson was in charge; so the Americans were running an American war, with the Vietnamese running their own. There hadn't been much chance for coordination, so General Westmoreland had a meeting where he called the Vietnamese and the American troops together and presented his plan for controlling the combined operations with the Republic of Vietnam forces and the United States forces. Included in this meeting were General Westmoreland, Lieutenant General Larson, General Vin Loc, Col. Mataxis, and some other staff officers from MACV. General Westmoreland decided to make the US IFFV commander a US three-star position, the new senior advisor to the ARVIN II Corps commander. This put the Vietnamese noses out of joint because they felt this was putting them in a secondary role in their own country. The United States was taking things over. It was like we were saying, "Step aside! We know how to run all these things after a couple of months in country." There could be no other way for the ARVIN to interpret that action. Col. Mataxis had been doing that job since October of 1964 and was now being replaced by an American three star, who had just recently arrived in Vietnam. Col. Mataxis argued vigorously against this, saying, "Look, we needed to keep the US MAG in Korea. That way if you wanted to work with the Koreans, you had an American advisor sitting in the hip pocket of the Korean commander and they were talking to each other, understanding each other, and working closely together. Here you will break it up, and you'll have the guy sitting down in IFFV telling the fellow on the hill what he wants him to do, basically, and having a US colonel there to ensure these things are done. I think this is wrong. This will break up the close coordination you need."

The ARVIN II Corps commander had two missions. His first mission was tactical and operational control of all divisions and troops in his area of responsibility. The second mission was the responsibility of overseeing the province chiefs who ruled over the people. These local province chiefs and district chiefs worked closely with the people and provided government support and coordination as required. Mataxis stated, "It's imperative that we can protect those people and provide security for them, that's what this war is all about; without the people's support we cannot win this war. Going off and chasing the VC and NVA in the woods won't do it. In addition to that, the Vietnamese will also have a system in place for the ARVIN when we leave." In a letter years later, Ted said, "So that was the end, and we shifted to the combined operations. I thought it was wrong at that time, and I still do, because we lost track of fighting to control and protect the people. It's the people, stupid."

"Westmoreland was pissed off at me, and he said, 'Ted, you're getting more like the Vietnamese instead of sounding like an American officer.'" The Vietnamese knew that Col. Mataxis would get whacked on the head for speaking out on their behalf. The Korean Military Advisory Group (KMAG), officially the United States Military Advisory Group to the Republic of Korea, was a US military unit during the Korean War. It helped to train and provide logistical support for the Republic of Korea Army.

Gone was the day of the Vietnamese infantry commander and his US counterpart facing the enemy on the ground alone. In a January 27, 1966 letter to Col. Mataxis, General Vinh Loc states, "I only regret that not much has been said about the worst hardships and tremendous job endured and achieved by the US Advisors and too much has been said about me, Which I myself sincerely feel not so praiseworthy."

Mataxis goes on to say, "I transferred to the 101st Airborne Brigade as the deputy commander. The Vietnamese were very happy with me, and we had been through Tet 1965 together. The ARVIN presented me with a very high Vietnamese decoration, one of the first the Americans had received during the war. This helped when I came back later in 1971 as chief of the Cambodian mission. I could go to an ARVIN general and sit down with him, discuss our needs and he gave me 10,000 shotguns for my village defenders and other things. I had a close personal rapport with the ARVINs, the only kind you can get when you've had guys who've fought together and trusted each other's lives on something."

In January 1966, Mataxis joined the 1st Brigade of the 101st as deputy commander to Col. James S. Timothy, the outgoing commander. Mataxis stated, "When I arrived at 101st Brigade, I had the expectation of taking over the brigade. Instead, General William Pearson was brought over from the 101st Division, where he was the deputy commanding general. He arrived at the end of January 1966, and I became his deputy. He was a good man and we worked well together. After I arrived, one of the first things I did was establish a standard operating procedure (SOP) that I drew up for US troops when working with ARVIN troops. Whenever we moved into a district or province, I'd go in to see the province chief, and they had known me for the last 18 months as an ARVIN advisor. They knew I had worked well with their generals and had their trust and respect. So, I could tell them, 'Hey, we need so many Regional Force platoons to go out with our artillery or other troops to guard roads or bridges,' and they would. So, our troops would have the local forces to assist them. If the brigade needed some ARVIN Regional Force units to deploy, they could assist by defending critical locations. Our personnel would be able to conduct combat operations, not tied down guarding static positions. It worked like ham and eggs, and we just worked together. I developed a SOP checklist for integrating US military operations and indigenous resources, civilian and military. It worked very well because we were still short of US troops."

Ted took a Rest and Recuperation leave (R&R) to Hawaii to visit with Helma and they took a cruise. In a letter to Helma prior to the cruise, Ted said, "I am taking an

5317 BRILEY PLACE
WASHINGTON, D. C. 20016

June 14, 1977

Brig. Gen. Theo C. Mataxis (USA, Ret.)
Valley Forge Military Academy
Wayne, Pennsylvania 19087

Dear Ted:

Thanks very much for your nice note about my appearance on the Susskind show. I certainly appreciate your comments about the importance of the advisory chain and the unfortunate way in which we really overpowered the Vietnamese who I really do think could have been brought to carry the main load. It's a tough job trying to get the facts straight against the common myth these days, but I sign up for sessions such as the Susskind show in order to do whatever I can in that direction.

Thanks again for writing. I hope to see you in the coming year.

Sincerely,

W. E. Colby

This letter was sent to Ted from William E. Colby in June 1977. Mr. Colby served as the deputy to the commander of MACV, General Abrams, with the rank of ambassador. He was in charge of US support for South Vietnam's pacification program and later became the head of the CIA.

These pictures show Ted and Helma on a cruise ship in Hawaii during his last rest and recuperation (R&R) leave in 1965.

R&R on 25 July and really looking forward to it and being with you. As I have so often said, 'Those who are never separated do not realize the joy of reuniting.'" After the cruise, in a letter dated September 27, 1965, he said, "I too really enjoyed the R&R. I really believe it is worth being separated so that we can realize how much we do love each other and do not take it all for granted and become complacent."

Mataxis stated, "When I arrived at the 101st Brigade, the troops had added two new scrolls to the 101st Airborne Division Screaming Eagle patch. Above it, it said, 'If you ain't,' and below it, it said, 'You ain't Shit.' I wrote a letter to S. L. A. Marshall, whom I had assisted with the book *Pork Chop Hill*, about my regiment, the 17th Regiment, in Korea. I invited him to Vietnam to do a book on our brigade. The 101st Separate Brigade Task Force was used like 'the firemen of the war,' being sent from one crisis to the next, putting out hot spots wherever they happened. This had the makings of a good book."

For its actions in Vietnam between July 1965 and October 1966, the brigade was awarded a Meritorious Unit Commendation:

>HEADQUARTERS
>UNITED STATES ARMY VIETNAM
>APO San Francisco 96307
>
>GENERAL ORDERS
>24 May 1967
>NUMBER 2337
>
>AWARD OF THE MERITORIOUS UNIT COMMENDATION
>1. TC 320. The following AWARD is announced:
>
>**Awarded:** Meritorious Unit Commendation
>**Date of Action:** July 1965 to October 1966
>**Theater:** Republic of Vietnam

Reason:
For exceptionally meritorious achievement in the performance of outstanding service: The 1ST BRIGADE, 101ST AIRBORNE DIVISION distinguished itself in support of military operations in the Republic of Vietnam during the period July 1965 to October 1966. Selected to be the first CONUS based unit to fight in Vietnam, the 1ST BRIGADE, 101ST AIRBORNE DIVISION has fought brilliantly, establishing a pattern of resounding victories in every major Viet Cong and North Vietnamese Army encounter and rendering ineffective several hostile battalions and one complete regiment.

Superb in its adaptation to jungle counterinsurgency warfare, the 1ST BRIGADE, 101ST AIRBORNE DIVISION developed and implemented a centralized base camp organization which enabled it with spectacular success to improve mobility, conserve supplies, and release many additional men for forward deployment.

While carrying a prodigious combat load, the members of this unit selflessly contributed their personal time to more than 2000 civic action projects which included transporting and supplying over 12,000 refugees, providing medical care for over 37,000 Vietnamese in outlying areas, and improving the political, psychological, and economic conditions in every area in which they traveled.

The 1ST BRIGADE, 101ST AIRBORNE DIVISION's exceptional standards of administration, maintenance, discipline, and morale, achieved these remarkable results without interrupting the vigorous search and destroy mission. The tenacity and dedicated devotion to duty displayed by the members of the 1ST BRIGADE, 101ST AIRBORNE DIVISION were in keeping with the highest traditions of the military service and reflect great credit upon themselves and the Armed Forces of the United States.

Authority: By direction of the Secretary of the Army, under the provisions of paragraph 203, AR 672-5-1, and DA MSG 793617, 10 Dec 66.

The first battle for the 101st came in February, after General Pearson's arrival. Operations were intense. Lieutenant Colonel Hank Emmerson, commander 2nd/502nd, referred to as the "Gunfighter," had heavy contact aided by the 1/327, resulting in 26 KIAs and 28 WIAs of the task force. Operation *Van Buren* resulted in 679 enemy KIAs and 49 captured; additionally, 200 Viet Cong defected, resulting in a treasure trove of intelligence. Col. Mataxis's future son-in-law, Vernon A. "Bud" Isaacs Jr., was the platoon leader of an engineer unit that captured many NVA while conducting a bomb damage assessment of a B-52 strike.

One mission required moving 4,700 peasants to safe areas in Thy Hoa Province, away from the control of the VC. Lt. James A. Garner received the unit's first Congressional Medal of Honor during this mission. Major Dave Hackworth was the task force commander.

When Kaye's fiancée, Bud Isaacs, volunteered for Vietnam, her father Col. Mataxis had been in Vietnam since 1964. Kaye had asked her father to find Bud a "good job." In her mind this represented a comfortable desk job in Saigon. Ted interpreted this using his definition of a "good job" for an airborne Second Lieutenant, which could only mean riding to the sound of the guns wherever and whenever the action was taking place.

The following quote is from Bud's biography, *Oil and Water: An Oilman's Quest to Save the Source of America's Most Endangered River*, written by Stephen Grace in 2015: "Amid the chaos of war, killing enemies is easier than capturing them." During Bud's battle, his troops became the first group of American soldiers to capture a significant number of North Vietnam prisoners. In the crucible of Vietnam, Bud discovered in himself a willingness to accept risk if he believed what he was doing was right. He said, "I realized I was willing to stick my neck out." He went to war because he believed his country was threatened by the spread of Chinese communism throughout Southeast Asia, and he felt a connection to that part of the world after spending much of his childhood in Indonesia. Isaacs stated, "I took prisoners because it was the right thing to do; even though it was the harder thing to do."

Bud was the first non-West Point officer to be assigned combat duty with the 101st Airborne Brigade, a position sought after by "ring knockers," graduates of military colleges and universities. He pulled this off by dating a general's daughter. He married her after returning from his service in Vietnam. During his tour of duty, Bud earned a Combat Infantryman's Badge, Silver Star, Bronze Star, ARVIN Cross of Gallantry, and a Purple Heart. Bud had been featured in the book *Battle In The Monsoon: Campaigning in the Central Highlands, South Vietnam, Summer 1966* by military historian S. L. A. Marshall.

This was quickly followed up by Operation *Harrison* in March 1966, which was an air assault that inserted troops in a blocking position, closing off the enemy's escape route, and another element to force the enemy into the blocking position. It was a "hammer and anvil ambush" against a significant enemy element. Operation *Fillmore*, in April–June, saw the brigade characterized by the company-sized immediate reaction forces responding to intelligence gathered by the numerous small reconnaissance elements that swept the area of operation. These tactics proved very effective and kept maximum pressure on both the NVA and VC units in the area. In the next few months, the brigade was working on intelligence reports indicating a significant VC stronghold located somewhere along the boundary between II Corps and III Corps. During this operation, the brigade worked with ARVIN forces, Civilian Irregular Defense Groups, Popular Forces, Regional Forces, and the National Police. A series of operations, codenamed Austin I–III, drove the enemy back to Cambodia, engaging them along the way.

Operations *Van Buren* and *Harrison* would lead to another award for the brigade: the Valorous Unit Award.

HEADQUARTERS
UNITED STATES ARMY VIETNAM
APO SAN FRANCISCO 96307

GENERAL ORDERS
21 June 1967
NUMBER 3038

AWARD OF THE VALOROUS UNIT AWARD
1. The following AWARD is announced:
Awarded: Valorous Unit Award
Date of Action: 17 January 1966 to 25 March 1966
Theater: Republic of Vietnam

Reason:
For extraordinary heroism while participating in military operations:
  The 1ST BRIGADE, 101ST AIRBORNE DIVISION distinguished itself by extraordinary heroism from 17 January 1966 to 25 March 1966 while conducting Operations VAN BUREN and HARRISON against armed hostile forces in the vicinity of Tuy Hoa, Republic of Vietnam.
  After commencing Operation VAN BUREN on 17 January, the 1ST BRIGADE deployed in the Tuy Hoa area to locate, fix, and destroy Viet Cong forces, while simultaneously protecting the local rice harvest from hostile seizure. The 1ST BRIGADE not only defeated the insurgents decisively in four major battles but also enabled the Vietnamese people to harvest a rice crop triple that of the previous year, when Viet Cong interference was unchecked. At Canh Tinh on 6 February, the 2D BATTALION (AIRBORNE), 502D INFANTRY killed 64 Viet Cong and completely routed a numerically superior hostile force from heavily fortified emplacements. On the following day, the 1ST BATTALION (AIRBORNE), 327TH INFANTRY took a toll of 66 insurgents in a savage conflict.
  During Operation HARRISON, that began on 21 February, the 1ST BATTALION (AIRBORNE), 502D INFANTRY continued maneuvers in the Tuy Hoa area by searching out and destroying 118 of the enemy in a five-hour pitched battle in the rice paddies around My Phu. After three days of difficult marching through mountainous jungle, the 2D BATTALION (AIRBORNE), 327TH INFANTRY discovered a Viet Cong regimental headquarters. The men fiercely broke the hostile defenses that were in a nearly impregnable cave complex, and uncovered one of the largest caches captured in the counterinsurgency efforts.
  While suffering only light casualties in both operations, the 1ST BRIGADE killed more than 500 Viet Cong, wounded hundreds more, and captured nearly 500 insurgents and suspects. Not content with merely defeating the enemy, the men of this exceptional unit strengthened the safety and health of the local Vietnamese population by tireless efforts in medical treatment, road building and protection of the valuable rice crop. Their extensive military and civic accomplishments deeply depressed enemy morale and struck an irreparable blow to insurgency efforts in the vicinity of Tuy Hoa.
  The extraordinary heroism and devotion to duty displayed by the men of the 1ST BRIGADE, 101ST AIRBORNE DIVISION, were in keeping with the highest traditions of the military service and reflect distinct credit upon themselves and the Armed Forces of the United States.

Authority: By direction of the Secretary of the Army under the provisions of paragraph 202.1, AR 672-51, and Department of the Army message 793617, 10 December 1966.
FOR THE COMMANDER:
FRANK D. MILLER
Major General, US Army
Chief of Staff

According to Mataxis, "All battalions conducted routine patrols during this period of relative inactivity; however, the bulk of their effort was focused on rebuilding their strength, training, and resupplying equipment. The brigade ordered an intensive critique of prior unit actions from battalion down to squad level to record the lessons learned." The brigade established a replacement training center, for new personnel assigned to the brigade as they arrived in the country. The Screaming Eagle Replacement Center (SERTC) provided all new personnel with an 80-hour block of instruction during a six-day period. Conducted during the night and day, this allowed the trainee to be acclimatized to Vietnam and significantly increased the ability to survive during his tour. NCOs were selected to teach squad leaders from each rifle company for six days of intensive leadership training known as a Squad Leader's Combat Reaction Course. These two courses increased the survivability of new arrivals in the country and cut down on the casualties. The brigade command group understood the importance of teaching lessons learned by the soldiers who had gone before, remembering the old army adage, "Sweat in training saves blood on the battlefield!"

John Wayne visited the 101st Division in Vietnam in 1965, doing field research in preparation for his movie *The Green Berets*. Ted presented him with an AK-47 and an SKS. At that time collecting war trophies was very typical, as in World War II and Korea. The army has since changed its policy and this is no longer permitted.

Operation *Hawthorn* was conducted immediately after this period of R&R. The established training paid great dividends in this operation. The brigade was airlifted to Dak To, located in the heart of the Central Highlands of II Corps. This was Col. Mataxis's old stomping ground and involved several ARVIN units he had worked with as a senior adviser to II Corps. The NVA had had months of preparing their defensive positions throughout the area and they selected to stay and fight. It was fierce fighting, day in and day out, sometimes resulting in hand-to-hand combat. Ultimately, the NVA was pushed back into Laos, and the operation was the most successful in the war. The 24th NVA regiment had suffered over 1,200 KIAs and these statistics quickly established the brigade as "the best fighting unit in Vietnam."

On this first tour in Vietnam, Mataxis won a number of decorations for his actions while with II Corps and the 101st Airborne:

HEADQUARTERS
UNITED STATES MILITARY ASSISTANCE COMMAND, VIETNAM
APO San Francisco 96243

GENERAL ORDERS
25 April 1966
NUMBER 575

AWARD OF THE ARMY COMMENDATION MEDAL
(Third Oak Leaf Cluster)

1. 320. The following AWARD is announced.
MATAXIS, THEODORE C. 034035 COL INF USA

Awarded: Army Commendation Medal (Third Oak Leaf Cluster) with "V" Device
Date of Action: 21 February 1965 to 24 February 1965
Theater: Republic of Vietnam

Reason:
For heroism in connection with military operations against a hostile force: Colonel Mataxis distinguished himself by heroic action from 21 February 1965 to 24 February 1965 while serving as Senior Advisor to II Corps, Army of the Republic of Vietnam. Informed that a series of Viet Cong attacks had isolated several friendly units, Colonel Mataxis immediately proceeded to the besieged areas to observe the tactical situation. Disregarding his personal safety, Colonel Mataxis repeatedly landed in small areas held by the friendly forces while maintaining a close surveillance of the battlefields and directing the deployment of the relief forces and the units that were still under attack.

Colonel Mataxis exposed himself to hostile fire to personally direct a heliborne operation, which resulted in the successful extraction of the beleaguered friendly forces. Colonel Mataxis's heroic actions were in keeping with the highest traditions of the United States Army and reflect great credit upon himself and the military service.

Authority: By direction of the Secretary of the Army under the provisions of AR 672-5-1.
FOR THE COMMANDER:
W. B. ROSSON
Major General, USA
Chief of Staff

E. D. BRYSON
Colonel, AGC
Adjutant General

HEADQUARTERS
I FIELD FORCE VIETNAM
APO San Francisco 96350

GENERAL ORDERS
13 December 1966
NUMBER 552

AWARD OF THE BRONZE STAR MEDAL WITH "V" DEVICE
(Third Oak Leaf Cluster)

MATAXIS, THEODORE C. 034035 COLONEL INFANTRY, United States Army
Headquarters and Headquarters Company, 1st Brigade, 101st Airborne Division
APO San Francisco 96347

Awarded: Bronze Star Medal with "V" Device (Third Oak Leaf Cluster)
Date of Action: 4 March 1966
Theater: Republic of Vietnam

Reason:
For heroism:
Colonel Mataxis distinguished himself while serving as the deputy brigade commander performing a liaison mission for the brigade commander. When Colonel Mataxis arrived at the scene of battle at about 2000 hours, he was advised by the battalion commander not to land his aircraft as the Viet Cong were raking the area with a torrid volume of machine gun fire.

 Realizing the immediate necessity of his mission, the battalion commander guided the chopper in at Colonel Mataxis's command. The chopper landed without the use of lights, and Colonel Mataxis jumped out and sent the aircraft airborne. Colonel Mataxis was then briefed by the battalion commander on the battle situation. Next Colonel Mataxis visited all of the units in the 1st Battalion (Airborne), 327th Infantry so that he could talk to as many troopers as possible. In so doing, he personally assessed the actual battle situation.

 Throughout this time, he was subject to hostile fire but continued to visit all of the units. He insured all of the wounded were being cared for. His presence in the battle area greatly inspired the troopers amd was a rare form of battlefield leadership. His estimate of the situation enabled the battalio to mass susfficient power to give the enemy a stunning defeat. Colonel Mataxis's actions reflect great credit upon himself, his unit, and the Armed Forces of the United States.

Authority: By direction of the President under the provisions of USARV Message 16695, 1 July 1966 and paragraph 31a, AR 672-5-1.
FOR THE COMMANDER:
LINTON S. BOATWRIGHT
Colonel, GS
Chief of Staff

OFFICIAL:
WILLIAM H. JAMES
Colonel, AGC
Adjutant General

DEPARTMENT OF THE ARMY
HEADQUARTERS 1ST BRIGADE 101ST AIRBORNE DIVISION
APO San Francisco 96347

GENERAL ORDERS
17 October 1966
NUMBER 1060

AWARD OF THE AIR MEDAL FOR HEROISM
1. TC 320. The following AWARD is announced:

MATAXIS, THEODORE C. 034035 COLONEL INFANTRY USA
HHC, 1st Bde, 101st Abn Div, APO 96347

Awarded: Air Medal with "V" Device, Seventeenth Oak Leaf Cluster
Date of Action: 9 June 1966
Theater: Republic of Vietnam

Reason:
For heroism in connection with military operations against a hostile force: Colonel Mataxis distinguished himself by exceptionally valorous actions on 9 June 1966, in the Republic of Vietnam. While flying in a helicopter as part of a reconnaissance team, Colonel Mataxis released his safety harness and leaned out of the aircraft door with a flashlight in order to better spot obstacles on the proposed landing zone.

His action was particularly hazardous as the aircraft was being maneuvered down a valley at night and was required to avoid heavy ground fire being directed at it. Colonel Mataxis, by heroically disregarding his personal safety, was instrumental in the team's quickly finding an adequate landing zone on which urgently needed reinforcements could be landed. His initiative and conspicuous valor are in keeping with the highest traditions of the military service and reflect great credit upon himself, his unit, and the United States Army.

Authority: By direction of the President under the provisions of Executive Order 9158 as amended by 9242-A, 11 September 1942.

FOR THE COMMANDER:
J. G. BROWN
Major, AGC
Adjutant General

WILLIAM O. HORGEN
Captain, AGC
Assistant Adjutant General

CHAPTER 12

82nd Airborne Division, 1967–68

Mataxis returned to the United States in July 1966 after serving in Vietnam for 25 months. He had volunteered while in the Pentagon, working for General Taylor, in 1964 and was excited to return to the Pentagon after Vietnam. Col. Mataxis was first assigned as Chief of the Far Eastern Pacific Division at the Pentagon. Then he was appointed deputy director of operations in the office of the deputy chief of staff for military operations (ODCSOPS) for eight months. He was promoted to brigadier general on March 1, 1967.

Helma and the family had remained living in their home in Bethesda, Maryland, which they bought in September 1961, long before Ted's time in Vietnam. Once again (like after the Korean War), Ted was reintroduced to his significantly older family. His children were not 10, seven, and five years old anymore. They were now young adults with their own lives. Shirley (23) had a well-paying job in Washington that she genuinely enjoyed. Ted Junior (20) was going to college in Georgia and had been in the local Special Forces Reserve unit for the previous two years. Kaye (18) was engaged and planned to marry Bud Isaacs once he returned from Vietnam. The family had settled into civilian life without the general. They were living in their house and putting down roots in the local community and truly enjoying this time. Ted was genuinely baffled to learn that his children were not excited about moving to another military community, even with their father's newfound status as a general. General Mataxis was a little disgruntled and needed to recalibrate his family into the warrior's philosophy of life. He expressed his frustrations in a letter to his youngest, Kaye. The family had, in his terms, become "too civilianized during their extended stay in Bethesda."

In April 1967, Mataxis was assigned to the 82nd Airborne Division, part of XVIII Airborne Corps at Fort Bragg. Upon coming down on orders for the 82nd Airborne Division, he was required to attend the Senior Officers' Preventative Maintenance Course at the United States Army Armor School. Helma and the children would return to a military community. Even Shirley would rejoin the family for this assignment. Although they had never been to Fort Bragg, in many ways, it was like

> Dear Kaye   January 1965
>
> Mother's last letter mentioned that you missed me and wondered why I had to be away. I thought by now,, you as an Army brat would understand. I guess the last 4 years among civilians, who in most cases have a different view of life, than we in the military profession has been responsible for this question arising in your mind. So under these circustances I thought I would drop you a line and explain my feelings on this subject.
>
> First we in the military are old fashioned incurable romantics--we still believe that all brothers are courageous and sisters virteous--and we hold to duty, honor and country above all. We exist to carry out our role in life--that of a professional soldier--as the most rewarding profession that life has to offer us. We get our reward in serving our country. We fully realize what this all means--the vesry leasat is seperation from our families.
>
> We are fully aware of this commitment and that it may lead to being killed on a battlefield far from home. But once again we look at it differently--. When we hear of a friend being killed we grieve for his family it is true -- but for him we feel a kind of pride that he had the courage to full fill his duty to his country. So you can see dear that a soldier's life is built on completely different standards than a civilians -- I can not say our way is better -- all I can say is that is suits those of us who follow it. Just as those priests and doctors who feel dedicated to their profession above all other things including money and all of those mundande things so dear to our civilian brothers. I feel proud to be one of this "bree of cat" -- I cannot help it -- or take credit for it, it's just the way I am. I fully subscribe to the old Greek saying of preChristian days:
>
> "It is a great thing to fight, and die if you must, in defense of your land, your home and your own true wife and children".
>
> I realize that what I have written must sound corny to your generation -- and that perhaps you won't understand the feeling in the back of it. But dear, be assured that it is there so strong it impells me to do my duty in spite of myself -- even if I wanted to take another path -- my sense of honor as a soldier would force me to do what is expected of me by my country.
>
> Your mother realizes this -- of course she has put up with me for over a quarter of a century and through World War II, Korea, Kashmir and now this. And believe you me it is even harder on her--- wondering what is happening thaan it is for those of us out in combat. It takes a strong willed women to survive these years as a soldier's wife -- and I do take my hat off to her and all others who must suffer in similiar cases.
>
> Well enough of this dear -- I hope it gives you an insight into my feelings and the reasons for my presence here in Vietnam. We must fight communism here -- or closer to home --and here is best -- no matter what the cost to us -- or to our country.
>
>   Dad

This letter (excerpt) was written by Colonel Mataxis during his deployment to Vietnam, October 1964–July 1966, trying to explain to his young daughter who had lamented to her mother about her father's absence. This letter explains his philosophy on life and why it required his absence.

the family was returning home. Many personnel from Fort Benning, the 505th Battle Group in Germany, and the 101st in Vietnam had also been relocated to Fort Bragg. The kids were pleasantly surprised to see many of their old friends who now had parents assigned to Fort Bragg.

A significant family event occurred soon after that would change the family's dynamics permanently. In June, their youngest daughter, Kaye, married Bud Isaacs and was the first to permanently move away from the family's nucleus. Kaye and Bud had been engaged before Bud went to serve his year in Vietnam. Kaye patiently waited at home for his return. While in Vietnam Bud had served at the same time as Ted in the 101st Brigade, and they had established a solid relationship and respect for one another. The general tried to talk young Isaacs into staying in the army, explaining that he would be promoted to captain in just a few weeks.

Bud had served in Vietnam as a second lieutenant and first lieutenant as an engineer platoon leader. He earned a Purple Heart, Silver Star, Bronze Star for valor, Combat Infantry Badge, and the Vietnamese Cross of Gallantry. At that time the army was promoting officers to captain after two successful years.

Ted being promoted to brigadier general by Helma and his boss on March 1, 1967.

Bud had served the army and his country quite well and yet he told the general that there were other things he would like to accomplish during his and Kaye's lifetime. Bud's father had been a successful oilman, and Bud had been exposed to the business and excitement of that life and he wanted to give it a try. The general was baffled as to why someone wouldn't want to stay in the army and become a captain. However, Bud was right; the young man had other things to do. Bud and Kaye were married for 56 years, had a wonderful family, and had a remarkable life together before he passed away in February 2022. Bud was known for living his life fully while establishing his own company and raising a successful family. He will always be remembered as a successful oil man and conservationist for his work on reconnecting the northern Colorado River.

Several men Bud had served with in Vietnam in the 101st were now part of the 82nd Airborne Division and participated in the wedding. They had been rotated back to Fort Bragg after their tour in Vietnam. Because the 82nd Airborne Division was the only airborne division, many of the men had requested to be assigned there. The military had converted the 101st to an airmobile division during its time in Vietnam. Once again, the small airborne community allowed soldiers and their dependents to be reunited at Fort Bragg. Kaye and Bud were married at the main post chapel and had an engineer battalion provide an earthmover with 55-gallon drums chained behind it as their sedan from the post chapel to the officers' club for the reception. The family had rented several of the cottages available through the Fort Bragg Officers' Club then, and it was a reunion of old and new friends. They partied like only the 82nd can.

The 82nd Division was constituted on August 5, 1917, and was organized on August 25, 1917, at Camp Gordon, Georgia. Since its initial members came from all 48 states, the unit acquired the nickname "All American," which is the basis for the famed "AA" shoulder patch. When the airborne concept was developed in World War II the 82nd Division became an airborne division with a proud history. As a result, it has earned the reputation for maintaining the highest state of readiness throughout the years. Generations of veterans have lived up to the division's motto, "All the way!" or their unit song that starts, "We're All-American and proud to be." They indeed went "All the way!" Military units across the world describe themselves through various mottos. The mottos of the 82nd Airborne Division were: "All the way!" or "Death from above." At the same time, their marching song was "The All-American Soldier." Their jump wings were and are more than an admirable uniform accoutrement; they represent a way of life for those who followed the airborne tradition for their careers. These tight-knit soldiers fought hard, trained hard and partied harder. They are today's "Band of Brothers."

The XVIII Airborne Corps headquarters was located at Fort Bragg, home of the army airborne troopers. Fort Bragg had taken on the role of the United States Strategic Reaction Force in 1965. Fort Bragg was contiguous with Pope Air Force Base, the home of operations for the US Air Force's transport aircraft, making deployment time even quicker and facilitating the airborne training required to stay continually certified. Fort Bragg also evolved into the home of Special Forces at Smoke Bomb Hill in the 1960s. Twenty years later, it became the home of Joint Special Operations Command, JSOC, with additional specialized units, all of which required immediate deployment airlift capability, which is located on Pope Air Force Base. The aircraft are also used in maintaining the required proficiency of the airborne troopers. The airborne division and Special Forces attract personnel who want to be challenged in all ways. An assignment to the airborne was desirable for junior and non-commissioned officers, and the Department of the Army traditionally assigned the very best.

Major General Richard Seitz, commander of the 82nd Division from April 1967 to October 1968. At this time Ted was serving as his assistant division commander for operations.

The 82nd Division had over 13,000 people, who were all constantly on the go maintaining proficiency and developing their capabilities and conducting the day-to-day operations of a tactical division. Physical conditioning is one of the hallmarks and is stressed in all they do, not only in operational activities, training, and professional development, but during their time off, unit team competitions and individual competitions among the units, and unique activities in almost all sports and recreational activities enable all to try to become the best of the best.

In addition to maintaining proficiency in airborne training, daily operations, command post exercises, field training exercises, and running the various professional development courses and schools for the division's soldiers, several other significant events occurred. Mataxis was assigned for the year as the division's assistant commander for operations. General Mataxis once again supported establishing a division-level sniper school. Having just returned from Vietnam and reflecting on all his previous experience, Mataxis believed in the value of snipers. In World War II, he learned the importance of snipers and had been on the receiving end of sniper fire in France, Germany, Korea, and Vietnam, and had a respect for their capabilities and realized the impact the snipers could provide psychologically against an enemy. At the time, the 82nd Division supported the only full-time division-level sniper school. Mataxis monitored the development of a two-week curriculum that included individual skills in marksmanship, range determination, target detection, observation and reporting of intelligence information, adjustment of indirect fires, and familiarization with foreign weapons systems. In November 1967, the division also prepared, coordinated, and supervised the testing of 75 long-range reconnaissance patrol personnel from divisional units at Camp A. P. Hill, Virginia. The course curriculum included patrol planning, infiltration, target surveillance, route reconnaissance, river reconnaissance, crossing site selection, point reconnaissance, exfiltration, and bridge classification. Both sniper skills and long-range reconnaissance patrols were needed in Vietnam then. Having lived a lifetime of hunting with long-range shots, Mataxis believed all infantry units needed this capability. This capability has come and gone many times over the years.

The division's other requirements included conducting the ROTC summer camp training for the East Coast universities and colleges at Fort Bragg and cadet training at West Point. General Mataxis's son Ted Junior attended a summer camp that summer as a cadet from the University of Georgia. Ted Senior's well-meaning orderly laid out Ted Junior's and Ted Senior's daily fatigues and boots every morning. One day the orderly confused Ted Senior's fatigue pants with Ted Junior's fatigue pants, and unknowingly they were switched. As a result, Ted Senior wore pants several sizes too small that day, while Ted Junior walked around trying to hold his pants up.

The 82nd was known to train for a wide variety of operational contingencies, covering every possible event. "Garden Plot" was the operational contingency plan in the event of civil disturbances throughout the United States. The 1967 Detroit Riots were among the most violent and destructive riots in US history. They took place in Detroit's predominantly African American neighborhood of Virginia Park, which was a simmering cauldron of racial tension. The entire city of Detroit was in a state of economic and social strife; middle-class flight to the suburbs, further gutting

Detroit's vitality, had left behind vacant storefronts, widespread unemployment, and impoverished despair. On Sunday morning, July 23, 1967, the Detroit Police Force conducted a raid downtown at an illegal after-hours establishment on 12th Street and Clairmont. The police arrested 85 people and while they were waiting on transportation for them, a crowd started to gather. Looting began and the closed shops and businesses were ransacked. The first fire broke out at 6:30 a.m., and soon much of the street was ablaze. By midmorning, every policeman and fireman in Detroit had been called to duty. On 12th Street, officers fought to control the unruly mob. The firemen battled the fires that were started and were then attacked and harassed, as were the police. Mayor Jerome Cavanagh requested state police support and received 300 men; they were totally insufficient to restore order. Then Governor Romney asked President Lyndon Johnson to send in US troops.

On July 24, 1967, XVIII Corps received an alert order to execute the operational contingency plan for civil disturbances. DA message 824879 ordered the conduct of "Garden Plot One-1967" and to form a Third US Army for Task Force Detroit. The task force would have elements of the 82nd Airborne and 101st Airmobile divisions. They had to be alerted and prepared to move one brigade from each division by 1200 hours local time that Monday to Selfridge Air Force Base. Upon arrival, the brigade from the 82nd moved to the State Fair Grounds to provide riot/civil disturbance control/assistance. The mayor established a curfew that was in effect from 11:00 p.m. to 5:30 a.m. and prohibited sales of alcoholic beverages. The air movement for these troops required aircraft to be recycled on a 24-hour airstream going to Michigan. Task Force Detroit combined these troops. Nearly 2,000 army paratroopers arrived on Tuesday and began patrolling the streets of Detroit in tanks and armored carriers.

The 46th Michigan State National Guard had 4,946 soldiers that were federalized and then assigned to the Task Force. On July 25, the 3rd Brigade of the 82nd relieved the 3rd Brigade of the 46th. The 82nd personnel remained at the state fairgrounds or strategic school sites throughout their responsibility. Governor Romney and Secretary of Defense Vance actively participated in the coordination and planning efforts with Lt. Gen. Throckmorton, task force commander from Fort Bragg.

On July 26, eight sniper incidents occurred overnight, and the troops conducted mounted patrols throughout the area. Air National Guard was called in to protect the telephone stations, and 127th Combat Support Squadron personnel were placed under the operational control of the Police Commissioner to provide guard details at various locations. Authorization was received that evening from the Army Chief of Staff to issue CS riot control grenades, with distribution down to the company level.

On the morning of July 27, to normalize appearances to the public, General Throckmorton directed all troops to unload weapons, remove all ammunition from sight, sheath all bayonets, and remove flak vests. It was believed this would help lessen the tension and normalize appearances to the public.

On July 30, Governor Romney agreed to remove the curfew from 11:00 p.m. to 5:30 a.m.; however, he did not lift the ban on alcohol. Governor Romney and Mr. Vance met with General Throckmorton, and all concurred on the redeployment of the troops on July 31. By the time the bloodshed, burning and looting had ended after five days, 43 people were dead, 342 injured and nearly 1,400 buildings had been burned. At noon on August 2, the task force was relieved of its mission. At that time, Michigan National Guard units reverted to state control.

The anti-Vietnam demonstration at the Pentagon was during 21–23 October 1967. On 21 October 1967, the day of the march, civilian and military protective forces were moved to their duty stations. Because of a possible threat of civil disobedience in the Washington area, the United States ordered the United States airborne division at Fort Bragg to form a brigade task force which would be flown to Andrews Air Force Base. The brigade provided the bulk of Task Force Washington, with 1,917 division personnel and augmented personnel. The protest involved more than 100,000 attendees at a rally by the Lincoln Memorial. Later, about 50,000 people marched across the Potomac River to the Pentagon and had a confrontation with the paratroopers on guard there. The demonstrations were highly polarizing and were supported by many with the same views.

As a direct result of Tet 1968, the 82nd Airborne Division was tasked to send one brigade to Vietnam. On January 30, 1968 the North Vietnamese and Vietcong forces launched the Tet Offensive, with thousands of troops being deployed, overrunning many parts of South Vietnam in a surprise attack. This attack was the largest military campaign of the war up until that time. General Westmoreland, commanding general of the US Military Assistance Command Vietnam, requested additional US combat forces be immediately deployed to Vietnam. He specifically requested those forces be paratroopers. The 3rd Brigade was notified and deployed to Vietnam within 24 hours. The soldiers flew by C-141 aircraft to Vietnam and were immediately deployed. The complete move of the brigade took 12 days and used 155 C-130 and six C-141 sorties. Before departing, the brigade was issued jungle fatigues, jungle boots, poncho liners, and other equipment required for that environment. They would return to the United States in December 1969. This brigade had had the opportunity to send personnel through the sniper schools that the division had established and was attributed to the first kills in Vietnam.

In 1968, in an already tumultuous decade, the United States experienced a significant wave of social unrest across the nation, one of the largest since the Civil War. The 1968 disturbances resulted in far more destruction of urban cores, which were already amid a years-long wave of disinvestment in the postwar period. In April 1968, Task Force 82nd was formed and assigned another civil disturbance mission, in Washington, D.C. The Washington riots of 1968 lasted four days following the assassination of civil rights activist Martin Luther King Jr. on April 4, 1968. The assassination riots affected at least 110 American cities, with reports of more than

40 casualties, another 3,500 injuries, and 27,000 arrests accumulating as a result. The District of Columbia Fire and Emergency Medical Services reported 1,180 fires between March 30 and April 14, 1968, as arsonists set buildings ablaze. President Lyndon B. Johnson called the National Guard and the 82nd Airborne Brigade to the city on April 5, 1968, to assist the police department in quelling the unrest. Ultimately, 13 people were killed, with approximately 1,000 people injured and over 6,100 arrested. Additional nationwide civil disturbances that followed the assassination of Dr. King were unmatched in scale until the protests and unrest of 2020 following the police killing of George Floyd.

In April 1968, the division conducted Exercise Clove Hitch III with a brigade to test the capability of mass tactical jumps from C-141s in Puerto Rico. The 3rd Brigade 82nd Airborne Division parachuted into Vieques Island, Puerto Rico. This exercise demonstrated that the C-141, a jet aircraft, was a new aircraft for parachute operations in 1967.

It was a busy year for the Mataxis family. In summary, the year went very quickly, and the family was reintroduced to military life. Helma thrived in her new role as a general's wife. Ted had volunteered to go to Vietnam; however, he came out on orders to Iran. Ted's captain aide at that time volunteered to accompany the general on the family's tour of duty in Iran.

CHAPTER 13

Iran, 1968–70

From April 1968 through May 1970, General Mataxis was assigned as the Army Senior Adviser to the ARMISH—Military Assistance Advisory Group (MAAG) to Iran. While serving as head of the army section, which was located at the headquarters of the Imperial Iranian Ground Force in Tehran, he advised the Iranians on their covert plans to assist Kurdish guerrillas in eastern Iraq. The Iranians had transitioned from grant aid, which gave their country old surplus equipment, to paying for current top of the line equipment to upgrade their armed forces. In the 1960s Iran began to prosper from oil revenues, and diplomatic relations were established with many countries. The Shah (king) of Iran set about expanding and modernizing the Iranian army. The Shah had the money and was intent on purchasing billions of dollars' worth of the most sophisticated, advanced equipment and weaponry through countries like the United States and the United Kingdom. Iran also received much of their ground armored equipment from the Soviet Union. These deals were usually bartered using cheap oil and natural gas from Iran to the Soviet Union and this equipment required integration into the MAAG planning for the Iranian forces.

The team planned for all foreign military sales, end item analysis, and equipment integration into the Iranian army. The team at that time had to ensure what the Shah ordered for the Iranians could be absorbed and they could actually use the equipment before they could receive it. Ted was responsible for supervising the activities of several widely scattered field advisory teams throughout Iran: in service schools, units, and at the three field army headquarters located in the north and west, with reserve units centrally located. These advisory teams were designed to upgrade the Iranian daily operational effectiveness, as well as tactical and technical employment of the new equipment. The training of ordering supply parts, preventive maintenance, and rebuilding were critical to long-range effectiveness. During this time the army was equipped with six divisions. The Iranians had tribal troops, located in their local geographic regions and equipped with older weapons. To back this up they had contingency plans to mobilize civilian trucks and hospitals, if needed for support. This was styled after the Israeli model of mobilization of civilian resources. Iran was also working very hard to increase the capability of its air force and navy.

The MAAG operation was part of an 850-man US advisory structure. The whole effort was commanded by Major General Hamilton Twitchell, who focused on the grinding load of staff work that had to be contended with around the headquarters. Mataxis, however, was the operations officer with the Iranian army and was field-oriented to troops on the ground. He said, "Frankly, I'm not sure an advisor can operate without always being in contact with his counterpart, without a real personal relationship at all levels in the country and army where he's assigned. I like people, I like them in all shapes, sizes, colors, and in any language. So, I like being an advisor and I enjoy getting out with the Iranian leaders to make it work on the ground using their new equipment." General Mataxis tried very hard to continually be wherever the action was taking place. While the Iranians were developing their brigades of airborne, air mobile, special forces, and Ranger units, MAAG was most challenged. These units were all highly mobile and provided additional skill sets to the Iranian army. They were designed for the contingency mission of jumping into Kuwait in case Iraq attacked the oil fields located there.

MAAG recommended that Soviet weapons be obtained with the $100 million that the Soviets owed Iran from the oil and gas sales piped into Russia. This included Soviet armored personnel carriers (APCs) to go with the Iranian tanks. They also set up production lines to rebuild tanks with new engines, and weapons like rocket-propelled grenades (RPGs), as well as others. Iran built a munitions plant to supply their ammunition requirements so that outside sources would not be required. They also purchased a fleet of operational hovercraft that would be able to patrol shallow areas in the Persian Gulf and avoid minefields.

As for the Mataxis family, this assignment was very engaging and provided quality family time and a multitude of social activities. It was a most enjoyable experience for Helma, Ted, and Shirley. Shirley decided going with Ted and Helma might just be a "great adventure." It provided an opportunity to observe the cultural and historical locations throughout Iran, the "cross-roads" of the Middle East. The assignment also provided opportunities to travel outside of Iran. Ted Jr. was in college and Kaye was happily married, living in Anchorage, Arkansas. The Shah of Iran, Mohammed Reza Pahlavi, made Iran a very interesting place. He was trying very hard to improve the economy, education, and skills of the people, so if oil and natural gas ran low, these would not be Iran's only source of revenue.

The Empire of Iran is in southwestern Asia between the Caspian Sea and the Persian Gulf. It shared borders with the USSR (now Armenia, Azerbaijan, and Turkmenistan), Afghanistan, Pakistan, Iraq, and Turkey. The topography consists mainly of interior desert plains and highlands. These are surrounded by a rugged mountain rim, 6,000 to 18,000 feet above sea level. Almost one half of the land area of Iran is dissected by deep valleys and gorges with a few plain areas. Its climate is very diverse, primarily because of its topography, but summers are hot in all parts of Iran except for the highest elevations. Tehran is the capital, with a population estimated in 1976 to be 4.2 million. Literacy was about 40 percent and life expectancy was 50 years. The Shah, Mohammed Reza Pahlavi, was trying to westernize Iran while Ayatollah Ruhollah Khomeini was still in exile. There was an extreme fundamentalist movement in Iran; however, they were watched very carefully. The SAVAK, the secret police, were charged with torture and abuse to suppress this movement.

Tehran was very cosmopolitan and there were many places to go for entertainment. The nightclubs and discos were plentiful and much like what would be found in any large city in the United States. For a city the size of Tehran, there was very little to offer the gourmet or food connoisseur. Only a few restaurants specialized in Iranian cuisine, except kebabs, with the best Iranian food still being served in private homes. "Continental" or "European" meant that the restaurant served a selection of hors d'oeuvres, soups, salads, steaks, fish, chops, or perhaps one or two additional entrées, and a dessert. Most of the menus were predictable and uninspired. Despite the international feeling of Tehran, there were very few ethnic restaurants. Prices were high in comparison to value and were no guarantee of quality. The family was in the "embassy circuit" for cocktail parties and dinners out, which were very frequent and consisted of quality food and refreshments. The Mataxis family was quite busy, and these parties provided many interesting and engaging evenings. Additionally, there was the international business community, MAAG personnel and expats living in Tehran. Helma and Shirley loved the lifestyle. They in turn were reciprocal and loved hosting parties in their home, with the help of their chef and household help.

The house to which they were assigned was very nice and was enclosed in a large compound. The house was spacious, all on one level, and well furnished. Like most Iranian houses, it had a flat roof for sunning or sleeping. Most of the homes were open and had large windows overlooking the compound's elegant landscaping. In the center of their home was a large gazebo with lovely greenery that surrounded a beautiful fruit tree. The property also included a beautiful swimming pool. As a result of the extreme heat, this became Ted's new physical fitness routine. This pool was where he began his habit of swimming an hour a day for the rest of his life. The most amazing feature of the compound was that outside the walls it was all sand and nothing grew; however, on the inside, with a gardener and a little water, anything grew. While they were stationed in Iran they often said, "Just another day in Paradise." This was rather ironic since "paradise" was from the old Iranian language. Used as a noun, *pairidaeza* meant "a wall enclosing a garden or orchard," which is composed of *pairi-* ("around") and *daeza* ("wall"). Over time, the word has evolved and expanded in meaning, but it continues to conjure images of peace and tranquility. Naturally, it required a full-time gardener to take care of the compound.

They had a chef who was a US soldier and an Iranian couple who lived on the property as housekeepers/guards. They were provided a car and driver; however, they had brought a Buick from the United States, which they were not encouraged to drive because of the traffic conditions. As a result of the crime rate, every compound had security and/or a watch dog called a "jube" dog. These guard dogs were specially trained and were like junkyard dogs on steroids. The dogs were trained to eat only the food that they were raised on, which smelled terrible. This training would ensure that if anyone was to throw food into the compound to poison the dog, the dog would not eat it. *Jube* was the Persian word meaning "gutter." There were neither adequate sewage nor garbage disposal systems in Tehran.

The drainage system for the streets in Tehran was still the *jube*, with an open ditch on both sides of the street. These ditches ran outside of the compound and all over the city and they served as water dumping points for toilets and other disposals, making them quite nasty.

Shirley was able to work with Northrop Page. She had a US Government secret clearance, from her previous job in D.C., which was very helpful in the job market. Since she was living with the general, she was given a diplomatic passport. This almost made her invisible to the Iranian government. Northrop Page had been contracted to put in the satellite system, as well as complete the expansion of Mehrabad Airport in Tehran. Shirley was not permitted to drive, so the company for which she worked provided a car and driver for her and her friend Penny, an English girl who also worked for Northrop Page. During their assignment in Iran, the family lived like the rich and famous. Quite a change from their 1950 Indian tour.

Ted and his deputy on a hunting trip in the Zagros Mountains, Iran, 1969.

Ted Jr. flew over for summer vacation from college. He was in the Army Reserve Special Forces, so it was arranged for him to make a parachute jump along with his father and his future brother-in-law from a C-130 with the Iranian Special Forces. Captain John Howell, who was the jump master, was also the aide to the general, as well as an advisor to the Iranian Special Forces.

Captain John Howell is being awarded his Silver Star and Air Medal from Vietnam. He was medevaced and spent several months in the hospital at Camp Zama, Japan. The awards did not catch up with him until Iran.

John had just returned from 18 months in Vietnam with the 1st Cavalry Division and extended for an additional six months with US Special Forces, receiving the Silver Star, Combat Infantry Badge, and Purple Heart. His wound was

A parachute jump from an Iranian Special Forces C-130 just north of Tehran in August 1968. Ted's aide was the jumpmaster. Ted Jr. was on college break visiting Iran from the University of Georgia. Ted Sr. was the US Army MAAG chief; John Howell was his aide and the Iranian Special Forces Advisor. Helma and Shirley were in the drop zone. The Iranian Colonel Khosrodad was the previous Special Forces commander; upon promotion he commanded the Airmobile Division. He refused to flee when Khomeini took over in 1979 and was executed; his body was on the cover of *Time* magazine.

quite serious, and he ended up at Camp Zama Hospital in Japan for several months. Shirley and John dated and eventually were married in Iran. Their wedding took place in Tehran and was a real happening. All the Mataxises' social circles were invited, which totaled about 500 people attending the church wedding and the reception. The wedding was quite elegant and could have been featured in any *Brides* magazine in the world. Kaye and Bud could not attend because airline tickets were outrageous. Lt. Ted Jr. started his active-duty service in January 1969. He received a picture of Shirley standing next to her wedding cake, which was as tall as her. This did not sit well with Ted Jr. since he was in the middle of Ranger School, where food was very hard to come by. Despite Shirley's good looks and beautiful wedding dress, all the Rangers could see was the wedding cake. Upon completion of John's period as aide to the general, he requested and received orders to Germany. At their new duty station, John served as an artillery battery commander.

One of Helma's favorite family traditions was having the family assemble from their various locations for the family Christmas and, of course, a family portrait. This perhaps was because she was an orphan. When she was five, her dad died of tuberculosis contracted during World War I and her mother died when she was seven. She didn't have any family growing up. The family never knew why, but she loved Christmas so very much. Over Christmas 1969 the Mataxis clan were spread

This picture of Ted and his deputy on a hunting trip in the Zagros Mountains, Iran, 1969.

out across the world. Helma and Ted were in Tehran, Iran; Shirley and John were in Germany; Kaye and Bud were in Anchorage, Alaska; and Ted Jr. was in Vietnam. So, this went down as the one year she did not try to con us into coming to her place for Christmas.

Since Ted's job was as an advisor to the Iranian army, he was required to visit all their military locations throughout Iran. The MAAG had a twin-turbo Beechcraft King Air and was able to fly the general all over Iran to visit the troops. Additionally, Ted and Helma took an overland journey to the Valley of the Assassins, which was most interesting. The general was able to hunt wild boar and a couple of different types of mountain goats. Ted always hunted wherever he was assigned.

They continuously saw the Soviet ambassador at many of the embassy circuit events. Ted had known some Soviet troops in Berlin after World War II and socialized with them, learning some of their language, war songs and the sword dance. Ted would always ask the ambassador if he had his royalty check for his book *Nuclear Tactics*, written in 1958. The Russians and several other countries had published it in translation for their armies. As a result of their friendship, they were able to arrange a trip to Russia for Ted and Helma. Ted received approval to take the trip, which was quite surprising. They stayed at the Hotel Rossia, located across the street from the Kremlin. It could accommodate 6,000 guests, having 3,182 rooms. It was the largest hotel in the world from 1967 to 1980; it was closed in 2006, but it remained the second largest hotel in Europe until that time. While traveling in Russia they were impressed by the orderly and neatness of Moscow. Visiting the University of Moscow, it appears as one giant structure; however, it was 37 separate buildings with a total of 3,500 rooms. Their guide gave them an interesting insight here: if a baby were placed in one room at birth and was moved to a different room each day, he would die an old man of about 95 years by the time he reached the last room. They saw a ballet at the magnificent Bolshoi theater and visited a Russian circus. After five days in Moscow, they moved on to Leningrad, which seemed a more relaxed, friendly, and casual atmosphere than they experienced in Moscow. The people seemed a lot more friendly. While there, they were able to visit the Hermitage Museum, the largest museum in the Soviet Union. After this eventful trip they left laden with balalaikas and souvenirs unique to Russia. Helma once again was able to shop for unique items and loved it. The Russian Ambassador to Iran was very interested in their impressions.

Ted had volunteered to go directly to Vietnam from Iran. Upon hearing this, the Russian ambassador gave him a card which, he said, "Will get you a bottle of vodka before they begin torturing you." Now that is a true friend. In September 1969, they flew down to see Ted Jr. in Istanbul, Turkey. Ted Jr. had just participated in Operation *Deep Furrow*, a long-range insertion non-stop into Turkey from Fort Bragg. He was a platoon leader with 1st Battalion, 504 Infantry Battalion, 82nd Airborne Division. This was the first exercise in which the 82nd undertook a long-distance, non-stop flight from Fort Bragg to Turkey, where they put their parachutes on in flight and parachuted into Turkey. Ted Jr. was on orders to Vietnam.

In 1968, during a discussion of the 1965 war between Pakistan and India with both the Pakistani and Indian ambassadors at another embassy party, both ambassadors invited General Mataxis to visit the western battlefields in their respective countries. Never being one to miss a trip or battlefield, Ted took them up on the offer. Mataxis said, "The Pakistani ambassador took me around openly in a helicopter and had me tour several of his units. The Indians took me around the battlefield at their sites; however, they were much more security conscience. At this time the Indians were beginning to depend on the Soviet Union for much of their military equipment and advice. After the visit to both sides of the battlefields and various interviews with participants in the battle, I had collected enough data to write a book." He had considered writing a book about the incident for the doctorate that he planned on getting; however, he became overcome by time. He did have the opportunity to visit his 1950 classmates and went to south India to give a presentation to their officers at the service schools on the war in Vietnam.

Helma was a collector of fine objects. Tehran's bazaars and open markets were places where you could find anything. There were objects from the world over. So, in Iran, she collected rugs, paintings, artwork, and jewelry. What separated Helma from the average shopper was that she was not just buying for herself but also for Shirley, Ted Jr., and Kaye. Kaye and Ted Jr. laughed because when they went into each other's homes, many of the objects were identical. The children realized that buying while overseas often allows one to afford quality items at a reasonable price point. This most definitely was a generational thing since all the Mataxis children enjoyed and valued their furnishings. Helma, Ted, and Shirley certainly took advantage of living in the Middle East and traveled as much as they possibly could. They enjoyed both the culture and the historical locations wherever they were. Traveling and living around the world was always relished by Helma and Ted and provided them with a lifetime of adventures. This carried over into their retirement years as they decided they would take two overseas trips every year.

The American presence in Tehran at this time was quite large and eclectic. Everyone from the US military, commercial and business world, as well as its large expatriate community, was trying to make a dollar off the Shah's programs. One thing that was a large morale builder was the embassy not only having a cafeteria, but also a commissary which received shipments from Europe weekly and a Class 6 store. This allowed the Americans to have a taste of home while they were in Iran. It also helped that the prices were much cheaper than on the economy for everything they carried. There was an Army Post Office (APO) combined with the Diplomatic Post Office (DPO), which enabled everyone living in Iran easy access for sending items cost-effectively anywhere in the world. Long-distance phone calls were quite expensive, including in-country calls. A call for three minutes from Tehran to Tabriz would cost you 20 times as much as a local call. Overseas calls were available; however, they were very expensive and seldom made.

General Mataxis was learning Farsi and attended Tehran University, taking courses in Iranian history and culture. Ted could arrange for visitors to see Iran's Treasury of National Jewels. The collection of the crown jewels went back to time unknown in Iranian history. Iran used the crown jewels to back their currency like the United States did with the gold at Fort Knox. The crown jewels were exhibited in the basement of the National Bank of Iran, a collection so unbelievably luxurious that they do not even put a value on it. For example, there is the World Globe of Jewels. Its frame and stand are set with 51,363 precious stones; the gems themselves amount to 18,200 carats. The world globe is made from 75 pounds of 24 karat gold, with the continents and islands outlined in diamonds, rubies, and emeralds, and the sea is indicated by a great sweep of large sapphires. There were many man-sized containers that were full of beautifully cut large diamonds.

Once again living overseas, Ted and Helma saw many of their friends as they came to visit or were passing through Iran with a layover in Tehran. When General Westmoreland visited Iran, he personally approved Ted's request to return to Vietnam for his next assignment. Once again, Ted volunteered to ride to the sounds of the guns in Vietnam rather than using the time to scout for a job after retirement. General Westmoreland said, "I was glad to have someone with his experience return because they were having so many disciplinary problems caused by the anti-war feelings in the country!" General Mataxis took 30 days of leave in the United States and then left for Vietnam in June 1970, first as acting commander of the 23rd Division and then as acting division commander. In January 1971, on one day's notice, he became head of the military mission in Cambodia. He held this position until his retirement in 1972 with 32 years of service.

Helma and Ted left Iran in May 1970. They missed the 2,500th anniversary of the Persian Empire, celebrating the foundation of the ancient Achaemenid Empire of Cyrus the Great. This celebration took place at Persepolis in 1971. When Helma and Ted left Iran, they went by way of Southeast Asia. They stopped in Vietnam to visit Ted Jr., who was serving with the 101st Airborne Division. Mataxis, having spent a lot of time in Vietnam (1964–66), was welcomed to Vietnam by his old counterpart General Vinh Loc. He greeted them with flowers for Helma. After a two-day visit with Ted Jr. in Saigon, upon trying to leave Vietnam, they found that they had never been recorded as arriving. General Vinh Loc had to be tracked down before they were permitted to leave Vietnam. Ted returned to the United States with Helma for a 30-day leave and then returned to Vietnam for his last assignment in June of that year.

CHAPTER 14

Vietnam and Cambodia, 1970–72

Mataxis returned to South Vietnam in June 1970, serving as deputy commander and acting commander of the 23rd Infantry Division (Americal), part of XXIV Corps. He served as the division commander during August and September. Then he served as assistant division commander for support until January 1971. The Americal division was the largest in the United States Army and was made up of 11 infantry battalions and six artillery battalions.

The counter-guerrilla war was winding down, and American forces were taking increasing casualties from mines and booby traps. Mataxis was two years away from retirement. Ted had once again volunteered and chosen to spend his last two years in the army serving in Vietnam and Cambodia rather than looking for a retirement job.

Upon arriving in Vietnam, Mataxis faced the 23rd Infantry Division's irreparable reputation. Their participation three years earlier in the My Lai Massacre, a mass murder of 350–504 unarmed men, women, and children, had permanently tarnished the division. US Army soldiers from C Company, 1st Battalion, 20th Infantry Regiment, and B Company, 4th Battalion, 3rd Infantry Regiment, and 11th Infantry Brigade killed the civilians. After the massacre, the division reverted to the 23rd Infantry Division nomenclature instead of Americal. Initially, three helicopter servicemen who tried to halt the slaughter and rescue the hiding civilians were shunned and even denounced as traitors by several US Congressmen. Thirty years later, the three servicemen were recognized and decorated by the US Army for shielding non-combatants from harm in a war zone. The massacre was one of the most shocking and heinous episodes of the Vietnam War. Later, the army tried an Americal assistant division commander for shooting civilians from helicopters. He was the highest-ranking officer to undergo a court-martial during the Vietnam War. The charges were eventually dropped due to a lack of evidence.

Mataxis recalls that time in later papers. He explains, "After processing in at Long Bien, I was informed that Major General Albert E. Milloy was the division commander. I went straight up to the division and relieved General Malloy so

These pictures of Ted were taken when he was the acting commanding general of the Americal Division in 1970.

that he could go on leave for a couple of months. He went home, and I was acting division commander during the summer.

I didn't even get a briefing in Saigon about what was happening. The MACV Headquarters said, 'You'll find out when you get up to the division!' The way they sent me was wrong because we got into the problem with herbicides and Agent Orange later. When I'd been in Vietnam in 1964–66, we used to duck under a tree when Agent Orange was sprayed so we wouldn't get the oily spots on our uniforms. MACV Headquarters did not indicate that we no longer used it in battle, nor did they update me on any of the tactical changes. Upon arriving at the division, I simply ordered it used just like before, not knowing anything had changed, and a shitstorm hit. The Inspector General came up from General Creighton Abrams, commander at MACV in Saigon, to investigate the order of the use of Agent Orange, which had been prohibited. I sat the investigating officer down and said, 'Say friend, I want you to take this to General Abrams. You didn't brief me in Saigon. You sent me up here to the division because I'd already been here for two years prior. Since I had been here in 1964–66, they said I knew what was going on, and MACV didn't need to brief me on the current changes in operations and procedures.' [The investigating officer] wrote that down and briefed General Abrams on it, and Abrams said, 'Forget about it. It was an error on his Headquarters' part, not mine.' It seemed to me they should have taken me by the hand and said, 'Now look, the things that make people excited are those things that have changed; here are the things not to do, you know, and the basic methods of current operations and here's what we'd like you to do.' That never happened."

"I immediately realized that the war had changed over the last four years. When I was here before and during the 'big battle' phase, our battalions were operating as a unit against large enemy forces. Deception plans were issued with every operation order, and conventional fire and movement plans were ordered daily. There appeared to have been a war slowdown, and tactics had turned towards fixed firebases and other fixed base complexes. Bunkers that would put Korea to shame had gone up. Our heavy hilltop firebases were so wired that they reminded me of World War I pictures I had seen. The unfortunate thing about these heavy firebases was that while they provided comfort to the command posts and the troops, they required excessive protection. We had to develop a system of multiple firebases providing mutual support for one another throughout the total division tactical area. At times, we would find a battalion operating on a mobile basis in the jungle with one company left to defend the battalion's firebase and command post. The battalion had a tactical command post deployed with the troops in the jungle. The battalion base was in the field, with their companies and platoons tactically operating away from the fire base. This would leave their fire bases very exposed. The rifle companies, due to a variety of things, were staffed at 85 to 90 percent of TOE strength and were usually fielded only with 50 to 60 men, with other men on special duties at the brigade base or the battalion rear. This operational procedure was very corrosive to deploying maximum firepower in the field." Mataxis explains, "The enemy troops' activities returned to phase one of small unit actions, consisting of three to four men up to squad size of ten personnel. So, we only upgraded to squad and platoon level. We must never forget that the enemy could suddenly form up larger units and hit our fragmented units. When larger units were formed by the enemy, they were able to chase or overwhelm our troops."

"When I returned on my second tour, I couldn't believe this was the American army. As division commander, I slept in the command post at our division headquarters with my gas mask beside me because damn antiwar soldiers would wait until the wind blew in a specific direction, and pop tear gas grenades which would float over the command post. The incidents of 'fragging' started to occur on their own officers and NCOs."

"The other thing that I'd mentioned was that the junior officers were under pressure from their own personnel. At night, the patrol would go out on offensive patrols and be prepared to move from one point to another location. They would report in, 'I'm at point 1, going to point 2, going to point 3.' At dawn, if the enemy overran a position, it was often the first position they had called in. They had not only lied about their locations, which made supporting operations to assist them next to impossible, but it also gave the enemy the tactical advantage to turn the table on our units. When young lieutenants came in, if they were too gung-ho, their soldiers threatened them. If they gave orders to the soldiers perceived as threatening, they would frag them. I'm sure that this was almost a mutiny, so to speak. If some senior guy came down to ensure everything was straightened out, the soldiers would refuse to do something. It was right on the edge of mutiny. We had companies that refused to do things until they came down with the battalion commander and threatened them with, 'If you don't do this, you'll end up at Long Bin in jail.' It was completely different. That was the way the war changed. I have always said, 'There are no bad units, just bad commanders.' The war was losing its popularity at home, and this impacted the beliefs and actions of our troops. Discontent on the home front provided a significant psychological impact on the soldiers fighting and dying for the cause of our country." In a letter to a friend describing the situation,

Mataxis wrote about his disappointment: "This time open[ed] my eyes on how far our units have gone down the slippery slope—drugs, racial problems, fragging. In six months', time, one battery commander and first sergeant were killed, and 18 officers and NCOs were wounded." He went on to say, "Well enough of this as it makes me heartsick."

As the assistant division commander of the 23rd Division, Mataxis shared the job of distributing Purple Hearts to the wounded with his fellow ADC. This required duty was the hardest one Mataxis ever faced over the years. In his own

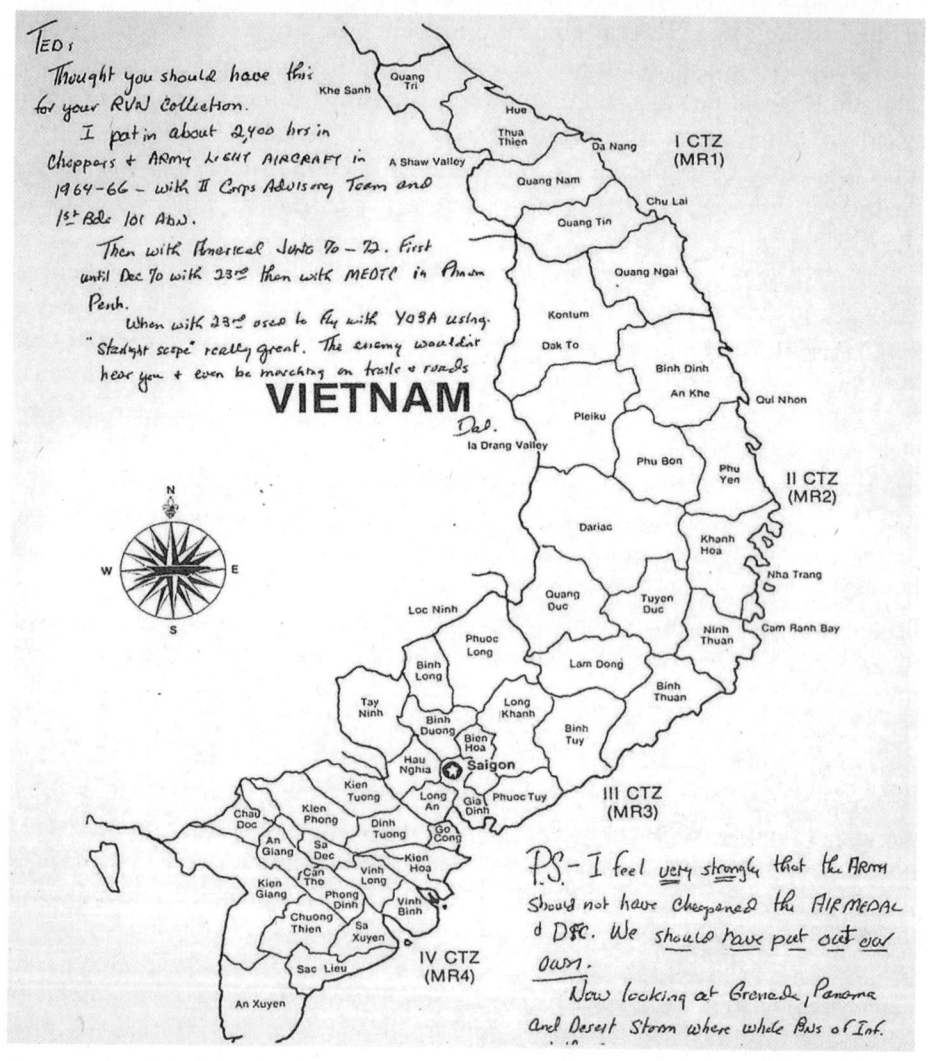

An army map showing all the districts of the four combat zones in Vietnam in the late 1960s. The comments were written by Ted for his son years later. (Map: US Army)

words, Mataxis explained, "It was the worst thing I've ever done from World War II, Korea, and Vietnam.... I remember seeing the young son of a very close friend of mine. I greeted him when he came in. He was so happy. The next time I saw him was in the hospital; he'd lost both legs and an arm.... The idea of going out and returning severely injured by a mine or booby trap, I think, was the greatest fear that our soldiers had at the time. At that time, many of our casualties were coming from booby traps and mines."

"At this stage of the war, it is a grim and dirty war, typical of Bernard Fall's book entitled *Street Without Joy*." Ted Jr. was operating with the 101st in the I Corps area of operation described by Fall. Ted Jr. and Ted Sr. were in Vietnam at the same time for 18 months, from when Ted Sr. arrived in June 1970 until Ted Jr. went home in January 1972. The worst encounter father and son experienced was when they were both waiting on a Red Cross death notification. When Ted Sr. first received the notification, he assumed it was about Ted Jr. Ted Jr. had been pulled out of the field and went to the Red Cross office, where they had gone to lunch. So, he sat there thinking that his father must have been shot down. The notification had been that Ted Sr.'s mother had died. The Red Cross representative was quite surprised at Ted Jr.'s remark: 'That is great!' After he explained that he thought it had been his 'father shot down,' the confused representative had to agree." Neither of the Teds wanted to leave Vietnam, so they both stayed and, in fact, extended their tours. Meanwhile, Helma had a son and a husband to worry about daily during the war.

Mataxis does not dwell on horrors, though, and in his journal, he explains, "The bright part of the picture is that we are upgrading the Regional and Popular Forces. They are gaining more confidence and moving out against the VC. This, in my mind, is where the war will finally be won or lost. It depends on how the peasant and his Regional and Popular Forces feel about the war; if they fight to win or even want to exist, they will make it. If they lose spirit and give up, we can only say we tried to do our best; however, we backed the wrong horse. With the ARVIN regular army increasing and staying to fight the NVA battalions in the jungle, I hope we will be able to leave South Vietnam strengthened by our logistical and advisory support. My previous experience working with ARVIN has paid off, and we can conduct combined air mobile operations with the ARVIN 2nd Division in our area of operations. We returned to Kham Duc to

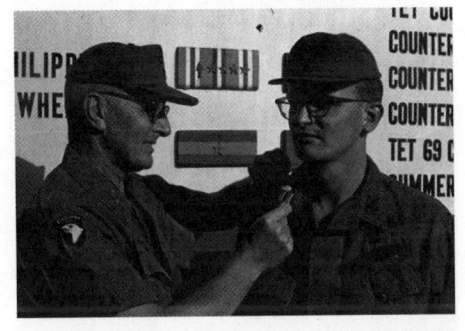

Ted Jr.'s promotion to captain in January 1971 in Vietnam. His father pins on the captain's bars he was promoted with in June 1942 during World War II. Years later Ted Jr. would promote his son, Ted III, with the same bars in 2009 at the Sainte-Mère-Église drop zone at Fort Bragg, North Carolina, in 2009.

disrupt the logistical base areas in fall 1970." Mataxis's citation for the Distinguished Flying Cross states, "General Mataxis consistently and unhesitatingly assumed the great risk inherent to flying over enemy territories while personally directing combat operations against a hostile armed force. Frequently taking his command-and-control helicopter into areas of heavy contact to maintain firm control over the action and assist in medical evacuations of units on the ground."

Some soldiers' actions at that time should not distract from those fine young men serving their country and protecting their unit; these honorable soldiers' bravery and sacrifices deserve to be remembered. During the Americal division's stay in Vietnam, there were 16 soldiers who earned earn the Congressional Medal of Honor. These awards speak very highly of the division's continual dedication over time. The officers, NCOs, and draftees all answered their call to serve our nation in its time of need. Over 58,000 paid the ultimate price by putting their lives on the line for the preservation of our freedoms and security of our nation. All endured the harsh realities of combat while demonstrating remarkable courage in the face of danger and willingly putting their life and limbs on the line for one another.

Mataxis once said, "America went into Vietnam with the best army we ever had. They were trained and ready. Most of us had been in World War II and Korea, and we ensured that we didn't come into Vietnam as we did in Korea. You know, not physically fit for the rigors of war and with units not trained to the required standards. We made sure we were prepared for what we would encounter. So that was as it should have been." Mataxis explained, "When we left Vietnam in the 1970s, it was the worst army I'd ever seen. I couldn't believe we were that bad; it was on the verge of completely collapsing." Years later, General Westmoreland called General Mataxis and asked why he had made a statement like that. He questioned Mataxis: 'What do you mean by saying that the army is the worst army you've ever seen?' Mataxis said, "Well, General Westmoreland, you and I have discussed this. Remember what we said about the fragging, how horrible it was, and the racial issues and lack of discipline in some parts? It simply was." Westmorland said, "Well yeah, I guess it was, you know, but that was the way. It's sad."

Ted departed for the Cambodian mission on February 1, 1971. Prior to his departure the Americal division's area of operation had a relatively low level of enemy activity and infrequent contacts. Ted had warned about the possibility of enemy concentrations and increased

Ted officiating at Lieutenant Colonel Norman Schwarzkopf's battalion's Change of Command Ceremony, which occurred in 1970. Here he is seen receiving his end of tour award. He was a heavily decorated combat veteran between both tours.

activity. As always, Ted had stressed being prepared for a worst case scenario, troubleshooting all the things that can go wrong, and having a course of action to deal with them if they were to occur. Murphy's Law has been around as long as the army itself. Mataxis stated, "If it can go wrong, it will." The division was engaged in turning over the fire support bases to the ARVIN, which resulted in the perimeter of the fire base not receiving the maintenance and care required. On the morning of March 28, 1971, Viet Cong (VC) overran Firebase Mary Ann, throwing satchel charges at the command bunker, troop bunkers, and communications bunkers, and killing many Americans in their sleep. At the time of the attack there had been 231 Americans and 21 ARVIN on the fire base. Of the American troops, 33 were killed and over 80 were wounded. Security had been very lax, and the base did not even have listening posts outside of the perimeter. The primary reason for this disaster was the failure to provide the required security by the officer and NCO leadership at the firebase. This was clearly a dereliction of duty. Some ARVIN artillery was on the firebase, supporting their operations in the area; this instilled a false sense of security in the US troops. The firebase seemed more like a rear echelon area rather than the division's most forward firebase. Major General James Baldwin was the commander of the division. He was held responsible for the disaster and relieved of his command.

Cambodia

In November 1953 the French granted Cambodia its independence, allowing King Sihanouk to take control of the government. At that time the French had been conducting the training for the army of Cambodia while the United States was providing the logistical support. In March 1970, while King Sihanouk was out of the country visiting China and Russia, there was a coup and Lon Nol took power as the president. One of the first ultimatums he issued as president was to demand that the NVA and Viet Cong units vacate the bases they had established in Cambodia. Up until that time those forces had been focused on ongoing operations in Vietnam. After the ultimatum from the president to leave Cambodia, there was an instantaneous backlash from the NVA/VC sanctuaries in the country. The Cambodian army was not trained and was caught off guard by the NVA and VC. Lon Nol requested immediate support from the United States.

On February 1, 1971, General Mataxis was reassigned to Cambodia with one day's notice. He became the chief of the Joint Military Equipment Delivery Team-Cambodia (MEDT-C) in Phnom Penh. The start-up mission was to build a Cambodian military force of 200,000 to take off some of the pressure caused by the NVA and VC reaction. However, the American Ambassador to Cambodia was Emory "Colby" Swank, who became ambassador after diplomatic relations were reestablished with Cambodia. He arrived in Phnom Penh in September 1970 and

Ted with Lieutenant General Lon Nol, the acting prime minister of Cambodia and head of the Generals' Council, February 1971.

served until 1973. As the ambassador, he believed the United States should be doing more to help the country and warned of a civil war. He clashed with State Department leaders about the policy towards Cambodia and was eventually reassigned to a dead-end desk job in NATO and retired shortly after. This was a case of a person who was trying to be doing the job he was assigned when the government did not want to hear his input. The door was left open to the Khmer Rouge, ruling 1975–79, during which time an estimated one million Cambodians were executed.

MEDT-C was organized on a crash basis with practically no institutional memory, except for the rudimentary working files that were inherited from its predecessor, which had conducted the military aid program to Cambodia before it was cut off. As a result, General Mataxis continually pleaded to CINCPAC for historical data on the previous Cambodian MAAG that had been run by Brigadier General Talbert. He had submitted a final report on their efforts at the termination of the mission in January 1964. It had been the first US military aid program in Cambodia, and the report was forwarded to the Saigon office. Although nearly seven years had passed, many of the conditions that were reported by General Talbert still existed and his recommendations were still valid. Influenced by the usefulness of this "historic report," MEDT-C was provided with information on specific areas. They were able to analyze not only what was done and not done but why it was done or not done. MEDT-C was a unique organization divided into two echelons: a rear echelon in Saigon and a forward echelon in Phnom Penh, Cambodia. Initially, 16 members of the MEDT-C were operating out of the American embassy in Phnom Penh while the other 44 were working out of Saigon. They later expanded to over 100 personnel. It operated under the commander in chief of Pacific Command (CINCPAC), Admiral McCain, with the supervision of the chief of the US diplomatic mission to Cambodia. According to Mataxis, "The team's mission was to plan, program, deliver, and check the end use of the American military assistance materials being provided. The command's mission also included overseeing Cambodia's congressionally approved materials assistance program, as required by statutes for evaluating requests, coordination, deliveries, observing and expediting distribution of equipment, and reporting on the auditing of US military equipment provided."

Mataxis recalls this time in his writings. "General Abrams told me I had been selected because I had just come from two years as chief of the army MAAG in

Iran. Clearly, his nose was out of joint because MEDT-C came under CINPAC, commanded by Admiral McCain, rather than his Military Assistance Command Vietnam (MACV)." MEDT-C's supervisor was the Chief of the US Diplomatic Mission to Cambodia. During the briefing by General Abrams, he stated that danger in Cambodia was a significant concern, and that's why MEDT-C was getting $200 million to build up the Cambodian army. Abrams said, "You're a MAAG chief, but we have to call it Military Equipment Delivery Team-Cambodia (MEDT-C) because of the State Department." The president and the Joint Chiefs were concerned about the perception of the Vietnam War being extended to Cambodia, and that country becoming another Vietnam. To give it a name like MAAG might do that, so MEDT-C was their work-around. They did not want any connection to Vietnam and thought this might accomplish that. As a direct result, Secretary of State William Rogers said, "The United States has no intention of escalating the air war over Cambodia or sending ground troops into the embattled nation."

The primary accomplishment of the first year was a successful application of the Nixon Doctrine to achieve US goals and objectives in Cambodia. With a minimal use of US manpower, the Khmer forces had been trained and equipped sufficiently, enabling the Khmer Republic to maintain its independence and neutrality while working against the NVA and VC.

The rapid training and equipping of combat units took place in the Republic of Vietnam. The Cambodian soldiers got their basic training from the South Vietnamese and US Special Forces. The US Special Forces personnel trained the Cambodians in battalion-size units, which performed well in combat and quickly became the backbone of the land component of the Khmer National Armed Force's (FANK) combat capability. While in Vietnam they were issued field radios, M16 rifles, and uniforms by the Americans. Helped by the equipment and training, the FANK began winning back some of the territory it had lost to the enemy. There was increasing pressure on the NVA and VC. The American military aid program consisted of $180 million initially, which included both the intensive training and equipping of the Cambodian troops in South Vietnam and delivery of other equipment for Cambodia.

General Mataxis used to spend a couple of days a week in Phnom Penh with his staff, which had more than doubled the size of the contingent. When it originally deployed it had 16 personnel; in May it had expanded to 23. There were also 63 other men attached to the team but based out of South Vietnam. One of the requirements for personnel assigned to the MEDT-C forward echelon was to be fluent in French. While the importance of language cannot be stressed enough, technical competency, professionalism, and the requisite experience in technical matters became very critical in the selection of personnel.

Mataxis explains, "The public was so much against the war in Vietnam that the United States pulled out. The President disengaged, and we started going down from 500,000 US troops." Ted's actions were at the center of all efforts to protect

> 30 Oct
>
> Dear Ted:
>
> I've just come from the WAR Room here at MACV — for the first time I've seen where you are at Polie Kleng. Watch yourself — going east over the road you come to Polie Krone — That was over run in the summer of 1964.
>
> Your Camp used to be an old French Outpost — I was on a combat assault there in the fall of 1964.
>
> In fact in Dec '64 I landed at Polie Krone — they had run into the first NVA in Country — that was their infiltration route. And they had captured the first SKS in South Vietnam. Later in Feb (TET) 65 they attacked and over ran part of our Compound at Pleiku etc. I dig deep. When they hit it will be the Kontum area. In fact I would plan to go back to Polie Krone — when you can be supported from Kontum if big numbers started coming in. They are pouring down through Laos now — !! So get all set. Recon E+E routes cup supplies & ammos up etc.
>
> I've just reread "Street without Joy" — the Chapter on "END of a Task Force" covers the fighting in Feb 1954. The French mobile group moved to Kontum in Dec 53. in — "At 1300, on Feb 2, all the posts to the northwest of Kontum, including the important post of Dak To were overrun by enemy troops in battalion strength attacking in waves." — Then Kontum fell — etc. beginning of end for the French on the highland plateau.
>
> I'll leave any article on the fighting in the Summer of 1966 on my desk you reread.
>
> Well this is my third letter today — but thought you should be updated — keep alert —
>
> Love, Dad

The following is a letter Ted wrote to Ted Jr. on finding out he had volunteered for the ARVN Border Rangers in II Corps at Poli Kleng. This fatherly advice was given in October 1971. Ted and Ted Jr. were in Vietnam for 14 months at the same time. No mother deserved something like that.

the United States interests and assist the brave people of the Khmer Republic. He goes on to say, "At that time the NVA had three divisions in the southern portion of Cambodia and three divisions in the Eagle Beak area. The danger was very real and when the US troop strength fell below 100,000, it would have been very easy if the NVA wanted to order these divisions to launch towards Saigon. They could have perhaps broken through and overrun South Vietnam in conjunction with all the other ongoing operations. Think of all the POWs and causalities that could have taken place with the remaining US troops."

For his service in Cambodia as head of the US Military Mission, Mataxis was awarded the US Distinguished Service Medal and the Cambodian Order of the Republic. He was known for inexhaustible energy and dedicated performance! His citation said, "Mataxis continued to demonstrate outstanding professionalism as his hallmark throughout his military career. From its inception through the time that Mataxis left, he consistently displayed a posture that was a tribute to his intense devotion to duty and the exemplary tact and diplomacy required to coordinate numerous highly complicated and potentially sensitive areas of interest in Southeast Asia. His guidance and direction to the Plans and Program Division assured a flexible and vibrant planning of the rapidly expanding Khmer force structure, which had quickly increased by over 500 percent, supporting a country in a full-scale war for its very existence."

General Mataxis stayed in Cambodia until his retirement on April 20, 1972, completing 32 years of service. For his last five years of service, he had been assigned out of the United States. While preparing for retirement when he was in Cambodia in January 1972, Ted requested to return to Fort Bragg for medical processing prior to his retirement in February 1972 so that he could be near Helma. The doctors had found some spots on an x-ray that needed to be checked out. On February 15, 1972 he received a message from the Lieutenant General at DCSPERD. Ted Jr. explains, "I read this message as a young captain having returned from a couple of years in Vietnam. I was amazed that after his service to this country he would receive something like this. So, I quote parts of the message. 'I appreciate your desire to return to Fort Bragg for medical processing but, unfortunately this will not be possible. Your mandatory retirement date is February 29, and it impacts on projected promotions and the necessity to remain within the authorized general officer strength militate against any decision which might cause your retirement to extend past your mandatory date. The conduct of your entire medical processing at Walter Reed will ensure expeditious handling of your case and afford us a reasonable opportunity to get you retired by the end of February. I regret the inconvenience caused by the extension of the separation from your wife and hope you will understand the necessity of this decision as in the long run it is in your best interest. Warm regards.' Dad had been diagnosed with artery blockages and would need a couple of operations later that year."

CHAPTER 15

Singapore, 1972–75

Upon returning home from Vietnam, Mataxis attended Duke University to work on his doctorate. While there, he was offered a position as a research associate at the Institute for Cooperative Studies of Southeast Asia. This position entailed giving some lectures and participating in seminars while he was working on his doctoral thesis. These tasks were things he loved to do. Alas, a doctorate was not in the cards.

According to Mataxis, "A couple of months after retirement, I was called by the Pentagon and asked if I would be interested in forming a new civilian type of Military Advisory and Assistance Group (MAAG) in the Republic of Singapore." Singapore had requested a MAAG for their country that the American government turned down because Vietnam syndrome was in full swing. In response, Singapore offered to hire a qualified officer and cover all expenses to establish a civilian organization to accomplish a MAAG-type mission. The US Army Judge Advocate Corps (JAG) investigated the request and set up a program where its personnel could be hired by a Singaporean firm, UMPC PTE. Ltd., and work as contractors for the Minister of Defense. As a result, Mataxis was offered a chance to go to Singapore to establish a management consultant organization as a private company. He faced the choice of becoming an aging graduate student, as Helma liked to call him, or accepting a fresh challenge overseas. This new career would provide a lifestyle that Helma and Ted would enjoy and deliver Ted the challenges he constantly sought out. There was not much of a debate. He accepted the position, enabling him to contribute to the ongoing Cold War effort.

Singapore became independent on August 9, 1965, when it was ejected from the Federation of Malaysia amid social unrest. Its strategic position on the straits between the Indian Ocean and the South China Sea enabled it to become the largest port in Southeast Asia. It owes its growth and prosperity to its critical position at the southern extremity of the Malay Peninsula, where it dominates. As a result of its natural deepwater harbor, it became one of the world's greatest commercial centers. The British founded modern Singapore as a trading colony on the site in 1819. It joined the Federation of Malaysia in 1963, but it was ousted two years later and became independent just 10 years before Ted went there. When he arrived, its fledgling armed forces and government were in the developmental phase and continued to grow, in population, capabilities, and wealth. It is connected to the mainland by a narrow channel crossed by a road and railroad causeway that is more than half a mile long, allowing its continual rapid development. Its critics say the rapid development has been accomplished by strict control on free speech and politics.

The Singapore Armed Forces (SAF) are made up of four branches—the army, navy, air force and intelligence services—under the umbrella of the Ministry of Defense. Today, Singapore has one of the most capable, robust, technically sophisticated and powerful militaries in Southeast Asia.

General Mataxis served as an independent contractor consultant to the Singapore Minister of Defense (MINDEF), Dr. Goh Keng Swee, from 1972 to 1974. The British had withdrawn their troops from Singapore, which made the newly independent nation vulnerable. Dr. Goh's mission was the defense of Singapore, with the main objective being to strengthen the country's military and domestic security capabilities. A key policy he designed and implemented was the creation of national service (NS), a mandatory conscription system for able-bodied young males. The US assistant secretary of defense, Berry Shillala, lined up the consulting business at the request of Mr. Ong Tech Chin and a consultant service for the Government of Singapore was established. The board of UMPC gave timely approval to the study conducted by Mataxis, with recommendations on how to proceed and operate. This gave him the go-ahead to start an autonomous management consultant division designed to meet the needs of the Singapore government.

Ted's role in working with UMPC was as head of their newly formed management consultancy department. They were attempting to establish a "Rand type of group" that would have the capability to take on civilian, municipal, and defense consulting jobs. One of his first assignments was working with Dr. Goh and the Government of Singapore to obtain the approval of a plan outlining the concept of development and implementation of a MAAG-type organization. As a consultant, Mataxis styled his team like a MAAG, only this was a civilian team. The management consultancy division of UMPC was an autonomous division. Ted was the head of a group of retired military officers hired to assist the Singapore Armed Forces. Ted instructed each of his consultants to deal directly with him, which prevented the consultants from responding directly with the officers of the Ministry of Defense of Singapore, which was led by Dr. Goh. He had identified a series of 14 projects where he felt their military was falling behind or needed to develop. One of the first approved studies was improving the logistical bases and schooling. It was practically non-existent and reminded him very much of Cambodia. The long-range projects were to follow the outlined plan. One example was the recommended action of establishing a logistical school for the Singapore Armed Forces. In a letter to General Westmoreland dated August 8, 1972, Ted says, "I couldn't ask for better working conditions or living conditions. Helma loves the shopping here and believes it is the best she has ever seen. With the ongoing activities in Vietnam and Cambodia there is a real threat of the communist penetration in the area. I feel I'm continuing to play a vital role in assisting our Allies in an effort to stabilize the area."

After the Army JAG gave the job the green light, Ted and Helma departed in late June 1972 on their new adventure to Singapore. Helma was not looking forward to their upcoming time in Singapore; something in her was not quite ready to leave the new retirement home she had built for them in Southern Pines, North Carolina. Helma's heart had been set on settling down in her home with her family and living a retired life. As a result, Helma did to her son what Ted Sr. had always done to her. When it was time to move, she left the house half-packed. Once Ted and Hema left the United States, her son and son-in-law had to pack up the rest of the house and move all the contents into storage. Ted Jr. was left with the unfinished state of his parents' home. He understood that his help was expected as payment for living in the house rent-free while he served at Fort Bragg.

While traveling from North Carolina to Singapore, Helma and Ted visited their family and friends. They eventually stopped on the West Coast and Hawaii. While on their trip, the 747 they were traveling in broke down on Guam, which caused them to miss their connecting flights. Another problem quickly arose when they realized they needed a visa to visit Guam. Ted called a Vietnamese friend, Lt. Gen. Lu Lan, with whom he served in II Corps in 1964–65. Gen. Lu Lan arranged for them to fly on to Vietnam for a short stay while they worked out their continuing travel arrangements to Singapore.

General Lu Lan had just visited Southern Pines and willingly agreed to serve as their special sponsor for their short stay in Vietnam. Once they landed in Vietnam, Helma and Ted had an excellent dinner with the general and his lovely wife. Unfortunately, when Ted and Helma got ready to leave the following day, immigration told them they could not leave the country. Once again, their passports had no stamps of entry to Vietnam. They had no visas in Guam, and now they had no passport stamps permitting them to enter Vietnam. It was reminiscent of their visit with General Vin Loc when they visited Ted Jr. in Vietnam in 1969. Eventually, they were cleared to leave, and they left for Singapore with their baggage and Sabrina, their Persian cat.

In Singapore, Ted worked as hard as he did on active duty and loved every moment. This assignment resembled the social life Helma and Ted had so enjoyed in Iran, and Helma quickly got in step with their new life. Ted and Helma became great friends with the United States Ambassador, Mr. Cronk, and his wife. Once again, they enjoyed the active lifestyle found in the embassy circle. In his spare time, Ted attended classes at the University of Singapore and worked on understanding the culture and language. Helma embraced the new shopping environment and all that it offered.

Ted's company held monthly meetings and published minutes of their ongoing activities and projects. It maintained appropriate paperwork showing they were in fact an independent contracting group working with a local Singapore business on a project for the local government. With this structure, they were not working directly for a foreign government. As a result of the initial study conducted, Ted was given the go ahead to hire three retired US Army colonels with experience in manpower, logistics, and technical ordinance to become part of the team. A study on the air force resulted in a contract for an additional three-man team to serve as consultants for the US Skyhawk planes that their air force had purchased. Next, the team hired a former government employee at level GS-15 to be a financial consultant for the defense director. Over time, this process allowed the company to expand its mission to include personnel to match the emerging requirements. Additionally, other special projects were approved such as transforming their commando unit into a special forces unit, upgrading their support services for the military, and reorganizing their army to accommodate expanding roles and missions.

One of their most notable projects was to improve the use of military history in training and effectiveness for the armed forces of Singapore. Appropriate levels of military history were integrated into all levels of officer and NCO training. This ranged from strategy at the staff college level to "heroic front line combat examples" for their NCOs and junior leaders. As a result, Ted integrated historical operations from World War II into the country's teachings of military history throughout the military school system. Additionally, General Mataxis was asked to set up an oral history program to gather information from local Singapore citizens who formed local defense units during World War II. This project concentrated on three main areas. The first area was to improve teaching history to the Singapore Armed Forces' officers. The second area created a current account of staff projects to gather yearly operational data. The third focus established an oral history project designed to collect data on the activities of Singapore's officers during several important events: the fall of Singapore, communist guerrilla warfare in Malaysia, and the Indonesian confrontation. Singapore's political leaders at the time were anxious to highlight their involvement in the Battle of Singapore, something British military historians had never evaluated. The British ignored the battle, while Singapore's leaders believed that this battle during World War II was a crucial historic moment for their newly formed island, citizens, and armed forces. Like the study of all history, it might provide some valuable lessons for the country's future operations and instill some pride in their civilian population for their accomplishments during World War II.

Ted's company was also responsible for recommending and advising new equipment purchases and arranging for the attendance of their military personnel at special forces courses at Fort Bragg. In special forces, Ted Jr. was quite surprised to find four Singaporeans in his high-altitude low opening (HALO) class at Fort

Bragg in 1972. It appeared as if Ted Sr. was ensuring the capability of Singapore's special forces.

They were very selective of the personnel they sent to attend Duke University and British universities. Mataxis arranged to upgrade the skill sets of the country's military historians by selecting intelligent, young officers to attend and earn master's degrees from these well-respected universities. The first officer sent to Duke later became head of the Ministry of Defense and after he retired, he became the ambassador to Australia. He is simply one example of the quality of the officers selected to participate in these programs during the start-up phase of this relatively new nation. These efforts and military arrangements included Ted teaching military history courses at two of Singapore's leading universities. During this time, Mataxis studied the files on the Japanese attacks on Singapore and the Malayan Emergency. He recalled, "I was also active in helping raise support for the anticommunist resistance to the Khmer Rouge in Cambodia. I attended many Singaporean and Indonesian military meetings to keep abreast of the ongoing issues of the time in Southeast Asia. The Vietnamese war was still going on and I was making several trips to Saigon, Bangkok, and Taiwan to stay abreast of the ongoing war, a key concern."

Upon arrival in Singapore, Ted and Helma moved into 4 Berkshire Road, a substantial British-type colonial home just down from Gillman Circle. It sat back from a main road in an old British staff officer-type housing compound—very peaceful, quiet, very spacious, and well-maintained grounds. The house had 16-foot ceilings, and every room had a huge ceiling fan and wooden shutters that could be closed during the monsoon rains. The doors provided extra security. The accommodation was rather lovely. The only exceptions were the 1936-style kitchen, which was 10 feet wide and 30 feet long, and the older bathrooms. Despite these minor annoyances, Ted and Helma enjoyed living there immensely.

Helma was in heaven. She had thrived over the years using retail therapy; she simply loved to shop. Singapore opened a whole new world of possibilities for her. Having arrived with only their luggage full of clothes and the cat, Helma had to buy new rattan furniture and other furnishings for their new home. She was up for the challenge. Since driving in Singapore was so tricky, Ted and Helma were provided a car and a driver. Unlike in India, servants in Singapore did not come running when one rang the bell; yet they were very efficient. The chauffeur was one of their favorites and he certainly earned his paycheck. He would drive Helma around while she filled the new house with numerous "bits and pieces" from around the island. For the first five months, Ted and Helma did not make any trips off the island; despite this, Helma's driver had already put 6,000 miles on their car. This statistic is made even more impressive when one realizes that Singapore is only 24 miles long from tip to tip, with a total land area of 283 square miles. Singapore is an island, city, state, and country.

The posting in Singapore was much like Iran; Ted and Helma would see more friends passing through than when they lived in Washington, D.C. Much to their surprise, several old friends had also moved to Singapore. This convergence of expats made their stay much more fun. The wives immediately reestablished friendships and began browsing through the markets together. They enjoyed being able to pick up where they had left off.

There were plenty of historical places scattered throughout Singapore for these friends to visit together. The Raffles Hotel was one such place. Ted and Helma visited the hotel for the first time during the 1950s on their way to India. Returning decades later, they realized that very little of the hotel had changed; Raffles was still as lovely as ever. Mataxis would continue his physical fitness regimen in Singapore by swimming 1,600 meters each night after work and on weekends at the Singapore Hilton Hotel. Helma and Ted were a daily feature at the hotel as Ted stuck to his daily swimming schedule. He clocked a mile without stopping every night. Helma secretly admired his persistence as she would sit poolside enjoying happy hour at the Tradewinds Bar on the top floor of the hotel and savor the fantastic view of Singapore as her husband swam. Everyone seemed to enjoy the older man swimming his daily hour, and none of the youngsters there ever tried to compete with him. The hotel staff not only adopted the couple but made Ted an honorary member of the hotel swimming pool, providing him with a plaque so stating.

Unlike Iran, there were plenty of unique places to eat. Ted liked going out to public places because in Singapore at that time, signs at bars and restaurants said, "If you have long hair, you are required to go to the back of the line." Thanks to Helma's perfect alibi of her dismally outdated kitchen, they ate out more in Singapore than they had while on any other assignment. The quality and the wide variety of food types added to their culinary experience. Only occasionally did they eat a meal at home that was not simply breakfast. It was a fascinating ride while it lasted.

Helma always said, "Along with the bad, some good always comes." Unfortunately, all good things must come to an end. Unexpectedly, Helma had to return to the United States for surgeries. In their 1973 Christmas letter from Singapore, Helma explained, "Ted was off on company business to Laos, Vietnam, Cambodia, and Thailand, where he visited many old friends." She said, "He met some English friends of ours in Bangkok, and they spent Christmas Day at the Bridge over the River Kwai." Helma briefly explained her health ordeal in the letter, "In March 1973, [I] returned to the States, had surgery, spent six weeks in the hospital, and then took some additional time to recover in April 1973. Ted returned for a month's leave from Singapore in July 1973, and we spent time visiting family and friends in the States." The time flew by for them, and they stopped at different friends' locations en route back to Singapore.

Helma would return to Singapore only to be hospitalized again in November 1973. She spent another week in the Singapore hospital, then was air-lifted to Clark

Air Force Base in Guam on December 7. While she was in the hospital, she had friends flying in to be with her. The staff and doctors worked hard to get her out of the hospital so that she could return to Singapore in time for Christmas. Christmas was always her favorite holiday, and this year was no exception. Despite her medical treatments, she was incredibly grateful to have so many friends supporting her when she needed them the most. Her trials and tribulations were not enough to stop the delivery of their yearly Christmas card.

According to Helma's annual Christmas card, "To close out 1973, Ted Jr. was married on November 17, 1973, to Kirby Jones, the girl next door, or at least the girl from across the street." As parents, Helma and Ted could not help but feel that this marked the end of their roles as parents and began their roles as grandparents. Always one for a goals list, Mataxis added being a great-grandfather to his list of desired accomplishments to complete during his lifetime. He would reach that great-grandfather goal several decades later, as he did so many other goals throughout his lifetime. Helma was sick again and had to be evacuated to the Philippines this time. After she got out of the hospital in May 1974, she left for her home in Southern Pines, North Carolina. She set up her retirement home once again. Ted was going on leave in August that year, and he was going to return for a stateside visit. During the leave he visited General Pearson at Valley Forge Military Academy en route to visit Shirley's family at West Point.

Upon returning to Southeast Asia after completing his contract in Singapore with UMPC, Mataxis joined another local Singapore business firm and moved to Phnom Penh in early 1975, three years after his retirement. Phnom Penh was under siege at the time and fell to the Cambodian communists, the Khmer Rouge, within a few weeks. The purpose of the business was to go into Cambodia and purchase weapons to prevent them from falling into the hands of the enemy. The plan did not work because things were too far gone in the besieged capital. They had been negotiating for about 31,000 weapons and didn't get any because rockets started landing in Phnom Penh and the team took off. Never one to be left out of a good fight, the retired general placed himself in the epicenter of the action. As the fighting closed around Phnom Penh, Mataxis woke up one morning to find his team gone. He looked around for them, only to realize upon finding their note that they had abandoned him. Their message was simple: "General, you might be used to this shit, but we are not. We got on the plane for Singapore last night!"

CHAPTER 16

Valley Forge Military Academy, 1975–83

After his visit to Valley Forge Ted sent General Pearson a letter in April 1975 stating, "I must say I really envy your job. I think the training of young men, particularly during this turbulent period in American history, is one of the most important jobs a person could have. It is much more important to my mind than getting out in the business world and merely 'making money.' After all, we professional army officers spend a lifetime being devoted to our jobs and not in a frantic search for jobs which would pay us more money, which is what I've seen in civilian life."

Mataxis served as assistant superintendent and commandant of cadets at Valley Forge Military Academy (VFMA) from 1975 through 1983. Lieutenant General Willard Pearson was the superintendent and president of the institution. General Pearson had been the commander of the 101st Brigade in Vietnam in 1965, where Ted served as his deputy commander. Lt. Gen. Pearson requested that Ted join him at VFMA as his deputy. Upon his arrival Lt. Gen. Pearson explained to Ted that the traditional role of the military academy was to build young men physically, mentally, and socially. In addition, they would provide a solid academic foundation for further study and prepare their graduates to assume leadership roles as citizens. Many of the students that attended came with a tinge of patriotism and they were eligible to receive a second lieutenant's commission upon completion of the school. He was asked by Lt. Gen. Pearson, "What better way to share your military knowledge and experience than with these young cadets over their years in attendance here?" Ted took that to heart and now had 600 students to mentor. He could ask for nothing more.

The curriculum at VFMA focused on total immersion in a unique educational experience centered on five cornerstones: academic

Ted served as the commandant at Valley Forge from 1975 to 1983.

excellence, personal motivation, character development, physical development, and leadership. College cadets were eligible to receive a commission into the army upon graduating. VFMA's administration and staff were composed almost entirely of current or retired military, and the board of trustees was almost entirely alumni.

The campus was on 130 acres of property and had about 120 buildings. It was like a self-contained city, with over 600 young men enrolled from 7th grade through junior college. Helma used to say that it brought tears to her eyes when she watched the young men perform on the parade field, polo field, or in chapel. It was all so beautiful and awe-inspiring. During the time they were there, refugees from Vietnam were fleeing to the United States. General Mataxis and the academy sponsored almost 30 refugees to work at the campus, helping to keep everything in pristine condition. The refugees loved the environment, and some third-generation refugees still work at Valley Forge. It was a lovely campus which included those amenities you would expect at a boarding college; in addition, they had a large parade field, a polo field, a museum, and a chapel.

The couple's time at Valley Forge would be the first time in their lives that Helma and Ted would have settled in and stayed in one spot for an extended period. They lived on campus in Wayne, Pennsylvania, for eight years. They were provided a four-bedroom house on the school's grounds that enabled Ted to walk everywhere, check on the cadets, and stay in touch with the pulse of the school. The extra bedrooms gave them plenty of room for visiting friends, which they enjoyed so much. Life at a private boarding school is not a job, it is a way of life that absorbs 24 hours a day, seven days a week, and there was always something going on with his newly acquired family of 600 young men. These years were hectic, but they gave the couple many fond memories. During his time at VFMA, he was paid $15,000 annually and provided a house for a monthly fee of $125. He was never concerned about making money; he focused more on the mission. After they left, they admitted that they genuinely missed the formal dances, teas, concerts, polo matches, and chapel services. Helma loved playing the role of hostess for everyone. Over the years, Helma enjoyed providing the cadets with formal teas and dinners to teach them proper etiquette, customs, and traditions. All five of Ted's grandsons were allowed to attend VFMA's annual summer camps. Ted and Helma's children always took advantage of this fun-filled activity and sent their children to camp looking forward to parent visits at drop-off and pick-up time.

The following description is from a civilian resume created by the general: "1975 through 1983, I was the Assistant Superintendent/Commandant of Cadets at Valley Forge Military Academy and Junior College in Wayne, PA. My wife and I lived there the entire time in a house provided by the Academy. I worked for General Pearson, whom I worked with in Vietnam in the 101st. In that position, I was the principal administrator of a $25 million complex of 100 buildings with over 200 educators, administrators, and support personnel. Since the school prepared junior college cadets to become second lieutenants, we maintained a close liaison with the Army Reserve Officers training program (ROTC) through frequent briefings and visits to training sites, active military bases, and military schools. During this period, I also worked part-time as a consultant to various Iranian projects, such as an organizational study, the re-establishment of the Iranian Merchant Marine Academy, and provided recommendations for Iranian cadets in the US attending VFMA. I also lectured at the Air Force Special Operations School at Hurlburt Field, Florida and the Special Operations Warfare School at Fort Bragg. I did this as a consultant under my company AZED Association, Ltd." Additionally, Ted was a member of the Speakers Bureau of the American Security Council and Commander of the Philadelphia Chapter of Military Orders of the World Wars. He also became involved with the Heritage Foundation as a representative on the status of Afghanistan to jump-start the Committee for a Free Afghanistan.

Ted enjoyed working and mentoring the young men. Perhaps one of the more famous students from that time frame was Lt. Gen. H. R. McMaster, who served as the 25th United States National Security Advisor, from 2017 to 2018, for President Trump. McMaster was a cadet officer while attending VFMA and Ted followed his career through West Point and into the army. They reconnected again while McMaster was taking graduate courses at the University of North Carolina, earning his PhD. His PhD thesis was critical of American strategy and military leadership during the Vietnam War and served as the basis for his book *Dereliction of Duty: Lyndon Johnson, Robert McNamara, The Joint Chiefs of Staff, and the Lies That Led to Vietnam*, which was widely read in the United States military. Ted was sent an unedited proof of Major McMaster's book and was impressed with the extent of the research. He had this to say upon reading it in a letter to the publisher: "I have read HR's book, and I am impressed with the extent of his research. It clarified questions I had which, even though I was a speechwriter for two chairmen [of the Joint Chiefs], had puzzled and frustrated me. His description of the feelings of the military for Secretary McNamara and his whiz kids is 'right on!' Even today I feel a rush of anger at their arrogance and ignoring of military advice which exacerbated the disaster in Vietnam." General McMaster sent Mataxis a copy of his book with the inscription: "To Brig. Gen. Theodore C. Mataxis, who has been a great inspiration to me for two decades and whose assistance with this project proved invaluable. H. R. McMaster."

One of the couple's favorite experiences during this time was, ironically, not wholly school-related. In 1981, the movie *Taps* was filmed on location. The movie is an American drama film starring George C. Scott, with Timothy Hutton, Tom Cruise, Ronnie Cox, Sean Penn, and Evan Handler in supporting roles. The film was directed by Harold Becker from the screenplay by Robert Carmen. It was based on the 1979 novel *Father Sky*. In the movie, a group of students attending the academy decide to take it over to prevent it from being closed. This movie was Sean Penn's first film role and Tom Cruise's second movie role. Stanley R. Jaffe bought the book rights when it was still in manuscript form. The movie took five months to film and required them to build a mockup of some buildings to correct the lighting. As the movie was being filmed, General Mataxis was provided a director's chair and served as the technical advisor on all things military. The production studio wanted to use many of the Mataxis family's furnishings for the movie. They had them appraised and paid 10 percent of the appraised value for their use. Helma worked with the set director in furnishing the dining room, study, and family room at the house and the office in which George C. Scott lived and worked. Helma and Ted appeared in three scenes: the opening at the chapel, the receiving line for a formal, and on the parade field. It was a unique experience for the couple, and they really enjoyed it.

Another exciting event occurred when, while visiting at VFMA, President Reagan was awarded the Order of Anthony Wayne. This is the highest honor presented by VFMA and reserved for those who demonstrated exceptional public service nationally or internationally. Prior honorees include Admiral John McCain, Secretary of State Alexander Haig, and General William Westmorland.

General Mataxis said before leaving in August 1983, "These eight years at Valley Forge have been among the most gratifying of my life." He added, "I felt it was time to try my hand at something else." Brig. Gen. Mataxis retired at 65 from VFMA because he wanted to become a consultant on international events, public education, and military affairs.

After Ted's retirement from VFMA in 1983, they once again moved back into Helma's retirement home. Valley Forge Military Academy had provided Helma with eight years of stability and now she was finally going to her retirement home, which she had built in 1972. She had set it up and furnished it with the family's possessions that they had collected while on various assignments. She was finally settling in and reconnecting with all her

Ted officiating at a banquet at Valley Forge. To his left is his old CINCLANT, Commander John McCain Jr. McCain was receiving his Order of Anthony Wayne.

President Reagan visiting Valley Forge Military Academy to receive the Order of Anthony Wayne Award.

Southern Pines and Pinehurst, North Carolina friends. She was living the retired life she had longed for so many years and enjoyed settling into her role as a grandmother. So, Helma had her "nest" the way she wanted it, displaying all their treasures and reflecting on memories of the times living abroad. It was her dream of retirement that had finally come true. The home was furnished exactly as she had envisioned it in 1972, prior to moving to Singapore. Ted Jr. was assigned once again to Fort Bragg in 1981 with the founding of the Joint Special Operations Command. Ted Jr. and his family had lived in Helma's retirement home while building their home in horse country in Southern Pines, North Carolina.

Upon returning to Southern Pines, retirement was the last thing on Ted's mind. Once he set up his file cabinets, library, and gun collection, he was actively pursuing things to keep his mind engaged. He did not want to fall into the easy life of golf, cocktail parties, and picking up pinecones. He also actively sought out a role in politics as an advisor to North Carolina's Republican Senate representatives, Jesse Helms and Lauch Faircloth, as a special advisor for military and veteran affairs.

Shortly after they had moved to Southern Pines, North Carolina, Ted was offered the position of field advisor to the Committee for a Free Afghanistan (CFA). In accepting the offer as a field advisor to CFA, he was locked into overseas travel. He immediately accepted the job, knowing that Helma was now settled, and he would not have to succumb to the retiree's life. In the years ahead, Ted would visit the mujahideen fighters every year until the end of the conflict. Ted often said, "The difficult we do immediately, the impossible takes a little longer." We never knew he was referring to settling down and retiring, which would only happen after the war in Afghanistan ended and the CAF was disbanded. Helma and Ted lived in Southern Pines until their move out to Denver, Colorado in 2001 to be close to Kaye and Bud's growing family.

CHAPTER 17

The Committee for a Free Afghanistan, 1983–89

When the Soviet Union invaded Afghanistan in December 1979 and killed the president of the country, they supported the Democratic Republic of Afghanistan. The Russians occupied the territory with an estimated troop strength of 100,000 personnel. During their time in Afghanistan the Russians carried out brutal atrocities, indiscriminately killing children, women, men, and animals, making the country a "free fire" zone. They used gas agents, booby-trapped toys, and saturated populated areas with small bomblets.

During the months before the Soviet invasion of Afghanistan, President Jimmy Carter's focus was on the Iranian hostage situation. By the middle of 1979, he had initiated a covert program through the CIA to financially support the Afghan rebels, the mujahideen.

Early in the 19th century, Afghanistan played a role as a geopolitical pawn between Tsarist Russia and Great Britain. This was often referred to as "the Great Game" and Great Britain fought three wars in Afghanistan. They were called the Anglo-Afghan Wars, also referred to as the Afghan Wars, and these three conflicts took place in 1839–42, 1878–80, and 1919. Britain, from its bases in India, sought to extend its control over its neighbor Afghanistan to prevent Russian influence from expanding into Central Asia. This would have positioned Russia too close to India, which the British did not want. Afghanistan remained on the front lines of the Cold War between East and West.

During his time in the army, Retired Brig. Gen. Theodore Mataxis served for several years in India, Pakistan, and Iran, and traveled extensively through the region, including Afghanistan. He was selected to advise and assist the "Mujahideen freedom fighters" in the capacity of field director for the Committee for a Free Afghanistan (CFA), a non-governmental organization (NGO). It was considered an educational group, headquartered in Washington, D.C. It was formed in 1980, and its purpose was to keep the Afghan war, and the plight of the guerrilla warriors, their families, and the refugees, before the American public. The committee supported the Reagan

Doctrine by assisting the Afghan freedom fighters who were struggling against the USSR's invasion of Afghanistan.

NGOs were basically ignored, except by President Reagan's outreach office in the White House. Later NGOs were well accepted and even mentioned in military field manuals taught at various service schools. Ted was an adviser to President Reagan's "freedom fighters," the mujahideen, from 1983 until 1990 for the CFA, providing support and advice to the Afghans as they fought the Soviets. Additionally, the committee worked closely with Doctors Without Borders and focused on humanitarian efforts, refugee camps, and medical issues. The president's policy was "peace through strength." As an advisor during this conflict, Mataxis (up until his 72nd year) made eight annual trips to Pakistan and Afghanistan, each lasting from one to three months.

This picture of Ted on one of his inspection tours with the mujahideen, date unknown.

In October 1983, Ted visited China at the invitation of the Peking Institute for International Strategic Studies. Ted had met a Chinese Ambassador to the United States at a function and the ambassador had extended an invitation for Ted to visit China and make a presentation at the institute. Ted's presentation was on the subject of "Mobilization for World War II and ROTC Programs." This visit had been cleared through proper channels and was encouraged by the military and State Department "to build better relations." Ted believed that the grassroots level among combat veterans was where "lasting friendships between nations are built!" The institute was most hospitable, furnishing an escort officer, translator, a car, and driver. During this time the Chinese didn't describe the land battles in Korea very much, but they did stress American airstrike power when discussing the war. Ted discovered that the Chinese had a different perception of what the Korean War was about. Mataxis said, "It's like different people looking at the same aerial photograph, some seeing hills and some seeing holes. I found out the Chinese believed that the United States was using the Korean War as an excuse to support an invasion of mainland China by Chiang Kai-Shek, whose nationalist Chinese forces retreated to Taiwan in 1949." He tried to explain that, "After the Soviet Union had taken over Eastern Europe and started a civil war in Greece, the United States saw the Soviet Union and China as a monolith bound together, getting ready to invade Japan through Korea." During this visit he was taken to many historical spots and was given a tour of Beijing's air raid tunnels and spent a day with the Chinese army's 196th Infantry Division. The division provided a demonstration for him and wanted his impression of the division. He told them, "I was impressed that the soldiers were alert, looked like soldiers, and were very well trained in basic infantry tactics." At that time, he told the Chinese, "I can't imagine anyone launching a conventional attack on China, not even the Russians." The Chinese had mentioned that divisions like the 196th were becoming obsolete. He immediately responded and took issue with the idea that such infantry units were obsolete, stating, "A capable infantry could cause an invading enemy terrific casualties." Here, Ted had the opportunity to meet and talk with some Chinese veterans of the Korean War. Wherever he went, he actively sought out opportunities to meet with veterans.

The CFA had planned for him to proceed on to Pakistan from China. Pakistan's Ambassador to the United States, Lt. Gen. Ejaz Azin (July 1981–September 1986), had arranged briefings for Ted in Islamabad and a tour of the Afghan border camps. This was fallout from an article Mataxis had written on Pakistan and Afghanistan earlier that spring after attending a Villanova seminar. The Pakistanis had been sent a copy of the article by the Villanova professor who conducted the seminar, and they were quite taken with it. Upon arrival, Mataxis was greeted by a political counselor and provided a car for the duration of the visit. He had been accompanied by another member of the Speakers Bureau of American Security Council. They received briefings on the Afghan mujahideen fighters and visited Afghan refugee camps in Pakistan so they could understand the gravity of the situation. Upon returning to the United States, they shared with CFA their findings, which allowed them to formulate additional planning.

After the election, President Reagan announced that the Reagan Doctrine supported the "freedom fighters" trying to regain their country from the communists. This created opposition among liberals in the media and Congress, who proclaimed that his aggressive anticommunism and support of the freedom fighters would lead to war! Frustrated by this opposition, President Reagan turned to his conservative supporters across the nation and ask them to use "grassroot public diplomacy" to support him. Members of the White House staff also encouraged conservative activists to form private volunteer organizations (PVO) which would generate support in Congress for the "freedom fighters." The CFA's mission was modified over the next decade as needs changed. The CFA's initial goal was to generate moral support among the public against the Soviet invasion. This first objective was to raise awareness at the grassroot levels for supporting the rebels. Then, as the freedom fighters' successful resistance against the Soviets continued, the next step was for the CFA to encourage congressional leaders to form Afghan support groups in Congress. According to Mataxis, "This move towards full political support was encouraged by the visit of the insurrectionist leaders in Washington to meet the president, Congress, and other key administrative officials. The Department of State noted that the CFA was instrumental in this public diplomacy aspect of promoting the Afghan cause." A key player in the clandestine support was covered in the book *Charlie Wilson's War:*

The Extraordinary Story of How the Wildest Man in Congress and a Rogue CIA Agent Changed the History of Our Time, written by George Crile. In 1983 the leadership from Afghanistan came to the United States and met with President Reagan and Vice President Bush Sr.

Ted was asked by the Pakistani military to visit Peshawar, Pakistan, to conduct a reconnaissance of the situation in Afghanistan and to make recommendations on weapons, training, and tactics for the mujahideen. The CFA also looked at bringing wounded soldiers to American hospitals and providing humanitarian aid for both the mujahideen and the swelling refugee camps. As the Russian invasion continued in length, the CFA efforts expanded as help was needed. CFA had a suite of offices in the Heritage Foundation office building in D.C. The foundation was a conservative public policy research institute which had been referred to as President Reagan's think tank. Initially, Mataxis provided reports on the conditions on the ground and updates on the situation to the various federal governmental agencies involved. He provided an independent viewpoint on the refugees, mujahideen, and Soviet activities. In a letter he said, "I must admit I was surprised by how much influence we were able to bring on key issues by assisting in areas that the official State Department couldn't handle. We understood that our clout came from phone calls from the president's 'outreach office' in the White House. We were taken seriously by the National Security Council, State Department, Department of Defense, Agency for Internal Development, and the Afghan support groups in the Congress and Senate."

Concurrently with these first two steps of gaining moral support at grassroots level and political support in Washington to provide material support for the freedom fighters, the CFA and other similarly fueled POVs raised funds for humanitarian assistance from individuals and organizations across America. The CFA initially funded a "wound program" which paid for transportation of seriously wounded mujahideen and refugees to the United States for medical treatment. This was accomplished by "walking the hill" and explaining these needs to Congress. Congress began by funding an expanded humanitarian assistance program for Afghan refugees and the mujahideen. Eventually, they fully funded a government program of using US Air Force planes to bring out seriously wounded Afghan fighters and refugees to Europe and the United States for treatment. Next, the CFA organized a war crimes project and funded a major fact-finding mission to the Pakistani refugee camps, which investigated violations of human rights and international law. Additionally, the CFA liaison office in Pakistan worked closely with several members of the mujahideen political offices, assisting them with special media enhancement projects and several other important ongoing projects.

During his stays in Pakistan, Ted was there as a private citizen without any security. He utilized an interpreter to talk with the guerrilla leaders, and they informed him of their need for weapons and the help needed for the millions of people in the refugee camps. The CFA assisted in the creation of a sanctuary across the border in northern Pakistan, which required the support of the Pakistani government. It was obtained by a large military assistance program that included providing Pakistan with F-16 fighters. The committee also sponsored medical evacuations and treatment for injured soldiers and civilians, as well as providing food, seeds, clothing, blankets, and other necessities of life to the fighters and refugees. The Pakistani government provided food and substance to some three million Afghan refugees for more than eight years. The CFA also continued to conduct fundraising activities for the Afghans' cause.

The term mujahideen is used in a religious context by Muslims to refer to those engaged in a struggle of any nature for the benefit of Islam, commonly referred to as a jihad. Over the centuries, Afghanistan's tribes have continually fought one another; however, they have always united quickly whenever their country is invaded, or another country tries to intervene in their affairs. The mujahideen continued to reflect the highly decentralized nature of Afghan society and strong loci of competing Pashtun tribal groups. Upon receiving pressure from the supporting nations, they formed a union with other Afghan groups for the benefit of all. The belief was, "That any enemy of my enemy is a friend."

Initially, the weapons supplied were antique British rifles, which were very accurate at long ranges but not at all effective when engaged in close combat with the overwhelming Russian firepower. To start with, Mataxis taught them things that were never solved by the United States when fighting in Vietnam, and lessons learned during his years of study of counterinsurgencies and guerrilla warfare. At first, these tactics and techniques were very rudimentary, such as placing mines on the trails to defend the camps and using the ridgelines to mask movements of the individuals. The placement of their mines in the entries and exits of the Soviet minefields was most effective. Another successful tactic used by the North Vietnamese was mortar raids. They would infiltrate the firing location and bury or conceal the mortar tubes with rounds. At the time of the mortar raid, all they would need to do was infiltrate the location, set up the mortar, fire, and flee.

The importance of "loya jirga" had not changed since Alexander the Great invaded Afghanistan centuries ago. Alexander said, "The village elders had a mullah who taught only religion." A significant difference between the people of Iraq and Afghanistan is that in Iraq they only stress loyalty to the family. The Afghans stress loyalty to the tribes, which were very decentralized. Mataxis gave presentations on the CFA's operations as a non-governmental agency during the Soviet Afghan war to the US Army Chief of Military History Conference and he submitted reports. He had long been a member of the National Security Speakers Bureau and presented lectures to anyone and everyone that had an interest in his lectures or his beliefs. He understood that the CFA and the lifeline they were providing for the mujahideen fighters and the people of Afghanistan were very good; however, that could easily change. He said, "When it comes to national interest, there are no eternal friends or eternal enemies, only self-interests. This was stated by a British statesman in the middle of the 1800s and still rings true today."

Even though the Russian army pulled out in February 1989, there was a constant battle to thwart the threat from the communist Kabul government the Soviets had left in place. Another key point was to keep the friction minimized between the seven different ethnic groups that were fighting for freedom. Once the Russians left, the people were struggling. The internal parties each wanted to come up with their own agenda. The Russian government continued pouring in $250 million monthly in aid through Kabul. They had withdrawn troop support, yet they were still providing logistical support. The Afghan groups were somewhat bonded through their religion and their shared struggle for freedom from the communists. The United States was attempting to help the mujahideen by sending arms through Pakistan at the rate of $400 million per year; however, the Americans failed to keep track of their shipments and the distribution of weapons. This resulted in one fundamentalist faction having an extreme advantage over the other six factions. Many of their weapons were American but the Afghans had additional support from many countries around the world.

The United States needed to help the country bond together through the Islamic religion and it needed to continue supporting its military. Mataxis said, "In the meantime America and the Western nations should not be fooled by smiling Soviets who encourage everyone to stop sending arms to Afghanistan." Mataxis also said, "The Soviets left a two-year supply of ammunition for the Kabul government on the ground. They can quit sending arms and still feel comfortable on how things are going there." He was quoted as saying, "I feel it necessary for the fighting to continue; however, restructuring and better tracking of weapon shipments and distribution of equipment is a must." These quotes were written in June 1990, in the *Citizen News-Record*, after the Soviets pulled out. Mataxis drafted a formal letter to President Bush regarding Afghanistan and its current needs. The letter stated to President Bush that the Afghan people could not be abandoned! At this point, pulling away from that country and leaving it to heal itself would be abandonment.

The CFA was one of the first PVOs that focused on the Soviet invasion of Afghanistan and its impact on the people of that country. The administration encouraged the PVOs to back the Reagan Doctrine by assisting anti-communist guerrillas. Mataxis stated, "As field director of the CFA, I constantly visited Peshawar, Pakistan, since it was the headquarters of the seven major Mujahideen factions and was the optimum site to coordinate CFA activities with the freedom fighters and the three million Afghan refugees living in squalor camps along the Pakistan/Afghanistan border. One of the first things I did was study the map and I was struck by a sense of déjà vu from my experiences in Vietnam. This time, however, I was sitting with the guerillas in the Eagle's Beak, which juts into Afghanistan, menacing Kabul. When I was in Saigon, years earlier, it was threatened by the enemy divisions in Cambodia located in the Parrot's Beak. During this same time, I made trips to Thailand to visit

Cambodian freedom fighters who were based there. We tried; however, we could not get any traction in the US because Vietnam was so fresh in the American mind."

The Russians divided the war into four phases. The first phase was from December 1979 to February 1980. This consisted of the introduction of Soviet forces into Afghanistan, establishing their garrisons and locations and securing various bases and installations. The second phase was from March 1980 to April 1985. During this time the Soviets carried out active tactical combat operations that maximized their use of the technical advantages of air power and artillery fire. These advantages inflicted significant losses, forcing the mujahideen to change tactics and take up guerilla warfare by moving back into the safety of the mountains. During the third phase from April 1985 to January 1987, the Stinger missile was provided. This was an absolute game-changer because the Soviets lost their air superiority. The Soviets turned the bulk of the fighting over to their Afghan allies and focused on their bases and security. General Mataxis was referred to as "the old American General who brought them the Stinger missiles." Mataxis said, "As a result of my name and Greek heritage I was referred to as Ouzo not Mataxis. It was not a very deep cover." The Russians started the deployment of their regiments back to Russia. During phase four, from January 1987 to February 1989, Gorbachev realized that he had to expand the war significantly or withdraw. He selected withdrawal as the better option. The Soviets were not conducting offensive operations and only initiated contact when they were attacked by the mujahideen or when they were supporting their Afghan allies in a fight. The Soviets were planning for total withdrawal of Russian forces from Afghanistan.

Ted on one of his trips into Afghanistan with the mujahideen, observing the recently acquired Stinger missile, 1985. The missile was a most significant game changer because of the Russians' effective use of technology and air superiority, which easily defeated the freedom fighters.

The mujahideen had a different perspective; however, they also divided the war into four phases. The first phase was the initial nationwide resistance to the invading Soviets. The Soviets initiated the conflict by air-dropping elite troops into the principal Afghan cities. Shortly after, they attacked with motorized divisions across the Afghan border. About the same time, the KGB infiltrated the Afghan presidential palace, poisoning the president and his ministers and assisting in launching a Moscow-backed coup, which installed a new puppet leader, Babrak Karmal. This Soviet invasion triggered a brutal attack on the Afghan people along with a nine-year-long Afghan civil war. This Russian action led to the Afghans' proclamation of jihad (holy war). The second phase was a reorganization phase, in which the mujahideen structured their headquarters, organized the receipt and distribution of weapons and materials, and began training their forces for the prolonged war to drive the invaders out. The third phase was simply surviving the Soviet technological onslaught brought to bear against the mujahideen. The Soviets had introduced remote electronic acoustic and seismic sensors that could detect the mujahideen moving some 12 miles away from the Soviet and Afghan communist positions. This, combined with the use of gas, sensors, and artillery fire, was devastating. Soviet radio-activated minefields, night vision devices, and subsonic bullets decimated the mujahideen ranks. However, nothing instilled a psychological impact like the introduction of Su-25 "Frogfoot" ground-attack aircraft and the Mi-24 "Hind" helicopter gunship, known as the "flying tank." Its infrared imaging was simply destructive to the mujahideen. The helicopter gunships and the "Frogfoot" close air support aircraft gave the Russians total uncontested control of the Afghan air space. The well-trained Spetsnaz forces, utilizing night vision capability, were increasingly effective, and as casualties soared mujahideen morale plummeted.

The year 1985 was in fact the decisive year. The most significant game-changer came about because of the effectiveness of the Russians' technology and air superiority, which easily defeated the freedom fighters. By September 1986, the program included state of the art American weapons, including the surface-to-air Stinger. The mujahideen started receiving the Stingers, which are shoulder-launched air defense missiles. It is believed that over 800 Stingers were ultimately shipped into Afghanistan. These missiles totally changed the dynamic of the war, allowing the mujahideen to take control of the skies over Afghanistan. This forced the Soviet gunships and attacking aircraft to fly much lower, losing their devastating capability and at the same time increasing their vulnerability. The Stinger changed the dynamics of the battlefield back in favor of the mujahideen. The fourth phase was signaled by the start of the Soviet withdrawal. This required the freedom fighters to increase their combat power to larger forces and begin to train conventional infantry battalions to fight the Afghan communists after the Soviet withdrawal. Mataxis remembers, "On the last trip at the end of June while the Russians were withdrawing, I infiltrated into the mountains to the north of Kandahar in Afghanistan. The CFA was assisting the rebels in building regular battalions to attack the communists after the Russians had pulled out."

The mujahideen learned to dodge Soviet attacks, work around Soviet technology, and how to survive to fight another day. In the end, the mujahideen's will was stronger than that of the Soviet leadership and the Soviet army simply withdrew. Once again, the will of the people allowed them to persevere and win in the end. It is believed by some that the defeat of the Soviet superpower brought the Cold War to an end.

A guerrilla group with inferior technology but smart leaders will avoid conflicts where technology will provide an edge against them. They will pick the time and the place of their battles, and they will opt for urban combat or combat in rough terrain or jungle. Guerrilla fighters using these forms of combat will need trained infantrymen to engage them, an increasingly rare commodity in armed forces throughout the world today.

The old saying goes that to win, all guerrillas must do is not lose too many battles and prolong the struggle until

Ted with a rocket launcher at a training camp somewhere in Afghanistan.

the other side loses interest in the conflict and ultimately pulls out, much like the American forces did in Afghanistan. This was a total disgrace to the American soldiers who fought, died, or were wounded, giving their all for their nation. The Soviet forces must have felt the same way! A country or faction within a country can effectively fight a technologically superior state or coalition using guerrilla warfare. Guerrilla warfare is a test of national will and endurance in which technological advantages are often degraded or negated. Simply stated, for guerrilla war to succeed, a portion of the local population must support or acquiesce to the presence of indigenous guerrillas in their midst. There must be a willingness to accept considerable casualties, combatant and non-combatant. Guerrillas must have a haven to retreat to when necessary, as well as a source of logistical supplies and support. What guerrillas do not need is a military victory. Guerrillas need to survive and endure over the years or decades of conflict. The guerrillas remained when the French left Algeria, the

United States left South Vietnam, and the Soviets left Afghanistan. The side with a greater moral commitment, be it patriotic, religious, or ideological, will eventually win because of their higher morale, greater obstinacy, stronger national will, and the determination to survive.

Guerrilla war does not fit into the popular image of the high-tech future war; however, it may well be the war that a high-tech country finds itself fighting around the world in future. The Soviet army, a modern, mechanized force, fought a guerrilla war for over nine years. Despite the their overwhelming air support, expenditure of national treasure, and young lives lost, the Soviets withdrew from Afghanistan, leaving the defiant mujahideen guerrillas behind. It was estimated that this conflict had cost the lives of over 1,000,000 civilians and combatants. The war did not just wreak havoc on Afghanistan; there were also millions of refugees in Pakistan and Iran. The last Soviet soldier did not leave until February 15, 1989, after the cost of 13,310 KIAs, 35,478 WIAs and 311 MIAs. This conflict contributed significantly to the loss of Soviet prestige and the later collapse and breakup of the Soviet Union.

As the Soviet army left Afghanistan in defeat, the mission of the CFA changed to keeping the public aware of the need to start negotiations under the UN to bring peace to Afghanistan. With the fall of Kabul and the outbreak of internal conflicts among various mujahideen groups, the CFA and other PVO support offices were closed. Not to be confused with the Taliban, the Afghan mujahideen were various armed Islamic rebel groups that fought against the government of the Democratic Republic of Afghanistan and the Soviet Union during the Soviet Afghan war and the first subsequent Afghan civil war.

This does not mean some Afghan mujahideen were not supported by or affiliated with the Taliban. In fact, Ted's good friend General Safi was one. Years later, Ted found out that General Safi had also worked for Britain's MI6 and would later work with the Taliban movement in Europe. General Safi visited Ted multiple times in Southern Pines, North Carolina. After Najibullah's government collapsed, the mujahideen factions (apart from Hezb-I Islami Gulbudin) signed a power sharing agreement, the Peshawar Accord. Kabul celebrated victory day on April 28, 1992. However, their new government was quickly fractured by rival factions, becoming

Ted with Afghan leader General Rahmatullah Safi in August 1993, visiting Ted's home in Southern Pines, North Carolina. The purpose of the visit was to try to get US support in having the United Nations bring peace to Afghanistan.

dysfunctional, and escalating into another civil war, from which the Taliban was formed. As a result, the mujahideen left a mixed legacy to Afghans.

One of the first issues dealt with in postwar rehabilitation in Afghanistan was working with the Kabul government and the UN to reopen medical facilities in each of the provinces. The CFA discussed the need for rapid economic rehabilitation to accommodate the several million refugees in Iran and Pakistan, plus rebuilding the destroyed infrastructure in the cities and towns across the country. Discussion of the need for lumber to rebuild would be critical since most of the concrete structure forms, wall footings, and prefab buildings had been destroyed. These events were all overcome by time because of the 9/11 attack and the follow-on war on terrorism. The United States became bogged down in Afghanistan even more than the Russians had. General Mataxis had strongly argued against this involvement by explaining their history, but it all fell on deaf ears.

The main weapons of the mujahideen resistance fighters evolved over time. Initially there were old British .303 Enfield rifles, which had both range and penetration power. The British Webley revolver was also popular early on. Ted had been presented a pair by General Safi to be used in his personal defense when in the country. Other early Soviet weapons were available but as the war progressed a wide variety of Soviet weapons and combat vehicles were captured and used by the mujahideen. The AK-47 assault rifle was plentiful and later upgraded with AKM, AKMS, Type 56, AK-74, and AK-74U models. A wide variety of World War II and later weapons also found their way, there such as the RPD, RPK, and Degtyaryov light machine guns, along with the general-purpose Soviet weapons such as the PKM and the Chinese Type 670; there were also several versions of heavy machine guns: DShk, Type 54 HMG, and SG-43. The Soviet RPGs—2, 7, Type 22 and 69—were used. The Soviet RPG antitank grenade launchers were very effective and used by both sides. The 82 mm and the 107 mm mortar, along with an Israeli model, were provided. The recoilless rifles, 73 mm, 75 mm, and 82 mm, were also used effectively. The real game changer for the mujahideen were the man-portable air defense systems—the Stinger and then FIM-92 Stinger missiles. Over 800 were delivered, starting in 1986. Two types of antitank weapons, the French MILAN and the US Tube-Launched, Optically Tracked, Wire Guided (TOW) antitank guided missile, with 80 launchers and 180 missiles, were provided in 1988.

In 1986 there was a book published by Kunhanandan Nair, a pseudonym for Thikkodiyan, an Indian playwright, novelist, and screenwriter. This book was published by Sterling Publishers in New Delhi and titled: *The Devil and His Dart: How the CIA is Plotting in the Third World*. The author called it a fact ledger and it had been suggested to him by a retired American World War I veteran, Brigadier General Hugh Hester. Hester was opposed to the United States Cold War policies and directives. He encouraged the author to research and study the CIA and their global covert operations. On page 82 of this book, he has this to say: "The agency also sends the best of its men to Afghanistan. One of those 'ugly Americans' is Theodore C. Mataxis. He is a decorated veteran of World War II, Korea, and Vietnam, who retired from the US Army in 1972 as a Brigadier General. The CIA gave him a new job. In Peshawar, he is now the field representative of the 'Committee for a Free Afghanistan,' a Washington lobby group that supports the Afghan and Contras. Theodore Mataxis also coordinates 'humanitarian aid' to the freedom fighters and arranges publicity visits to the United States for the rebel leaders." The writer attributes this quote to the *International Herald Tribune*, May 16, 1986.

The following speech was written by General Mataxis and presented at the US Army Center of Military History Conference. Although this may appear to be a repetition of things that have been written about previously, this presents his words in greater detail on the CFA history and President Reagan's "Peace Through Strength Policy."

Mataxis said, "The Carter regime's view of the world reflected the post-Vietnam War liberal malaise in America which favored a diminished role in the world for America and a close detente with the Soviets. Under President Carter, American defenses were cut back, the Panama Canal had been given away and a political furor erupted over his plan to pull back from Korea. These actions caused the Soviet Union to view the Carter Administration as weak and unlikely to take a strong response against future Soviet expansionist moves. The Iranian's Hostage Crisis had been dragging on and when the American raid failed at 'Desert One' President Carter looked weak. The hostages were released shortly after President Reagan was sworn in as President.

"Emboldened by our post-Vietnam War syndrome, which had led to the Carter administration's inactivity in the international arena, the Soviets felt that 'the correlation of powers' had shifted in their favor encouraging the invasion of Afghanistan. As explained by the DOD booklet *Soviet Military Power-1987* a stronger more adventurous Soviet Union had begun to view the conflicts in the third world as a venue for furthering Soviet interests!

"The Soviet invasion of Afghanistan triggered the next change in not only the US but also in world opinion towards the Soviet Union and the Cold War. When the Soviets blocked action in the United Nation's Security Council with their veto, it resulted in the United Nations' General Assembly condemning the invasion and calling for a 'withdrawal of foreign troops!' In the US this brutal invasion destroyed the existing public consensus for the detente and reignited the Cold War antagonism and suspicion against the USSR which contributed to the defeat of President Carter and the election of President Reagan. President Reagan's popular Campaign for 'Peace Through Strength' reflected the call of conservatives in the past of 'Keep your powder dry' of our early history and President Teddy Roosevelt 's call 'to carry a big stick!' Reagan's position was based on a firm conviction that trying to appease the USSR would only convince them that the correlation of power had shifted in their favor.

"The plans for the USSR's invasion of Afghanistan by the 40th USSR's army on December 27, 1979, was drawn up by two generals who had been involved in the planning of the invasion of Hungary in October 1956 and the invasion of Czechoslovakia in August of 1968. However, this wasn't Eastern Europe, and the entire countryside erupted as their mullahs declared a jihad, a holy war against the invaders! Armed groups under their tribal leaders reinforced by deserters from the Kabul's Communist army embarked on a prolonged guerrilla war to drive out the 'godless invaders' from their homeland.

"When the Soviet army invaded, they seized Kabul with their 105th Guards' Airborne Division and their special Commandos Task Force and assassinated President Amin replacing him with their puppet Babrak Karmal. Their mechanized task forces drove South along the two roads in eastern and western Afghanistan to seize the border crossing points into Pakistan thus isolating the country. President Carter was personally shaken by the invasion, which toppled his world view of a future based on a close detente with the USSR, which would allow a reduction of the defense budget and reduce the US military presence overseas. Carter's administration cancelled our participation in the Olympic Games, cut our grain shipments, and withdrew our support for the Salt II treaty. In addition, spurred by a fear that this invasion was only the first move towards obtaining access to the Arabian Sea, the US announced the Carter Doctrine which stated that the US would view the security of the Persian Gulf oil routes as a vital American interest!

"As the Mujahideen's stubborn resistance against the Soviet invaders continued the US, supported by Saudi Arabia, Egypt, and China with the assistant of the Pakistani Inter Service Intelligence (ISI), set up a covert weapon supply route to the Mujahideen. The objective was designed to 'bleed the enemy' and cost them so much that they would agree to withdraw their troops and end the war.

"The frustration over the inability to take effective action by the Carter administration against the Soviets resulted in a bipartisan group of conservative organizations in Washington taking action to find a new 'single issue' private organization. The Committee for a Free Afghanistan (CFA) with an objective to keep the Afghan invasion on the media's 'front burner' started a public relations campaign designed to bring public pressure on the Soviets to withdraw.

"To expedite action by the CFA this group decided to provide funds to set up an office. This office would initially be responsible for publishing and mailing a newsletter 'Free Afghan News' plus timely 'Fact Sheets' to make sure the Soviet invasion was kept in the news, maintaining pressure on the Carter administration. As a result of my past military service in this region and my contacts with the Afghans, I was asked to join the CFA's Advisory Council.

"After winning the election President Reagan embarked on a wide-ranging buildup of strategic and conventional forces to give the US a strengthened military position from which to negotiate with the Soviets; the basis for his 'Peace through Strength Strategy.' With this military buildup underway he next turned his concerns to the Soviet communist expansion. In a clear break from past strategies the President worked directly with the Director of the Central Intelligence Agency, the Secretary of Defense, and a small group on the National Security Council on a 'close hold basis' to draw plans for a series of Top-Secret National Security Decision Directives (NSDDs) which would place pressure on the overextended Soviet empire. These NSDDs were the basis for the Reagan Doctrine which visualized not merely containing but also a rollback of the Soviet empire which would directly challenge the Brezhnev Doctrine of 'Once a communist government, always a communist government.' These plans were highly classified to ensure that they would not 'be leaked' and cause a domestic political firestorm before Reagan gathered additional support for his new rollback strategy!

"As early as 1981 he began a public grassroots domestic counterattack against communism which he felt would develop 'Public Diplomacy' support for his administration's strategy. His speech to the students at Notre Dame in May stressed that 'we will not only contain communism but dismiss it as a sad bizarre chapter in human history whose last pages are being written.' In 1982 he stepped up his attack against communism in a speech before the British Parliament in which he predicted that 'the Evil Empire's' Communist government would be left on the ash heap of history by internal upheavals in Eastern Europe and Russia itself.

"His Bully Pulpit Rollback Strategy campaign against communism was strongly attacked by liberals and many in Congress who feared his approach would lead us to war. The liberals soon deemed him 'a cowboy who would embroil us in war.' To neutralize these bitter opponents the President spoke out on TV, radio, and made public appearances to encourage conservatives to become active and make their views known through 'Public Diplomacy.' He was effective marshalling 'the silent majority's support' to pressure Congress to support his new aggressive attack on the Brezhnev Doctrine.

"His administration's anti-communist campaign illustrated the influence of the continued Afghan resistance against the Soviet invaders not only in the American public's opinion but also on the decision makers in the government. This anti-communist campaign was also actively supported by his cabinet and the vigorous activities of his White House Staff's Public Relations Office which coordinated closely with grass roots conservative organizations. This office also initiated a series of conferences which were held to develop tactics and techniques on how best to implement the new Freedom Fighter strategy. It also stressed the objective for this strategy dealing with the USSR and its allies, forcing them to fight against local guerrilla movements, and was designed to further increase financial pressure on the Soviets.

"Conventional wisdom holds that a government must expand ten times as much as the insurgents in their effort to contain an insurgency. This strategy had been used against the West in the new wave of National Liberation movements in the third world by Soviets since World War II. Now for the first time it was turned back against the communists, forcing them to spend billions in support of their communist allies now being pressured by anti-communist Freedom Fighters.

"Reagan's concept of assisting those fighting against the takeover of their government by the communists goes back to 1967. This idea was amplified in an article in the US News and World Report saying 'Maybe part of the answer in hotspots such as Vietnam is to give the enemy something else to worry about. Maybe he ought to have some interest in some other corner of the world to worry about.'

"As noted on becoming President he maintained this appreciation for the need for the public to support his initiatives. He continued to use his Presidential Bully Pulpit Campaign to maintain support at the grassroots for his rearmament program and his aggressive freedom fighter strategy which was heating up the Cold War. He needed this public support against his opposition which ranged from the liberals in academia, the media, those in Congress and the State Department who favored the detente and strongly disagreed with the President's new rollback strategy. The White House staffers held publicized conferences and forums highlighting Freedom Fighters from anti-communist movements around the world. They actively encouraged concerned citizens at these meetings to join to form Private Volunteer Organizations (PVOs) which would network with Congress and provide unofficial interim grassroots support for the Freedom Fighters until government funding supporting Reagan's program could be passed by Congress. This call for action by the President's administration struck a responsive note among conservative activists who began to form PVOs to generate public and congressional support for the Freedom Fighters and causes they supported.

"The CFAs Progress in this program was already well underway. The White House staffers provided key 'points of contact' (Conservatives) within the government with whom they could actively network in support of the Reagan Doctrine. As a result of these contacts CFA was able to develop its plans in coordination with key officials in Defense, the National Security Council, the Department of State, USAID, and the Intelligence community. This coordination allowed CFA to utilize their limited funds to plan programs that would best complement the ongoing Reagan Administration's Freedom Fighter initiatives. Utilizing the mailing list provided by sponsors CFA's initial mailings alerted the public of the dangers of not resisting the Soviet invasion. This general thrust was highlighted by CFA's first bumper sticker, 'AID AFGHANS NOW or FIGHT SOVIETS LATER.' The success of these bumper stickers was surprising as they tapped into conservatives and their organizations, such as the NRA, which provided a surprisingly effective recruiting ploy! CFA also soon found out that its publication 'Free Afghanistan Report' had tapped into the deep sense of public frustration over the ineffectual response of the Carter administration. As a result, with additional members available, CFA was able to expand its staff and operations!

"Since information about the war was difficult to obtain at this time, CFA's 'Free Afghan News' and 'Fact Sheets' based on visits and direct contact with the Mujahideen leaders were eagerly sought in Washington and across the country. With a mailing list which rapidly grew to over 12,000 the CFA established an office in The Heritage Foundation Building only two blocks from the Senate and house office buildings.

"With regular mailings of the "Free Afghan News' underway, CFA initiated a more active role coordinating with other POVs and conservative groups supporting the Reagan Doctrine in D.C. It also started a regular schedule of 'walking the hill,' now only two blocks away, seeking support in Congress for the Mujahideen. They soon found there was also a sense of keen frustration in Congress as noted by congressman Charlie Wilson. He said strong action was favored by many to 'pay them back for Vietnam.' Once the CFA's appeal for public support and funds were underway its next move was to call on its supporters to contact Congress and the administration by letters, phone calls, and personal visits to the Capital to support congressional action assisting the Mujahideen.

"CFA's initial staff visit to Pakistan developed 'points of contact' among the Mujahedeen. During its visit in Peshawar, CFA stressed the importance for their leaders to furnish representatives to come to the US to explain what was happening in the Afghan War. Schedules were developed for speech tours across the country to go to groups who wanted to hear more about Afghanistan. An important element of this program was meetings with legislators, congressional aides, key staff members at the White House and other Department and Government Agencies working on this issue. Initially even the strongest CFA supporters of the Afghan Mujahideen felt it would only be a matter of time until they were crushed by the Soviet military. Even so, supporters continued to come forward full of admiration and most importantly funds to assist the freedom fighters. The objective early in this program was twofold, to assist the refugees and make the invasion so costly that the Soviets would withdraw!

"Support continues to grow as the Soviets were unable to crush the Mujahideen. As the war continued several million refugees were driven into Iran and into camps on the northern Pakistan border. The United Nations and Pakistan tried to organize support for the 3.5 million refugees in these camps. During the CFA's liaison visits it soon became evident that the magnitude of the problem was far beyond the capability of the United Nations to handle. As a result, CFA intensified their public campaign and called on their supporters to request Congress to provide direct humanitarian assistance for these Afghan refugees. This Public Relations initiative was complimented by Winston Churchill, a British member of Parliament, who noted that 'the greater pressure that can be brought on the Soviets the sooner they will be forced to retire.'

"At this time, with membership growing, a special drive was launched to organize Regional CFA Groups around the country. Once these regional offices were organized Afghan leaders were sent to speak before various local businesses, patriotic and academic groups across the country. A direct fallout from these visits was an increase in donations of medicine, boots and warm clothing by people who had been touched by the Mujahideen leaders' accounts of a lack of supplies for their resistance to the Soviet invaders. One of CFA's most challenging administrative problems became shipping of these donations.

"The committee also initiated a 'Wounded Program.' This program brought a limited number of severely wounded Afghans to the US via commercial airliner for treatment. CFA and the regional CFAs coordinated arrangements with local hospitals to sponsor medical care for these wounded. Careful planning also ensured that the maximum publicity and fundraising drives were also organized around these events. This program was so successful that Congress funded Representative McCollum's Program to utilize United States Air Force aircraft to bring supplies to the refugees and to return to the US with these serious wounded, who could not be treated in Pakistan.

"In early 1983 I met with the Pakistan Ambassador Ejaz Azm and Congressman Coughlin at Villanova University's International Seminar 'Pakistan and the Arc of Crisis.' We discussed CFA and its support of the Afghans' struggle against the Soviet invader. They both recommended that I visit them in D.C. to discuss the situation in more detail. When I visited the Ambassador, I brought two local news articles I had written stressing the Soviet threat of their continual drive to secure a warm water port in Pakistan. He asked me to write a magazine article on the same subject since the media coverage on this subject was very poor. This I did and brought him copies on my next trip to D.C.

"During my next visit I noted that I had been invited by the Chinese to present a paper to their Strategic Study Institute in Beijing in the fall. The Pakistan Ambassador Ejaz Azm suggested that he could set up a visit to the Pakistan military for a visit to the Mujahideen groups in Peshawar to evaluate their operations based on my four-year service fighting the guerrillas in Vietnam. I agreed and after my visit to the combat leaders including Brigadier Safi, former head of the King's Afghan Army Commandos, I reported to the Pakistani Army Headquarters in Rawalpindi to discuss my observations. A major recommendation stressed the need for cooperation between several of the Mujahideen parties for their attacks on the Soviets. In addition, I recommended that they utilize more Chinese 107 mm rockets which had proven so effective against us in Vietnam.

"When I returned to D.C., I also debriefed the Pakistan Ambassador and his military attaché. At that time, he encouraged me to make regular visits to Peshawar noting that the Army Attaché would assist me in obtaining Visas and liaison with the Pakistani Refugee Officials and the Mujahideen Political groups being supported by the Pakistani Government through the ISI, the Pakistani Intelligence Agency in charge of the covert arms distribution to the Mujahideen groups.

"As a result of this visit, I was appointed CFA's 'Field Director' responsible for making regular visits to Peshawar to evaluate how best to assist the Mujahideen. The CFA visits to Peshawar expanded to regularly scheduled liaison visits to the Pakistan Refugee Officials and the key Mujahideen political groups! On a personal note, one of the retired Brigadiers on their refugee staff had been a student of mine at the Army Infantry School at Fort Benning in the 1950s and this 'old boy' relationship added greatly to our effectiveness. The Pakistanis added CFA to the list of nearly 50 NGOs due to the contributions of clothes, boots and other materials donated through our organization from members in the US. In addition, their virtual sponsorship of the CFA allowed us not only to set up regular visits to key Mujahideen Groups being supported by the ISI, but also arranged for messages to be sent and received through the Pakistan military attaché in Washington.

"Key contacts by the CFA with the Mujahideen in Peshawar depended upon personal meetings with key leaders and their staff to organize selection of wounded to be sent to the States and selection of key leaders and staff members who were sent to the States for lectures at universities, CFA regional meetings, interviews with Congressional staff, and the press.

"Once these normal CFA duties were completed, I worked with various training camps and guerrilla leaders on improving their specialized skills, such as mine clearing, by bringing Field Manuals to be translated for their training camps. The most difficult task was convincing them of the necessity of coordinating their guerrilla attacks on the enemy in several widely separated sections of the country so that the enemy's reaction by air strikes and availability of helicopter assets would be hampered by the need to cover different areas. A major problem that surfaced was the need for medical assistance. This included not only the need for 'aid men' to accompany the fighters but also a program to improve care for those severely wounded Afghans who were being treated in understaffed hospitals in Pakistan.

"This desperate need for medical assistance reported by the Mujahideen leaders and CFA's reports and Fact Sheets was confirmed by the medical community supporting the US hospitals caring for the Afghan wounded. Doctors soon began to question CFA on how they could help. A visit to the refugee camps in Pakistan was arranged by CFA to analyze this problem. After several visits by different volunteer medical groups, it was determined that the problem fell into two categories. short-term and long-term.

"The short-term problem was to assist the local Pakistani hospital staffs when they were periodically overwhelmed by casualties caused by large Soviet offensives. This was resolved by American doctors volunteering to come to Peshawar for short periods to supplement local hospital staff during these Soviet offensives.

"The long-term problem of providing training for aid men to accompany the Mujahideen into combat was resolved by several medical volunteer groups raising funds to establish medical training facilities in Pakistan. To assist with these programs CFA served as a point of contact in Washington and Peshawar. CFA also assisted some volunteer medical groups in obtaining surplus medical hospital equipment being released by the government.

"By the mid-1980s CFA's program to 'educate' Americans about the Afghan war had hit its full stride. CFA had 15,000 supporters and was continuing to grow. The availability of the services of the liaison office in Peshawar resulted in still closer coordination with the staff of the new Special Joint Congressional Task Force on Afghanistan. CFA not only provided them with current information on the status of the war but also brought key Afghan leaders to testify before their Congressional Committees.

"The networking in Washington between various POVs supporting the freedom fighter groups in Africa, Asia and Central America also changed from its original ad hoc contacts to regularly scheduled bimonthly meetings. These were held at the Stanton Club, a conservative activist organization which acted as a clearinghouse and coordination center for the various conservative programs.

"The turning point came when President Reagan issued a Proclamation which established 21 March 1985 as 'Afghanistan Day." This proclamation not only called for the American people to remember and support the Afghans gallant struggle, but also condemned 'the atrocities and human rights violations being committed.' With this proclamation and the use of Vice President Bush's quarters for a fundraiser, CFA's public relations battle for support of the Afghans was won in the US! With this government backing the POV Freedom Fighters, support groups stepped up operations.

"The American Security Council subsequently sponsored a Worldwide Conference for the Freedom Fighters in Washington, D.C. This initial meeting was attended not only by the freedom fighters, but also a prestigious group of administration leaders and legislators. The tone was set by the Secretary of Defense who stated our message must be what it has always been. 'We shall not abandon you.' With the worldwide support for the freedom fighters, growing hope spread that finally a 'window of opportunity' existed to drive back the Soviet empire from its invasion of Afghanistan.

"With congressional funding finally approved for the refugees, the Agency for Internal Development (AID) moved quickly to assume responsibility for the Humanitarian Assistance Programs. With this expansion of US AID programs, CFA's

'Wounded Program' was taken over by a new official Afghan Medical Project. With many of its other humanitarian assistance programs also being taken over by AID CFA, through its Peshawar Field Directors office, initiated a program to identify unfunded projects which needed assistance. Among these projects were food and clothing for the newly unregistered refugees and medicine to the small hospitals and clinics in the refugee camps.

"With government assistance being publicized the Soviet/Afghan war became a hot subject! CFA began to be deluged with calls from media, press and TV crews planning to 'cover the war!' Close liaison was also maintained with the new volunteer medical groups arriving in Pakistan to assist hospitals and provide training programs for the Mujahideen combat aid men.

"During this period CFA was also requested by the State Department to assume the responsibility of assisting an 'official visit of the Afghan Resistance leaders to meet with President Reagan and key Administrative and Congressional leaders.' After this visit the deputy assistant secretary of state sent a letter of congratulations to the committee. He said, 'It is fitting that the Committee for a Free Afghanistan, which has done so much to promote the Afghan's cause, played a key role in organizing this important event.' Following this official visit CAF was increasingly called on by Afghan leaders coming to the United States, American media, and civilian volunteer groups going to Peshawar for liaison assistance and networking with the Mujahideen to expedite their projects.

"Brigadier General Safi, a senior Afghan commander was also brought to Fort Bragg, NC to brief personnel from the 5th Special Forces Group who were being sent to Peshawar to assist in Operation *Salaam*, the new UN Demining Program. Arrangements were also made to provide Mujahideen training camps with US Field Manuals on mine clearing and other military subjects which would be translated and used for training to increase pressure on the Soviets.

"CFA initiated and funded a major new program which responded to the concerns expressed by the President about Human Rights violations. This council consisted of a group of international lawyers who traveled to Pakistan to investigate and document accounts of torture and gross violations of human rights by the Soviets and Afghan communist troops in Afghanistan. Their complete report was briefed to Congress and the report was later presented to the United Nations. Senator Humphrey, chairman of the congressional task force on Afghanistan, noted that this report was a 'valuable and painstaking document of the effort to destroy a nation and its people.'

"Another major change in the war came in 1986 with the furnishing of the Stinger missile, a US army handheld ground to air missile, to the Mujahideen. This missile was a game changer and completely neutralized the Soviet air force's tactical firepower and mobility advantage, which combined with the increasing use of mobile special operation forces, had caused the Mujahideen heavy casualties. Taking heavy losses in both helicopter and fixed wing fighter bombers from the

Stinger, the Soviet forces were forced to drastically cut back on their helicopter and close air support.

"The changes in tactics so limited their mobility that the Soviets pulled their forces out of isolated positions and virtually left the Kabul government's forces on their own, while the Soviets concentrated in large garrisons and limited their offensive sweeps. This caused momentum on the battlefield to shift to the Mujahideen. Faced with this prolonged 'bleeding wound' in Afghanistan the Soviets began to seriously participate in a series of long drawn out 'UN Proximity Talks' which finally resulted in their withdrawal of forces by February 1989."

"With this Soviet shift into the defense, some Afghans from liberated areas near the border started to move back to their villages. A new CFA fundraiser was created titled 'In Afghanistan You need a Stinger to till your Soil.' I loved this new phase of the war. There was a request to fund support for 'Project Plowshare' which was designed to buy seeds and simple tools in the local bazaars to assist these villagers to start farming.

"After their withdrawal from Afghanistan, Moscow launched a full-scale propaganda offensive to erode the worldwide support. Blame was placed on the US and Mujahideen for continuing the war after the Soviets and Kabul regime 'had seen the light' and now only wanted to stop the killing.

"Charles Lichtenstein, Former Ambassador to the United Nations countered this propaganda. He said, 'To end the war at this time would allow the Soviets to steal victory from the jaws of defeat.' To improve the ability to publicize the war and counter Soviet propaganda Congress funded the Afghan Media Resource Center. This media project was designed to assist the Afghans to assume responsibility for their own public relations. To assist with this effort to improve western media access to Mujahideen news releases the CFA sent an experienced foreign correspondent to staff its Liaison Office in Peshawar to assist their PR offices in preparing news releases and press conferences. CFA also assisted with several 'psychological warfare' type projects during this.

"Concurrently with their propaganda campaign the Soviets launched a massive arms resupply effort to ensure that the Mujahideen would be outgunned on the battlefield even after their withdrawal. During this phase of the war CFA assisted in countering this wave of Soviet propaganda by publishing the Mujahideen's position. An example was the statement made by a commander sent to the UN. He said, 'For us to agree to a peace settlement now is tantamount to Washington's Army at Valley Forge laying down their weapons and joining a coalition dominated by the British.' The CFA also publicized the report of the Congressional Task Force on Afghanistan which stated the Soviets were pouring in military supplies, to include SCUD missiles, at the rate of 250–300 million a month, 10 times that of the US military assistance. Highlighting this new phase of the conflict was CFA's new bumper sticker 'Trust the Soviets? Ask the Afghans!'

"After the Soviet Army's withdrawal differences of opinions arose over what responsibility the US had for continuing to support Afghanistan. This controversy was highlighted by Robert Kimmet, Under Secretary of State for Political Affairs, when he stated, 'For more than a decade while Soviet troops occupied the country our Afghan policy enjoyed strong support from Congress and the American public. Now that the Soviets have gone the problem is more complex.' This difference of opinion on how to deal with the Soviets resulted in strained relations between Congress and the State Department. CFA swung into action to gain public support for the Congressional Task Force's position in this controversy. CFA organized meetings and public demonstrations and furnished 'Fact Sheets,' press releases and speakers to publicize the Congressional Task Force's position. Other key issues the Congressional Task Force was having difficulty agreeing on with the State Department ranged from expediting the selection of 'an ambassador at large' to the Mujahideen, to groups providing military support for the Mujahideen as long as the Soviets supplied Communist forces in Kabul. This controversy between Congress and State Department escalated to the White House and was highlighted by a front-page story in The Washington Time, 'White House and State Department in Conflict over Afghan Aid.' The seriousness of this problem was explained by senator Humphrey who said, 'We must ensure the US is not party to any settlement which would help the Soviets achieve diplomatically what they cannot achieve militarily.' By the second year of Soviet withdrawal support in the United States had rapidly eroded triggered both by a lack of success on the battlefield and the increased fighting between the contending Mujahideen groups.

"Another issue which surfaced at this time, causing concern among the Afghan supporters in Congress, was the favoritism shown by Pakistanis Internal Service Intelligence Afghan Bureau to the fundamental political parties. This was exacerbated by complaints from more moderate parties that they were not receiving supplies. This 'skewing of supplies' denied by the ISI is covered in detail by Kurt Lobeck, the only reporter assigned full time to cover the Afghan war, in his book, *Holy War, Unholy Victory*.

"The anger in Congress grew to such an extent that they considered cutting back on the F 16 Military Assistance Program for Pakistan. CFA was encouraged by Congressional Task Force members to send a representative to impress on the Pakistanis Congress's anger over the issue. A meeting was arranged initially in D.C. with the Pakistan Ambassador to address this issue. He noted that he had informed his Foreign Office of the congressional concern over the issue, and he said he felt the CFA's visit could be helpful. He would arrange it with the Foreign Office in Islamabad.

"Upon arrival in Pakistan a meeting was held with two Foreign Office representatives. They said they had to discuss this matter with the State Department representatives from Washington who told them that this issue would 'soon blow over.' When they met with ISI officials, they denied this allegation and planned to visit a newly formed infantry battalion. A trip was scheduled by ISI to inspect the new battalion near Kandahar in southwest Afghanistan. The inspected unit was completely equipped with new infantry heavy weapons to include the long new range Egyptian multi barreled rocket launchers.

"It was clear from this visit that ISI was concerned over the issue and willing to compromise if pressed. Prior to leaving Islamabad the state representative's statement that 'it would soon blow over' was discussed with the Ambassador. He said they must have misunderstood and that he would clarify the matter. Upon returning to the States a trip report recommending that inspectors be assigned to monitor covert arms shipments was prepared and briefed to the Congressional Task Force and other interested governmental agencies.

"By 1991, plagued by an increase of infighting between Afghan parties, it was clear that with the withdrawal of the Soviets and the collapse of the communist government in Kabul, the days of the 'jihad' were over. The fighting which continued at a high level between Mujahideen parties led to chaos and threatened to turn Afghanistan into another Lebanon or Yugoslavia. Faced with this situation the CFA made plans to disband. One of its last official acts was the receipt of an award from the Department of Defense. This award was given on the 100th flight of the Afghan medical project which brought wounded Afghans to the States for treatment. DOD commended the committee 'for their outstanding support of the Afghan medical project.' CFA turned over its files to the American Security Council with whom they had worked supporting the Reagan Doctrine. The Reagan era of public diplomacy which had effectively generated PVO the Freedom Fighters in Afghanistan ended; its mission successfully accomplished."

CHAPTER 18

The Later Years

After the CFA disbanded, Ted settled into an actual retirement lifestyle in Southern Pines. His hobbies were hunting, writing, and collecting books and guns. During the time he was at Valley Forge Military Academy he used his GI Bill to take a course in gunsmithing, in Scottsdale, Arizona. Once he completed the basic course he then signed up for and completed their advanced gun repair course for senior repairman. While attending the University of Washington, Uncle Sieg had shown him how to work on various surplus weapons so he could repair them and sell them to hunters in the Seattle area for pocket money. Now he had time to work on his collection of weapons that covered several wars. During his lifetime he saw the collecting of war trophies going from the norm to being illegal. While stationed at Fort Bragg and en route to Iran, he recognized the shifting winds and reregistered his DWATs (Deactivated War Trophies) during the 1969 amnesty period. During the Congressional hearings in 1965, the Treasury Department proposed registration of all "destructive devices" such as bazookas, antitank rifles, landmines, hand grenades, and similar items that previously did not require registration. The Treasury also allowed registration (or in some cases reregistration), of these DWATs which had been deactivated or removed from purview of the NFA under the program that the Treasury created and subsequently revoked. Finally, the Treasury proposed to double the transfer tax on NFA firearms from $200 to $400 (and the $5 transfer tax on "any other weapon" to $10.)

There were two overarching time bites that kept Ted engaged in life and in the role of a mentor. He loved sharing his life experiences with others who could benefit from them. The first was becoming a professor for American Military University. The other role was taking an active role in working with Texas Tech University's Vietnam Center, which was being formed.

American Military University (AMU) was established by James P. Etter, in Charles Town, West Virginia, in 1991. As a major in the Marine Corps, Mr. Etter recognized the need for active-duty personnel to find a source for continuing education while on active duty. So, he established American Military University with

Ted with an American Military University student in his library in Southern Pines, North Carolina, in the 1990s.

the specific goal of meeting the unique educational needs of military personnel needing courses in specialized areas, such as counterterrorism and military intelligence, that were not currently included in university course offerings. Teaching began in 1993 with 18 graduate students. By June 1995, AMU was nationally accredited in distance education and training and online classes started in 1998. All classes are offered online. Active-duty personnel could use Tuition Assistance, and retired personnel the GI Bill, making it very attractive, along with their college transfer program and credits for military education. AMU now offers associates, bachelors, masters, and doctoral degrees, in addition to dual degrees, certificate programs and learning tracks. Degrees are offered in Homeland Security, Intelligence Studies, Emergency and Disaster Management (Coast Guard only), Criminal Justice, Management, and Business Administration.

Ted started teaching there in the early years, when instruction was conducted through the conventional correspondence course, which required telephone conversations with the professor. Ted took several trips to West Virginia to look at the curriculum requirements and the distance learning processes that they learned as teachers. The process used was continually upgraded based on developing technologies. Each professor had to be experienced in the field they were teaching and design the course syllabus and supporting academic curriculum for their courses. Ted's first class was Insurgency and Counter Insurgency. An anthology was selected that was originally printed by the Industrial College of the Armed Forces, located in Washington, D.C. The service schools and universities did not offer these courses; however, some of their classes had appropriate and relative material that they published which was public domain, thus allowing them to be reproduced with no permission required. College publications like these were sent to the students by post. Additionally, all instructors were required to develop an instructor's research package to prepare them for class. At the start of each course the student would be provided with the core scope and objectives, which gave an overview of the timeline and material to be covered. In some cases, a text was provided in the course for required reading. The course also required four quizzes, four reading reports, a book report, a term paper, and a final examination. The syllabus explained the requirements due for each of the lessons. There were typically 15 lessons per course. The end of course tests were prepared for each course and were sent to military test centers to be administered to the students.

Classes were at taught undergraduate level and graduate levels. The courses Ted taught were:

L 508 American Military University History of Guerrilla Warfare
R 226 Insurgency and Counterinsurgency
LW 518 History of Guerrilla Warfare
MS 643 United Nations Peacekeeping and Peacemaking Operations

Ted was qualified with a master's degree from George Washington University in International Relations. Additionally, he was an instructor at the Infantry School for four years and a graduate of the War College and Command General Staff College. He was an author, lecturer, and reviewer of military articles and books. He wrote extensively for military magazines, and was the co-author of a book, *Nuclear Tactics, Weapons and Firepower in the Pentomic Division, Battle Group, and Company*, a primer for the use of tactical nuclear weapons which had been translated into Russian, Spanish, Yugoslavian, and Portuguese. While on active duty he lectured on various subjects at the defense colleges of India, Canada, Iran, and Vietnam; after retirement he continued lecturing at US military schools, civilian universities, various businesses, and social service organizations. In 1984 he was contacted by a lifelong friend, John E. Jessup, who was the editor-in-chief of *Encyclopedia of the American Military*, a three-volume set consisting of 2,157 pages on the study of the history, traditions, and policies of the armed forces in war and peace. With Jessup, Ted co-authored chapters on military coalitions and advisors.

Mataxis also brought to the instructional table years of actual experience in the subjects he taught. Since he was in his 70s, he wanted to assure Mr. Etter that each year he would submit annual papers at the collegian conference or at a military institution to reinforce his bona fides as a professor. He insisted on this since he was familiar with the accreditation process from Valley Forge Junior College.

The other overarching time bite was the Texas Tech University (TTU) Vietnam Center and Archives. In 1989 a group of Texas veterans of the Vietnam War and TTU personnel tried to identify some ways to look objectively at the war. Dr. James Reckner was a military history professor at the university who had served two tours in Vietnam. It was his vision, dedication and hard work that enabled the creation of the Vietnam Center at TTU. The university quickly approved the establishment of the Vietnam Center and Archives and immediately began collecting, documenting, and preserving donated materials that related to the war.

This naturally became one of Ted's pet projects because of his and his immediate family's involvement in the war, along with his contemporaries from his tours there. Ted's first tour was from July 1964 until August 1966 (senior advisor and 1st Brigade, 101st), his second was from June 1970 until February 1972 (Americal division and MEDTC). John Howell, his son-in-law, served from December 1965 until June 1967 (1st Cavalry Division and an extension with Special Forces). Bud Isaacs, his son-in-law, served from January 1966 until February 1967 (101st), and Ted Jr. served from November 1969 until January 1972 (101st Division as platoon and company commander in 3/187 (Rakkassan) and extensions as commander G Ranger Company and advisor to ARVIN airborne and Ranger Units).

The university immediately started an oral history program to document the veterans' experiences. On March 31, 2000, Ted Sr. did an oral history interview conducted by Dr. Stephan Maxner and on April 13, 2002, Ted Jr. did an oral history interview conducted by Dr. Stephan Maxner. Initially these interviews were transcribed and made available in their virtual archives for any interested researchers. The center's strength is the fact that it looks at all perspectives of the war and provides greater understanding for everyone. The center's objective is to guide the development of the Vietnam Archive and encourage continuing study of all aspects of the American experience in Vietnam. The Vietnam Center holds an annual conference on a particular topic and invites papers to be presented. Every third year it holds a triennial symposium that focuses on several topics and is open to anyone that is interested. These presentations are filmed and then placed in the archives for viewing by any interested researcher. One of the center's developmental strengths was that they sought comments from the attendees at the conclusion of the conference and looked for recommendations to better organize and conduct future conferences.

The Third Vietnam Triennial Symposium was held during April 15–17, 1999. Symposium Panel 3a was "US Military Support of the Lon Nol Government." Ted's presentation covered "The Activation and Operations of the US Military Equipment Delivery Team Cambodia (MEDTC)." Major General (Ret.) John Cleland covered "Operations of MEDTC Before and After Cut Off of USAF Air Support (15 Aug. 1973)." He covered the problems he had with trying to keep the Cambodian government supplied without US air support. Major General Ken Bowra, commander of the US Army Special Warfare Center and School, presented "Operations and Withdrawal of MEDTC (Operation Eagle Pull)." He covered the collapse of the war in Cambodia and the withdrawal from the embassy.

Ted cherished his role as a professor and mentor to young service personnel, enthusiastically trying to increase their value to the military through their continued education. This provided Ted with an opportunity to interact with his students, share his knowledge, and stay abreast of the services. The size of his classes normally ranged between six and 14. After he became a known commodity, his classes had to be capped at 20 so he would have the time he needed to spend with each student. He would rotate his courses, teaching a different one each semester. The UN class appealed to many who were doing UN missions during President Clinton's administration. He would get phone calls from all over the world, including Germany, Bosnia, Okinawa, and Japan, requesting extensions for the course because of their work.

THE LATER YEARS • 241

As much as Helma had grown to love the retired life that she embraced, they realized that they loved to travel. So, they quickly agreed that every year they should plan on taking two trips someplace in the world that they wanted to visit to fulfill that wanderlust. They did this every year after retiring until the trips became too much for them. The center of their focus was each other, their children, their grandchildren, and finally their great grandchildren.

In 1988, they took off for Bergen, Norway, for a 14-day coastal trip to include the Arctic Circle. Ted was researching the German invasion of Norway and the resistance activities in World War II. While taking the fjord and glacier tour, Ted ran into a veteran of World War II and received a firsthand account of the veteran's experiences. During this same year, Ted went to Israel with a group of retired military officers.

In 1989 the 62nd Annual Scripps National Spelling Bee was held on May 31 through June 1, 1989, in Washington, D.C. It was won by their grandson Scott Isaacs, a 14-year-old eighth grader, sponsored by the *Rocky Mountain News* of Denver, Colorado. His winning word was "spoliator," and he was faced with becoming a brief celebrity. Ted Jr. was in El Salvador that year as a lieutenant colonel with the operational planning and training team at the embassy in El Salvador. That same afternoon he had just returned from the field, set down his weapon and his rucksack,

Brigadier General and Mrs. Helma Mataxis of Southern Pines, North Carolina, celebrate their 50th anniversary at the officers' club at Fort Bragg on August 18, 1990. Attending were family and friends, gathered over the course of 32 years of military life, his work on behalf of Afghanistan, and since their retirement in Southern Pines.

Committee for a Free Afghanistan
(Member of the Coalition for Peace through Strength)

214 Massachusetts Avenue, N.E., Suite 480, Washington, D.C. 20002 • (202) 546-7577

Board of Directors
Maj. Gen. J. Milnor Roberts AUS (Ret.)
Reed Irvine
Accuracy in Media
David C. Isby
Attorney at Law
Mars Lewis
Council for the Defense of Freedom
William F. (Bill) Roorbat
Col. John Shelley AUS (Ret.)
National Association of Uniformed Services

Council of Advisors
The Hon. Richard V. Allen
Terry Cannon
Young Americans for Freedom
Rep. Bill Chappell, Jr. (D-FL)
Arnaud de Borchgrave
Washington Times
The Hon. Edward J. Derwinski
Col. Samuel T. Dickens USAF (Ret.)
Council for Inter-American Security
Prof. Louis Dupree
US Military Academy
Rep. Mickey Edwards (R-OK)
M. Stanton Evans
National Journalism Center
John Fisher
American Security Council
Rep. Barney Frank (D-MA)
Prof. Richard Frye
Harvard University
Jeffrey Gaynor
The Heritage Foundation
Steve Girsky
College Democrats of America
Lt. Gen. Daniel O. Graham USA (Ret.)
Project High Frontier
Sen. Charles Grassley (R-IA)
Jake Hanson
American Conservative Union
The Hon. S. I. Hayakawa
Joan Heuter
National Association of Pro-America
RADM Mark Hill USN (Ret.)
Rep. Robert J. Lagomarsino (R-CA)
The Hon. Charles M. Lichenstein
The Heritage Foundation
Dr. Edward D. Lozansky
Sakharov International Committee
Sen. John McCain (R-AZ)
Cpt. Eugene "Red" McDaniel USN (Ret.)
American Defense Foundation
Brig. Gen Theodore Mataxis USA (Ret.)
Adm. Thomas H. Moorer USN (Ret.)
David Miner
College Republican National Committee
Philip Nicolaides
Accuracy in Media
J.A. Parker
The Lincoln Institute
Sen. Claiborne Pell (D-RI)
Rep. Thomas Petri (R-WI)
Howard Phillips
The Conservative Caucus
Prof. Richard Pipes
Harvard University
The Hon. Joel Pritchard
Rep. Don Ritter (R-PA)
Sen. Paul Simon (D-IL)
Maj. Gen. John K Singlaub USA (Ret.)
U.S. Council for World Freedom
Cabot Sedgewick
Attorney at Law
Rep. Samuel S. Stratton (D-NY)
Rep. Gerald B. Solomon (R-NY)
The Hon. Paul Tsongas
Dr. Jack Wheeler
Freedom Research Foundation
Rep. Charles Wilson (D-TX)

27 May '90

LTC. KEN BOWRA
CO. 2ND BN. 5TH SPECIAL FORCES GP.
473 TURNER LANE
FT. CAMPBELL, KY. 42223

Dear Ken:

Just a quick note. Am working in D.C. two weeks a month, mainly on Afghanistan. Was in SEA (SINGAPORE, MALAYSIA & BANGKOK) in Feb. on CAMBODIAN RESISTANCE, MILITARY HIST PROJECT (FALL OF SING) and flogging the OWL (seaborne unmanned recon veh.)

Returned a couple of weeks ago from my 7th trip to survey the Afghan war. Had a good tour went "inside" to inspect newly organized MUJAHIDEEN BN with new 30K Egyptian SAKR Rocket. They're well trained — time will tell what happens — key meeting between GORBY / PRES. next week. Am busy on Hill Senate For Relations Comte, Cong Task Force on AFGHAN & STATE!

New SUBJECT, Have decided to "PUSH" on ORAL HISTORY PROJECT for MEDT-C. XEROXED ccy of letter gives status of this project. Have seen Chief Mil. History, his ORAL HIST. Staff — all busy. Best approach seems to be one outlined in LTR. Saw your ORAL DEBRIEF in files at War College.

Perhaps when you're at Carlisle you can convince ORAL HISTORY staffer to pick up on other two Chiefs.

Warm Regards, TED MATAXIS Sr.

P.S.- Thanks for invitation to your change of cmd ceremony. Would be there — but unfortunately in Seattle for 50th yr grad ceremony. Best to your family.

Your contributions are tax-deductible

TEM/

A letter from General Mataxis, written in May 1990, to the commander of the 2nd Battalion of the 5th Special Forces Group, Lieutenant Colonel Ken Bowra. He mentored Ken over the years he was on active duty. Ken retired as a major general. This letter shows what Ted was contributing in this phase of his life.

and turned on CNN World News for an update. He was quite shocked to see that his nephew Scott had just won the National Spelling Bee. This was also the year that TTU established the Vietnam Center and Archives.

In 1990, Ted Sr. and Helma celebrated their 50th wedding anniversary, with friends coming from everywhere to attend their celebration—it was a memorable year. Ted Jr. was still on active duty and assigned to activate the 3rd Special Forces Group at Fort Bragg, having just returned from a year in El Salvador. His family had built a home at the Country Club of North Carolina, just outside the back gate of Fort Bragg, resulting in Ted and Kirby becoming the hosts of the event. In honor of Helma and Ted's 50 years together, Shirley and her family gave them a first-class ticket anywhere in the world, while Bud and Kaye's family gave them a week's lodging anywhere in the world. It was a week of old friends reconnecting after years, very much like Kaye and Bud's wedding at Fort Bragg years earlier. According to Ted, "Nothing better than that!" It was like they were never separated from their friends, despite the fact in some cases years had passed. That same year Shirley and John Slack moved to Satellite Beach, Florida.

In 1991, Ted and Helma went to Vienna. They then went on to visit Prague, Budapest, Germany, and then Denmark to trace her grandparents' place of birth and the birthplace of her father. Helma and Ted really got a lot of information about her great-grandfather and visited the barracks where he had been stationed. He was the head veterinarian in a Danish dragoon division and had been knighted. So, there was quite a bit of information available about him and they found it was very interesting going through his records. In November they took a trip to Spain, Portugal, Tangiers, and then back to Gibraltar, which Helma had not seen since the return trip from India. After that they went to London for a week of Christmas shopping. They ended the year in Colorado, spending 10 days with Kaye and Bud. Helma flew home and Ted went to visit his dad's old village in Greece, where Kim, his granddaughter, linked up with him. For his 75th birthday he took a grandson to Guatemala for an immersion class in Spanish, staying at a local indigenous house. In November Jacqueline Maslen came to the United

Ted and Helma in their home, 1990s.

States for a tour and they went to Seattle, then Vancouver, had high tea at the Empress Hotel in Victoria, Canada, and then back to Seattle. They then went to San Francisco and from there on to Shirley and John's in Florida. They went back up to North Carolina and on to Williamsburg to visit the Goldbergs. Helma and Ted ended the year in Colorado, splitting time between Denver, where Kaye and Bud had a home at Cherry Hills Country Club, and a house of theirs in Vail. Vail always reminded Helma of 1947–48 in Garmisch, with so many pleasant memories being relived in Vail. Seeing the snow, trees, and the mountain view always made her relax. She didn't mind being cabin-bound at all. It was a great year for snow and Helma and Ted believed the dry cold didn't affect their old bones as much. Ted was writing for a military encyclopedia that year. Ted ended the year with a West Point visit with Patrick, who was a professor there.

In 1993, Ted went with a US military delegation to Greece and was part of the symposium on the Balkan wars of 1910 through 1912. He received a briefing on Yugoslavia from their military personnel. Ted and Helma took a 16-day trip to Russia, first visiting Moscow and then on the MS *Lenin* cruise ship, down the River Volga, the river of the tsar, for eight days visiting towns and cities along the way and ending at Saint Petersburg. The highlight of Ted's trip was to visit with veteran Spetsnaz troopers who were in Afghanistan. One of the Russians, Retired Major Eugene Khruschev, visited him at Fort Bragg in August 1993 to study soldiers transitioning out of the military. One night in Ted's map room, the major asked him if he had ever heard about one of the rogue battalions that the major had tried unsuccessfully to track down. It turned out that Ted had created a ghost battalion to confuse the Russians. They had Korans printed up with the unit designation and left them scattered throughout Afghanistan. That year Ted made four trips to Russia and Ukraine with the Military History Institute of Moscow, who wanted to establish a working relationship with the West. There were unique opportunities courtesy of the military institute and the faculty at Frunze Academy. They were coordinating visits to the Russian archives for people who had specific research topics. It was very easy to obtain access to the Russian archives, which had just been opened. They also coordinated trips and seminars related to anything Russian. At this time the Russians had thrown off the fetters of communist ideology and they were trying to develop professional relationships with institutions of higher education and veteran US soldiers.

In 1994, Ted was on a week's cruise visiting various Greek islands as a guest of the Greek government. He was one of the six American historians presenting at the XXI Congress of the International Commission of Military History. Ted gave a talk on "The Afghan Insurgency and the Reagan Doctrine." He gave the same presentation later at the US Army 2002 Bicentennial Conference of Military Historians in Washington. His major thrust these days was the Cold War and getting recognition that Korea and Vietnam were hot wars in the 40-year Cold War of containment

> Dear Ted:
>
> You are right, the battles of the Cold War spanned peace and conflict. Too frequently, in our euphoria over the end of a half-century of confrontation, the service and sacrifice of those that made this great victory possible have been ignored. Thank you for your poignant and proper reminder of the debt we owe to several generations of Americans.
>
> Sincerely,
>
> Dennis J. Reimer
> General, United States Army
> Chief of Staff
>
> *[handwritten: You're right — I flew it — Thanx for keeping me straight.]*

Letter to Brig. Gen. Mataxis from General Reinier, August 23, 1997.

against communist expansion. This was a recurrent theme for Ted as upon hearing a speech given by the Army Chief of Staff in 1997, Brig. Gen. Mataxis wrote a letter reminding General Reinier that the hot wars of Korea and Vietnam were in fact part of the Cold War. This letter (excerpt) was a response from the General thanking Brig. Gen. Mataxis for his reminder and for "setting him straight." The United States lost the Vietnam War; however, it won the 40-year Cold War.

Also, in 1994 Helma said: "Life is so different when we are out in Colorado. The altitude and dry weather really agree with us, plus it is a state for very active people. No one sits around inside watching TV when you can be outside exercising or participating in outdoor activities. Ted continues his hour a day regimen of swimming. Kaye's active family also engaged us in many get-togethers, activities and travels. Ted and I really liked their Vail house and their main house in Cherry Hills is quite nice. Their family is always doing some sort of family activity. Ted really loves the opportunity of being forced into thinking, writing, and socializing with the young soldiers that he works with." In July and September 1993, Ted had surgeries to repair his carotid artery, which was 99 percent blocked. He finally got a computer. It had taken several years to be convinced that he needed one. However, it was life-changing for him. He did a lot of op-eds and he did 900 letters and articles in a little over a year. It was quite an accomplishment.

The 50th anniversary of VE Day was celebrated on May 8, 1995. Across France there were many French ceremonies and World War II veterans gathered to commemorate the end of the war. At Spécheren Heights, a battlefield of the Franco-Prussian War, 1870–71, when Germany defeated the French and seized Alsace-Lorraine, the French erected a monument to the 70th Infantry Division for liberating the area in the last Allied offensive of World War II in spring 1945. General Blanchard and

Ted participated, as both had been members of the division. After the dedication of the monument, which was near the 1871 German monuments, the French mayor asked them to obtain a World War II tank to go with the monument. When Ted asked the mayor why the French had paid for the monument, he said, "Up until that time the only monument there had been the Germans', and we want one also." It seemed like an impossible task; however, USAREUR Headquarters in Heidelberg was contacted and there was a Kaserne closing which provided a tank. It only took a year and a half to have this idea come to pass. The tank was installed on the site where Hitler had commemorated the seizure of Alsace early in World War II with a speech saying, "Alsace will remain a part of Germany for 1000 years." At the 50th anniversary the veterans commented that at the next anniversary, rather than marching in the parade they wanted to be jeep-borne.

In 1996, Ted and Bud went to the 30th anniversary of the 101st at Fort Campbell, Kentucky. Bud met with many of his Vietnam buddies there. General Buck Kernan was the division commander and an old family friend. He was the son of Col. Kernan, whose regiment in Korea was next to Ted's. They were instructors at the Infantry School, attended the War College together, and were then assigned to Germany as brigade/battle group commanders.

The year 2000 started off with coordinating a trip to France in May. Visiting the 70th Infantry Division monument at Spectrum Heights and the Franco/Prussian battlefield of 1870 was going to be the first visit of the 21st century. That year they also visited Maui, Hawaii, with Kaye's family. In March they went to Belgium, Holland, and Germany with the band from Valley Forge Military Academy. On this trip they visited a local cemetery of soldiers from World War II and the band placed wreaths on the graves and played "Taps." It was amazing how beautifully the cemeteries were maintained over the years. Then in September and October they took a cruise along the Norwegian coast for 11 days, stopping at many locations along the way. Then they went 300 miles above the Arctic Circle to a port near the Russian border. The trip was fantastic, and a Russian outpost was visited. According to Helma, "We thought the Cold War was over, but it certainly did not seem like it was here. Ted met a man on the cruise ship who was on the German invasion force, which really gave him inside information on the invasion, and he loved it. This year we reached the conclusion that at this stage of our lives we'd better stay on two overseas trips a year since more than that is really pushing our endurance."

In June 2001, Helma and Ted packed their bags and their household and moved out to Colorado to be near Kaye and Bud's family and the Rocky Mountains that they loved so dearly. Helma had reached a point where she could no longer run a house and Kaye had suggested that they move out there so she could be of assistance. Ted considered it a very prudent move since they were only 20 minutes away from their daughter and 15 minutes away from their granddaughter, a pediatrician, who had two daughters, aged four, and six months. Psychologically this was great for

Helma as she could play grandmother once again. Kaye took care of taking her out to lunch and shopping. Kim visited at least once a week, and they had dinner once a week with the whole family. Kaye or Kim also accompanied them to medical appointments. Ted Jr. drove Ted out in their little station wagon, carrying all their high-value items that they did not want shipped with the moving company. For their retirement community they selected Park Place, which was a converted hotel and centrally located in downtown Denver. It was very close to the river walk of Denver which is a stretch of 20–30 miles where one can run, bike, or hike. After years of collecting, it was hard to choose what possessions they now wanted in their small two-bedroom apartment. Their apartment was on the ninth floor, which gave them an outstanding view of the mountains to the west. Ted's paperwork could have easily filled the place.

Ted Jr. built an addition onto his house in Pinehurst, North Carolina, which turned out to be a library and a bedroom suite so Ted could come and visit a couple of times a year. Ted's books and papers were kept there. Ted would visit his son in North Carolina and have access to his books and papers, which was time he thoroughly enjoyed.

Ted died on March 8, 2006, at the age of 86. For the last 11 years of his life, he was able to stay engaged as a professor for the American Military University, teaching and mentoring young active-duty students.

Helma Jensen Mataxis stayed in their apartment at Park Place in Denver. Kaye's family and her grandchildren kept her actively engaged for her remaining years. She had 32 years as a devoted army wife and was married to Ted for 66 years. She had spent numerous years raising the children single-handedly while Ted served his country in World War II, Korea, and Vietnam. She had eight grandchildren and 15 great-grandchildren. Helma died on April 13, 2011, at the age of 91.

***

This book began with President Roosevelt's "The Man in the Arena," and it is only appropriate to end with the words of President Ronald Reagan: "Freedom is never more than one generation away from extinction. We didn't pass it to our children in the bloodstream. It must be fought for, protected and handed on for them to do the same, or one day we will spend our sunset years telling our children and our children's children what it was once like to live in the United States where men were free."

Reagan's words highlight the fragility of freedom and the responsibility Americans each have to preserve it. The United States is at a crossroad and as a nation must end the deep divisions. We must focus on our core American values—freedom, justice, the rule of law, pursuit of happiness, and the opportunity for success in our lives based on the efforts and sacrifices we make to accomplish our dreams.

COMMANDER
UNITED STATES TRANSPORTATION COMMAND
SCOTT AIR FORCE BASE IL 62225-5357

> 3 MAR
>
> Dear General Mataxis,
>
> I had the great pleasure of meeting your grandson in Iraq a few weeks ago. I write you to let you know that the warrior spirit of the Mataxis clan is very much alive and well in Iraq. Those who succeeded you in military service, like Ted, are grateful for your service and example. Please know that my generation shares that sentiment too!
>
> Sincerely, Norty

When Ted was taken ill and while on his death bed, he received this letter from General Norton A. Schwartz, who was commander of the United States Transportation Command from September 2005 to August 2008. The letter was to inform Ted "… that the warrior spirit of the Mataxis clan is alive and well in Iraq." General Schwartz had met Ted's grandson, Ted III, in Iraq a few weeks earlier.

However divided we are politically, all Americans share these ideals. As individuals, communities, and leaders, we need to bridge the gaps and create common ground.

"And I heard the voice of the Lord saying, 'Whom shall I send, and who will go for us?' Then I said, 'Here I am! Send me.'" (Isaiah 6:8) This is the question today when we are called upon to serve our country and preserve our freedoms. In every chapter of General Mataxis's life, there was a choice—and each time, he chose to serve. In World War II, Korea, and Vietnam, and Afghanistan he answered the call, sacrificing comfort, safety, and time with family to uphold ideals he believed in deeply. His service was never without hardship, nor his sacrifice without cost.

Now is the time for you, the reader, to reflect: when the call comes, whether in ways grand or humble, will you be ready to step forward? Will you be willing to give of yourself for a cause greater than your own? These choices define us, just as they defined him. Let his story be not just one of remembrance, but of inspiration—calling on all of us to honor our freedoms with our actions, our sacrifices, and our service.

Thank you for reading this. May God continue to bless the United States.

APPENDIX

Recommendations for Awards, World War II and Early Vietnam

```
                HEADQUARTERS 70TH INFANTRY DIVISION
                       APO 461  U S ARMY

GENERAL ORDERS)                              20 June 1945
NUMBER      49)

                        ++ EXTRACT ++

I ---- AWARD OF THE SILVER STAR. By direction of the President,
under the provisions of Army Regulations 600-45, 22 September 1943,
as amended, the Silver Star is awarded to the following individuals:

       THEODORE C MATAXIS, O 392 185, Lieutenant Colonel, (then Major
Infantry, Headquarters 2d Battalion, 276 Infantry, for gallantry in
action on 10 January 1945, near Rothbach, France. When two companies
had lost their commanding officers as a result of enemy action, Lieu-
tenant Colonel Mataxis, then Battalion Executive Officer, went for-
ward to coordinate these units in a night attack. He maneuvered one
company into action, and aided the other by bringing effective fire
upon enemy machine guns which had halted the rifle platoons. Moving
forward, he reorganized the front line troops, in complete darkness
and under heavy artillery fire. While thus engaged, he captured two
prisoners, and killed three enemy soldiers at an automatic weapons
position. His aggressive leadership at a critical juncture was an
inspiration to the officers and men of the battalion, and a major
factor in accomplishment of his unit's mission. Entered military
service from Seattle, Washington.

                BY COMMAND OF MAJOR GENERAL BARNETT:

                                        JAMES L RICHARDSON JR
                                        Colonel   GSC
                                        Actg Chief of Staff

OFFICIAL:

    /s/ B V Merrick
    /t/ B V MERRICK
        Lt Col  AGD
        Adj General

                          CERTIFIED TRUE COPY

                                     ELLEN P. TALBOTT
                                     1st Lt., WAC
                                     Adjutant
                                     7734 EUCOM Historical D
                R E S T R I C T E D   APO 172, U. S. Army
```

Award of the Silver Star from 70th Infantry Division for Ted Sr.'s gallantry on January 10, 1945. As the battalion commander, he single-handedly took out a machine gun position, killing three SS troopers and capturing the remaining three German troops.

```
GO 285 Hq 7th Inf Div APO 7, 2 June 53

                    Section II

      AWARD OF THE BRONZE STAR MEDAL (SECOND BRONZE OAK LEAF CLUSTER).--By
direction of the President, under the provisions of Executive Order 9419,
4 February 1944 (sec. II, WD Bul. 3, 1944), and pursuant to authority in
AR 600-45, the Bronze Star Medal (Second Oak Leaf Cluster) with Letter "V"
device for heroic achievement in connection with military operations
against an enemy of the United States is awarded to the following-named
officer:

      Lieutenant Colonel THEODORE C. MATAXIS, 034035, Infantry, United
States Army, a member of Headquarters, 17th Infantry, distinguished him-
self by heroic achievement near Haugae, Korea. On the night of 20-21
February 1953, when a friendly patrol was engaged by a numerically
superior enemy force, Colonel MATAXIS, upon hearing of the ensuing action,
hurried to the Fire Support Coordination Center where he oriented him-
self on the situation and advised the battalion commander on courses of
action. Colonel MATAXIS also heard that communications to the supporting
tanks had failed and that their fires were endangering friendly units
sent to relieve the original patrol. Realizing the gravity of this new
development, Colonel MATAXIS went two hundred yards forward of friendly
lines to locate the tank platoon. When he arrived, Colonel MATAXIS
calmly redirected their fire to give maximum support without endangering
the friendly forces. The heroic actions of Colonel MATAXIS reflect
great credit on himself and the military service. Entered the Federal
service from Washington.

            BY COMMAND OF MAJOR GENERAL TRUDEAU:


OFFICIAL:                           THOMAS J. ELDER
                                    Lt Col, GS
                                    Acting Chief of Staff

C. W. COPP
WOJG, USA
Asst AG

DISTRIBUTION:
  X, plus
  TAG, ATTN: AGAO-I (4)
       ATTN: AGPO-A (3)
  Hq USAFFE, ATTN: AG-DA (3)
  Hq Eighth Army, ATTN: KAG-PD (1)
  I Corps (2)
  PIO (4)
  Ea individual concerned (5)
```

Award of the Bronze Star for "Valor" while acting as the 17th Regimental Executive Officer from the 7th Infantry Division on June 2, 1953.

HEADQUARTERS
7TH INFANTRY DIVISION
APO 7

GENERAL ORDERS
NUMBER   298

4 June 1953

Section I

AWARD OF THE BRONZE STAR MEDAL (FIRST BRONZE OAK-LEAF CLUSTER).--By direction of the President, under the provisions of Executive Order 9419, 4 February 1944 (sec. II, WD Bul. 3, 1944), and pursuant to authority in AR 600-45, the Bronze Star Medal (First Oak-Leaf Cluster), with Letter "V" device for heroic achievement in connection with military operations against an enemy of the United States is awarded to the following-named officer:

Lieutenant Colonel THEODORE C. MATAXIS, 034035, Infantry, United States Army, a member of Headquarters, 17th Infantry, distinguished himself by heroic achievement near Song Ch'on-dong, Korea. On the night of 6-7 February 1953, Colonel MATAXIS, in his capacity as Regimental Executive Officer, moved up to the scene of enemy action in order to obtain a more exact and complete report for his superior officers. When Colonel MATAXIS reached the lines he found the friendly troops nervous because they believed the enemy was within their tactical defensive wire. Colonel MATAXIS talked to the men to bolster their morale and personally led a group of men to screen the defensive wire. While moving to the wire, an enemy searchlight illuminated Colonel MATAXIS and his men. Taking cover until the searchlight had swung its arc in another direction, Colonel MATAXIS, with complete disregard for his personal safety, moved to an exposed position to observe the enemy and call in heavy mortar fire on them. After the hail of friendly fire had demolished the enemy, Colonel MATAXIS continued on his original mission to check the defensive wire. The heroic actions of Colonel MATAXIS reflect great credit on himself and the military service. Entered the Federal service from Washington.

Section II

AWARD OF THE COMMENDATION RIBBON WITH METAL PENDANT.--By direction of the Secretary of the Army, under the provisions of AR 600-45, the Commendation Ribbon with Metal Pendant for meritorious service during the period indicated is awarded to the following-named enlisted men:

Master Sergeant LEONARD SPANGLER, RA38472751, Corps of Engineers, United States Army, in Korea, Headquarters and Service Company, 13th Engineer Combat Battalion, 1 June 1952 to 1 June 1953. Entered the Federal service from Oklahoma.

Sergeant BENJAMIN I. CAMPBELL, US52121916, Infantry, United States Army, in Korea, Service Company, 32d Infantry, 22 May 1952 to 1 June 1953. Entered the Federal service from Maryland.

Sergeant DAVID R. JONES, US52095455, Infantry, United States Army, in Korea, Headquarters Company, 7th Infantry Division, 20 February 1953 to 18 May 1953. Entered the Federal service from Virginia.

Award of the Bronze Star for "Valor" on the night of February 6/7, 1953, as the 17th Regimental Executive Officer from the 7th Infantry Division on June 4, 1953.

HEADQUARTERS
UNITED STATES ARMY VIETNAM
APO San Francisco 96307

GENERAL ORDERS
NUMBER 2337

24 May 1967

AWARD OF THE MERITORIOUS UNIT COMMENDATION

1. TC 320. The following AWARD is announced.

Awarded: Meritorious Unit Commendation
Date action: July 1965 to October 1966
Theater: Republic of Vietnam
Reason: For exceptionally meritorious achievement in the performance of outstanding service: The 1ST BRIGADE, 101ST AIRBORNE DIVISION distinguished itself in support of military operations in the Republic of Vietnam during the period July 1965 to October 1966. Selected to be the first CONUS based unit to fight in Vietnam, the 1ST BRIGADE, 101ST AIRBORNE DIVISION has fought brilliantly, establishing a pattern of resounding victories in every major Viet Cong and North Vietnamese Army encounter and rendering ineffective several hostile battalions and one complete regiment. Superb in its adaptation to jungle counterinsurgency warfare, the 1ST BRIGADE, 101ST AIRBORNE DIVISION developed and implemented a centralized base camp organization which enabled it with spectacular success to improve mobility, conserve supplies, and release many additional men for forward deployment. While carrying a prodigious combat load, the members of this unit selflessly contributed their personal time to more than 2000 civic action projects which included transporting and supplying over 12,000 refugees, providing medical care for over 37,000 Vietnamese in outlying areas, and improving the political, psychological, and economic conditions in every area in which they traveled. The 1ST BRIGADE, 101ST AIRBORNE DIVISION's exceptional standards of administration, maintenance, discipline and morale, achieved these remarkable results without interrupting the vigorous search and destroy mission. The tenacity and dedicated devotion to duty displayed by the members of the 1ST BRIGADE, 101ST AIRBORNE DIVISION were in keeping with the highest traditions of the military service and reflect great credit upon themselves and the Armed Forces of the United States.
Authority: By direction of the Secretary of the Army, under the provisions of paragraph 203, AR 672-5-1 and DA MSG 793617, 10 Dec 66.

Award of the Meritorious Unit Commendation 1st Brigade, 101st Airborne Division, for actions taken July 1965–October 1966, while dealing with the North Vietnamese regiments and the local Viet Cong in close combat.

> **HEADQUARTERS**
> **UNITED STATES ARMY VIETNAM**
> **APO SAN FRANCISCO 96307**
>
> GENERAL ORDERS   21 June 1967
> NUMBER   3035
>
> ### AWARD OF THE VALOROUS UNIT AWARD
>
> 1. TC 320. The following AWARD is announced.
>
> Awarded: Valorous Unit Award
> Date action: 17 January 1966 to 25 March 1966
> Theater: Republic of Vietnam
> Reason: For extraordinary heroism while participating in military operations: The 1ST BRIGADE, 101ST AIRBORNE DIVISION distinguished itself by extraordinary heroism from 17 January 1966 to 25 March 1966 while conducting Operations VAN BUREN and HARRISON against armed hostile forces in the vicinity of Tuy Hoa, Republic of Vietnam. After commencing Operation VAN BUREN on 17 January, the 1ST BRIGADE deployed in the Tuy Hoa area to locate, fix, and destroy Viet Cong forces, while simultaneously protecting the local rice harvest from hostile seizure. The 1ST BRIGADE not only defeated the insurgents decisively in four major battles, but also enabled the Vietnamese people to harvest a rice crop triple that of the previous year, when Viet Cong interference was unchecked. At Canh Tinh on 6 February, the 2D BATTALION (AIRBORNE), 502D INFANTRY killed 64 Viet Cong and completely routed a numerically superior hostile force from heavily fortified emplacements. On the following day, the 1ST BATTALION (AIRBORNE), 327TH INFANTRY took a toll of 66 insurgents in a savage conflict. During Operation HARRISON, that began on 21 February, the 1ST BATTALION (AIRBORNE), 502D INFANTRY continued maneuvers in the Tuy Hoa area by searching out and destroying 118 of the enemy in a five-hour pitched battle in the rice paddies around My Phu. After three days of difficult marching through mountainous jungle, the 2d BATTALION (AIRBORNE), 327TH INFANTRY discovered a Viet Cong regimental headquarters. The men fiercely broke the hostile defenses that were in a nearly impregnable cave complex, and uncovered one of the largest caches captured in the counterinsurgency efforts. While suffering only light casualties in both operations, the 1ST BRIGADE killed more than 500 Viet Cong, wounded hundreds more and captured nearly 500 insurgents and suspects. Not content with merely defeating the enemy, the men of this exceptional unit strengthened the safety and health of the local Vietnamese population by tireless efforts in medical treatment, road building and protection of the valuable rice crop. Their extensive military and civic accomplishments deeply depressed enemy morale and struck an irreparable blow to insurgency efforts in the vicinity of Tuy Hoa. The extraordinary heroism and devotion to duty displayed by the men of the 1ST BRIGADE, 101ST AIRBORNE DIVISION, were in keeping with the highest traditions of the military service and reflect distinct credit upon themselves and the Armed Forces of the United States.
>
> Authority: By direction of the Secretary of the Army under the provisions of paragraph 202.1, AR 672-5-1, and Department of the Army message 793617, 10 December 1966.
>
> FOR THE COMMANDER:
>
> OFFICIAL SEAL   FRANK D. MILLER
> HEADQUARTERS   Major General, US Army
> U.S. ARMY VIETNAM   Chief of Staff

Award of the "Valorous" Unit Award, 1st Brigade, 101st Airborne Division, for actions taken January 17, 1966–March 25, 1966, for heavy fighting that took place with the North Vietnamese Regiments and local Viet Cong in close and personal combat.

```
                    DEPARTMENT OF THE ARMY
           HEADQUARTERS 1ST BRIGADE 101ST AIRBORNE DIVISION
                       APO San Francisco 96347

GENERAL ORDERS                                          17 October 1966
NUMBER   1060

                   AWARD OF THE AIR MEDAL FOR HEROISM

     1. TC 320. The following AWARD is announced.

MATAXIS, THEODORE C. 034035 COLONEL INFANTRY USA
HHC, 1st Bde, 101st Abn Div, APO 96347
     Awarded:  Air Medal with "V" Device Seventeenth Oak Leaf Cluster
     Date action:  9 June 1966
     Theater:  Republic of Vietnam
     Reason:   For heroism in connection with military operations against a hostile
               force: Colonel Mataxis distinguished himself by exceptionally valorous
               actions on 9 June 1966, in the Republic of Vietnam. While flying in a
               helicopter as part of a reconnaissance team, Colonel Mataxis released
               his safety harness and leaned out of the aircraft door with a flash-
               light in order to better spot obstacles on the proposed landing zone.
               His action was particularly hazardous as the aircraft was being manuvered
               down a valley at night and was required to avoid heavy ground fire being
               directed at it. Colonel Mataxis, by heroically disregarding his personal
               safety, was instrumental in the team's quickly finding an adequate landing
               zone on which urgently needed reinforcements could be landed. His init-
               iative and conspicuous valor are in keeping with the highest traditions
               of the military service, and reflect great credit upon himself, his unit,
               and the United States Army.
     Authority:  By direction of the President under the provisions of Executive
                 Order 9158 as amended by 9242-A, 11 September 1942.

          FOR THE COMMANDER:


                                        J. G. BROWN
                                        Major, AGC
                                        Adjutant General


WILLIAM O. HORGEN
Capt, AGC
Asst AG
```

Award of the Air Medal for "Valor," 1st Brigade, 101st Airborne Division, for actions taken on June 9, 1966. This Air Medal was his 17th Oak Cluster for this award.

HEADQUARTERS
UNITED STATES MILITARY ASSISTANCE COMMAND, VIETNAM
APO San Francisco 96243

GENERAL ORDERS   25 April 1966
NUMBER   575

AWARD OF THE ARMY COMMENDATION MEDAL
(Third Oak Leaf Cluster)

1. TC 320. The following AWARD is announced.

MATAXIS, THEODORE C. 034035 COL INF USA
  Awarded: Army Commendation Medal (Third Oak Leaf Cluster) with "V" Device
  Date action: 21 February 1965 to 24 February 1965
  Theater: Republic of Vietnam
  Reason: For heroism in connection with military operations against a
          hostile force: Colonel Mataxis distinguished himself by heroic
          action from 21 February 1965 to 24 February 1965 while serving
          as Senior Advisor to II Corps, Army of the Republic of Vietnam.
          Informed that a series of Viet Cong attacks had isolated several
          friendly units, Colonel Mataxis immediately proceeded to the
          besieged areas to observe the tactical situation. Disregarding
          his personal safety, Colonel Mataxis repeatedly landed in small
          areas held by the friendly forces while maintaining a close
          surveillance of the battlefields and directing the deployment
          of the relief forces and the units that were still under attack.
          Colonel Mataxis exposed himself to the hostile fire to personally
          direct a heliborne operation which resulted in the successful
          extraction of the beleaguered friendly forces. Colonel Mataxis'
          heroic actions were in keeping with the highest traditions of
          the United States Army and reflect great credit upon himself
          and the military service.
  Authority: By direction of the Secretary of the Army under the provisions
             of AR 672-5-1

FOR THE COMMANDER:

W. B. ROSSON
Major General, USA
Chief of Staff

E. D. BRYSON
Colonel, AGC
Adjutant General

Award of Army Commendation Medal for "Valor," third oak leaf cluster, 1st Brigade, 101st Airborne Division, for actions taken February 21–24, 1965.

HEADQUARTERS
I FIELD FORCE VIETNAM
APO San Francisco 96350

GENERAL ORDERS
NUMBER   552

13 December 1966

AWARD OF THE BRONZE STAR MEDAL WITH "V" DEVICE
(Third Oak Leaf Cluster)

1. TC 320. The following AWARD is announced.

MATAXIS, THEODORE C 034035 COLONEL INFANTRY United States Army Headquarters and Headquarters Company, 1st Brigade, 101st Airborne Division, APO San Francisco 96347.
  Awarded: Bronze Star Medal with "V" Device (Third Oak Leaf Cluster)
  Date action: 4 March 1966
  Theater: Republic of Vietnam
  Reason: Heroism: Colonel Mataxis distinguished himself while serving as the deputy brigade commander performing a liaison mission for the brigade commander. When Colonel Mataxis arrived at the scene of battle at about 2000 hours, he was advised by the battalion commander not to land his aircraft as the Viet Cong were raking the area with a torrid volume of machine gun fire. Realizing the immediate necessity of his mission, the battalion commander guided the chopper in at Colonel Mataxis' command. The chopper landed without the use of lights and Colonel Mataxis jumped out and sent the aircraft airborne. Colonel Mataxis was then briefed by the battalion commander on the battle situation. Next Colonel Mataxis visited all of the units in the 1st Battalion (Airborne), 327th Infantry so that he could talk to as many troopers as possible. In so doing, he personally assessed the actual battle situation. Throughout this time, he was subject to hostile fire but continued to visit all of the units. He insured that all of the wounded were being cared for. His presence in the battle area greatly inspired the troopers and was a rare form of battlefield leadership. His estimate of the situation enabled the battalion to mass sufficient power to give the enemy a stunning defeat. Colonel Mataxis' actions reflect great credit upon himself, his unit, and the Armed Forces of the United States.
  Authority: By direction of the President under the provisions of USARV Message 16695, 1 July 1966 and paragraph 31a, AR 672-5-1.

FOR THE COMMANDER:

OFFICIAL:

LINTON S. BOATWRIGHT
Colonel, GS
Chief of Staff

WILLIAM H. JAMES
Colonel, AGC
Adjutant General

Award of the Bronze Star for "Valor," third oak leaf cluster, 1st Brigade, 101st Airborne Division, for valorous actions on March 4, 1966.

References by Chapter

Chapter 1

Childhood Metaxas vs. Mataxis by Ted.
Descriptions of very early family years 1453, escaping from the fall of Constantinople and Ted growing up.
Mataxis, Theodore C. "Christopher Peter Metaxas AKA Christopher Peter Mataxis."
Mataxis, Theodore C. "Metaxas Family 1081–1963, Early family history."
Metaxa's Family 1081–1961.
Metaxas, Christo (1907–1961). Untitled poem written upon his return to Greece. Translated from Greek by Amphitrite Constantelos Manuel, November 2010.
Miscellaneous family papers.
Pratt, Michael. *Britain's Greek Empire*. London: Rex Collings, 1978.
Ross, William F. and Charles F. Romanus. *United States Army in World War II. The Technical Services. The Quartermaster Corps: Operations in the War Against Germany*. Washington, D.C.: Center of Military History, United States Army, 1991. https://www.govinfo.gov/content/pkg/GOVPUB-D114-PURL-gpo77874/pdf/GOVPUB-D114-PURL-gpo77874.pdf.

Chapter 2

Mataxis, Theodore C. Personal notes.
Quotes from ROTC Professor of Military Science, University of Washington, Lieutenant Colonel Delphin Thebaud.
Remembrances of Ted.
University Of Washington. *Tyee*. Seattle, WA: 1936. University of Washington Libraries UW Yearbooks and Documents. https://digitalcollections.lib.washington.edu/digital/collection/uwdocs/id/18781/rec/33. Accessed March 11, 2025.
University Of Washington. *Tyee*. Seattle, WA: 1937. University of Washington Libraries UW Yearbooks and Documents. https://digitalcollections.lib.washington.edu/digital/collection/uwdocs/id/19059/rec/9. Accessed March 11, 2025.
University Of Washington. *Tyee*. Seattle, WA: 1938. University of Washington Libraries UW Yearbooks and Documents. https://digitalcollections.lib.washington.edu/digital/collection/uwdocs/id/30456/rec/1. Accessed March 11, 2025.
University Of Washington. *Tyee*. Seattle, WA: 1939. University of Washington Libraries UW Yearbooks and Documents. https://digitalcollections.lib.washington.edu/digital/collection/uwdocs/id/30830/rec/2. Accessed March 11, 2025.
University Of Washington. *Tyee*. Seattle, WA: 1940. University of Washington Libraries UW Yearbooks and Documents. https://digitalcollections.lib.washington.edu/digital/collection/uwdocs/id/35029/rec/3. Accessed March 11, 2025.

Chapter 3

Ambrose, Stephen E. *Citizen Soldiers: The U.S. Army from the Normandy Beaches to the Bulge, to the Surrender of Germany.* New York: Simon & Schuster, 1997.
Cardozier, V. R. *The Mobilization of the United States in World War II: How the Government, Military and Industry Prepared for War.* Jefferson, NC: McFarland & Co., 1995.
History of the 91st Division—US Army, 1942.
Letters to Helma.
Mobilization Plan.
Mobilization for World War II. October 1940. Draft notes from Ted.
The Officers' Guide. 4th ed. Harrisburg, PA: The Military Service Publishing Company, 1941.
Original operations orders and documents.
Personal papers.
Ted's reflection papers of the time.
War Department. *Basic Field Manual: Infantry Drill Regulations.* FM 22-5. Washington, D.C.: U.S. Army Military History Institute, 1941.

Chapter 4

Arnold, Edmund C. *The Trailblazers: The Story of the 70th Infantry Division.* Richmond, VA: Seventieth Infantry Division Association, 1989.
Blanchard, George. Speech dedicating the Trailblazer monument, October 6, 1997.
Bonn, Keith E. *When the Odds Were Even: Vosges Mountains Campaign, October 1944–January 1945.* New York: Presidio Press, 1994.
Bonn, Keith E. *With Fire and Zeal: The 276th Infantry Regiment in World War II.* Hampton, VA: Aegis Consulting Group, 1998.
Cheves, Wallace Robert. *L'Operation Nordwind et Wingen-sur-Moder* [Operation Nordwind at Wingen-sur-Moder]. Published privately by the author, 1978.
Department of Defense. *70th Division (Training) 50th Anniversary Issue: A Historic Profile of the 70th Division (Training).* Benton County Historical Society Collection, James M. Collins (Major General) Collection, 1993.
Eisenhower, Dwight D. *Crusade in Europe: A Personal Account of World War II.* New York: Vintage Books, 2021.
"General Marshall's Report: The Winning of the War in Europe and the Pacific; Biennial Report of the Chief of Staff of the United States Army July 1, 1943 to June 30, 1945, to the Secretary of War." Washington, D.C.: War Department in cooperation with the Council on Books in Wartime by Simon & Schuster, 1945.
Goodwin, Mark. *US Infantry Weapons in Combat: Personal Experiences from WW II and Korea.* Scott A. Duff Publications, 2005.
Grossjohann, Georg. *Five Years, Four Fronts: The War Years of Grossjohann.* Bedford: Aegis Consulting Group, 1999.
Letters to Helma.
Original operations orders and documents.
Personal notes of Mataxis and Leo Cooper, 1986.
Personal papers.
Quinn, William. *The 7th Army Concept of Operations,* Volume I–III, 1946.
Rothman, Stewart N. *17th Infantry Association Scrapbook.* Fairbanks, AK: The Lens Unlimited, 2005.

Samsel, Harold J. *The Operational History of the 117th Cavalry Reconnaissance Squadron (Mech.) World War II*. 117th Cavalry Association, 1982.
US Army, History of the 91st Infantry Division, August 1942.
Whiting, Charles. *Operation Northwind: The Other Battle of the Bulge*. Stroud: Spellmount, 2007.
XXI Corps. The Story of the 70th Infantry Division, April 1945.
Zoepf, Wolf T. *Seven Days in January: With the 6th SS-Mountain Division in Operation Nordwind*. Bedford: Aberjona Press, 2001.

Chapter 5

Background of Establishment and Operations of 7734 USFET Historical Detachment—An extract from the personal papers and files of Brig. Gen. Theodore C. Mataxis.
Helma's impression of the time.
History of the 3rd Infantry Regiment, 106th Infantry Division.
Letter to Chief of Military History, BGen. Mountcastle, December 14, 1995.
Letter Order #58, February 10, 1947.
Orders Travel Authorization of Dependents 23 May 1946 AGAO-0 510.
Organization Orders of 7734 Historical Detachment, GO 347, December 7, 1946.
Personal letters.
Personal papers.
US Government. Introduction to Germany for Occupational Personnel Guide, 1947.

Chapter 6

Defense Service Staff College. Student Guide, Memos, Demonstration Tour Guide 1851, Records and Publications.
Division of Information, India Tourist Information, 1949.
Guest List Round World Services, American President Lines.
India Tourist Information, Government of India, 1950.
Jamieson, Norma. *Memoirs of a Memsahib: India 1950–1951*. Australia: Self-published, 2007.

Chapter 7

Buffalo Bugle. Copies of original unit newsletters.
Department of Defense. The 7th Infantry Division in Korea. FEC Printing Plant, 1955.
Department of Defense. Freedom's Frontier Korea, 1970.
Eighth Army Staff Historian's Office. "Key Korean War Battles Fought in the Republic of Korea." March 1972.
Gonsalves, Joesph. *Battle at the 38th Parallel: Surviving the Peace Talks at Panmunjom*. Central Point, OR: Hellgate Press, 2001.
Goodwin, Mark. *US Infantry Weapons in Combat: Personal Experiences from WW II and Korea*. Scott A. Duff Publications, 2005.
Guardia, Mike and Harold G. Moore. *Hal Moore on Leadership: Winning When Outgunned and Outmanned*. Maple Grove, MN: Magnum Books, 2017.
Korean Government. *Korea Reborn: A Grateful Nation Honors War Veterans for 60 Years of Growth*. Remember My Service Productions, 2013. https://www.veterans.nd.gov/sites/www/files/documents/resource/Korea-Reborn-Book.pdf.

Letters to Helma.
Moss, James A. *Trench Warfare*. Menasha, WI: Geo. Banta Publishing Company, 1917.
Operation orders.
Personal papers.
Rees, David. *The Korean War: History and Tactics*. New York: Crescent Books, 1984.
Quinn, William W. *Buffalo Bill Remembers: Truth and Courage*. Fowlerville, MI: Wilderness Adventure Books, 1991.
XXI Corps. The Story of the 70th Infantry Division, April 1945.

Chapter 8

Goldberg, Seymour L. and Theodore C. Mataxis. *Nuclear Tactics, Weapons, and Firepower in the Pentomic Division, Battle Group, and Company*. Harrisburg, PA: Military Service Pub. Co., 1958.
Personal letters.
Personal papers.
US Army Infantry School. *Infantry Magazine*. Fort Benning, GA.

Chapter 9

8th Infantry Division.SS *America* pamphlet for passengers August 1, 1958.
Hackworth, David H. and Julie Sherman. *About Face: Odyssey of an American Warrior*. New York: Simon & Schuster, 1989.
Herbert, Anthony B. and James T. Wooten. *Soldier*. Holt, Rinehart and Winston, 1973.
Personal letters.
Personal papers.

Chapter 10

Personal letters.
Personal papers.
Taylor, Maxwell D. *The Uncertain Trumpet*. New York: Harper & Row, 1960.

Chapter 11

Cash, Captain. Interview with General Mataxis. The Pentagon, 1967.
"God's Own Lunatics," narrated by Joe Galloway in *In the Shadow of the Blade* (documentary film). Directed by Patrick and Cheryl Fries, 2004.
Goodwin, Mark. *US Infantry Weapons in Combat: Personal Experiences from WW II and Korea*. Scott A. Duff Publications, 2005.
Grace, Stephen. *Oil and Water: An Oilman's Quest to Save the Source of America's Most Endangered River*. Denver, CO: UCRA Publishing, 2015.
The Green Berets. Directed by John Wayne and Ray Kellogg. Batjac Productions, 1968.
Hackworth, David H. and Julie Sherman. *About Face: Odyssey of an American Warrior*. New York: Simon & Schuster, 1989.
Interview with General Theodore Mataxis Sr., OH0111. 31 March 2000, Theodore Mataxis Sr. Collection, Vietnam Center and Sam Johnson Vietnam Archive, Texas Tech University, https://www.vietnam.ttu.edu/virtualarchive/items.php?item=OH0111. Accessed March 11, 2025.

Letters to Helma.
Marshall, S. L. A. *Battle In The Monsoon: Campaigning in the Central Highlands, South Vietnam, Summer 1966*. New York: Warner Books, 1989.
Marshall, S. L. A. *Pork Chop Hill*. New York: Permabooks, 1958.
Mataxis, Theodore C. "The War in the Highlands—Attack and Counterattack Along Highway 19." *Army Times*, October 1965.
Mataxis, Theodore C. "Monsoon Offensive in the Highlands." Unpublished manuscript, 1966.
Mataxis, Theodore C. "Enemy Summer Offensive in II Corps." Unpublished manuscript, 1967.
Mataxis, Theodore C. "1965 Tet Offensive." Unpublished manuscript, 2001.
Mataxis, Theodore C. Military Equipment Delivery Team, Cambodia, Presentation. Texas Tech University, 2003.
Moore, Harold G. and Joesph L. Galloway. *We Were Soldiers Once… And Young: Ia Drang—The Battle That Changed Vietnam*. New York: Random House, 1992.
Operation orders.
Personal letters.
Personal papers.
Shock and Awe. Directed by Rob Reiner. Castle Rock Entertainment, Savvy Media Holdings, and Acacia Filmed Entertainment, 2017.
We Were Soldiers. Directed by Randall Wallace. Icon Entertainment International and Wheelhouse, 2002.

Chapter 12

82nd Airborne Division. Historical Summaries 1966, 1967, and 1968.

Chapter 13

Embassy Handbook, 1964.
Goldberg, Seymour L. and Theodore C. Mataxis. *Nuclear Tactics, Weapons, and Firepower in the Pentomic Division, Battle Group, and Company*. Harrisburg, PA: Military Service Pub. Co., 1958.
Personal letters.
Personal papers.

Chapter 14

DCSPER Message, O 150026, February 1972.
Fall, Bernard B. *Street Without Joy*. Mechanicsburg, PA: Stackpole Books, 1994.
Interview with General Theodore Mataxis Sr., OH0111. 31 March 2000, Theodore Mataxis Sr. Collection, Vietnam Center and Sam Johnson Vietnam Archive, Texas Tech University, https://www.vietnam.ttu.edu/virtualarchive/items.php?item=OH0111. Accessed March 11, 2025.
Mataxis, Theodore C. "End of Tour Report." US Military Equipment Delivery Team Cambodia, 1972.
Mataxis, Theodore C. Military Equipment Delivery Team, Cambodia, Presentation. Texas Tech University, 2003.
Personal letters.
Personal papers.
Personal tapes.

Chapter 15

Personal contract.
Personal letters.
Personal papers.

Chapter 16

Freeman, Devery. *Father Sky: A Novel.* New York: Morrow, 1979.
McMaster, H. R. *Dereliction of Duty: Lyndon Johnson, Robert McNamara, The Joint Chiefs of Staff, and the Lies That Led to Vietnam.* New York: HarperCollins Publishers, 1997.
Personal letters.
Personal papers.
Taps. Directed by Harold Becker. Twentieth Century Fox, 1981.

Chapter 17

Asprey, Robert B. *War in The Shadows: The Guerrilla in History.* New York: Morrow, 1994.
CFA Factsheet. "In Afghanistan You need a Stinger to Till the Soil!" Washington, D.C. May 1986.
CFA Pamphlet. "War Crimes in Afghanistan." Washington, D.C. August 1986.
CFA. Trip Report, DA. June 1990.
Churchill, Winston, MP. Letter to Chmm. CFA. July 25, 1985.
Citizen News-Record. June 1990.
Crile, George. *Charlie Wilson's War: The Extraordinary Story of How the Wildest Man in Congress and a Rogue CIA Agent Changed the History of Our Time.* New York: Atlantic Monthly Press, 2003.
Department of Defense. *Soviet Military Power.* 6th ed. Washington, D.C.: US Government Printing Office, 1987.
Dupree, Louis. *Afghanistan,* Princeton, NJ: Princeton University Press, 1973.
International Herald Tribune, May 16, 1986.
Mataxis, Theodore C. "Afghanistan-Soviet Miscalculation? Drive to Warm Water?"
Nair, Kunhanandan. The *Devil and His Dart: How the CIA is Plotting in the Third World.* New Dehli: Sterling Publishers, 1986.
Personal letters.
Personal papers.
United Nations Security Council. "Security Council Committee, Established by Resolution 1267 (1999) Concerning Afghanistan, Issues Consolidated List." Press release AFG/ 131.SC/7028. https://press.un.org/en/2001/afg131.doc.htm. Accessed March 12, 2025.
Writers & Speakers for Freedom. "The Soviets in Afghanistan, Not SO Quietly In to the Night." California, May 1988.

Chapter 18

Bowra, Ken. "Operations and Withdrawal of MEDTC (Operation Eagle Pull)." Paper presented at the Vietnam Triennial Symposium, Texas Tech University, Lubbock, TX, April 1999.
Cleland, John. "Operations of MEDTC Before and After Cut Off of USAF Air Support (15 Aug. 1973)." Paper presented at the Vietnam Triennial Symposium, Texas Tech University, Lubbock, TX, April 1999.

Goldberg, Seymour L. and Theodore C. Mataxis. *Nuclear Tactics, Weapons, and Firepower in the Pentomic Division, Battle Group, and Company.* Harrisburg, PA: Military Service Pub. Co., 1958.

Interview with Theodore Mataxis Jr., OH0134. 31 March 2000, Vietnam Center and Sam Johnson Vietnam Archive, Texas Tech University, https://www.vietnam.ttu.edu/virtualarchive/items.php?item=OH0134. Accessed March 12, 2025.

Interview with General Theodore Mataxis Sr., OH0111. 31 March 2000, Theodore Mataxis Sr. Collection, Vietnam Center and Sam Johnson Vietnam Archive, Texas Tech University, https://www.vietnam.ttu.edu/virtualarchive/items.php?item=OH0111. Accessed March 11, 2025.

Jessup, John E. ed. *Encyclopedia of the American Military.* 3 vols. New York: Scribner, 1994.

Mataxis, Theodore C. "The Activation and Operations of the US Military Equipment Delivery Team Cambodia (MEDTC)." Paper presented at the Vietnam Triennial Symposium, Texas Tech University, Lubbock, TX, April 1999.

Mataxis, Theodore C. "The Afghan Insurgency and the Reagan Doctrine." XXI Congress of the International Commission of Military History, 2001.

Mataxis, Theodore C. "The Afghan Insurgency and the Reagan Doctrine." US Army Bicentennial Conference of Military Historians. Washington, 2002.

Index

Abrams, General Creighton, 160, 188, 194–95
Active-Duty Mobilization, 21–37
Aesop's Fables, 5
Afghanistan, x, xi, xvi, 1, 45, 97, 178, 209, 211, 213–25, 227–35, 241, 244, 249 *see also* Committee for a Free Afghanistan (CFA), Kabul
Agency for Internal Development (AID), 216, 231–32, *see also* Humanitarian Assistance Programs
Agent Orange, 188
Air Force, 50, 72, 80, 97, 104, 131, 136, 141, 153, 155, 172, 174–75, 200, 202, 205, 209, 216, 229
    German, 35, 74
    Indian, 81, 83
    Iranian, 177
    Japanese, 35
    South Vietnam, 145
    Soviet, 232
    US Air Force Color Guard, 62
    US Twelfth Air Force, 76
Alabama, 69, 78
Alsace, 41, 51, 54, 60, 245–46
American Military University (AMU), 1, 237–39, 248
Anabasis, 7
Ardennes Forest, 43
Arizona, 91, 237
ARMISH—Military Assistance Advisory Group (MAAG), 177
Armistice Day, 8
Army (non-US)
    Army of the Republic of Vietnam (ARVIN), 139–41, 144–49, 153–59, 163, 166, 191, 193, 240
    Chinese People's Volunteer Army (PVA), 104
    Indian Army, xv, 80–81, 87–90, 92, 116, 136 *see also* Madras Regiment
    Khmer National Armed Forces (FANK), 195
    Madras Regiment, 80
    Philippine Army, 23, 26
    Singapore Armed Forces (SAF), 200, 202
Army (US)
    1st Cavalry Division, 149, 153, 155–56, 180, 240

3rd Armored Cavalry Regiment, ix, x
3rd Infantry Regiment, 22, 59, 65–66, 187 *see also* Old Guard, The
6th Infantry Division, 23, 27, 29, 32
7th Infantry Division, 40, 102, 104–5, 107, 109, 113, 252, 253
17th Buffalo Regiment, 110–11
17th Infantry Regiment, xvi, 99, 101–9, 111–13, 139
20th Infantry Regiment, 23, 25, 27, 187
23rd Infantry Division, 187
41st Infantry Division, 16
42nd Infantry Division, 59 *see also* Task Force Linden
45th Infantry Division, 43–44, 50
63rd Infantry Regiment, 22, 59 *see also* Task Force Harris
70th Infantry Division, 32–33, 36, 43, 46, 50, 52, 54, 56, 60, 63, 89, 245–46, 251 *see also* Task Force Herren
79th Infantry Division, 41
80th Infantry Division, 42
82nd Airborne Division, 129, 138, 169, 171–76, 183
91st Infantry Division, 32–33, 36
101st Airborne Division, xvi, 138, 159, 161–64, 166–67, 184, 254–58
276th Regiment, 34, 41, 44, 50–51, 57–58 *see also* Task Force Herren
504th Airborne Battle Group, 125–26, 128–29
505th Airborne Battle Group, 125–26, 128–29
505th rifle company, 129
884th Field Artillery Battalion, 50
7734th Historical Detachment, 68, 70–71
Continental Army Command (CONARC), 116
Eighth Army, xv, 100–106, 111, 124
Headquarters Company, 32, 45, 166
I Field Force Vietnam (IFFV), 149, 158, 166
Infantry School, 19, 23, 115–19, 230, 239, 246
Military Equipment Delivery Team for Cambodia (MEDT-C), xvi, 193–95
Old Guard, The, 15, 58–59, 65–66, 68, 89 *see also* 3rd Infantry Regiment

Seventh Army, 39–43, 50, 52, 54, 56–57, 76, 121, 130, 138
Strategic and Tactical Analysis Group (STAG), 133
Task Force Harris, 39, 59
Task Force Herren, 39–43, 45, 50, 54, 59
Task Force Linden, 39, 42, 59
Third Army, 31, 42, 57–58
Trailblazers *see* 70th Infantry Division
USAREUR, 127, 246
US Army Special Forces, xi, 135
US Army Strategic & Tactical Group, 132
Wild West Division *see* 91st Infantry Division
atomic bomb, xv, 59, 65, 109, 115–16, 120, 124, 136

Baden Powell, Lord, 118
Bad Kreuznach, 59, 123, 125, 129, 131
Bangladesh, 80
Battalion Field Firing Test (BFFT), 33–34
Battle of Pork Chop Hill, 109, 113
  First, 109
  Second, 113
Battle of the Bulge, ix, 40, 126 *see also* Western Front
Bavaria, xv, 57, 71
Beckwith, Major Charley, 154–55
Belgium, 100, 132, 246
Berlin, xi, xv, 65, 67–68, 70–71, 75–76, 121, 123–25, 182
Berlin Wall, 125
Big Louisiana Maneuvers, 29
Bischwiller, 41–42, 44
Bremerhaven, 65, 123, 132
Brezhnev Doctrine, 226
Bush, President George W., 157, 218, 231
Byzantine Empire, 6

California, 22, 24, 29, 78
Cambodia, ix, xvi, 1, 140, 142, 153, 155, 159, 163, 184, 187, 189, 192–97, 200–201, 203–5, 218–19, 240 *see also* Phnom Penh
Camp Adair, 22, 32–34
Camp Kilmer, 59
Camp Leonard Wood *see* Fort Leonard Wood
Camp Myles Standish, 36
Camp White, 22, 32
Carter, President Jimmy, 213, 224–25, 228
Ceasefire Line, 92–93, 95–96
Center of Military History, 17, 224
Central Intelligence Agency (CIA), 134, 140, 160, 213, 216, 223–24, 226
Central Treaty Organization (CENTO), 100
Ceylon, 78, 90, 92
Checkpoint Charlie, 71, 125
Churchill, Winston, 229

Civil War, 4, 8, 175, 194, 214, 220, 222–23
Cold War, 68, 74–76, 99–100, 125, 134–36, 199, 213, 221–24, 227, 244–46
Colombia, 100, 110–11
Colorado, 95, 171, 211, 241, 243–46
commander in chief of Pacific Command (CINCPAC), xvi, 194
Committee for a Free Afghanistan (CFA), xvi, 209, 211, 213–35, 237
Commonwealth, 80, 100
communism, 17, 68, 76, 88–89, 98, 100, 133–34, 136, 163, 201–3, 205, 215, 218, 220–21, 227, 234–35, 244–45
Congo, 125
Congress, xvi, 17, 21, 134, 215–16, 226–29, 232–34
Congressional Task Force, 231–35
Constantinople, 6
crown jewels, 184
Cuba, 134–36
Cuban Missile Crisis, 135–36

Darmstadt, 58, 66
D-Day, 34, 130, 138
Deactivated Military War Trophies (DMWTs), 117
Defense Service Staff College (DSSC), 80–81, 83, 90
Delinquent Report (DR), 99, 117, 126–27
Denmark, 11–12, 100, 243
Denver, 89, 91, 97, 116, 132, 211, 241, 244, 247
Detroit, 173–74
displaced people (DP), 58, 67
Duc Co, 153–54, 156
Duke University, 199, 203
dysentery, 86–87

Eastern Bloc, 76
Eastern Front, 70, 72
East India Company, 83
Eisenhower, General Dwight D., 31, 39–40, 59, 75, 109, 117, 124, 137
Ellis Island, x, 1–3
El Salvador, xi, 241, 243
Emmersweiler, 50–51
esprit de corps, 28, 109, 126

Federal Republic of Germany (FRG), 76, 123
Finland, 47–48
Floyd, George, 176
Forbach, 49–56, 62
Fort Benning, xv, 19, 23, 32–35, 78, 113, 115–21, 127–28, 157, 170, 230
Fort Bragg, 125, 138–39, 169–75, 183, 191, 197, 201–2, 209, 211, 232, 237, 241, 243–44
Fort Hamilton, 65

Fort Leavenworth, 28–29, 33, 78
Fort Leonard Wood, 29–32, 34, 36
Fort Warren, 19, 23–26, 28, 29
France, xv, 16, 36, 38, 39–45, 47, 54, 60–61, 66, 100, 130–31, 137–38, 173, 245–46, *see also* Marseille, Rothbach
Frankfurt, 59, 68, 71, 74
Freedom Fighters, 1, 213–16, 218–20, 224, 227–28, 231, 235
Fulda Gap, 124, 131

Garden Plot (operational contingency plan), 173–74
Garmisch-Partenkirchen, 71–72, 75
Gavin, Lieutenant General James, 124, 130, 138
George Washington University, 239
Georgia, xv, 19, 35, 117, 157, 169, 171, 181 *see also* Fort Benning
German Democratic Republic (GDR), 76, 125
Germany, xv, 10, 16, 22, 39, 41, 50–62, 65–76, 79, 91–92, 97, 101, 112, 116, 121, 123, 125–27, 129–32, 138, 170, 173, 180–82, 240, 243, 245–46 *see also* Berlin, Federal Republic of Germany (FRG)
East Germany, 65, 76, 125
West Germany, 68, 76, 123, 131
Gestapo, 51, 62
GI Bill, 237–38
Goh Keng Swee, Dr., 200
Gorbachev, Mikhail, 125, 219
Governor's Island, 75–76
Great Depression, 9
Greece, x, 1–3, 100, 214, 243–44
Greek Orthodox Church, 9
Guam, 201, 205
guerrilla, 89, 145, 177, 187, 202, 213, 216–18, 221–22, 225–26, 229–30, 239

Hackworth, Major David, 129, 156, 162
Hafner, Lieutenant Claude, 57
Haguenau, 42, 44
Harris, Colonel Benjamin T., 112
Hawaii, 21, 78, 159, 161, 201, 246
helicopter, 138, 140, 143, 145, 147–48, 150, 156, 168, 183, 187, 192, 220, 230, 232
Herbert, Lieutenant Tony, 129–30
Herren, Brigadier General Thomas, 36, 39–43, 45, 50, 54, 59
Hill 414, 45–46
Hindu, 92
Hitler, Adolf, 10, 42, 54, 56–58, 60, 63, 246
Humanitarian Assistance Program, 216, 231

Ia Drang Valley, 156–57
India, xi, xv, 69, 77–78, 81, 83–98, 99–100, 103, 110, 114, 116, 119, 131, 135–37, 180, 183, 199, 203–4, 213, 223, 239, 243

Indian Staff College, xv, 69, 77, 82, 89, 91
Infantry Magazine, 115
Infantry School, 19, 23, 115–19, 230, 239, 246
Iran, xvi, 1, 176, 177–85, 195, 201, 204, 209, 213, 222–24, 228, 237, 239 *see also* Tehran
Iranian Special Forces, 180–81
Isaacs Jr., Vernon A. "Bud," 162–63, 169–71, 240–41
Islamabad, 215, 234–35
Italy, 10, 22, 36

Japan, 10, 21–22, 31, 35, 58–59, 65, 78–79, 98–99, 102, 104, 180–81, 203, 214, 240
Jensen, Julia Drankey, 11–12
Johnson, President Lyndon, 137–38, 139, 174, 176, 209
Jump School, 119, 127
Indian, 88–89

Kabul, 218, 222–23, 225, 233–35
Kashmir, xi, xv, 77, 88–97, 103, 110, 116, 137
Kennedy, President John F., 133–36
Kernan, Colonel William B., 111, 121, 246
Kesselring, Field Marshal, 72
Khyber Pass, 96–97
King Jr., Martin Luther, 175–76
Kleinwald, 51, 53
Korean Military Advisory Group (KMAG), 159
Korean War, ix, xi, xv, 60, 88, 98–100, 113, 116, 124, 130, 157, 159, 169, 214–15
Kuchler, Field Marshal Georg Carl Wilhelm Fredrick Von, 73

Laos, 142, 165, 204
Lebanon, 121, 235
Lentaigne, Major General Walter, 81, 88
Lincoln High School, 10–11

MacArthur, General, 23, 26
McNamara, Secretary of Defense Robert S., 137, 148–49, 209
Magellan Club of World Navigators, 91
Mainz, 58, 123, 125–32
Malaysia, 78, 199, 202
Manhattan, 75
Mao Zedong, 99–100
Marine Corps, 89, 237
Marseille, 38, 91
Master Training Plan (MTP), 27–28, 32, 34–35, 39
Mataxis, Helma Jensen, x, xi, 11–12 , 23–27, 29–33, 35–38, 65, 68–72, 75–80, 84, 86–88, 90–92, 101–3, 105, 107, 109–10, 116–18, 120–21, 131–32, 136, 151, 159, 161, 169, 171, 176, 178–79, 181–85, 191, 197, 201, 203–5, 208, 210–11, 241, 243–48

Mataxis Sr., Lieutenant Colonel (then Major) Theodore Christopher (Ted)
  1st Battalion of the 3rd Infantry Regiment (Old Guard), 22, 59, 65–66, 68, 89, 187
  1st Brigade of the 101st Airborne Division, 159, 161
  6th Infantry Division, 23, 27, 29, 32
  7th Infantry Regiment, 23
  70th Infantry Division, 32–33, 36, 43, 46, 50, 52, 54, 56, 60, 63, 89, 245–46, 251
  82nd Airborne Division, 129, 138, 169, 171–76, 183
  505th Airborne Battle Group, 125–26, 128–30
  7734th Historical Detachment, 68, 70–71
  academic career, 10, 13
  Afghanistan, 215–18, 220, 223
  birth, 1
  Berlin, 67–71
  Buffalo, 110–12
  Cambodia, 195–97
  death, 248
  Duke University, 199, 203
  father, x, xi, 32, 68
  field director for the Committee for a Free Afghanistan, x, 213, 218, 230, 232
  Fort Benning, xv, 19, 23, 32–35, 78, 113, 115–21, 127–28, 157, 170, 230
  France, 40–47, 55–58
  Garmisch military post, 74–76
  husband, 24, 68–69
  immigrant, 1–2
  India, 78–90, 92, 98
  injury, 49, 72
  Iran, 177–78
  Japan, 59
  Korea, 99–110, 113, 214, 245
  military decorations, x, 113, 168
  Minister of Defense in Singapore, 1
  National Guard, 17
  Rue du Général Mataxis, 60–61
  Scouts, 9, 118
  Singapore, 1, 199–205, 207
  Strategic and Tactical Analysis Group (STAG), 133–35
  Strategic Intelligence School, 77
  United Nations Military Observer Group, 92–95
  Valley Forge Military Academy (VFMA), ix, 207–10
  Vietnam War, x, 139–47, 150–55, 157–66, 170, 173, 183–84, 187, 191–93, 245
  weapons, 47–49, 219
  World War II, 38–47, 55–59
Mataxis, Shirley Jean, 32, 36, 68–69, 78, 87–88, 116–20, 131, 135, 169, 178–83, 205, 243–44

Mataxis Jr., Theodore Christopher (Ted), ix, xi, xiii, 35–36, 38, 62, 68–69, 78, 87–88, 116–21, 131, 169, 173, 178–83, 248
Mediterranean, 36, 132
Metaxas, Christos Peter, 1–2, 6
Metaxas, General Ioannis, 3
Middle East, 38, 100, 178, 183
Military Advisory and Assistance Group (MAAG), 1, 139, 177–79, 181–82, 194–95, 199–200 *see also* ARMISH—Military Assistance Advisory Group (MAAG)
Military Assistance Command Vietnam (MACV), 142, 147–50, 158, 160, 165, 175, 188, 195
military decorations
  Bronze star, x, 60, 102, 107–8, 113, 156, 163, 167–68, 171, 252, 253, 258
  Combat Assault Badge *see* Combat Infantryman's Badge
  Combat Infantryman's Badge, 1, 59, 163
  Congressional Medal of Honor, 162, 192
  Distinguished Service Cross, 14, 44, 57, 142
  Purple Heart, x, 14, 44, 66, 102, 109, 113, 129, 156, 163, 171, 180, 190
  Silver Star, x, 43, 47, 102, 129, 156, 163, 171, 180, 251
Military Police (MPs), 57–58, 104, 127
Minnesota, 12
Mobilization Plan, 22, 27–28
Moder River, 44, 57
Montagnards, 140–41, 150, 154, 157
Montreal, 4
Moore, Captain Hal, 105, 109–10, 114, 156–57
Morgan, Colonel Al, 34, 41, 44–46, 49, 53, 55
Moscow, 135, 182, 220, 233, 244
Mount Rainier, 4, 7, 10
mujahideen, xvi, 96, 211, 213–25, 228–35
Muslim, 80, 92, 217
Mussolini, Benito, 10
My Lai Massacre, 187

National Guard (NG), xv, 13, 16–19, 21–22, 28–29, 32, 174–76
  205th Coastal Artillery, 16–17
  Washington, xv, 16
National Rifle Association (NRA), 118–19, 227
Natzel, Bob, 41
Navy
  British, 80
  Indian Navy, 81, 83, 155
  Iranian, 177
  Singaporean, 200
  US naval forces, 8, 17, 76
Nazi, 51, 56, 112 *see also* Third Reich
New York City, 3, 75, 90–92, 116, 119, 120, 123, 132 *see also* Manhattan, Staten Island
Nilgiri Mountains, 80

North Atlantic Treaty Organization (NATO), 76, 125, 129, 133–35, 194
North Carolina, 24, 125, 191, 201, 205, 209, 211, 222, 238, 241, 243–44, 248 *see also* Pinehurst
North Korea, xv, 76, 99–100, 102, 104, 109–10, 113
Northrop Page, 180
Northwest Frontier, 92, 96
Norway, 12, 100, 241 *see also* Oslo
Nuclear Tactics Weapons and Firepower in the Pentomic Division, Battle Group, and Company, 116, 182, 239
nuclear war, 91, 131, 135
Nuremberg trials, 74

Oeting, 43, 49–53, 60–63
Officer Candidate School (OCS), 34
Officer's Guide, The, 24–25
office of the deputy chief of staff for military operations (ODCSOPS), 169
Operation *Big Switch*, 113
Operation *Deep Furrow*, 183
Operation *Dragoon*, 44
Operation *Harrison*, 163–64
Operation *Hawthorn*, 165
Operation *Nordwind*, 42, 44, 50
Operation *Van Buren*, 162, 164
Oslo, 12 *see also* Norway

Pakistan, x, xvi, 80, 88, 92–97, 114, 178, 183, 213–18, 222–23, 225, 228–34 *see also* Peshawar
Pahlavi, Mohammed Reza *see* Shah of Iran
Parachute Landing Fall (PLF), 88–89, 119
Patton, General George, 31, 42, 72
Pearl Harbor, 21, 31
Pearson, Lieutenant General Willard, 159, 162, 205, 207–8
Pentagon, 17, 79, 113, 121, 136–37, 149, 153, 169, 175, 199
Pentomic Division, 124, 130, 239 *see also* Reorganization of the Current Infantry Division (ROCID)
Peshawar, x, 216, 218, 222, 224, 228–33
Philippines, the, 23, 26, 100, 147, 205
Philippsbourg, 42, 44
Phnom Penh, xvi, 193–95, 205
Pinehurst, 211, 248
Pleiku, xvi, 139, 140, 143, 146–48, 150, 153–55, 157
Poland, 16–17
prisoner of war (POW), 56, 70–71, 73, 104–5, 196
Puerto Rico, 176

Quetta, 80
Quintana, Sergeant A., 44, 112

Reagan, President Ronald, 125, 210, 213–16, 218, 224, 226–28, 231–32, 235, 244, 248
Red Cross, 118, 191
Reorganization of the Current Infantry Division (ROCID), 124–25 *see also* Pentomic Division
Reserve Officers' Training Corps (ROTC), xv, 11, 13–19, 25, 83, 173, 209, 214
Reynolds Jr., Colonel Royal, 102
Rhine River, 41–42, 58
Ridgway, General Matthew, 105, 124, 138
Romney, Governor, 174–75
Roosevelt, President Franklin D. (FDR), 16–17, 22
Roosevelt, President Theodore (Teddy), 16, 224, 248
Roscoe, 68–70, 7–80, 84, 123, 131
Rothbach, 45, 47, 49
Rue du Général Mataxis, 60–62
Russia, xvi, 1, 16, 62, 71–74, 81, 96, 124, 131, 178, 182–83, 193, 213, 215–21, 223, 226, 239, 241, 244–46 *see also* Moscow, Soviet Union, USSR

Saarbrucken, 50–52, 56, 58
Saar River, 49, 51–52, 56–57
Saigon, xvi, 134, 137–38, 142, 144–46, 153, 162, 185, 188, 194, 196, 203, 218
Sainte-Mère-Église, 130, 137–38, 191
San Francisco, 78, 161, 163, 165–67, 244
Savalis, Telly, ix
Seattle, 1–9, 11–12, 14, 16, 30–33, 35, 47, 237, 244
Secretary of War, 39, 59
Scabbard and Blade Society, the, 14
Schlossberg Castle, 51, 53
Schongau, 71–72, 130
Scout, 8, 118 *see also* Baden Powell, Lord
  Boy, 8–10, 16, 118, 128
  Eagle, 9–10, 118, 128
  Girl, 118
Seibert, Colonel Donald A., 60
Seoul, 105–6
Shah of Iran, 177–79
Siegfried Line, xv, 52, 56–57
Sihanouk, King, 193
Singapore, 1, 78–79, 199–205, 211
Singapore Armed Forces (SAF), 200, 202
Sino-Soviet Bloc, 100
smallpox, 86
Smith, Major General Wayne C., 102, 104, 106
Southeast Asia, 10, 100, 134, 163, 184, 196, 199–200, 203, 205
Southeast Asia Treaty Organization (SEATO), 100
Southern Pines, 24, 201, 205, 211, 222, 237–38, 241
South Korea, xv, 79, 99–100, 110, 113 *see also* Seoul

Soviet Union, 66, 123–24, 134–35, 177, 182–83, 213–14, 222, 224 *see also* USSR
Spanish-American War, 8, 10, 15
Special Forces, xi, 30, 133, 135, 140–41, 148, 150, 153–54, 169, 172, 178, 180–81, 195, 202–3, 232, 240, 242–43
Spicheren Heights, 52, 60, 63
Sri Lanka *see* Ceylon
SS (*Schutzstaffel*), 47–48, 57, 251
SS *America*, 38, 123 *see also* USS *West Point*
Stalin, Joseph, 75, 99
Stalingrad, 73
standard operating procedure (SOP), 17, 28, 35, 159
Staten Island, 75, 116
Suez Canal, 59, 65, 78, 90
Sweden, 3–4, 100

Table of Organization and Equipment (TO&E), 18, 40
Taliban, 222–23
Tehran, 177–84
Texas, 22, 29, 237, 239
Thailand, 100, 204, 218
Thebaud, Lieutenant Colonel Delphin, 14–15, 18, 82, 114
Third Reich, 51 *see also* Nazi
Triangle Hill, 104, 112
  Battle for, 104, 112
Tripartite Pact, 22
Trudeau, General, 103, 108
Truman, President Harry S., 76, 99
tuberculosis, 11, 103, 181

United Nations (UN), xv, 88–90, 92–94, 97, 100, 102, 104, 109–11, 113–14, 222, 224, 228, 232–33, 239
  General Assembly, 224
  Military Observer Group, 90, 92–93, 95, 97
  Peacekeeping, 92, 95, 239
United Kingdom, 124, 177
United States Forces European Theater (USFET), 70
United States Military Academy, ix
University of Washington, xv, 11, 13, 17–18, 30, 82–83, 114, 237
USSR, 99–100, 135, 178, 214, 224–26 *see also* Soviet Union
USS *West Point*, 38 *see also* SS *America*

Valley Forge, ix, xvi, 1, 6, 205, 207–10, 233, 237, 239, 246
VE Day (Victory in Europe Day), 59, 245
Viet Cong (VC), 134, 137, 145–49, 157–58, 162–63, 164, 166–67, 191, 193, 195, 254–55

Vietnam, x, xi, xvi, 1, 24, 45, 60, 76, 88–89, 100, 117, 129, 134, 137–38, 139–59, 160–68, 169–76, 180, 182–85, 187–93, 195–97, 199, 201, 203–4, 207–9, 217–19, 222, 224, 227–29, 237, 239–40, 243–46, 248–49, 251–55, 257 *see also* Saigon
  Archive, 240
  Center, 237, 239–43
  War, 60, 144, 155–56, 187, 195, 209, 224, 239, 245
Volkssturm, 58
Vosges Mountains, xv, 43, 49, 51, 55

War Department, 17
War Memorial, 62, 138
Washington, D.C., 65, 77, 108, 133–37, 175, 204, 213, 231, 238, 241
Washington, George, 16
Wayne, John, 165
weapons
  AK-47, 165, 223
  antitank grenade launcher, 223
  antitank gun, 23, 28, 30, 40–41, 99
  atomic artillery/bomb, xv, 59, 65, 115, 130
  bayonet, 53, 57, 174
  bazooka, 46, 57, 237
  Browning Automatic Rifle (BAR), 15, 23, 48, 143
  cannon, 41, 47–48, 50, 125, 130, 141
  Enfield rifle, 30, 223
  M3 howitzer, 40–41, 99
  machine gun, 15, 18, 23, 46–48, 52, 57, 96, 101, 112, 145, 223, 251
  mine, 48, 58, 83, 187, 191, 217, 230, 232, 237
  rocket-propelled grenades (RPGs), 178, 223
  Stinger, 219–20, 223, 232–33
Western Front, 40, 70
Westmoreland, General, 138, 140, 144, 146–48, 153–58, 175, 184, 192, 200
West Wall *see* Siegfried Line
White House, the, 4, 134, 214–16, 226–28, 234
Wingen, 42, 44
World's Fair, The, 119, 132
World War I, 1, 4, 8, 10–12, 14–18, 22–23, 27, 30–32, 41, 52, 70, 74, 80–81, 103, 181, 188
World War II, xv, 1, 4, 9, 21–22, 24, 31, 35–36, 38, 41, 52, 58–63, 66–67, 74–76, 77, 81, 89, 92, 97–100, 102–3, 106–7, 110, 112, 114, 117–18, 121, 123–24, 126, 129–32, 138–39, 146, 165, 172–73, 182, 191–92, 202, 214, 223–24, 227, 241, 245–46, 248, 249, 251–53
Wyoming, 19, 23–24, 29 *see also* Fort Warren

Yugoslavia, 72, 235, 239, 244